The
Mixer

The Mixer

The Story of Premier League Tactics, from Route One to False Nines

MICHAEL COX

HarperCollins*Publishers*

HarperCollins*Publishers*
1 London Bridge Street
London SE1 9GF

www.harpercollins.co.uk

HarperCollins*Publishers*
1st Floor, Watermarque Building, Ringsend Road
Dublin 4, Ireland

First published by HarperCollins*Publishers* 2017
This edition published 2018

11

A catalogue record of this book is
available from the British Library

ISBN 978-0-00-821555-2

Printed and bound in Great Britain by
CPI Group (UK) Ltd, Croydon, CR0 4YY

Contents

Introduction

'Get it in the mixer!'

These five words represent the simplest tactic in football: launch the ball into the penalty box, take advantage of the ensuing chaos, perhaps following a goalmouth scramble, and hope to pinch a scruffy goal.

It's an approach rightly ridiculed today, but as recently as the 1980s it was English football's most popular tactic. During this period tactical thinking was influenced heavily by Charles Hughes, the Football Association's director of coaching, who clumsily employed statistics to illustrate the value of launching the ball quickly downfield. He effectively formulated English football's national coaching curriculum, as well as working alongside England managers Bobby Robson, who was sceptical about Hughes's methods, and Graham Taylor, who was altogether much keener.

Hughes was obsessed with players thumping the ball into the 'position of maximum opportunity' (POMO) – inside the box, level with the far post – as often as possible. Hughes did have other, more sophisticated ideas, but his obsession with POMO dominated, and harmed, English football by creating predictable, simplistic teams and one-dimensional, brain-dead players. At the time of the Premier

League's formation in 1992, therefore, English football was considered to be about long balls, about route one, about POMO, about getting it in the mixer.

But this was a darker period for more significant reasons, as an overwhelming hooligan problem meant English football was derided both in the national media and across Europe. The nadir came with the 1985 European Cup Final at the Heysel Stadium in Belgium, when Liverpool supporters charged at Juventus fans, resulting in 39 people being killed by a collapsing wall. English clubs were subsequently banned from European competition for five years, and English footballing culture, traditionally slow to embrace tactical innovations from abroad, consequently became even more insular.

There were other tragedies. A fortnight before the Heysel disaster, 56 people were killed at Bradford City's Valley Parade by a fire that engulfed an entire stand within minutes. Four years later, grave policing errors at Hillsborough resulted in the deaths of 96 people, a tragedy subsequently blamed, consistently and incorrectly, upon supporters.

In the aftermath of the Bradford fire a leading article in the *Sunday Times* described football as 'a slum sport played in slum stadiums, increasingly watched by slum people'. It was a desperately distasteful description, but serves as a useful low-water mark for measuring English football's subsequent development. Slum people? The problem of hooliganism was largely defeated in the years that followed. Slum stadiums? The Taylor Report recommended all-seater grounds, and the Premier League's formative years were dominated by new or dramatically renovated stadiums. Slum sport? English football changed enormously during the Premier League era, its popularity rising dramatically, first within England and then across the world.

While the Premier League was identical in its basic sporting structure to its predecessor, the old First Division, England's top flight benefited from something of a rebrand considering the aforementioned problems, and 1992 isn't an entirely arbitrary start date for football's modern age – as explained in the opening chapter.

The concept of the Premier League enabled top-flight clubs to gain independence from the Football Association and the Football League, allowing them to negotiate lucrative broadcast and sponsorship contracts. The broadcasting aspect proved most significant; a bidding war between ITV and Sky ensued, with the latter securing TV rights in a move that completely transformed its previously loss-making satellite subscription service. Incidentally, Manchester United manager Alex Ferguson was one of the fiercest critics of the Premier League, ridiculing the concept as a 'piece of nonsense' that would 'sell supporters down the river'. But Ferguson would define the division more than anyone, winning 13 of the first 21 titles before his retirement in 2013.

This book isn't an account of the Premier League's business development, but it's impossible to ignore the extraordinary surge in TV revenue. The Premier League received £51m per season in broadcasting rights between 1992 and 1997, then considered an astounding amount. This sum increased exponentially over the next two decades, reaching £2.75bn per season by 2016, 50 times more than in 1992. Sky were effectively paying over £11m to screen each live match, a staggering figure when you consider rights to the entire final old First Division season cost less than £15m. A division essentially created to provide televisual entertainment has proved successful beyond anyone's wildest dreams.

It's worth remembering, too, that these figures weren't plucked out of thin air. Broadcasters could justify paying these eye-watering sums because of the huge public demand, which was fuelled by the Premier League becoming such a fantastic spectacle, the world's most thrilling league. Set against the dark days of the 1980s, it represents an incredible turnaround. How did the football – the 'product', as the marketing men would say – become quite so good?

This book seeks to explain how. Although the 25 years are represented by 25 chapters, this is a thematic rather than a literal season-by-season account. The focus is upon the revolutionaries: the innovative managers, the game-changing players, the inspirational teams, the new tactical concepts, the off-field developments that influenced playing styles. The story is about the Premier League becoming universal, in two different ways.

First, it became universal on a tactical level. In the early 1990s there were very specific demands for every position – defenders simply defended, attackers simply attacked. But gradually positions became more all-encompassing, with defenders expected to start attacking moves and attackers encouraged to start defensive pressure. Players were increasingly all-rounders rather than specialists.

Second, it also became universal on a geographical basis, as English clubs broadened their horizons and became increasingly dependent upon foreign players and managers. Amazingly, on the Premier League's opening weekend in August 1992, just 11 foreign players started for the 22 clubs combined, and there were no foreign managers. By its 25th season, the majority of Premier League players and managers were foreign – and almost every major footballing nation on earth was represented. Of the top 25 countries in the FIFA rankings, only Mexico didn't have a Premier League representative in 2016/17.

The combination of these two factors saw Premier League sides abandon ugly, straightforward, direct football and embrace a more cultured, continental, technical style. This is the story of the Premier League's remarkable tactical evolution – from pie to paella, from route one to false nines.

Part One

In the Beginning

1

A Whole New Ball Game

'The back-pass law is the best rule change ever
– it has changed the game.'

Peter Schmeichel

We are constantly reminded that 'football didn't start in 1992' in response to Premier League-centric historical records, but 1992 effectively marked the beginning of modern football. It was the beginning of a new, exciting, more entertaining era of the game, the watershed moment that prompted sweeping changes to create a more fast-paced, technically proficient sport.

However, it had absolutely nothing to do with the formation of the Premier League.

The introduction of the back-pass law in 1992 had a transformative effect upon football. Not since 1925 – when the offside law was altered so that only two opponents, rather than three, needed to be goalside of an attacker – had a law change been so effective at improving the spectacle of the world's most popular sport. There have been minor alterations to the Laws of the Game during the Premier League era: different interpretations regarding offside, stricter laws governing tackles, revisions to kick-off. But 1992 was literally a game-changer.

The law change was simple. Previously, goalkeepers were allowed to use their hands if the ball was deliberately kicked to them by a teammate. Now, they were not. They could still handle the ball if a teammate headed, chested or even kneed it back, and throw-ins back to the goalkeeper could be picked up until 1997, but goalkeepers were forced to use their feet more than ever before, effectively becoming part of passing moves.

There was an extremely good reason for the law change. Hitherto, teams could time waste infuriatingly when leading matches; the goalkeeper would roll the ball out, the defenders would retain possession until an opponent challenged, then return the ball to the goalkeeper, who would pick it up and restart the process. It was often very tedious, and in hindsight it's incredible that any team ever contrived to lose a lead. The ultimate example came in the dying seconds of Rangers' European Cup first round tie against Dynamo Kiev in 1987. With Rangers 2–1 ahead on aggregate and building an attacking move, midfielder Graeme Souness received the ball midway inside the opposition half, immediately turned towards his own goal and thumped a 70-yard backward ball to his goalkeeper Chris Woods. Souness, incidentally, would later suffer from the back-pass change more than most.

Examples of negative play became particularly obvious at the 1990 World Cup, a tournament so dreadfully negative that FIFA felt compelled to take action. The new law came into effect two years later, in time for the inaugural Premier League campaign.

While some managers, like Luton Town's David Pleat, spoke in favour of the change, there was a significant backlash from most top-flight managers, including the last two title-winning bosses. 'I don't think this is going to enhance the game at all,' complained

Arsenal's George Graham, while Howard Wilkinson, who had taken Leeds United to the final pre-Premier League title in 1991/92, suggested the new laws would simply encourage long-ball football. 'If the new rule is the authorities' idea of how to foster better football, then the experiment will prove counter-productive,' he declared. 'The new ruling will be manna from heaven to a coach working with his long-ball side.'

Wilkinson predicted teams would concentrate on pumping long balls in behind the opposition and use a 'goalie-blocker', lingering in an offside position, to intercept potential back-passes from defenders to the goalkeeper's feet, forcing them to hack the ball into touch instead. 'FIFA have inadvertently encouraged more long-ball football,' he maintained. 'This isn't a mad, scientific nightmare, this is the reality as stipulated by the overlords of the world game.' Wilkinson's view, that route one football would become dominant, found support from many managerial colleagues.

But the back-pass law served its initial purpose, and teams were no longer able to time waste so blatantly. Wilkinson's predictions about long-ball football weren't entirely inaccurate immediately following the law change – Leeds's matches in a pre-season friendly tournament against Stuttgart and Sampdoria were notable for the opposition repeatedly playing hopeful balls in behind the Leeds defence, hoping for errors – but he failed to foresee how goalkeepers and defenders would adjust and gradually become comfortable in possession, creating a more technically advanced sport.

There were significant knock-on effects. Teams had a greater incentive to press in advanced positions, forcing defenders into mistakes, and managers were less inclined to play stiflingly aggressive defensive lines, because covering the space in behind now involved playing out of trouble. As a result the game became stretched, which created more room in midfield. Arguably the biggest change was in the speed of matches – players had previously become accustomed to breaks in play while goalkeepers held onto the ball. Suddenly the action had become non-stop.

These developments, the consequence of one simple law change, played into the hands of the Premier League, a division created specifically to provide televisual entertainment. Sky Sports introduced plenty of innovations, including a simple idea that has become universally established: displaying the score and clock on the top-left of the screen. Other Sky gimmicks were less successful: pre-match firework displays were scrapped after a stray rocket was launched out of The Dell and into a nearby petrol station, while the use of cheerleaders was short-lived, possibly after concerns from the presenter over their understanding of the offside rule. But none of this artificial razzmatazz was as crucial as the back-pass law in making the Premier League a fantastic show, and Sky were hugely fortunate that world football took an enormous step forward ahead of 1992/93. Without this significant improvement in the spectacle of matches, the Premier League wouldn't have developed into the multi-billion-pound product it is today.

While supporters quickly realised the benefit of the back-pass change, many players found themselves exposed. The impact was first noticed in pre-season, when Manchester City goalkeeper Andy Dibble suffered a broken leg in a friendly against a League of Ireland XI, struck by sudden indecision as a slow back-pass approached, eventually attempting to tackle the opposition striker. 'I wasn't sure whether to kick the ball or pick it up,' Dibble complained, describing himself as 'the first victim' of the law. However, defenders struggled more than keepers, and the Premier League's opening day, 15 August 1992, was a comedy of errors.

Fourteen minutes into Leeds's 2–1 victory over Wimbledon, Dons right-back Roger Joseph panicked inside his own penalty box, caught in two minds – should he pass back to goalkeeper Hans Segers or simply clear the ball? Eventually he did neither, scuffing the ball barely two yards, allowing Leeds's Lee Chapman to pounce – and presumably leaving Leeds manager Wilkinson unsure whether he should celebrate or ruefully shake his head at the 'reality as stipulated by the overlords of the world game'. Down at Highbury, Norwich recovered from 2–0 down to defeat Arsenal 4–2, a victory secured with a classic example of back-pass confusion. Norwich launched a high pass into the opposition half, forcing Arsenal captain Tony Adams to deal with a bouncing ball. He nervously glanced back to his goalkeeper, realised David Seaman didn't want the ball, so instead attempted a square pass to centre-back partner Steve Bould. But Adams missed the ball completely and stumbled, allowing Mark Robins to steal in and chip Seaman, scoring the goal that ensured Norwich were the Premier League's first-ever leaders.

Both goals in Chelsea's 1–1 draw with Oldham at Stamford Bridge were related to the back-pass law: Oldham centre-back Ian Marshall, troubled by his inability to play the ball back to his keeper, slipped when attempting to control a long ball and allowed Mick Harford to open the scoring. But then Chelsea goalkeeper Dave Beasant, having received the ball from a defender, scuffed his kick, allowing Nick Henry to equalise. The new rules were causing chaos.

There was also a 'positive' goal scored from the back-pass rule, however. Sheffield United's Brian Deane had headed the Premier League's opening goal against Manchester United, then scored another from the penalty spot. This second arose because Blades midfielder John Gannon looked set to play a back-pass, saw an opponent making a run to intercept his potential pass (although he wasn't quite a 'goalie-blocker') and so turned his way out of danger before playing a left-footed pass into the channel. Striker Alan Cork raced onto it, was tripped by Gary Pallister, and Deane converted the penalty. There were just seven seconds from Gannon's turn until the penalty award – without the new law, the ball would still have been in the goalkeeper's hands at the opposite end.

Compilers of 'football's funniest gaffes' VHS tapes must have been delighted. The most comical error came in early September at Tottenham, and resulted in the dismissal of Sheffield United goalkeeper Simon Tracey. He'd already been booked for handling the ball outside the box, and then, when presented with a back-pass in the second half, panicked. He was closed down quickly by Spurs' Paul Allen, and proceeded to dribble the ball sideways, taking it directly out of play for a Tottenham throw. When Tracey tried to retrieve the ball from next to the advertising hoardings to prevent Spurs taking the throw, a quick-thinking ball boy snatched it away, chucked it to Spurs sub Andy Gray, which prompted Tracey to rugby-tackle Gray to the floor. He was dismissed. Blades manager Dave Bassett wasn't impressed. 'He's got the brains of a rocking-horse – and I told him so.'

This was not simply an English phenomenon, of course, and there were similar problems across Europe. North of the border, Rangers opened the scoring in October's Scottish League Cup Final when Aberdeen goalkeeper Theo Snelders bizarrely chested a wayward clearance from a teammate straight into the path of a grateful Stuart McCall. It wasn't an intentional back-pass anyway, and wouldn't have been penalised, but Snelders was clearly unaware of the regulations and was left screaming at his defenders, 'I can't pick it up!' The biggest impact came in Italy. Serie A was traditionally Europe's most defensive division, and following goals-per-game averages of 2.11, 2.24, 2.29 and 2.27 in the four seasons before 1992/93 it suddenly jumped to 2.80, an unprecedented rise. The Premier League didn't witness such a surge, rising from 2.52 in the final old First Division season to 2.65 in the opening Premier League campaign, but the back-pass law clearly affected the nature of the division, with certain teams particularly struggling.

The most famous victims were Liverpool. Many have linked their inability to win a Premier League title, having dominated the 1970s and 1980s, to the introduction of the back-pass law. In reality they finished sixth in both the final First Division season and the first Premier League season, but Liverpool's players admit it affected them badly. 'It was constantly in your mind as a defender – you can't play the ball back,' remembered defender Nick Tanner. 'Previously, Liverpool would just kill the game off. We'd be 1–0 up, play the ball back to Bruce Grobbelaar. He'd bounce the ball a bit, Phil Neal would drop off, and Bruce would roll it out to him. That all stopped.' Their manager during this period was Souness – the man responsible for the back-pass to end all back-passes.

Arsenal also suffered. They were the bookmakers' title favourites, having scored the most goals in the top flight during 1991/92, but they struggled to build play from deep and scored the fewest goals during 1992/93, underlining the extent of the back-pass change. However, they adapted well defensively and remained an excellent side in knockout competitions, winning the League Cup and FA Cup – both, coincidentally, with 2–1 victories over Sheffield Wednesday.

But the biggest losers, significantly, were a very direct side – Wilkinson's Leeds. Having triumphed the previous season, they slipped backwards alarmingly and finished 17th in the Premier League's inaugural campaign, failing to win away all season. Considering that Wilkinson predicted route one football would prosper under the new regulations, it was ironic that his own players suffered precisely because they could no longer play that way. Goalkeeper John Lukic became the first Premier League goalkeeper to be penalised for handling a back-pass, from centre-back Chris Whyte – whom Wilkinson had rated as the division's best centre-back in the previous campaign but who struggled considerably with modern football. 'The back-pass law affected us particularly,' midfielder Gary Speed later admitted. 'The centre-backs used to stroke the ball back to the goalkeeper, and John Lukic used to launch it up to me and Lee Chapman. Suddenly we weren't allowed to play that way anymore.'

Fellow midfielder Steve Hodge agreed. 'Previously John Lukic would hold the ball and he'd launch it to us high up the pitch,' he explained. 'Now, Lukic would have to launch it from the floor and the ball wasn't going far enough down the pitch. We were much less of a threat because the ball wasn't landing or being flicked to the edge of our opponents' area, it was bobbling around in the midfield. Also, teams would now really push up and made Lukic kick it quickly.' It's notable how much emphasis was placed upon the simple concept of how far the goalkeeper could kick, indicating the accepted method of distribution at the time.

Nottingham Forest also paid a heavy price for the new regulations, finishing bottom. Legendary manager Brian Clough had other problems by this stage, particularly his alcoholism, which, as he later admitted, clouded his judgement significantly. But his side's style of football didn't suit modern football, as Gary Bannister outlined. 'Where we've suffered is when we've had the ball, we've played it back to Mark Crossley and he has cleared it,' he said. 'On most occasions the ball has come straight back at us, putting us under pressure. Mark having to hump the ball up the field has not helped us at all. Last season, a back-pass would have kept us possession and Stuart Pearce, Brian Laws or Gary Charles would have picked the ball up from the keeper to start us off again.'

Pearce, slightly surprisingly for a regular set-piece taker, looked particularly nervous when forced to play out and was responsible for the most famous misplaced back-pass of this era. After eight seconds of a November 1993 World Cup qualifier against minnows San Marino, he underhit the ball towards David Seaman, allowing Davide Gualtieri to give San Marino a shock 1–0 lead over England, who nevertheless won 7–1. That match was also the final England appearance for Pearce's ex-Forest teammate Des Walker. He'd raced to 59 caps in the space of five years and was described as 'the outfielder England manager Graham Taylor can least afford to lose' in the *Guardian* a year earlier. But Walker discovered his talents no longer suited the modern game, and his England career was over at the age of 27. As Harry Redknapp later said, 'When they did away with the back-pass in 1992 it made a huge dent in Des's game. He used his speed to nip in front of the striker, mop up the ball and knock it back for the goalkeeper to pick up … suddenly, he was being required to play his way out of trouble, and that wasn't his style at all.'

Indeed, one of the notable features of the early Premier League seasons – in line with Wilkinson's prediction – was the frequent sight of defenders, when chasing long balls back towards their own goal, simply hacking the ball out of play to concede a throw-in. 'I've told the players, "If you're in doubt, kick it out," said Coventry manager Bobby Gould. '"Stop fannying about and put it in Row Z."' It's no coincidence that the first PFA Player of the Year during the Premier League era was Paul McGrath, the Aston Villa centre-back who played the ball comfortably with both feet. No other defender adjusted so impressively to the new law, and the Irishman became the template for the modern centre-back, as managers increasingly required ball-playing defenders rather than old-fashioned cloggers. A player like Rio Ferdinand, for example, would have been a midfielder rather than a centre-back were it not for the back-pass change.

* * *

Inevitably, the role of goalkeepers changed enormously. It was the first time that they had been forced to adjust since the 1912 law change that ruled they could handle only inside the penalty box rather than in the entirety of their own half. Goalkeepers, rightly famous for moaning, were outraged. 'The new rule is making a mockery of my profession,' complained Alan Hodgkinson, the ex-England shotstopper who became renowned as the country's first specialist goalkeeping coach. 'I know people will assume I'm biased but I can't see the value of setting up goalkeepers so they look foolish. There's not one who hasn't been caught out. Is that good for the game? You have to remember that keepers have spent 20 years learning to catch the ball. It's second nature to them. It's not easy to adjust.' Tough luck. The rules were here to stay, and goalkeepers were forced to spend long training sessions practising an entirely new skill – kicking a moving ball. The goalkeeper, football's most specialised position, needed to become more of an all-rounder.

One of Hodgkinson's key achievements was recommending Peter Schmeichel to Manchester United manager Alex Ferguson, before acting as the Dane's coach. Schmeichel would define goalkeeping during this period, and was the only Premier League player who was the world's greatest in his position. He was physically imposing, capable of tremendous close-range reaction stops and a master of the double save, springing up quickly to thwart rebounds. Schmeichel's approach wasn't textbook, and his positioning wasn't as flawless as Arsenal's Seaman, his goalkeeping rival of the 1990s. The Arsenal shotstopper was his opposite: quiet, understated and solid, whereas Schmeichel was loud, bold and unpredictable. Schmeichel introduced English football to the 'starjump' save – where he would spread arms and legs while leaping towards a striker – having borrowed it from handball, which Schmeichel played regularly as a teenager. 'A goalkeeper is not a footballer, a goalkeeper is a handball player,' former Manchester City manager Malcolm Allison declared in the 1960s. For Schmeichel, that was literally true.

Schmeichel had benefited heavily from the pre-back-pass situation. He started the Premier League era on a completely unexpected high, having won Euro 92 with Denmark – who hadn't even qualified for the tournament initially, but were handed a late reprieve when civil war forced Yugoslavia to withdraw. In the last major tournament before the back-pass change, Denmark demonstrated why reform was desperately required, with centre-back Lars Olsen continually knocking balls back to Schmeichel to pick up, an approach that gradually spread to the rest of the side. The second half of the final, a 2–0 victory over Germany, featured particularly infuriating examples of time wasting. With five minutes remaining, Danish forward Flemming Povlsen collected the ball midway inside his own half, dribbled determinedly towards the opposition goal, but was tripped on the halfway line. He picked himself up, dusted himself down, then turned around and fired the ball 50 yards back to Schmeichel. 'Every time we got into the German half and couldn't find someone to pass to, players would turn around and pass to me, and I would pick it up,' Schmeichel later recalled somewhat sheepishly. 'How can you win football matches like that?!'

The new law forced goalkeepers to become more comfortable in possession, and Schmeichel was proactive in evolving. Upon arriving at Manchester United the previous summer, with back-pass reform on the horizon, Schmeichel insisted that the goalkeepers should play a more active role in training. Rather than being separated from the main group, Schmeichel wanted to take part in passing sessions with the outfielders, an important change both tactically and psychologically. He would later stun opponents by charging upfield for corners when United were behind in the dying seconds, sometimes with great success. This has become accepted practice in modern times, but Schmeichel introduced the concept to English supporters, first showcasing his attacking qualities on Boxing Day 1994, when United were 1–0 down at home to Blackburn Rovers. With three minutes remaining, Schmeichel raced forward into the opposition box, distracting three startled opponents and enabling Gary Pallister to find space; he headed towards goal, and Paul Ince smashed in the equaliser.

Schmeichel had already scored multiple times in Denmark, and later netted a consolation goal for United with a powerful header in a 1995 UEFA Cup tie against Russian side Rotor Volgograd. He also had an overhead kick against Wimbledon disallowed for offside – surely the first-ever goalkeeper penalised for that offence – and would, fittingly, become the first Premier League goalkeeper to score, during his sole season at Aston Villa. Schmeichel was a genuine revolutionary, convincing fellow goalkeepers that they weren't simply about defending their own goal from opposition attacks and that they could launch – and indeed finish – attacks of their own.

But Schmeichel wasn't particularly reliable with his feet in traditional goalkeeping areas. In Manchester United's second-ever Premier League game, a 3–0 home defeat to Everton, the great Dane made the first possession-based goalkeeping error of the post-back-pass era when he was tackled by Everton's Mo Johnston, who curled the ball home. The majority of Schmeichel's errors came with his feet or when sweeping outside his penalty box; he kicked the ball straight to West Ham's Matthew Holmes in February 1994, allowing the winger to cross for a Trevor Morley goal, then three months later gifted Ipswich's Chris Kiwomya an open goal when air-kicking outside his box, and he was dismissed in an FA Cup quarter-final against Charlton when handling 15 yards outside his penalty area.

Other, less celebrated goalkeepers adjusted well, like Norwich's Bryan Gunn, who contributed to his side's excellent passing football.

Seaman also coped admirably, partly because he was accustomed to playing behind Arsenal's famously aggressive offside trap and was encouraged to sweep proactively by George Graham. Even before the back-pass change, Graham had Seaman working on kicking the ball with his weaker foot, then an extremely rare skill for a goalkeeper, although the rule change did cause him problems. 'When the rule came in, first of all, you went to the safety route,' he admitted. 'If someone passed it back to you, just booted it, you just made sure you got good contact. Then you develop that and get a bit more confident with the ball, so you try to control it ... the more you do it, the better you get – you learn who to pass to, where to find players.' As goalkeepers increasingly passed the ball rather than hoofed it, they acted as an eleventh outfielder, and teams started playing out from the back.

Schmeichel, meanwhile, once had a blazing row with Ferguson over the subject of his kicking. Manchester United were 3–0 up at Anfield in January 1994, but contrived to blow their lead and drew 3–3. Ferguson was understandably furious, but surprisingly targeted Schmeichel for continually sending balls up the middle of the pitch, where Neil Ruddock was heading them back, allowing Liverpool to maintain their pressure. Schmeichel didn't appreciate the criticism, and after Ferguson had threatened to throw a cup of tea over his goalkeeper, he launched a volley of abuse. He later phoned his agent demanding a transfer, although Ferguson called him into his office the next day and told him that he was going to be sacked anyway. After the Dane apologised, both to his manager and his teammates, Ferguson reversed his decision, and Schmeichel spent five more years at the club, ending his extraordinary spell by lifting the European Cup as captain in 1999.

Schmeichel never entirely solved his kicking problems, however, making two atrocious errors with his feet both home and away in a

1998 FA Cup tie against relegation strugglers Barnsley, who won the replay. Considering the nature of his international success with Denmark, and his subsequent struggles with kicking, it's impressive Schmeichel put personal preferences aside to declare that 'the back-pass law is the best rule change ever – it has changed the game.'

Significantly, however, Schmeichel popularised the concept of a goalkeeper acting as a playmaker – but with his hands rather than his feet. His incredible long-range, overarm throws had barely been witnessed before in English football, and became a fundamental part of Manchester United's attacking weaponry. Ferguson's side largely played counter-attacking football at this stage, based heavily around wingers Ryan Giggs and either Andrei Kanchelskis or Lee Sharpe, who frequently received the ball on the run, because Schmeichel could accurately hurl the ball half the length of the pitch. 'When I get hold of the ball, I try to create counter-attacking opportunities,' Schmeichel explained. 'It's not always successful, but the tactic forces the opponents to turn around and head for their own goal, which is both strenuous and demoralising.' Schmeichel even recorded assists with his hands. In February 1994, away at QPR, he launched the ball straight up the centre for the speedy Kanchelskis to dribble forward and open the scoring in a 3–2 win. Two years later, in a 5–0 thrashing of Sunderland – a game better remembered for Eric Cantona's legendary chip into the top corner – Schmeichel caught a tame header and immediately, from three yards off his line, chucked the ball into the opposition half for Ole Gunnar Solskjær, who raced clear of the defence and finished calmly.

Not until Pepe Reina, who joined Liverpool in 2005, did the Premier League witness a goalkeeper so adept at these immediate, accurate long-range throws to launch counter-attacks. By this stage goalkeepers were generally also extremely comfortable with their feet, the majority growing up accustomed to the modern laws. 'I was ten years old when they changed the back-pass rule,' said Reina, who won the Premier League Golden Glove award three consecutive times. 'I was still young enough, thankfully. It caught me just in time, as I was beginning to develop my skills.' But even by this stage, in the mid-2000s, Reina's kicking received significantly less attention than his throwing, indicative of how Schmeichel had created the template for the Premier League goalkeeper. 'Schmeichel's long throws were so powerful and allowed his team-mates to create danger at the other end … his approach was clearly ahead of his time,' said Serie A veteran Samir Handanović. Nigeria's Vincent Enyeama summarised the thoughts of a generation of keepers: 'Even though Edwin van der Sar was my role model, Schmeichel brought in a different kind of goalkeeping.' Schmeichel was the first Premier League player to provide inspiration across the world.

Van der Sar, who excelled for Manchester United around the same time as Reina was doing so for Liverpool, was famed for his quality in possession, primarily because he grew up at Ajax, where the visionary Johan Cruyff had inisisted that the goalkeeper be an eleventh outfielder long before the back-pass change. Van der Sar became the accepted goalkeeping role model, with Thibaut Courtois and Manuel Neuer citing him as their inspiration because he was so comfortable on the ball. Kicking had become an essential part of modern goalkeeping, and those poor in possession found themselves marginalised.

Meanwhile, Schmeichel also helped revolutionise the Premier League in a different manner entirely. Of the 242 players who started a Premier League match on the Premier League's opening weekend, just 11 were foreign. By virtue of simple probability, you'd expect only one of the 11 to be a goalkeeper. Instead, it was four: Schmeichel, plus Wimbledon's Dutchman Hans Segers, Canadian international Craig Forrest at Ipswich and Czech Jan Stejskal for QPR. A year later, with overseas outfielders still rare, there were six more foreign regulars between the posts: Australian Mark Bosnich at Aston Villa, Russian Dmitri Kharine at Chelsea, Norwegian Erik Thorstvedt at Tottenham, Zimbabwe's Bruce Grobbelaar, who had regained his place at Liverpool, and two more Czechs, Luděk Mikloško of West Ham and Pavel Srníček of Newcastle. Jim Barron, then the goalkeeping coach at Aston Villa, noted how foreign goalkeepers were more proactive than their English counterparts, commanding their box better and possessing superior distribution. England had always prided itself on the quality of its goalkeepers, but foreign imports were evolving the role.

Goalkeepers in the Premier League's first couple of seasons were therefore significant for two clear reasons. First, the change to the back-pass law meant they broadened their skill set and became all-rounders rather than specialists, a development subsequently witnessed in every other position. Second, there was a concerted shift towards foreign players at the expense of homegrown talent, another process that would be replicated across the pitch. Goalkeepers were traditionally considered outsiders, but now they were leading the way into football's modern age.

2

Cantona & Counters

*'Being French, to me, is first and foremost
being a revolutionary.'*

Eric Cantona

Upon the formation of the Premier League, Manchester United hadn't lifted the league trophy in a quarter of a century, which made their dominance of its early years even more remarkable. Alex Ferguson's side triumphed in four of the first five seasons.

These five years coincided with the half-decade reign of Eric Cantona – and United's only failure during this period, finishing second in 1994/95, came when the fantastic French forward was suspended for half the campaign. His impact upon United was extraordinary, turning them from also-rans to consistent champions almost overnight, and his influence on the Premier League was unparalleled. Cantona, more than anyone else, popularised technical football.

At a time when foreign players were still rare, this was a Frenchman of Italian and Spanish descent who strolled into English football stadiums, collar upturned, as if he owned them. Cantona was unlike anything England had previously encountered: when listing his inspirations, he mentioned Diego Maradona and Johan Cruyff, but also Pablo Picasso, Jim Morrison and Wolfgang Amadeus Mozart. Brilliantly, when he referenced French poet Rimbaud, journalists mistakenly believed he was talking about 1980s action movie character Rambo. Cantona was almost a satirical character, a French philosopher trapped in English dressing rooms, where cutting up teammates' clothes was considered the height of wit – and he clearly played along with the act. Teammates said he spoke English well, yet when quizzed by tabloid reporters his language skills suddenly deserted him, preserving his status as the baffled outsider. When Manchester United's squad went for a post-match drink, the standard round was 17 lagers and one glass of champagne.

It wasn't entirely about Cantona being from abroad, however. He'd earned a similar reputation in France, where he bounced between various Ligue 1 clubs with alarming regularity, usually after serious breaches of discipline. In his enlightening biography of the man, Philippe Auclair notes that in the late 1980s Cantona had become 'the first celebrity footballer in his country's history', known primarily for his peculiar cultural references rather than his pure footballing ability. He'd risen to national prominence following his displays for France's U21 side, who featured heavily in the sports programming of the new, innovative subscription TV channel Canal+. Cantona was the perfect protagonist for the trendy channel's focus and, sure enough, he became the ideal figurehead for Sky and the Premier League, too.

Cantona's most infamous moment in English football came in January 1995. Just after being dismissed for kicking out at Crystal Palace defender Richard Shaw, he reacted to abuse from Palace supporter Matthew Simmons by launching himself over Selhurst Park's advertising hoardings to perform an extravagant 'kung-fu' kick on Simmons, an incident that brought an eight-month worldwide football ban and effectively ended his international career. While a disgraceful act, it was nevertheless a momentous incident for the Premier League; it featured heavily on news bulletins in countries as distant as Australia and New Zealand, the first time that England's new top flight had become a genuinely global story.

It was probably inevitable the division would initially receive attention for negative reasons, considering the problems of the 1980s, but as reports explained Cantona's background, they introduced viewers to the most intriguing character in English football, some-one who clearly bucked the stereotype. British newspapers went to town: the *Sun* featured the incident on their front page two days running, on the second with a panel reading 'The Shame of Cantona: Full story pages 2, 3, 4, 5, 6, 22, 43, 44, 45, 46, 47 & 48'. The Premier League was big news. After Cantona successfully appealed against a two-week prison sentence for his attack, he reluctantly attended a press conference, where he slowly, thoughtfully told the assembled press: 'When the seagulls ... follow the trawler ... it's because they think ... sardines ... will be thrown into the sea. Thank you very much.' He then stood up, shook the hand of his lawyer and swiftly departed to stunned laughter.

The crucial factor in Cantona's image, however, was that he wasn't simply different to every other Premier League player in terms of personality; he was also different to every other Premier League player in terms of footballing style. The references to philosophers and artists worked precisely because he was a footballing genius who boasted guile, creativity and unpredictability. He thrived upon space between the lines and was a creator as much as a goalscorer, boasting the Premier League's best-ever assists-per-game record. He loved chipping goalkeepers, he casually rolled home penalties, and he produced a succession of outside-of-the-foot flicks and elaborate, stabbed, dinked passes to teammates.

Cantona was also exceptional in a physical sense, ready for the rough and tumble of the English top flight. When Cantona had finally burnt his bridges in his home country, France assistant manager Gérard Houllier – keen to find Cantona a top-level club for the sake of the national side – suggested England specifically because Cantona possessed the strength and aerial power to survive. Cantona was six foot two, and his most distinctive physical feature was his chest, eternally puffed out. He held up the ball excellently, shrugged opponents aside nonchalantly, and a surprising number of his goals and assists came with his head. He was also quicker than assumed, as his speedy Manchester United teammate Ryan Giggs often mentioned.

Cantona didn't move straight from France to Manchester, however, and his introduction to English football was somewhat inauspicious. Sheffield Wednesday accommodated him for a week, although the precise purpose of this exercise was seemingly lost in translation; Cantona believed he was coming to sign, journalists assumed it was a trial, while manager Trevor Francis insists he was simply doing a friend a favour by letting him train. Whatever the truth, Cantona's only appearance in a Wednesday shirt was, utterly bizarrely, in a six-a-side friendly against American indoor specialists Baltimore Blast, which ended in an 8–3 defeat at Sheffield Arena, where Francis had enjoyed a Simply Red concert earlier in the week.

Cantona ended up 35 miles north, signing for Leeds United midway through their 1991/92 championship-winning season. Although he only scored three goals in 15 appearances that season – none of them directly winning a point – he became something of a cult figure among Leeds supporters, who once improvised a questionable version of 'La Marseillaise' in tribute to their star centre-forward. But Leeds didn't suit Cantona; manager Howard Wilkinson distrusted flair players and stated bluntly that no foreign forward had ever succeeded in English football, underlining how Cantona was fighting against the tide. 'Can Eric adapt to life in England or can we adapt to Cantona? Do I ask him to change or do I ask Leeds to change to the French style?' pondered Wilkinson, before declaring, 'There will be no French revolution because that, in our football terms, would inevitably suffer a defeat.' Cantona was often bypassed as Leeds played a succession of long balls, although he started 1992/93 in tremendous form, hitting the only hat-trick in Charity Shield history, then the first-ever Premier League hat-trick. Still, his relationship with Wilkinson, and his history of rebelling against authoritarian managers, meant that he never had a long-term future at Elland Road. Ferguson and Manchester United pounced.

The story about Cantona's transfer is famous – Wilkinson phoned Manchester United to enquire about the availability of full-back Denis Irwin, and Ferguson took the opportunity to ask about Cantona. But it wasn't simply a fortunate swoop: Ferguson had already been seriously interested, and had specifically asked centre-backs Gary Pallister and Steve Bruce for their opinion after Leeds's visit to Old Trafford. Both suggested he was a difficult opponent because he took up unusual positions, and Cantona had also produced a spectacular bicycle kick, saved by Peter Schmeichel, that drew an unusual round of applause from across Old Trafford for an away player.

Crucially, as revealed in Auclair's biography, Ferguson had recently attended a Rangers v Leeds Champions League tie, sitting alongside Houllier, and after Cantona reacted angrily when substituted, Houllier expressed concern, wryly remarking that he'd need to find Cantona another club. Ferguson was immediately interested, but only pounced after youngster Dion Dublin, a considerably more straightforward striker, suffered a broken leg. Ferguson sniffed around other players: creative forwards like Matt Le Tissier and Peter

Beardsley, but also more typical strikers like David Hirst and Brian Deane. He was open-minded about the type of forward he required, because first-choice striker Mark Hughes was a one in three rather than one-in-two goalscorer, and many suggested he needed to play alongside a ruthless goalscorer, prompting Ferguson's interest in Alan Shearer before he joined Blackburn that summer. But Cantona was for sale when others weren't, and joined United for the ludicrously small fee of £1.2m – incredible considering Ferguson had unsuccessfully offered over £3m for Hirst.

The purchase of a player in Cantona's mould revolutionised United's tactical approach overnight. While Ferguson unquestionably deserves enormous credit for United's success during this period, his side lacked a defined style until the Frenchman's arrival. Ferguson encouraged attack-minded football with width, in keeping with United's traditions – but there was a rudimentary approach in the final third, epitomised by the time winger Andrei Kanchelskis stormed off the training pitch in frustration at yet another crossing drill, muttering 'English football is shit' on his way – not an unreasonable comment at the time. Ferguson was considered a man-manager rather than a footballing philosopher or astute tactician. Schmeichel, who would become Cantona's roommate on away trips, summarised Cantona's first training session concisely. 'From that day, Manchester United's style of play changed,' he said. 'The arrival of Cantona suddenly made it clear to the coaching staff exactly how the team should play to be successful.' Cantona was the catalyst for United's revolution, and their success set the tone for the tactical development of rival Premier League clubs, which was initially accelerated by the influence of inspirational foreign players rather than managerial philosophies.

Cantona was capable of playing either as a traditional centre-forward or as a playmaker, having filled both roles at various stages of his career. For United, he was generally used in the number 10 role behind a traditional striker, effectively turning United's 4–4–2 system into a 4–4–1–1. The Premier League had very few deep-lying forwards in this mould; Teddy Sheringham, who would later replace Cantona at United, became renowned as an excellent 'withdrawn' forward, although at this stage was more of a target man, winning the inaugural Premier League Golden Boot with 22 goals, having transferred from Nottingham Forest to Tottenham three games into the campaign. Southampton's Matt Le Tissier was in a similar mould to Cantona, but was suffering under the management of Ian Branfoot, who wanted his defenders to thump long balls downfield. Neither Sheringham nor Le Tissier had yet been capped by England. Peter Beardsley, another of Ferguson's targets, was the most similar type of forward, although often found himself out of the Everton side. Besides, Beardsley lacked Cantona's flamboyance and wasn't superstar material – he was among the quietest, humblest players in the top flight, whereas Cantona was surely the most arrogant, albeit with some justification.

English football was historically suspicious of deep-lying forwards, despite the likes of Ferenc Puskás and Diego Maradona causing the national team so much misery over the years. It was considered a foreign role, and extravagance in English football was usually the domain of tricky wingers, with Tom Finney, Stanley Matthews and George Best among the most revered players. Even Paul Gascoigne, England's most talented player of this era, was a number 8 rather than a number 10, a midfielder who burst forward from deep. It was unfortunate the Premier League didn't witness Gascoigne at his best: he spent its first six years with Lazio and then Rangers, only returning to England with Middlesbrough and Everton in his thirties. Ferguson, incidentally, says being beaten by Spurs to Gascoigne's signature in 1988 is one of his biggest regrets in football, and

Gascoigne would later phone Ferguson in the summer of 1995 (when Cantona was serving his eight-month ban and intending to leave England) begging for a move to United. Ferguson, however, concentrated on convincing Cantona to stay.

Ferguson had a close relationship with Cantona throughout his five years at Old Trafford. Whereas Ferguson took a schoolmasterly approach to the majority of his players, Cantona was afforded the rare privilege of a cup of tea with his manager before training every day, and while it's difficult to imagine anyone entirely understood Cantona, Ferguson came closest. Managers often suggest the toughest part of their job is affording star players special treatment without prompting dissent from the rest of the squad, and Ferguson quickly realised he needed to make allowances for Cantona, sparing him from blasts of 'the hairdryer', as Manchester United players called Ferguson's tendency to scream in their faces after bad performances.

Winger Lee Sharpe tells an amusing, revealing anecdote about the United squad's reception at Manchester Town Hall shortly after their first title victory. The rest of the squad wore smart black suits, but Sharpe arrived in an olive-green silk outfit with a green tie. This inevitably prompted Ferguson to come over and admonish him, at which point Cantona strolled into the room with a suit, no tie – and red Nike trainers. Ferguson let out a cry of frustration and simply stormed off. A similar incident occurred when Ferguson was about to criticise Sharpe for getting a skinhead haircut on a pre-season tour, only to suddenly notice Cantona had the same, forcing him to bite his tongue. 'There were times when the different treatment Eric got was laughable,' Sharpe complained. 'It was one set of rules for him, and another for the likes of me.' After Cantona's infamous kung-fu kick at Selhurst Park, Ferguson's first instinct in the dressing room afterwards was to complain about sloppy defending for Crystal Palace's equaliser.

In general, footballers accept a star teammate being indulged, and on the pitch Cantona was effectively handed a free role with licence to roam wherever he pleased. He contributed little in defensive situations, as Roy Keane later recalled. 'Often we'd give him a bollocking for not tracking back. We certainly did more than our share of running for him. Then, just when exasperation was being felt, and expressed, Eric would produce a bit of magic to turn the game our way.' English football was learning that players in Cantona's mould were worth embracing, worth freeing from defensive responsibilities, and a footballing culture that valued hard work and commitment above everything else was forced to reconsider its principles. United's youth coach Eric Harrison, upon first seeing Cantona in training, said he 'wanted to kidnap him and spend a week talking to him about football'.

Tactically, opponents simply weren't structured for stopping Cantona. Ordinarily, centre-backs were fighting against centre-forwards, and central midfielders were involved in running battles with their opposite numbers. Players like Cantona, who interpreted the game differently and dropped into the space between opposition defenders and midfielders, were able to enjoy plenty of time on the ball. 'Eric, no matter the tempo or the maelstrom of Premier League football,' Ferguson said, 'has that ability to put his foot on the ball and to make his passes. That in itself is almost a miracle.' So much of this, however, was simply about Cantona's initial positioning, combined with his ability to hold off defenders when they approached. Previously, United had focused on attacking down the flanks, or hitting longer passes to centre-forward Hughes, who was superb at bringing down high balls and feeding teammates. But Cantona orchestrated United's attacking play wonderfully, and like the very best number 10s – particularly Maradona, but also, in Premier League terms, Dennis Bergkamp and Gianfranco Zola – was a selfless footballer who recognised that his individual freedom should be used for the collective good.

In addition to Cantona's on-field contribution, he was also a tremendous example to his teammates in training. He insisted upon some level of autonomy – his own warm-up routines before joining in with the other players' warm-up, for example – but United teammates agree he raised the standard of training considerably. His professionalism inspired the club's emerging youngsters, including the 'class of '92', featuring Giggs, David Beckham, Nicky Butt, Paul Scholes, and Gary and Phil Neville, surely the greatest set of footballers ever produced by an English youth academy.

'During my time at Manchester United I was lucky enough to have a lot of people who put in countless extra hours to get better,' Ferguson wrote in his autobiography. 'Gary Neville turned himself from an average footballer into a wonderful one because of his work ethic, as did David Beckham. I remember Eric's first day, and after the training session had finished he asked for a goalkeeper, two players from the junior team who were still there, and a few footballs. I asked him what he needed those for, and he said he wanted to practise. When word got back to the other players, one or two more turned up the next day for an extra session and so the number grew. That was all because of Cantona's work ethic and influence.' Phil Neville has a slightly different interpretation, which makes more sense considering there are plenty of tales about the incredible dedication of him, his brother and Beckham before Cantona joined. He says that Cantona didn't inspire the youngsters to work hard – they did that already – but he made it 'acceptable' to do so, ensuring they weren't seen as teacher's pets by experienced members of the squad.

Where it counted, on the pitch, Cantona made an immediate difference. His stunning, instant impact is occasionally overlooked:

he arrived at Old Trafford in late November 1992 with United in eighth place, nine points behind surprise leaders Norwich City, having scored a pitiful 17 goals in 16 league games. A title challenge was unthinkable. But with Cantona's arrival United's scoring rate doubled and they rose to top of the table after the first game in January.

Manchester United's most famous victory during the title run-in was unquestionably their 2–1 victory over Sheffield Wednesday at Old Trafford, when United found themselves 1–0 down going into the final five minutes, before two headers from centre-back Steve Bruce produced an unlikely turnaround. Bruce's second arrived deep into an unusually extended period of stoppage time – the referee had been replaced because of injury – which was the start of Manchester United's habit of scoring crucial late goals throughout the Premier League era, and gave rise to the expression 'Fergie time'. Ferguson and his assistant Brian Kidd famously spilled onto the Old Trafford pitch in their jubilant celebration of a winner that put Manchester United top of the table, a status they wouldn't relinquish. However, United's most tactically significant victory occurred five days earlier, away at Norwich. This display would dictate the big-game approach under Ferguson for years to come, and is the single most influential team performance in the history of the Premier League.

For a significant period of 1992/93, Norwich were title favourites. They'd been the first Premier League leaders after a surprise 4–2 victory over Arsenal, which appeared nothing more than a freak opening-day result, Norwich having only escaped relegation on the final day of the previous season and being widely tipped for the drop having sold star striker Robert Fleck to Chelsea. However, Norwich's key man was actually Mike Walker, a likeable, calm, silver-haired Welshman and among the most promising managers in the country.

In an era when route one remained dominant, Norwich's passing football, their tendency to score spectacular goals and their underdog status ensured they became the neutral's favourite. Other Premier League managers were man-managers and disciplinarians, but Walker loved discussing tactics and offered a clear, forward-thinking philosophy. He'd been dismissed from his only previous managerial job, at Colchester, because his chairman considered Walker's brand of passing football 'too soft' for the lower leagues – despite the fact Colchester were only one point from the top of Division Four. Walker claimed he was 'happy to win every match 4–3', although Norwich actually suffered several heavy defeats and, peculiarly, finished in third place despite a goal difference of –4.

Norwich's default formation was 4–4–2, but it was a flexible system most notable for the advanced positioning of the two full-backs, Mark Bowen and Ian Culverhouse. Right-winger Ruel Fox was among the quickest wingers in the league, central midfielder Ian Crook boasted a fine passing range and Mark Robins banged in the goals up front. They were the Premier League's first good footballing side, and when they defeated Wimbledon 2–1 in December, their lead at the top was an incredible eight points after 18 games.

But then Norwich somehow failed to score in their next five games, almost proving the old-fashioned British dogma that continental football wasn't suitable when winter arrived and pitches became boggy. Norwich recovered to play a significant part in the title fight, and started April top of the Premier League once again, with Aston Villa and Manchester United a point behind. The Canaries' next fixture was a home match against Ferguson's side, and while Villa couldn't be ignored, this felt like a title decider. United appeared to be wobbling; winless in four matches, and without suspended centre-forward Hughes. It was widely anticipated that Ferguson would introduce veteran Bryan Robson in central midfield, with Brian McClair returning to the striking role he'd played before Cantona's arrival.

Instead, McClair stayed in midfield alongside Paul Ince, and Ferguson deployed three natural wingers at Carrow Road, with Andrei Kanchelskis in the same team as Sharpe and Giggs, who essentially played as a centre-forward in advance of Cantona. The outcome was a quite astonishing spell of counter-attacking football, with Norwich dominating possession but United scoring on the break three times in the first 21 minutes.

The goals were incredibly direct. For the opener, Schmeichel typically hurled the ball 40 yards to Sharpe, on the left, who prodded the ball with the outside of his left foot to Cantona, waiting between the lines. The Frenchman controlled the ball, paused briefly as he waited for midfield runners, then played a through-ball that found no fewer than three United players – Sharpe, Ince and Giggs – beating Norwich's offside trap simultaneously. Giggs collected the ball, rounded goalkeeper Bryan Gunn, could have passed, but rolled the ball home himself. From penalty box to goal in 12 seconds and eight touches.

The second featured even better interplay. Schmeichel moved to collect a loose ball inside the penalty area, but Steve Bruce thumped it to the right – straight to Kanchelskis, who volleyed the ball into the centre circle for Ince, who volleyed it back out to Giggs, who knocked the ball backwards for McClair, whose first-time pass found Kanchelskis running through on goal. The Russian winger had Cantona in support, but dribbled past Gunn and converted. From penalty box to goal again in 14 seconds and nine touches.

Just a minute later, Ince – the man supposedly anchoring the midfield behind five attackers – collected a loose ball in central midfield and immediately stormed past one, two, three challenges, bore down on Gunn and then flicked the ball right for Cantona, who fired into an empty net. This time, the move had only started from midway inside United's half, but it took nine seconds and six touches for the ball to end up in the net.

The counter-attacking looked so simple; United simply waited for Norwich to push forward, then attacked into space with frightening speed. Each time they broke in behind with multiple players, each time they took Gunn out of the game before converting into an open goal. 'We were a good counter-attacking side, but our performance exceeded even our own expectations,' raved Bruce. 'The speed and incisiveness of our movement, the quality of the passing, it was right out of the top drawer and Norwich couldn't live with it.'

Ferguson could barely contain his excitement, saying, 'Some of our football was breathtaking, unbelievable stuff,' while Cantona later provided the best summary. 'That was the turning point,' he said. 'We played a perfect game. We played perfect football.' United went on to win the title, and that performance pointed the way to Premier League glory. Had Norwich defeated United and gone on to win the title themselves, their incredible underdog success might have popularised possession football. Instead, inspiration came from United's speed.

Manchester United's first Premier League title was achieved when things fell into place almost accidentally, but the following season, 1993/94, saw them reach a different level entirely. Players often remark upon the difficulty of defending a title – there's less motivation to succeed, and opponents up their game against the champions – but Ferguson, who had retained the Scottish title with Aberdeen in the mid-1980s, astutely ensured his players maintained their desire. Before the start of the campaign he announced to United's squad that he had a sealed envelope in his office drawer, containing a piece of paper with a list of players he believed lacked the hunger to win a second title. The trick proved highly effective, with his players determined to prove him wrong.

Ferguson, typically for this period, canvassed the views of his players about potential new recruits, and after they unanimously agreed that Nottingham Forest's Roy Keane was a top-class midfielder, Ferguson broke the British transfer record to make one of his most important signings. This changed the balance of United – with McClair relegated to the bench, Keane formed a brilliantly aggressive, combative central midfield partnership with Ince. Cantona's influence was naturally greater because he was present from the outset, while Giggs became a greater goal threat from the left and Kanchelskis, peripheral in the previous campaign, was outstanding down the right. Such was the emphasis upon battling central midfielders and electric wingers, some journalists depicted United's formation as 4–2–4, although in reality it was a 4–4–1–1, and not dissimilar to the 4–2–3–1 that only became a recognised Premier League system a decade later.

United were utterly dominant throughout 1993/94. Within the opening fortnight they'd won away at their two title rivals from the previous campaign, Norwich and Aston Villa, and topped the table from the end of August onwards. They only lost twice until the end of March, both against Chelsea – although United defeated them 4–0 in the FA Cup Final, which clinched the club's first-ever double. Ferguson's first-choice XI played together 13 times, and won 13 times.

Subsequent United teams would become more cultured, particularly when Paul Scholes and David Beckham emerged to provide passing quality from midfield, which helped United progress in Europe. But in Premier League terms, Ferguson's 1993/94 first-choice XI was perfectly suited to the week-in, week-out challenges of a division still based around physical football, with tough tackles, poor pitches and 42 games – four more than from 1995/96 onwards, when the division was reduced from 22 to 20 teams. They were 'real tough bastards' in Ferguson's words, and he later suggested that his 1993/94 side were as good as the treble winners of five years later.

Manchester United's 4–4–1–1, with combative central midfielders and speedsters out wide, would essentially become the standard tactical template throughout the Premier League's first decade. The difficult part for teams hoping to follow in their footsteps, however, was obvious: finding their Cantona.

3

The SAS
& The Entertainers

*'I'll tell you, honestly,
I will love it if we beat them. Love it.'*

Kevin Keegan

Sir Alex Ferguson famously described his greatest challenge at Manchester United as 'knocking Liverpool right off their fucking perch'. He had turned United into English football's dominant side, and they would eventually overtake Liverpool in terms of league titles. During the mid-90s, however, United's greatest title fights were not against Liverpool, but against clubs managed by two ex-Liverpool forwards: Kenny Dalglish's Blackburn Rovers in 1994/95 and Kevin Keegan's Newcastle United in 1995/96.

Under these managers, Blackburn and Newcastle did everything a year apart. Dalglish had taken charge of second-tier Blackburn in 1991 and achieved promotion in 1992. Keegan took charge of second-tier Newcastle in 1992 and won promotion in 1993. Blackburn hadn't won the championship since 1928, Newcastle not since 1927. There were similarities between Keegan and Dalglish, too; they were born within a month of one another in 1951, and when Keegan left Liverpool for Hamburg in 1977, his replacement up front was Dalglish.

Tactically, both sides played 4–4–2, concentrating upon width, crosses and a towering number 9, and there was also a common link in defensive midfielder David Batty, who came into the side towards the end of both Blackburn's 1994/95 triumph and Newcastle's 1995/96 campaign. Both clubs, meanwhile, suffered a significant late-season slump during their title challenge. That might sound peculiar, considering Blackburn triumphed in 1994/95 and Newcastle are remembered as 'bottlers' for blowing a 12-point lead the following season, but Blackburn's collapse had been equally dramatic. They contrived to lose three of their final five games during their title-winning season, including a dramatic final-day defeat at Anfield, where even Liverpool supporters wanted Blackburn to win, to deny rivals Manchester United another title and to witness Dalglish, an Anfield legend, lift the trophy.

Left-back Graeme Le Saux later outlined the extent of Blackburn's nerves in the final weeks, admitting that the players became obsessed with Manchester United and claiming that Dalglish didn't know how to control the situation. At half-time on that final day at Anfield, winger Stuart Ripley sat down in the dressing room and declared he was so nervous he couldn't get his legs to work properly. Blackburn were saved by Manchester United's failure to win away at West Ham. In the 'bottling it' stakes, therefore, there was minimal difference between Blackburn in 1994/95 and Newcastle in 1995/96 – aside from the fact that Dalglish convinced the outside world he had things under control, while Keegan had a meltdown live on TV with his famous 'I will love it if we beat them' rant.

Dalglish and Keegan were primarily man-managers and motivators rather than tacticians or training-ground coaches; they attracted players through their reputation as legendary players and broadly left them to their own devices. The most significant difference was the nature of their assistants. Dalglish's only previous managerial post was at Liverpool, where he maintained the pass-and-move football his predecessors had introduced. At Blackburn, however, he was starting from scratch, and with more limited players, so his approach was much simpler. Dalglish decided he wouldn't take charge of Blackburn without Ray Harford, widely considered one of the most intelligent, inventive English coaches of his generation.

Harford boasted managerial experience, having been promoted from assistant to manager at Fulham, Luton (where he won the League Cup) and Wimbledon. He would later succeed Dalglish at Blackburn, too. His Luton and Wimbledon sides were renowned for their direct football, and he provided the coaching expertise that Dalglish lacked for creating a straightforward but effective crossing side. Dalglish said his 'coaching, organisation, his deep knowledge of football' made him the perfect assistant, and Harford took almost every Blackburn training session, concentrating heavily upon 'pattern of play' sessions that improved Blackburn's passing and movement.

Keegan, on the other hand, appointed his old Liverpool teammate Terry McDermott. Not only did McDermott, like Keegan, boast absolutely no previous coaching experience, he also had no coaching badges, had no intention of becoming a coach and had recently been spotted manning a burger van at a racecourse. 'He's not here in any capacity other than to help the atmosphere of the club,' said Keegan, who personally paid for McDermott's employment from his own salary. McDermott concentrated on taking players aside after training and improving a specific part of their technique. Blackburn had an assistant manager who took every training session and focused upon the collective, while Newcastle's assistant manager didn't take any sessions and focused upon individuals. Ultimately, that was a perfect microcosm of the sides' approaches.

Blackburn were new kids on the block. Before the Premier League era they hadn't featured in the top flight since before England won the World Cup, even dropping into the third tier during the 1970s. Their sudden rise owed much to the wealth of Jack Walker, a Blackburn-born millionaire who had inherited Walkersteel, a scrap-metal business, from his father and turned it into the largest steel stockholder in Britain. His munificence explains how second-tier Blackburn managed to attract Dalglish, already a multiple title winner as both player and manager with Liverpool, and how, having won promotion in time for the Premier League's inaugural campaign, they promptly finished fourth, second and then first. Dalglish insists Blackburn's title wasn't solely about Walker's millions, with some justification – although the signings of centre-forwards Alan Shearer and Chris Sutton both broke the record for the highest transfer fee paid by a British club. Both were old-fashioned number 9s who thrived on crosses, in keeping with Blackburn's simple footballing approach, and they quickly became nicknamed 'the SAS' because of their ruthlessness in front of goal. They contributed 49 goals during Blackburn's title-winning campaign and remain arguably the Premier League's most famous strike partnership. Their off-field relationship, however, was less successful.

When Shearer signed for Blackburn in 1992 he was befriended by new strike partner Mike Newell on a pre-season tour of Scotland, and as he waited for his wife to move to Lancashire he spent plenty of time at Newell's house. It was a classic footballing friendship; they played golf together, they travelled to training together, they were roommates on away trips and their great relationship continued on the pitch. Newell had previously been an out-and-out striker, but after Blackburn recruited the country's hottest young goalscorer, Newell adjusted and played a deeper, supporting role. 'He was an ideal striking partner, so unselfish and willing to cover every blade of grass,' Shearer said. 'Sometimes he gave the impression he would rather lay on goals for me than score himself ... with him just behind the attack, opposition teams would push a defender out to mark him and that would give me more room in which to operate. He was a big reason for my success.' Shearer won the Golden Boot in three of the first five Premier League seasons, and finished on a record 260 Premier League goals.

The arrival of Sutton, who had only recently become a permanent centre-forward at Norwich having often played in defence, changed things in two ways. Most obviously, Newell was the major victim and started just twice in Blackburn's title-winning season. Meanwhile, Sutton stole Shearer's thunder, taking his status as Britain's most expensive player. He briefly became Blackburn's highest-paid player, too, although Blackburn immediately handed Shearer a rise to reflect his seniority. 'Suddenly, Alan was being asked to play with a guy who wanted to score as many goals as him,' said Le Saux. 'That was when I saw a side of Alan that I wasn't keen on ... Alan knew his relationship with Mike revolved around himself, and neither he nor Mike reacted well when Chris broke up their partnership.'

Sutton, a fearsome striker but a sensitive character who occasionally lacked confidence, later recalled the 'lack of warmth' from Shearer, blaming his friendship with Newell. When Sutton hit a hat-trick in a 4–0 victory over Coventry in Blackburn's third game of the season, he was upset when Shearer didn't celebrate with him. Publically, Dalglish insisted there were no problems between his two star strikers, but with Blackburn's attacking play no longer based entirely around him, Shearer wasn't best pleased.

It was nevertheless a stunningly effective strike partnership. Blackburn's opening goal of their title-winning season, away at

Southampton, set the scene. Captain Tim Sherwood lofted a long pass into the box, Sutton nodded the ball down, and Shearer smashed the ball home. Simple, but effective. Blackburn now had two strikers in the penalty box whenever possible, and without Newell playing the link role, focused heavily on getting the ball wide and sending in a stream of crosses.

As much as the SAS, Blackburn's football was defined by their two wingers. Right-sided Stuart Ripley and left-sided Jason Wilcox were classic, touchline-hugging dribblers who sprinted to the byline and hung crosses into the box. As Dalglish put it, they were 'proper wingers, not wide midfielders'. Nor were they goalscorers like Manchester United's pairing of Ryan Giggs and Andrei Kanchelskis, who were capable of reaching double figures in a season, but rather facilitators, assisters and, unlike many wingers, extremely hard workers without the ball. Blackburn's central midfielders, Sherwood and Mark Atkins (who played the majority of the season before being replaced by Batty, who returned from injury for the final five games), pushed forward in turn, the other protecting the defence. Sherwood was better in possession, Atkins cool in front of goal – the best finisher at the club, according to Dalglish – but they seldom played throughballs and instead passed calmly out wide. It was a system 'designed for a centre-forward to score goals', as Shearer said.

Critics claimed Blackburn's approach play was too predictable, but opponents found it difficult to stop, partly because of the cohesive interplay stemming from the training sessions directed by Harford, whose favourite phrase was simply 'If it ain't broke, don't fix it.' Blackburn's training ground, incidentally, was astonishingly basic: a patch of land covered in dog mess, with no changing facilities. The players drove to Ewood Park, got changed, then drove to training. Most problematically, the training ground was adjacent to a cemetery, so sessions were frequently interrupted out of respect when a hearse slowly crept up the driveway. Harford's 'pattern of play' sessions involved Blackburn lining up in their 4–4–2 formation on the training pitch, and practising their build-up play. Their passing and movement was very structured and always ended with Blackburn working the ball into crossing positions.

There were three major approaches. Ideally, Blackburn found a winger in a position to dribble forward, their most obvious route to goal. If not, the wingers were instructed to come short, bringing the opposition full-back up the pitch and allowing Shearer or Sutton to drift wide into space. Shearer implored Sutton to do the majority of the running so he could remain in the penalty box, but actually became an excellent crosser himself, ending the campaign as Blackburn's most prolific assister as well as their top scorer. Finally, Dalglish and Harford recognised that full-backs were the players with the most time on the ball when 4–4–2 played 4–4–2, invariably the battle of formations during this period. Right-back Henning Berg was more of a converted centre-back, so there was a huge emphasis on left-back Le Saux to push forward, and he had a fine relationship with Wilcox and Shearer, supplying many key assists, most notably hanging a cross up for Shearer to nod home in Blackburn's penultimate match of the campaign, a 1–0 victory over Newcastle.

Crucially, Harford demanded that crosses were played from what he termed 'the magic box', the space in the final 18 yards, as if the penalty area extended across the entire width of the pitch. Shearer disagreed with this concept and was confident he could convert crosses played from deeper – the type of ball David Beckham would later supply him with at international level – but Harford believed crosses from advanced positions created better chances, and Wilcox and Ripley depended upon getting into this 'magic box' to a staggering extent. Midway through the title-winning season, Dalglish called

Ripley aside in training and attempted to devise a plan B. Eventually, he reasoned, opposition full-backs would work out Blackburn's plan and usher Ripley and Wilcox inside. In that situation, 40 yards from goal, in a narrower position and forced onto his weaker foot, Dalglish asked where Ripley wanted the strikers to position themselves to be a target for crosses. Ripley looked at him blankly. 'Are you taking the piss?' he asked. No, insisted Dalglish. Ripley thought about it some more. 'I don't know,' he admitted. The thought had never occurred to him; Blackburn's wingers literally only knew how to play one way.

Blackburn's tactical naivety was highlighted when they encountered continental opposition. In the opening round of the UEFA Cup, the club's first-ever game in European competition, they were drawn against Swedish part-timers Trelleborg. The nature of Trelleborg read like a stereotypical 'European minnow' checklist; they boasted just one full-time professional footballer, alongside a carpenter, a shopkeeper and an insurance salesman. They'd recently lost a domestic cup tie to third-division opposition, and had progressed through the UEFA Cup qualifying round with an unspectacular victory over the champions of the Faroe Islands. They arrived at Ewood Park to discover their kit clashed with Blackburn's, so were forced to borrow Rovers' red away shorts. Journalists had researched Blackburn's record victory, suspecting it could be surpassed, while the Swedes later claimed they would have considered a 2–0 defeat a decent result. Instead, Trelleborg's Frederik Sandell latched onto strike partner Joachim Karlsson's flick-on to score the game's only goal. Trelleborg defended deeper than anyone Blackburn faced in the Premier League and focused on doubling up against Blackburn's wingers. 'If you were organised you could stop them,' said captain Jonas Brorsson.

'There was potentially a bit of naivety in the way we played,' Ripley later recalled. 'We were steamrollering teams in England and I think we tried to do the same, but they came with a defensive formation and nicked the win.' Le Saux, meanwhile, admitted Blackburn's style didn't suit European competition. The second leg finished 2–2 – the SAS both scored close-range efforts in the aftermath of set-pieces – and ten-man Trelleborg progressed 3–2 on aggregate. The early exit emphasised English clubs' tactical inadequacy, but allowed Blackburn to concentrate on domestic football.

There were no defining victories during Blackburn's title campaign – they lost home and away to their closest challengers, Manchester United, and stuttered badly during the run-in, but their simple approach proved enough to consistently defeat run-of-the-mill Premier League sides. Blackburn weren't doing anything different, they were simply doing it in an extremely cohesive manner, with excellent players. Six of their starting XI (goalkeeper Tim Flowers, commanding centre-back Colin Hendry plus Le Saux, Sherwood, Sutton and Shearer) featured in the PFA Team of the Year, which was announced before Blackburn sealed their title.

Manchester United had clinched the first two Premier League titles anticlimactically when rivals slipped up, but 14 May 1995 was truly memorable, as the Premier League's first final-day decider. Blackburn went 1–0 up at Liverpool when Shearer typically converted Ripley's right-wing cross, and had Rovers maintained that scoreline, they were champions regardless of United's result. But Liverpool produced an unlikely turnaround, with Jamie Redknapp's superb late free-kick confirming a 2–1 home victory. Dalglish spent much of the second half watching a TV close to the dugouts, showing the action from Manchester United's game at Upton Park: Sir Alex Ferguson's decision to play a lone striker backfired, and West Ham's Luděk Mikloško provided one of the Premier League's all-time great goal-keeping displays. United could only draw 1–1, which meant Blackburn's defeat was irrelevant – they were champions. Dalglish was congratulated by old friends from Liverpool's backroom staff, Shearer and Sutton warmly embraced, Sherwood lifted the trophy.

For all this incredible drama, Blackburn's previous visit to Merseyside was more significant stylistically. On April Fools' Day, Blackburn stormed into an early 2–0 lead at Everton; the first goal came inside 13 seconds, then the quickest to date in the Premier League, when Berg's long ball was headed on by Sutton, then by Shearer, and Sutton fired home. The second came after a free-kick found Sutton, who stumbled and allowed Shearer to fire home. It was textbook Blackburn. But then, after Graham Stuart got Everton back into the game with a stupendous chip, Blackburn embarked upon a remarkably blatant display of cynical football, concentrating upon breaking up play and time wasting. It was an incredibly fierce, frantic contest, with the highlight an incredible goalmouth scramble in front of Tim Flowers, which featured no fewer than 14 players inside Blackburn's six-yard box. The climax saw Shearer thumping a clearance so far that he nearly sent the ball out of Goodison Park entirely. At full-time, Everton's fans booed Blackburn off. Dalglish couldn't care less about whether opposition supporters appreciated his side's style of play. To him it was three points, and job done.

In stark contrast, when Kevin Keegan was asked for his favourite memory from Newcastle's 'nearly' campaign of 1995/96, he recalled his players being applauded onto the pitch by opposition fans during the final few days of the season, away at Leeds and Nottingham Forest. Dalglish called his Blackburn side the 'people's champions', playing on their underdog status, but Newcastle were the true neutral's favourite, a team who played enthralling, attack-minded football. Keegan's impact during this period was incredible; he took the club from the bottom-half of the second tier to the top of the Premier League, galvanising a whole city. Newcastle's shirts displayed the blue star of the Newcastle Brown Ale logo, their goalkeeper's shirt during 1995/96 depicted the city's skyline, while Keegan spoke about the club's cultural importance to the city in a manner that recalled Barcelona. At times their football was comparable too, and Newcastle were referred to as, simply, The Entertainers.

Newcastle earned that nickname a couple of seasons earlier, with a 4–2 victory over Sheffield Wednesday, but 1995/96 took things to a new level, and Newcastle's title challenge was somehow befitting of British pop culture at the time. 1996 was the year of England hosting, and threatening to win, Euro 96, soundtracked by Baddiel and Skinner's 'Three Lions'. 1996 was when Britpop still reigned supreme. 1996 saw the launch of Chris Evans's *TFI Friday*, a programme based largely around wackiness, and the debut of the loud, extroverted Spice Girls. 1996 was the year of *Trainspotting*, a film about a group of heroin addicts that managed to become a feelgood story. Somehow 1997 felt very different, a melancholy year dominated by the film *Titanic*, Radiohead's *OK Computer* and the death of Princess Diana. 1996 was about mad-for-it extravagance, and here were Keegan's Newcastle, The Entertainers, playing all-out-attack football with no regard for the consequences.

Newcastle started the season, like Blackburn the previous year, with tactics based around crossing. Left-winger David Ginola was signed from Paris Saint-Germain and bamboozled opposition right-backs with his pace and ambidexterity, able to receive the ball with his back to goal, before spinning either way, cutting inside or going down the touchline. He won Player of the Month immediately. On the opposite flank Keith Gillespie was a typical winger of that period, always reaching the byline. Keegan's instructions to his wingers were simple: new signing Les Ferdinand was the best target man in the business, and he was to be supplied with constant crosses. 'The way the side was playing, with Ginola on the left and Gillespie on the right, was ideal for a striker like me,' Ferdinand recalled. 'Both David and Keith were raining balls into the penalty area from all over the place.'

Surprisingly for such an aerial threat, Ferdinand was only five foot 11, but was blessed with a prodigious leap. He hit 21 league goals by mid-February, while Keegan encouraged him to develop his game and bring teammates into play, having become frustrated with his predecessor Andy Cole's single-mindedness. Whereas Blackburn used two target men up front, Keegan played Peter Beardsley in a deep-lying forward role, linking attacks. With Rob Lee bursting forward from central midfield, this was the most complete attacking force the Premier League had witnessed. Newcastle started at an incredible pace, attempting to win matches within the opening half hour, and weren't involved in a single goalless draw all season. 'The Entertainers' tag, however, also underlined Newcastle's defensive frailties. Keegan had openly preached a 'you score two, we'll score three' philosophy, although the defining game in Newcastle's season – and the most memorable in the Premier League era – was the defeat at Liverpool in April, which was 'we'll score three, you score four'. Many attributed Newcastle's title failure to their leaky defence, although the truth is more complex.

Keegan made no attempt to hide his attacking approach. He was determined to satisfy the Geordies' thirst for positive football, and considered himself part of a wider movement to make football more exciting, at a time when managers frequently highlighted the fact their team had 'put on a show' when matches were live on Sky. 'A lot of forwards are coming into management,' he said at the time. 'You look at Brian Little, Glenn Hoddle, myself. We are all forwards who wouldn't really know enough about defending to coach it.' It was a selective argument, though. Arsenal boss George Graham had been a forward, then later an attacking midfielder so languid he was nicknamed 'Stroller', but he had assembled the most disciplined defence in English football.

Keegan's defenders were, originally, midfielders and attackers. It's common for players to be shifted into a different position as they develop, but Newcastle's situation was quite remarkable, particularly with their three main centre-backs. Darren Peacock had been a centre-forward in the Bristol Rovers youth team. Steve Howey had risen through Newcastle's ranks as an attacking midfielder, occasionally used in defence during training – but when Keegan arrived, he told Howey he was either a centre-back or he was leaving. Belgian Philippe Albert, meanwhile, started his career as a midfielder and was recruited on the strength of his displays at the 1994 World Cup, where he continually brought the ball forward from the back. Keegan, working as a TV pundit for the tournament, witnessed him score against both the Netherlands and Germany, and snapped him up.

First-choice full-backs Warren Barton and John Beresford were encouraged to push forward simultaneously and, by the end of the campaign, were replaced by hometown lads Steve Watson and Robbie Elliott, both forwards when rising through the ranks at Newcastle. Another Geordie, holding midfielder Lee Clark, had played an attacking midfield role the previous season, hence his number 10 shirt. It was, more or less, a team of forwards, as Keegan acknowledges in an admirably honest passage from his autobiography. 'Were my full-backs too adventurous? Yes! Were my centre-backs too skilful, better going forward than going back? Yes! But that is what we built.' That was that, and Keegan wasn't going to change. Towards the end of the campaign, his back four – Watson, Howey, Peacock and Beresford – approached him, suggesting they were being overrun and Newcastle should play more cautiously. Keegan's response to the critique was simple – 'Do you wanna play on Saturday?'

He ignored defending to a remarkable extent. Newcastle had a rare defensive training session ahead of the long trip down to Southampton in September, lost 1–0, and Keegan never bothered with defensive drills again. Later, after Newcastle failed to win the Premier League, Keegan appointed former Liverpool defender and BBC pundit Mark Lawrenson as a defensive coach. Lawrenson, however, spent his time merely observing training and didn't take a single coaching session under Keegan, at one point confessing to him that he wasn't sure what he was being paid for. His appointment was Keegan's attempt to fight the criticism rather than a genuine attempt to fix the problem.

But, amazingly, Newcastle's defensive record in 1995/96 was actually reasonably good, and that famous 4–3 defeat at Anfield has exaggerated their weakness at the back. They conceded 37 goals in 38 matches, only two more than Manchester United, and considering the subsequent four title winners conceded 44, 33, 37 and 45 goals, Newcastle's defensive record wasn't a barrier to success. Instead, their problem was that they didn't score enough, managing only 66 goals – lower than every single Premier League title winner. The 'Entertainers' tag wasn't entirely true, and for all their individual brilliance, Newcastle lacked cohesion. It wasn't simply that they ignored defensive work in training, more that they didn't do any tactical work whatsoever. No work on shape, no work on build-up play, no work on set-pieces. Nothing that makes a group of players into a team.

Training was extremely simple, and the players loved it – as did the supporters. Newcastle used the facilities at Durham University, which meant training was essentially public and often watched by thousands of people during the title run-in. The players would arrive early and play head tennis, with Keegan and McDermott among the most feared doubles partnerships. They'd then play high-intensity, match-speed, small-sided games, the teams often determined by playground-style 'pick teams'. They would end with skills and shooting drills, and some players would stay behind to work on individual technical aspects. But Newcastle never discussed team shape.

Keegan had a similarly relaxed attitude towards opponents. Alex Ferguson was increasingly adjusting small details to counter an opponent's strengths and provided specific information on their weaknesses. But Keegan wouldn't mention Newcastle's upcoming opponents in training and would simply read out the opposition's team sheet in the dressing room shortly before the warm-up. He'd add a couple of words to rubbish his opponents – 'wouldn't have any of them', or, if he'd recently signed one of their players, 'I've got the one I wanted.' It was all about individuals. Ignoring the opposition proved particularly problematic in away matches, where Newcastle were literally only half as good as at St James' Park – they won 52 points at home, just 26 away.

Keegan's team talks rarely included specific instructions for coping with the opposition, although there was one notable exception. Ahead of a mid-April meeting with Aston Villa, Keegan realised Brian Little was using three centre-forwards – Dwight Yorke, Savo Milošević and Tommy Johnson – and therefore instructed left-back Beresford to defend narrower, helping Newcastle's two central defenders. Beresford, however, complained that Keegan was ignoring the knock-on effect; Villa's right-back, Gary Charles, would overlap into his left-back zone because Ginola wouldn't track back. Keegan wasn't interested. When the inevitable repeatedly happened – Charles found space on the right – Keegan shouted instructions to Beresford rather than Ginola. This infuriated Beresford, and the two had a blazing row by the St James' Park touchline, which ended when Beresford told Keegan to 'fuck off', prompting his immediate substitution. 'You can't have players saying what he said to me,' said Keegan afterwards. Beresford had started 32 of the 34 games until that point, but was dropped entirely for the final four games.

The cause of Newcastle's decline, however, was related to the addition of two signings in the New Year. Unpredictable Colombian forward Faustino Asprilla was signed on a snowy Friday in February, the day before Newcastle made the short trip to Middlesbrough. On matchday Keegan assured Asprilla he wouldn't be playing, and at lunchtime poured him a glass of wine. But incredibly, the Colombian was introduced as a second-half substitute just hours later and created the equaliser for Watson almost immediately, bamboozling opposition centre-back Steve Vickers with a wonderful Cruyff turn before crossing. Watson pointed to Asprilla in celebration, and his teammates instinctively congratulated the assister rather than the goalscorer. Asprilla had provided Newcastle with a spark.

While his signing is sometimes blamed for Newcastle's collapse, in the second half of the season Asprilla was Newcastle's best player. He was fantastic in the unfortunate, and fatal, defeat to Manchester United, when the combination of Peter Schmeichel's saves and Eric Cantona's finish resulted in a barely deserved 1–0 win for the eventual champions. He was pivotal in the 3–0 victory over West Ham and was Newcastle's best player in that 4–3 defeat to Liverpool, grabbing a goal and an assist. The problem, though, was that his arrival changed Newcastle's shape entirely – and Keegan didn't explain how he wanted his players to adjust. Asprilla was very different to Beardsley, who switched to an unfamiliar right-sided midfield role, and Ferdinand was left perplexed by the change, especially as Asprilla was immediately the main man. 'I haven't bought Asprilla to play with you, I've bought him for you to play with him,' Keegan somewhat bluntly told Ferdinand. There were no attempts to get them on the same wavelength in training, and Keegan later told Ferdinand he simply needed to 'expect the unexpected' from Asprilla – a reasonable summary of his style, but hardly useful advice. Ferdinand, having been scoring at roughly a goal per game beforehand, now scored one in three.

The Colombian's full debut coincided with Keegan's surprise decision to switch from Newcastle's usual 4–4–2 to a more flexible system often appearing like a 3–5–2 for a 2–0 defeat to West Ham and a hugely entertaining 3–3 draw at Manchester City. The biggest beneficiary was Albert, as the moustachioed Belgian centre-back was deployed as a sweeper with licence to burst forward. Against City he scored twice and created the other for Asprilla, all from open play, a perfect demonstration of how he was a footballing centre-back ahead of his time. Asprilla was Newcastle's most dangerous attacking weapon in both games, but got away lightly with a one-match ban for elbowing and headbutting City centre-back Keith Curle. 'He's from Latin America, that's the way they are,' offered Keegan. That dominated the headlines, but the greater issue was that Newcastle's lack of shape had never been more obvious. Newcastle won 43 per cent of matches with Asprilla, compared with 75 per cent without him.

For the next game, a 1–0 defeat to Manchester United, Newcastle returned to 4–4–2 but boasted another new signing: David Batty, the circumstances of whose arrival were peculiar. Sir John Hall, Newcastle's chairman, wanted to sign a centre-back to improve Newcastle's defence. Keegan was having none of that, however, so they compromised and bought a defensive midfielder, which doesn't seem a particularly logical approach to recruitment. Even Batty was surprised. 'They were flying at the top of the table and I couldn't imagine why they'd want to change things,' he admitted. Batty, a pure defensive midfielder, replaced the forward-thinking Clark, and once again, Newcastle attempted to play similar football with an entirely different player in a key position – the problem, of course, was the system rather than individuals. Batty slowed Newcastle's passing and didn't perform his defensive midfield role perfectly either – in the late-season 1–1 draw with Nottingham Forest, for example, Ian Woan dribbled past him easily before smashing into the top corner from 25 yards. Keegan considered Batty an excellent signing – although, typically, believed his long-term future was as a forward-thinking centre-back, bringing the ball forward from deep. Keegan's logic was that this would allow him to play yet another attacking player in midfield. He simply couldn't get enough.

Newcastle's gung-ho approach was epitomised by that 4–3 defeat to Liverpool at Anfield in early April 1996, a game widely considered the Premier League's greatest. It was an action-packed, end-to-end thriller, the goals starting in the 2nd minute and not ending until the 92nd. Newcastle led for the majority of the contest, both 2–1 and 3–2, but somehow conceded a late-minute winner to Stan Collymore, to leave Keegan slumped over the advertising hoardings.

Newcastle entered the game in disastrous form, having collected just seven points from their previous six matches. Keegan made one change, with Watson replacing Barton at right-back, probably linked to the fact Watson had already scored two winners that season against Liverpool, in the reverse league fixture and the League Cup.

The ludicrously open nature of the contest was summarised by the positioning of Ginola. Newcastle played a 4–4–2 system while Roy Evans' Liverpool played 3–5–2, which meant an inevitable question about whether or not Ginola would track Liverpool's right-wingback Jason McAteer. The answer was simple – he didn't. This had both positive and negative consequences; after Robbie Fowler had opened the scoring and Les Ferdinand equalised, Ginola's advanced positioning behind McAteer meant he streaked away on a counter-attack. Liverpool's centre-backs played very narrow, and Ginola had the entire left flank to himself, finishing coolly.

In the second half, however, Liverpool exploited the space behind Ginola, in particular with Steve McManaman's constant drifts to that flank. He crossed for Fowler to equalise and had another dangerous cross sliced just wide of the far post by Steve Howey. Newcastle raced down the other end and scored again through Asprilla, in part because Liverpool centre-back John Scales had dropped very deep to cope with Ginola's advanced positioning, playing the Colombian onside. Liverpool soon equalised again with a right-wing cross – this time a beautiful curled ball by McAteer, with Ginola nowhere to be seen. 3–3, and arguably two goals at either end came from Ginola's positioning. The final five minutes were even more open, after Evans boldly introduced veteran striker Ian Rush for left-wing-back Rob Jones, with Collymore moving left. After interplay between Rush and John Barnes in the centre, the ball was switched wide to Collymore, who smashed home the winner. Liverpool had won the game with the type of attacking gamble that Keegan greatly admired. Keegan loved contributing to such a legendary, attack-minded game. 'After the match I turned to Terry Mac and said, "I know I should be disappointed, but I'm elated,"' he later recalled.

Newcastle's players gave various tactical explanations for their decline. Ferdinand was frustrated the attack was now built around Asprilla. Gillespie believed his omission meant Newcastle weren't stretching the play properly, something Lee agreed with, as Beardsley wasn't at home on the right. Goalkeeper Pavel Srníček suggested Batty upset the rhythm of the side, and also accepted that Newcastle were simply found out by better sides in the second half of the campaign. The experiment with Albert as a sweeper in a rough 3–5–2, meanwhile, lasted two games, cost Newcastle five points and was immediately abandoned. Ginola's decline in the second half of the season was also significant; his defensive sluggishness was criticised, but it wouldn't have been problematic had he contributed the attacking efficiency of earlier in the season.

More than anything else, however, Newcastle's problem was their overall lack of cohesion, surely due to omitting any collective work on the training ground. Keegan's threw together talented individuals and let them run free, which largely worked with a simple, old-fashioned 4–4–2 that everyone knew how to play. But this laissez-faire style proved problematic when Keegan suddenly switched shape, when he signed a different type of centre-forward and a different type of deep midfielder. Newcastle simply didn't have any tactics; their approach was a consequence of the 11 players Keegan assembled on any particular day.

But while Newcastle ultimately fell short of winning the Premier League, it was unquestionably a glorious failure; the players remain heroes in the city, the team still admired across the country. Keegan's achievement in taking Newcastle from the second tier to the brink of the title shouldn't be underestimated, and while naivety may have cost Newcastle the title, the most pertinent story is that they came so close with such basic tactics, highlighting the primitive approach of most Premier League sides at this point.

The title was presented in the north-east – but at Middlesbrough, where Manchester United ended the season with a 3–0 victory. Keegan was magnanimous in defeat, immediately congratulating Manchester United and predicting they would be 'fantastic representatives of the Premier League in the Champions League' the following season. It recalled the way he'd referred to Asprilla, upon the Colombian's arrival, as 'a real asset to the Premier League – and Newcastle United, I hope'. Perhaps it was just semantics, but it's difficult to imagine Ferguson, who cultivated an 'us against the world' approach, caring about the benefits to the league as a whole.

Newcastle responded to their failure in dramatic fashion, breaking the world transfer record to sign hometown boy Shearer from Blackburn. Keegan lasted just half of the following campaign before suddenly resigning, to be replaced by, inevitably, Dalglish. With Batty, Shearer and Dalglish, it was clear Newcastle were trying to be Blackburn – but tactically, the Premier League was already moving in a different direction.

Part Two

Technical Progress

4

Between the Lines

*'Cantona's supporters loved him, and so did the
media. He was this foreign fella, different.
Everyone wanted one like him, but it didn't
mean players like that grew on trees.'*

Roy Evans

As Eric Cantona's influence ensured Manchester United became the
Premier League's dominant force, other clubs desperately searched
for their Cantona equivalent. A wave of talented, mercurial but often
inconsistent number 10s joined the Premier League during the
mid-1990s, with mixed success. England wasn't producing players in
that mould, so clubs looked abroad – often to relatively obscure footballing nations. Supporters of unglamorous, mid-table Premier
League sides could now get excited by exotic, mysterious foreign
deep-lying forwards whose presence was meant to inspire more
aesthetically pleasing football.

Ipswich Town, for example, had Bulgarian Boncho Genchev, who
opened his goalscoring account with a wonderful bicycle kick against
Blackburn. He positioned himself between the lines to encourage

passing football, but struggled to exert a consistent impact upon Premier League games. After a brief spell back home, he ended his career with a couple of spells at non-league Hendon, taking a break in between to run a short-lived Bulgarian café in Kensington called 'Strikers'. Genchev himself wasn't actually a striker, of course, although he was presumably comfortable in the serving role.

Southampton found the diminutive, extraordinarily gifted Israeli Eyal Berkovic, who featured decisively in the Saints' famous 6–3 victory over Manchester United in 1996, his second league start. Berkovic enjoyed a successful Premier League career, although he is probably most famous for being booted in the head during a West Ham training session by teammate John Hartson.

Derby County signed Aljoša Asanović, a wonderful left-footed creator who played a significant part in Croatia's journey to the Euro 96 quarter-finals and the 1998 World Cup semi-finals, and who is quite possibly the most underrated Premier League player. Unsurprisingly, he insisted on taking the number 10 shirt. Coventry City signed Moroccan Mustapha Hadji, a direct dribbler with a fine passing range, and he also took number 10. At West Ham, Harry Redknapp signed the Premier League's first two Portuguese players – first Dani, then Paulo Futre. To Futre's disgust, he wasn't handed the number 10 shirt.

Ahead of his first game against Arsenal, West Ham's kitman Eddie Gillam handed Futre the number 16 shirt, and promptly had it thrown back in his face. Not understanding that the Premier League had switched to permanent squad numbers that were consistent throughout the season and that number 10 had already been allocated to John Moncur, Futre shouted at Redknapp, 'Futre 10, not 16! Eusebio 10! Maradona 10! Pelé 10! Futre 10! Not fucking 16!' Redknapp told Futre to either wear the number 16 shirt or go home. So Futre went home. He later insisted the number 10 shirt was written into his contract, and when Redknapp pretended West Ham's club shop had shifted so many shirts with Futre's name and '16' on the back that they couldn't change it, Futre offered to refund any disappointed supporters up to a total cost of £100,000. Eventually West Ham sought permission from the Premier League for Moncur to change numbers, allowing Futre to wear 10; he thanked Moncur by allowing him a fortnight's stay in his holiday villa on the Algarve. It's surprising something similar didn't happen at Sheffield Wednesday a couple of years later – two brilliant Italians, Benito Carbone and Paolo Di Canio, had serious claims to the number 10 shirt, but were forced to wear 8 and 11 respectively, with their favoured number taken by the somewhat less spectacular Andy Booth.

During this period, a relatively limited number of games were broadcast live on TV, while *Match of the Day* showed extended high-lights from only a couple of big matches, screening just goals and major incidents from others. These players' subtle, constant influence upon matches was therefore not overwhelmingly obvious to the majority of supporters, so they needed to provide concise summaries of their quality with outstanding individual moments.

Between November 1996 and August 1997 the BBC's Goal of the Month competition was won by Dennis Bergkamp, Eric Cantona, Trevor Sinclair, Gianfranco Zola, Juninho, Zola again, Juninho again, then Bergkamp again – who, ludicrously, finished 1st, 2nd and 3rd that month. Sinclair's famous bicycle kick aside, the Premier League's greatest moments were being provided almost exclusively by four magical foreign playmakers: Cantona, Bergkamp, Zola and Juninho. These players fundamentally changed their clubs' footballing style, but required their sides to be built entirely around them. This proved problematic. Depending upon a newcomer to English football was risky, especially when foreign imports were still a relatively recent phenomenon and clubs did extremely little to help them settle.

If Cantona was the trailblazer, Bergkamp and Zola followed closely behind in his slipstream. They weren't, however, joining title challengers; Arsenal had finished in the bottom half of the Premier League immediately before signing Bergkamp in the summer of 1995, as had Chelsea just before their purchase of Zola the following year. Like Cantona, both players had an immediately positive effect on their teams, and the fact that Manchester United, Arsenal and Chelsea have been the three most successful clubs in the Premier League era can, in part, be traced back to the arrival of these three brilliant deep-lying forwards.

Bergkamp and Zola were unquestionably top-class footballers. Bergkamp had finished second in the 1993 Ballon d'Or, one place ahead of Cantona and behind only Roberto Baggio, the greatest number 10 of this generation. Meanwhile, Zola finished sixth in 1995. They were revered across Europe because of their creativity, their selflessness and the spatial awareness that allowed them to thrive between the lines. Both arrived from Serie A, with Bergkamp – whose influence upon Arsenal would become clear later on – outlining why he discovered the Premier League suited him. 'English defences always played a back four, with one line, which meant they had to defend the space behind. In Italy they had the libero [a sweeper who would cover behind his fellow defenders], but the English had two central defenders against two strikers, so they couldn't really cover each other. As an attacker I liked that because it meant you could play in between the lines. They couldn't come off their line. So I used that.'

Zola discovered something similar. 'At the beginning, the open English football really helped me, as I was coming from tighter marking in Serie A,' he explained. Zola only arrived in England because his former club, Parma, had an inflexible coach who was unwilling to deviate from 4–4–2. Surprisingly, this was Carlo Ancelotti, who would later become the go-to manager for continental giants awash with superstars – including Chelsea – precisely because he was flexible enough to build teams around star individuals. Back then, however, Ancelotti – who had been Italy's assistant coach under legendary manager Arrigo Sacchi, the man who popularised a pressing 4–4–2 system – simply wouldn't accommodate a number 10, turning down Baggio for similar reasons, and attempted to play Zola out wide. 'I will be able to play my proper role in England,' Zola declared upon his arrival in London.

Zola had served his apprenticeship at Napoli under the best possible mentor. 'I learned everything from Diego Maradona,' he admitted. While famous for his ego, Maradona was also renowned for being extremely generous with his praise of his Napoli teammates, and he loved Zola so much that, ahead of a Coppa Italia tie against Pisa, he handed the Sardinian his famous number 10 shirt, and wore number 9 instead. Zola was forced to settle for 25 at Chelsea, with Mark Hughes in his favoured 10 shirt, but it became an iconic number. Although not officially retired by Chelsea, no one has dared to wear Zola's number 25 since his departure in 2003.

Zola's technical ability was outstanding. His first goal was a magnificent free-kick in a 2–2 draw with Everton, and only David Beckham has scored more Premier League free-kicks. Zola confirmed his status as Chelsea's dead-ball specialist after a training-ground competition with Dennis Wise. A sock was tied to the crossbar – both were five foot six, so this presumably involved one sitting on the other's shoulders – and they stood outside the box and attempted to curl the ball against the sock. Zola won 10–1, and the matter was settled. Dismayed by the lack of equipment at Chelsea's old training ground near Heathrow Airport, Zola purchased his own mock defensive wall and spent hours practising.

While Cantona was tall and physically commanding, Zola was small, slight and wore size 5 boots. He was strong for his size, however, and used his body excellently. Chelsea teammate Graeme Le Saux considered him the joint best forward he'd ever seen, along with Kenny Dalglish, at the art of shielding the ball from defenders. But more than anyone else of this era, Zola thrived upon space, a classic example being his winner in the 1997 FA Cup semi-final against Wimbledon at Highbury. Initially positioned high up against the opposition defence, Zola watched teammate Roberto Di Matteo moving between the lines, dragging Wimbledon's right-sided centre-back Chris Perry up the pitch. Zola then sprinted into the space Perry had vacated, pulling Wimbledon's left-sided centre-back Dean Blackwell across to cover. Di Matteo played the ball into Zola's feet, and Chelsea's number 25 immediately backheeled it into the zone Blackwell had vacated, changed direction, collected the ball and fired home. In a few seconds, he'd seen space, exploited it, created more space, exploited that, and scored. For a player in his mould, it was the perfect goal.

Crucially, Zola was allowed a 'free role' behind the main striker, in a Chelsea side formatted specifically to bring out his qualities. Centre-back Steve Clarke remembers a team talk in which the message was simply 'get the ball to Zola', while Wise referred to Zola as a 'showhorse' and labelled himself a 'donkey'. The donkey's job, he said, was simply to do the hard work and pass to the showhorse. 'Historically [English sides] have been set up with two strong strikers, two sitting midfielders and two wingers,' Zola said after his retirement. 'You never used to play the ball through the middle. What you used to do was play the ball down the sides and cross the ball to the tall player.' Zola, like Cantona and Bergkamp, helped to change that.

'He's a clever little bugger ... a better player than I thought he was,' Alex Ferguson had conceded two months earlier, after Zola scored a fine second-minute goal against Manchester United, dribbling inside from the right before finishing with his left foot. 'I thought we could push my full-backs forward, but he was smart enough to go and play wide. He has got a good head on him.' Later, Ryan Giggs claimed that such was Zola's ability to find space that he was the only Premier League player United man-marked, although this often proved unsuccessful. For Chelsea's 5–0 thrashing of United in October 1999, Ferguson was without Giggs and played Phil Neville in his place, but instructed him to play centrally, man-marking Zola. United largely nullified the Italian but left a gaping hole on their left, which meant Chelsea's Albert Ferrer and Dan Petrescu, two right-backs in tandem, assisted the opening two goals with deep crosses.

While Premier League observers marvelled at these majestic, game-changing foreign number 10s, there was nevertheless an acknowledgement that many arrived in Britain because they had limited options elsewhere. Cantona had effectively been run out of France, Bergkamp struggled in Italy with Inter Milan, while Zola had recently turned 30, then considered the cut-off for forwards' peak years, and admitted he only expected to play for a couple more seasons. There was a sense that the Premier League was gaining top-class players when they were on the way down. Therefore, in one respect the most significant arrival during this period was another foreign number 10: Juninho. Newly promoted Middlesbrough's purchase of the diminutive Brazilian in 1995 was a truly remarkable transfer coup, because he was unquestionably on the way up.

Juninho had impressed on English soil that summer, when world champions Brazil competed alongside England, Sweden and Japan in the Umbro Cup, a tournament held as preparation for the following summer's European Championships. Juninho wore Brazil's number 10, the most iconic shirt in world football, played in a 4–3–1–2 system based around him and was inspirational in the 3–1 victory over England. He opened the scoring with a classic Brazilian 'folha seca' (dry leaf) free-kick, played with topspin, which surprised goal-keeper Tim Flowers with its sudden dip. Simply being allowed to take free-kicks ahead of Roberto Carlos was an achievement in itself. Brazil's second goal, meanwhile, showcased Juninho's playmaking skills perfectly; he received the ball between the lines, glanced up and sidefooted a through-ball into the path of another promising young-ster, Brazil's number 9, who finished confidently by rounding Flowers and converting into an empty net. It was English football's introduc-tion to Ronaldo, and yet everyone was talking about Juninho.

In the home dugout at Wembley that sunny afternoon was Bryan Robson, then acting as assistant to England manager Terry Venables in addition to his role as player-manager of Middlesbrough. Mesmerised by the opposition number 10's performance, Robson convinced Middlesbrough's board to sign Juninho, beating the likes of Arsenal, Inter and Porto to the Brazilian's signature. Middlesbrough chief executive Keith Lamb referred to his new recruit as 'the most sought-after player in the world'. Hyperbole, certainly, and some-what undermined by the fact that Juninho cost less than Middlesbrough's other major arrival that summer, Nicky Barmby, but this was a landmark purchase, a rising player joining a rising team in a rising league.

His unveiling was a huge event in Middlesbrough. Fans greeted him at the airport with Brazilian flags, more cheered as he arrived at the new Riverside Stadium in scenes reminiscent of a papal visit, then 6,000 moved inside to watch him play keepy-uppies with Robson. His first press conference didn't pass without one inevitable question. 'Does he know how cold it gets in Middlesbrough in January?' asked one journalist. Juninho, through a translator, insisted it wouldn't be that bad, although he was often criticised by pundits for playing in gloves, and during his first winter stuffed newspaper inside his boots in an attempt to keep his feet warm. Robson responded by describing Juninho as a 'tough character' – and most top-class Brazilian attackers are. The cliché about Brazil suggests it's non-stop samba football, played by technical players who learn their trade playing on the Copacabana. Realistically, the Brazilian top flight is extremely aggressive: it's not simply that defenders kick attackers ferociously, it's that referees allow it, and so Juninho's transition from Brazilian to English football wasn't as tough as many anticipated.

Immediately afforded a free role by Robson, Juninho used that licence fully on his debut against Leeds, starting on the right flank before quickly drifting across to the left. He played two killer through-balls inside the first half, setting up Jan Åge Fjørtoft for the opener. Inevitably, Leeds's response was to kick him, and both Carlton Palmer and John Pemberton were booked for fouling the Brazilian. The *Independent*'s match report remarked upon his 'surprising courage' and ended with an acknowledgement that 'perhaps he is tougher than anyone thought.' Indeed, his final significant contribution before being substituted was a thundering tackle on legendary crossbar-botherer Tony Yeboah, one of the Premier League's most powerful players, which earned a booking. That went down well, as fans wanted proof he would get stuck in.

A fresh-faced, slender creator whose name meant 'Little Junior' – so small they named him twice – the Brazilian wasn't expected to thrive in English conditions, but Juninho loved the north-east and loved English football. The club found him a house in Ingleby Barwick, a large housing estate, and he moved in with his entire family, which helped him settle. Juninho's house became something of a local landmark, with children queuing outside for his autograph. His mum made them cookies, and Juninho wasn't averse to the occasional kickabout in the street.

Juninho was tricky but direct in possession, efficient with the ball rather than a showboater. He was an instant hit, and unquestionably in the class of the aforementioned number 10s, later playing a significant role in Brazil's 2002 World Cup triumph. In Juninho's second season, Alex Ferguson described him as the Premier League's best player and later considered signing him. His finest moment in English football arrived during that campaign, a 1–0 home victory over Chelsea in March. He outshone Zola and created a succession of chances, wasted by Craig Hignett and Mikkel Beck. Eventually, he settled things himself. Receiving the ball wide on the left, he slalomed between Wise and Di Matteo and evaded a desperate lunge from Chelsea's third central midfielder, Craig Burley, before slipping the ball into the left-hand channel for Beck. The Danish striker paused, and then chipped the ball into the box for a perfect diving header from – of all people – five-foot-six Juninho. The Brazilian magician wasn't simply performing the duties expected of a Brazilian number 10, outwitting the entire opposition midfield, but also the duties of an English number 9, beating Chelsea's centre-backs to score a header. 'I don't know what Juninho's running on at the moment,' Robson said afterwards. 'He isn't looking tired, he's keeping pace with the game – and he's tackling back!' Make that the qualities of an English number 4, too.

In his second season Juninho was handed Middlesbrough's number 10 shirt, having worn 25 in his debut campaign, and was also named the Premier League's Player of the Season. Admittedly not as prestigious an award as the PFA or FWA Player of the Year, it was nevertheless an acknowledgement of his great influence. And yet, staggeringly for one of the league's most revered players, Juninho ended the campaign sobbing on the pitch as Middlesbrough were relegated.

Basing the side around Juninho didn't pay dividends. When Juninho made his debut for Middlesbrough in November 1995, the

Teesiders were sixth, having lost to only the two title challengers, Manchester United and Newcastle. Despite Juninho's impact, their form nosedived dramatically. They were atrocious in the second half of the season, winning just two of 19 matches. They finished 12th, but in points terms, were closer to relegation than 11th.

The 1996/97 relegation campaign was also strange for Middlesbrough. They reached both the League Cup and FA Cup finals, losing to Leicester City and Chelsea respectively – a devastating double blow for a club that had never won a major honour (although Juninho would later help them to League Cup success seven years later, then into his third spell on Teeside – he simply couldn't stay away). Granted, Middlesbrough's relegation was partly because they were deducted three points for withdrawing from a December fixture at Blackburn when half their squad had been wiped out by flu, but you can't ignore the fact that they had the division's worst defensive record. There were also major problems in the dressing room, particularly involving star striker Fabrizio Ravanelli, a divisive influence. He once interrupted a team meeting with a lengthy rant in Italian about wanting to leave, and had a fight with Neil Cox before the FA Cup Final after the right-back suggested Ravanelli wasn't fit enough to start. 'Half the squad hated him and the other half loved him,' said Hignett. 'He was one of the best finishers I've seen, but he rubbed people up the wrong way. He was selfish in everything he did.'

Meanwhile Juninho, while individually brilliant and very popular with teammates, caused Middlesbrough problems. Like Cantona, Bergkamp and Zola, he thrived in space between the lines, but was a different type of footballer. An advanced midfielder rather than a withdrawn forward, he ventured into deeper positions to collect possession. He therefore wasn't suited to a deep-lying forward role in a 4–4–1–1 like the aforementioned players, and Robson constantly changed his shape in an attempt to base the side around both Juninho and Barmby, deploying 4-3-2-1 or 3-4-2-1 in his first season. It didn't quite work defensively, and getting the best from two players between the lines was difficult. Both Juninho and Barmby had a better relationship with the underrated Hignett, and Barmby departed after 18 months for Everton, leaving Juninho as the sole creator. His form improved, and a 6-1 thrashing of Derby demonstrated Middlesbrough's potential. 'I am now playing as well as I ever did in Brazil, but I think that is because I have found my best position,' Juninho said. In other words, the system was based around him.

In that second season Juninho suffered from fatigue, not helped by Middlesbrough's double cup run – or by international trips to South America, then an unprecedented problem for Premier League clubs. His biggest problem, though, was man-marking – Middlesbrough didn't have a Plan B when Juninho was nullified. The most famous example came during the 1997 League Cup Final defeat to Leicester. Two weeks beforehand in the league, Juninho had torn apart the Foxes in a 3-1 victory, so for the trip to Wembley, Leicester boss Martin O'Neill deployed Pontus Kåmark to follow the Brazilian everywhere across the pitch. In a 2011 interview discussing nearly 25 years in management, O'Neill said he'd never sent his teams out to be anything other than positive – apart from that final, when he knew he needed to concentrate on stopping Juninho. 'If you had seen him a fortnight before running riot at Filbert Street, only a fool would have chosen not to man-mark him,' he said. Many other managers thought the same; stop Juninho, and you stopped Middlesbrough. Ultimately, it ended with their relegation.

* * *

This became a familiar pattern among bottom-half clubs – brilliant individuals who weren't necessarily conducive to Premier League success. Bolton spent a club record £1.5m on Yugoslav playmaker Saša Ćurčić, who scored one of the goals of 1995/96 against Chelsea, ghosting past five challenges and playing a one-two with Alan Thompson before firing home. Bolton finished bottom that season. 'I was a crowd pleaser, everywhere the fans loved me,' Ćurčić recalled. 'But I wasn't very good for the team because I wasn't a team player.'

Another inventive playmaker who scored a memorable solo goal that season was Manchester City's Georgi Kinkladze – the epitome of a frustrating genius – who demonstrated the dangers of building your side around a number 10. Like Juninho, Kinkladze was recruited after a sensational performance against British opposition, at a time when Premier League scouts rarely looked abroad for new players. Kinkladze was inspirational in Georgia's 5–0 thrashing of Wales in November 1994, a seismic result; just three years after Georgia had gained independence, it was their first-ever competitive victory. Deployed behind Temuri Ketsbaia and Shota Arveladze in a 4–3–1–2, Kinkladze ran the game and grabbed his first international goal. 'They murdered us,' Wales goalkeeper Neville Southall later recalled. 'Kinkladze was different class and the best player on the pitch by a mile.' In the return fixture the following summer – four days before Juninho's performance at Wembley captured Middlesbrough's attention – Kinkladze again dominated. This time he scored the game's only goal, an incredible 25-yard, left-footed chip over Southall.

The Georgian was tracked by other clubs, and had unsuccessful trials at both Real and Atlético Madrid – and, intriguingly, a month-long loan at Boca Juniors, who revere the number 10 role more than any club in world football, where Kinakladze met his idol Maradona. None of them signed Kinkladze permanently, however, and instead he joined Manchester City as Alan Ball's first signing. Ball and Kinkladze's City experience started disastrously. City collected two points from their first 11 games, scoring just three goals, while Kinkladze struggled; homesick, unable to speak English and living in a Manchester hotel on his own for three months. Juninho was happy in Middlesbrough partly because he'd emigrated with his parents, and Kinkladze's improvement coincided with the arrival of two Georgian friends and his mother, Khatuna, who brought some home comforts: Georgian cognac and walnuts, and spices to make Kinkladze his favourite dishes.

Kinkladze scored his first goal in November, a late winner in the 1–0 victory over Aston Villa at Maine Road. 'He was bewildered to start with,' Ball said afterwards. 'He spoke very little English and it was foreign to him to tackle and scrap and fight like you do in England. But the boy's got an immense talent.' His Premier League spell is best remembered for a couple of truly magnificent goals. The first opened the scoring against Middlesbrough in December 1995, when he collected the ball on the right and dribbled into an inside-left position, before suddenly cutting back inside Phil Stamp and sidefooting the ball firmly into the far corner. Middlesbrough eventually won 4–1, however, with Juninho completing the scoring.

Kinkladze's other superb strike, later voted March's goal of the month, came at Southampton. Having already scored the first with a close-range tap-in, and hit the crossbar from outside the box, Kinkladze collected the ball on the right, dribbled directly towards goal while evading four increasingly desperate challenges, dummied to put goalkeeper Dave Beasant on the ground, then lifted the ball over Beasant's head and into the net. 'It was the closest thing I have seen to Maradona's goal against England!' Ball raved, before somewhat unnecessarily clarifying: 'Not the one with his hand, the one where he did everyone and put it away. People ask why we are bringing this type of player to this country. If that wasn't the answer today, nothing is.'

City supporters were already tired of United's dominance and Cantona's cult-like status, and they absolutely worshipped Kinkladze – the best Georgi in Manchester since Best. The love was reciprocated; after his initial alienation in Manchester, Kinkladze grew to love the city and married a Mancunian. 'If he'd been playing with a successful team,' said striker Niall Quinn at the time, 'then he would have won Player's Player of the Year because it's quite breathtaking what he's done in English football. He's a lovely guy as well – I think, because he doesn't speak a word of English – but he seems nice.'

This was at the height of Britpop, and Kinkladze was rewarded for his fine form with a chant to the tune of Oasis's 'Wonderwall'. 'All the runs that Kinky makes are blinding,' it ran, before ending with a brilliant: 'And after all … we've got Alan Ball.' The composer of the original song, City fan Noel Gallagher, also offered a wonderful Kinkladze summary. Describing him as 'either the most frightening thing I've ever seen or the best thing I've ever seen', Gallagher predicted Kinkladze would either lead City to the European Cup, or take them down to the Fourth Division. He was nearly right; when Kinkladze left City in 1998, they were in the third tier.

City were relegated because Ball built the entire team around Kinkladze, as winger Nicky Summerbee outlined. 'Bally loved him. Georgi could do no wrong – I got on very well with him and we weren't jealous because we could all see how talented he was, but some hated Alan Ball for doing that – except Georgi, because he loved all the praise … the problem with Georgi was that you couldn't play 4–4–2 because to get the best out of him you wouldn't want him playing a conventional running midfield game, and if there are two men wide, that leaves only one in midfield. Ball changed formation all the time, a sure sign he didn't know what he was doing.'

Keith Curle, then City's captain, later recalled the extent of the free role Ball afforded Kinkladze. 'I remember losing away to Arsenal that season and one of the goals we conceded came because Georgi hadn't tracked a runner. The lads were not happy and some said as much to the manager after the game. In reply, he told them that if they were as talented as Georgi, they wouldn't have to track back either.'

After City's relegation, Ball lasted just three games before he was replaced by Frank Clark, who tried a similar approach. 'I wanted to build the team around Kinkladze because that's the ideal way to get the best out of him. He's an incredible talent … [but] he certainly didn't like running if he didn't have the ball at his feet and I thought there was a certain amount of resentment towards him from some of the squad.' Like Ball, Clark ended up changing formation to change Kinkladze's role. He initially played a 4–4–2 with the Georgian as a deep-lying forward, then switched to 4–3–1–2, fielding him behind a strike duo. 'We tied ourselves up in knots trying to accommodate Kinkladze,' Clark continued. 'The [4–3–1–2] system suited Kinkladze perfectly because it gave him great freedom, but it didn't suit the other players and it didn't work.' Incidentally, Kinkladze switched to number 10 after City's relegation, having previously worn number 7.

Clarke was replaced by Joe Royle, less of a footballing romantic, whose first words to the board about footballing matters were simple: 'We have to sell Kinkladze.' He would no longer be indulged. 'Kinkladze was not a team player, and had a disturbing habit of disappearing for long periods during games,' Royle said. 'To the supporters he was the only positive in all that time. To me he was a big negative.' The Georgian was sold to European giants Ajax, a club who love technical players but play 4–3–3, so manager Jan Wouters had no space for a number 10. 'I could have been Maradona and he wouldn't have changed the system to accommodate me,' he complained. By this point, managers had tired of basing the side around Kinkladze, who needed a manager like Ball.

Chiefly remembered for his high-pitched voice, his red hair, his flat cap and for being the standout player in the 1966 World Cup Final, Ball was also the first footballer in England to wear white boots – the ultimate sign of a flair player – and clearly wanted like-minded footballers in his sides. Before Kinkladze, Ball had also adored England's truest number 10 during this period, Southampton's Matt Le Tissier.

Avoiding the hatred that comes with playing for a title challenger, Le Tissier was the most popular player in the country and a regular winner of Goal of the Month competitions. He scored a wide variety of incredible strikes: there was a chip-up-and-volley from a free-kick against Wimbledon and a legendary strike against Newcastle that involved backheeling the ball over his own head, before flicking the ball over two defenders in a row and volleying in. He lobbed Blackburn's Tim Flowers from 35 yards and chipped Manchester United's Peter Schmeichel from 25. He had enough natural ability to be an England regular but, fittingly for a man born in Guernsey, was distinctly un-English. His name added to the foreign feel, and in his younger days his father was contacted by France assistant manager Gérard Houllier, a keen fan of players in Cantona's mould, who unsuccessfully enquired whether Le Tissier had any French relatives.

Ball declared his love for Le Tissier immediately upon arrival at Southampton, with the south-coast club languishing in the relegation zone. In their first training session Ball and assistant manager Lawrie McMenemy pulled ten players onto the training pitch and assembled them in a defensive shape, leaving Le Tissier wondering if he'd be omitted, as had often happened under previous coach Ian Branfoot. Instead, Ball then dragged Le Tissier into the centre of the group and announced to the other ten players, 'This is the best player you've got on your team. Get the ball to him as often as you can, and he'll win games for you.' Le Tissier, a humble man, felt slightly uncomfortable being elevated to this status, but it provided an enormous confidence boost and he scored six goals in his first four appearances under Ball.

Just as Ferguson made allowances off the pitch for Cantona, Le Tissier's free role extended to socialising. On a rest day midway through a pre-season trip to Northern Ireland, Southampton's squad had planned a round of golf, but Ball suggested they went to a local pub instead. This was a bad move. After Ball retired to the hotel it turned into an all-day drinking session, capped by the players venturing out to a nightclub. They arrived back at 2 am, blind drunk, with training the following morning. Ball was furious, screaming at Beasant, Iain Dowie and Jim Magilton before sending them to bed. He then took Le Tissier aside and told him, 'Look, our senior players are setting a bad example … but the way you're playing, you can do what you like!' Le Tissier, incidentally, was routinely mocked by teammates for his drinking habits. He didn't drink beer, preferring Malibu and Coke, although this wasn't because of a revolutionary, forward-thinking diet – he admits consuming sausage and egg McMuffins ahead of training sessions, and fish and chips the evening before a game. Le Tissier wasn't the fittest or the hardest-working, and recalls an incident later in his career when then-Southampton manager Gordon Strachan shouted from the technical area to a particularly languid Le Tissier, walking back from an attacking move, 'Matt! Get yourself warmed up, I'm bringing you off!'

'Those 18 months Ball was there were the best of my career,' Le Tissier recalled. 'Ball built the team around me, instead of trying to fit me into the team.' Despite playing as an attacking midfielder rather than a forward, Le Tissier hit 45 goals in 64 games in all competitions under Ball, many of them spectacular. Southampton avoided relegation at the end of Ball's first season, and finished in the top half in his second.

Unfortunately, England managers didn't share Ball's enthusiasm for Le Tissier. There was still a suspicion of number 10s in his mould, even among managers like Terry Venables and Glenn Hoddle, who appreciated flair players. English football now adored foreign number 10s but didn't trust its own, and Le Tissier made the familiar complaint of the 1990s number 10: 'I think maybe England managers weren't brave enough to change their formation to accommodate me.' That said, Hoddle – who was Le Tissier's boyhood hero – used both him and Liverpool's Steve McManaman behind Alan Shearer in a fluid 3–4–2–1 shape for a 1–0 defeat to Italy in 1997, England's first-ever World Cup qualifying defeat at Wembley. It was a performance that encapsulated such an enigmatic footballer; Le Tissier was constantly second to loose balls, conceded possession regularly, and his lack of energy was juxtaposed by the constant running of the wonderful Zola, who played the same role for Italy and fired in the only goal when sprinting in advance of his strike partner. Nevertheless, Le Tissier came closest to scoring for England.

'It is not a gamble [to play Le Tissier] when you feel the game is going to be tight and the door might need to be unlocked,' said Hoddle afterwards. 'Le Tissier, with his talent, could do that.' Nevertheless, he lost faith in his most creative talent – presumably his faith-healer Eileen Drewery hadn't been able to help – and failed to include Le Tissier in his 30-man provisional 1998 World Cup squad, a blow Le Tissier admits he never recovered from. The ultimate 1990s Premier League player discovered the devastating news in a brilliantly 1990s way: by reading Teletext.

English football had learned to appreciate the quality provided by number 10s, but was still largely fixated on variations on 4–4–2.

Therefore, while the entire definition of a number 10 is that he's neither a forward nor a midfielder and instead is somewhere in between, realistically almost every number 10 is one or the other. And while withdrawn forwards like Cantona, Bergkamp and Zola thrived by dropping deep and turning their side into a 4–4–1–1, attacking midfielders like Juninho, Kinkladze and Le Tissier caused problems, because they generally needed more unusual formations that their English teammates simply weren't accustomed to. The Premier League was evolving in terms of personnel, but not yet in terms of tactics.

5

Arsènal

'Wenger doesn't know anything about English football. He's at a big club – well, Arsenal used to be a big club – he's a novice and should keep his opinions to Japanese football.'

Alex Ferguson

The sheer scale of revolution during the Premier League's formative years is best summarised by Arsenal. When the division was formed, Arsenal were the most traditional, conservative club in English football; the chairman was an Old Etonian from a family of cricketers, while the beautiful old marble halls at Highbury underlined the old-fashioned, if unquestionably grand, nature of the club. In footballing terms, Arsenal's players were old-school and British, the team most famous for its offside trap and for winning 1–0. 'Boring, boring Arsenal' was the standard jeer from opposition fans.

After just six years of the Premier League, however, Arsenal had become the model for futuristic football. They were the division's most attractive side, the most forward-thinking club in terms of physiology, they recruited footballers from untapped markets across

Europe and were the first team in English top-flight history to win the league with a foreign manager. The revolution, however, was not solely about Arsène Wenger.

Arsenal had enjoyed tremendous success in their eight seasons under George Graham, who won six major honours, including two league titles and the European Cup Winners' Cup. When Graham was suddenly sacked midway through 1994/95 after accepting an illegal payment from an agent, Arsenal vice-chairman David Dein wanted to appoint former Monaco manager Wenger, who he'd encountered by chance at Highbury six years earlier. Dein realised the need for revolution; whereas most directors of English clubs surrounded themselves with like-minded figures and lived in a rather small world, Dein also had a prominent role at the Football Association, which meant he was frequently travelling abroad, moving in international circles and discovering how antiquated English football had become. The move didn't happen this time. Wenger went to Japan – at this stage a complete footballing backwater, having never qualified for the World Cup – to coach Nagoya Grampus Eight. Japan had recently launched an extraordinary 100-year football plan with the intention of winning the World Cup by 2092, the type of long-term thinking Wenger would become closely associated with.

Instead, Arsenal appointed Bruce Rioch. He was a considerably safer choice, and somewhat reminiscent of Graham, both being ex-Scottish international midfielders and strict disciplinarians. Rioch's reign was troubled, as he ostracised senior players, but during his sole season in charge, 1995/96, he recorded a respectable fifth-place finish – and more crucially set the wheels in motion for the Wenger revolution, introducing a passing game that was distinctly different from the direct style Graham had favoured towards the end of his reign. He had two major objectives: encouraging Arsenal to play out from the back and ensuring there was less dependence upon Ian Wright in terms of goalscoring. 'Bruce encouraged us to pass the ball through midfield more,' goalkeeper David Seaman said. 'Had he stayed longer, I am sure he would have gradually changed the whole way we played – as was to happen later with Arsène Wenger.'

England captain David Platt, who arrived at Arsenal shortly after Bergkamp, had been playing in Serie A under revered coaches like Giovanni Trapattoni and Sven-Göran Eriksson, yet said that Rioch 'deeply impressed me with his vision of how the game should be played'. Martin Keown underlined the difference between Graham and Rioch: 'Under George the emphasis was to win the ball back, press as a team, deny the opposition space and have lots of offsides … Bruce began by introducing the passing game. We would work on keeping the ball, whereas with George we worked on winning it back.' Rioch was a huge admirer of flair players, and the board provided him with the transformative footballer Arsenal desperately needed: Dennis Bergkamp.

In terms of stylistic impact upon the Premier League, Bergkamp is second only to Eric Cantona. They could, in slightly different circumstances, have ended up at one another's clubs; Alex Ferguson had explored the possibility of recruiting Bergkamp before eventually signing Cantona, who, upon leaving Leeds, supposedly wanted to join one of Manchester United, Liverpool or Arsenal. When Cantona finished third in the 1993 Ballon d'Or, he made a particular point of paying tribute to Ajax's Bergkamp, who had finished second behind Roberto Baggio. He recognised a kindred spirit.

When Bergkamp left Ajax for Inter Milan that year, he was signed specifically because Inter were desperate to evolve from a defensive, unattractive side to a more aesthetically pleasing outfit. They were tired of the plaudits showered upon city rivals AC Milan, who had become Europe's most celebrated side courtesy of Arrigo Sacchi's revolutionary coaching and the efforts of three brilliant Dutchmen: Marco van Basten, Frank Rijkaard and Ruud Gullit. Inter had challenged them with a team featuring three Germans: Jürgen Klinsmann, Andreas Brehme and Lothar Matthäus. But at this stage there was a huge difference in the perceptions of Dutch footballers (intelligent, creative, dynamic) and German footballers (efficient, ruthless, boring) and Inter attempted to becoming more stylish by signing two Dutchmen of their own, Bergkamp and his Ajax teammate Wim Jonk.

But Inter's revolution never occurred. After poor initial results, they became more defensive and sacked their manager, leaving Bergkamp playing in a more direct side and unable to link attacking moves. He managed just 11 goals in two Serie A campaigns combined. It's fascinating, therefore, that Bergkamp put that frustrating experience aside and made a second transfer to a club who required a catalyst for technical football. After retirement, Bergkamp outlined his determination to be a revolutionary: 'Like when I chose Inter instead of Milan or Barcelona, I thought: "I'm the sort of player you don't see at Arsenal, so maybe I can show people this is my way of playing."'

Arsenal, who had generally been reluctant to pay large fees and therefore missed out on top talent during the Premier League's first three seasons, broke their club record fee three times over to sign Bergkamp and immediately reallocated Paul Merson's number 10 shirt to their new technical leader. The *Independent*'s headline read, 'Rioch signs Bergkamp to signal new era'. That would prove particularly prescient, but there were sceptics – England left-back Stuart Pearce said it was a 'massive gamble', pundits questioned his value when he took seven games to score, while Tottenham chairman Alan Sugar said his arrival amounted to 'cosmetic surgery'. Instead, it was more like a brain transplant. 'He was the one that changed our whole attitude towards training,' said Ray Parlour. 'Just watching the way he handled himself from day one was an eye-opener. It made you think: hold on a second, I need to up my effort here.'

Rioch, in particular, offered tremendous support, defending him staunchly from the early criticism and encouraging Bergkamp's teammates to supply him frequently between the lines, although Arsenal were sometimes crowded in that zone, with Bergkamp, David Platt and Paul Merson broadly playing similar roles. It was a notable shift, however, from Arsenal's previous approach of incessantly knocking long balls over the top for Wright. Bergkamp's first campaign was patchy – and he endured more quiet seasons at Highbury than his reputation might suggest – but he was unquestionably Arsenal's game-changer, someone who brought the best out of others. Bergkamp had finished as Eredivisie top goalscorer three times, but said his role changed upon arriving in the Premier League, becoming an assister more than a goalscorer, as shown by the fact that he collected 93 Premier League assists compared with 87 goals. Tellingly, the only other players to have scored 50+ Premier League goals but been more prolific assisters are all midfielders: Ryan Giggs, David Beckham, Damien Duff, Gareth Barry and Danny Murphy.

There were many similarities to Cantona; Bergkamp was also a perfectionist who worked upon his game tirelessly after training, practising seemingly simple passes repeatedly, setting the standard in terms of technique and professionalism. Supporters instantly recognised his ability, but teammates raved about the things you can't fully appreciate from the stands: the weight of his passes, the spin on the ball. Similar to Cantona, his pace was often overlooked – before the 2003/04 season, when Bergkamp was 33, he recorded the third-fastest 60m sprint time at Arsenal, behind Thierry Henry and Jermaine Pennant, but ahead of Ashley Cole, Robert Pirès, Gaël Clichy and Sylvain Wiltord. And as with both Cantona and Zola, opponents often remarked upon his surprising strength for a primarily creative player, enabling him to compete with aggressive centre-backs. 'People don't think that Dennis had such strength,' said Sol Campbell, a future teammate, 'but believe me, he was one of the strongest I played with or against.' Early in 1997/98, he scored a brilliant long-range strike having shoved aside Southampton left-back Francis Benali, considered the dirtiest defender in the Premier League. For all his technical quality, Bergkamp also had a petulant streak. He was dismissed four times throughout his Arsenal career, all straight red cards: an elbow, a push and two wild tackles, so 'the Iceman' always seemed a peculiarly inappropriate moniker. Besides, as nicknames go, considering Bergkamp's famous refusal to board an aeroplane, 'the Non-Flying Dutchman' was difficult to beat.

Bergkamp was, aesthetically, among the Premier League's greatest players and scored some wonderful goals during his 11 years at Arsenal. His classic strike was receiving the ball just outside the box in an inside-left position, before opening up his body and curling the ball into the far corner, a goal he scored four times in the space of 18 months, against Sunderland, Leicester and both home and away against Barnsley in 1997/98. Bergkamp also netted two of the Premier League's most famous goals. The first was against Leicester in 1997, where he brilliantly brought down a long ball, turned inside and finished coolly – a goal which foreshadowed his similar World Cup winner against Argentina the following summer – and there was also the astonishing, extravagant opener against Newcastle in 2002, where he flicked the ball one way around Nikos Dabizas with the inside of his left foot, then spun in the opposite direction before collecting the ball and converting with his right. It prompted years of debate about whether it was intentional, and when Arsenal commissioned a statue of Bergkamp outside their Emirates Stadium, the sculptor complained that goal was simply impossible to depict.

Bergkamp only played for a year under the manager who brought him to Arsenal, and the circumstances of Rioch's departure were peculiar. He was dismissed shortly before the start of 1996/97, a fortnight after signing a new contract. This time around, Dein got his wish and Wenger was appointed. But as Arsenal chairman Peter Hill-Wood admitted, both he and Dein had already been in regular dialogue with Wenger, who later accidentally revealed that he'd been consulted about Bergkamp's arrival. It seems Rioch was unwittingly a caretaker manager, a short-term stopgap between two very different eras of Arsenal, but he nevertheless deserves great credit for starting the revolution.

Back in 1996 hiring a foreign coach was considered extremely dangerous. There was one other in the Premier League, as Ruud Gullit had recently been appointed Chelsea player-manager, but the Dutchman was a world-renowned footballer who had already played in the Premier League. Wenger was understandably unheard of in England, at a time when there was minimal coverage of foreign football aside from Channel 4's *Football Italia*, and before the internet was widespread. Six years earlier Aston Villa had appointed the first-ever overseas manager of a top-flight side: the mysterious Dr Jozef Vengloš. It was a disastrous experiment. Villa had finished second the previous campaign, but under the Slovakian (he was then considered Czechoslovakian) they finished two places above relegation. He appeared incompatible with the English approach, but the man with a doctorate in physical education was essentially a forerunner of Wenger, and not simply because he was foreign – he attempted to professionalise English football. 'Never had I imagined it was possible for human beings to drink so much beer,' he gasped shortly after his arrival. Years later he took a more considered view. 'A few things in those days were a bit different to what we had been doing in central Europe – the methodology of training, the analysing of nutrition, and the recuperation, regeneration and physiological approach to the game.' The Premier League desperately needed a foreign coach like Wenger to successfully implement modern methods. As Dein said, 'The combination of Arsène and Dennis changed the culture of Arsenal.'

Wenger was completely different from anyone else in the Premier League, frequently described as looking more like a teacher than a football manager; he spoke five languages, had a degree in economics and had briefly studied medicine. More than anything, he appeared extraordinarily calm, a quality he's occasionally lost in recent years. Football managers were supposed to be ranters, ravers, eternally angry people; Alex Ferguson famously dished out the 'hairdryer treatment'. A year before Wenger's appointment, Leyton Orient manager John Sitton had been the subject of a Channel 4 documentary that recorded him threatening to fight his own players in a famously bizarre dressing-room outburst. 'When I tell you to do something, do it, and if you come back at me, we'll have a fucking right sort-out in here,' he roared at two players. 'All right? And you can pair up if you like, and you can fucking pick someone else to help you, and you can bring your fucking dinner, 'coz by the time I've finished with you, you'll fucking need it.' That was the 1990s football manager. Wenger was the opposite, stunning his players by demanding a period of complete silence at half-time. More to the point, he certainly wasn't asking players to bring their dinner.

Wenger's major impact upon English football was revolutionising his players' diet. Before the Frenchman's arrival, Arsenal's squad – in common with the majority of Premier League teams – had the culinary preferences of a pub team. They'd enjoy a full English breakfast before training, and their pre-match menu included fish and chips, steak, scrambled eggs and beans on toast. Post-match, things became even worse. On the long coach journey back from Newcastle, for example, some players held an eating competition, with no one capable of matching the impressive nine dinners consumed by centre-back Steve Bould. When Tony Adams and Ray Parlour were given a police caution for spraying a fire extinguisher at abusive Tottenham supporters, the incredible thing wasn't that the incident had taken place at a Pizza Hut, but that when the police pulled up outside Adams's house later that night, the pair had recently taken delivery of a Chinese takeaway, too.

Wenger, meanwhile, had been impressed by the healthiness of Japanese cuisine, noticing the low level of obesity throughout the country. He quickly overhauled the dietary options at Arsenal's training ground, banning sweets, chocolate and Coca-Cola, and encouraging his players to eat steamed fish, boiled chicken, pasta and plenty of vegetables. Whenever Arsenal stayed in a hotel before an away match, Wenger banned room service and insisted that the mini-bars were emptied before the team's arrival. Crucially, he introduced dieticians who educated the players about good nutrition, and concentrated heavily upon the benefit of chewing slowly to digest food properly. Wenger knew there would be a backlash, and intelligently ensured that meals were particularly bland and flavourless in the opening weeks. Then, when the players complained, Wenger made concessions – allowing them tomato ketchup, for example – so the new arrangement appeared a compromise. Wenger set the example, always eating exactly the same meals as his players.

The previous innovator in this respect was Australian Craig Johnston, who played for Liverpool in the 1980s and was one of football's most intelligent, innovative characters, designing the Adidas Predator boot after his retirement. He was inspired by a book called *Eat to Win* by Robert Haas, and eschewed Liverpool's steaks in favour of rice, soy bacon and egg, initially prompting mockery from teammates. But when they noticed his tremendous stamina, they gradually switched to his diet. Intriguingly, Adams says he and a couple of Arsenal teammates read the book in 1987, nearly a decade before Wenger's arrival, but if it provoked them to eat some healthy food they were clearly cancelling out any benefits by also consuming pizzas and Chinese takeaways.

It wasn't all about food, however. Wenger also encouraged his players to take supplements, an unorthodox concept at this stage. Vitamin tablets were placed on tables ahead of training, and many players started taking Creatine to build muscle and improve stamina. Again, everything was explained by experts, and while an improved diet was mandatory, the supplements were optional. Bergkamp was sceptical and didn't take anything, while goalkeeper David Seaman started off without them, then noticed how his teammates were improving physically, so changed his mind. Ray Parlour admitted he simply took whatever was given to him without a second thought. Arsenal's physical improvement was obvious, and on international duty, England teammates asked the Gunners contingent what they'd been taking, and quickly copied, which annoyed Wenger, who was understandably determined to maintain Arsenal's competitive advantage. Unintentionally, the Frenchman was revolutionising the whole of the Premier League, not simply his own club.

The arrival of Wenger, who had grown up in his parents' pub near Strasbourg, also coincided with the end of the drinking culture at Arsenal. Regular boozing was a widespread practice at Premier League clubs, but appeared particularly prevalent at Arsenal, with captain Adams the ringleader of the famous 'Tuesday club', when a group of players would follow a heavy training session with a heavy drinking session, safe in the knowledge that Wednesday was a rest day. Even then, however, drinking the night before training was common, and turning up hungover wasn't frowned upon by teammates if the player got through training properly. On Bergkamp's first pre-season tour of Sweden, he was dismayed when, midway through an evening stroll with his wife, he spotted the rest of the team drinking at a local pub.

But everything changed a fortnight before Wenger's arrival, when Adams shocked his teammates by announcing he was an alcoholic. Two of his teammates immediately wondered, if Adams was an alcoholic, whether they had a drinking problem too. This worked out perfectly for Wenger, who would have encountered serious problems overhauling the drinking culture himself. When Ferguson had attempted to solve this problem at Manchester United, he was forced to sell the two chief culprits, Paul McGrath and Norman Whiteside, who were among United's star players and fan favourites, and he initially struggled. Wenger, luckily, found his captain did the job for him, and Parlour admitted Adams quitting drinking was the best thing that could have happened for his own football career, never mind Adams's.

Similarly, Wenger was fortunate that Arsenal had signed Platt the previous summer, shortly after Bergkamp's arrival. The midfielder had spent the previous four seasons in Italy and introduced new practices to the Arsenal dressing room: the use of a masseur, for example. Again, the introduction of foreign concepts was more likely to be accepted coming from Platt, who had captained England 19 times, rather than from an unknown Frenchman who had been working in Japan. Bergkamp's professionalism, Adams's new lifestyle and Platt's Italian innovations were a series of happy coincidences that prepared Arsenal for Wenger's new regime. Even Platt, however, hated one of Wenger's ideas: stretching sessions. Ahead of Wenger's first game, away at Blackburn, Wenger called an early-morning meeting in the hotel ballroom and instructed his players to go through a mixture of yoga and Pilates routines. Eventually, stretching became an accepted, regular part of training – albeit not on matchdays – and Arsenal's veteran defenders credit this practice for extending their careers.

All these physiological innovations were crucial tactically, because while Wenger's Arsenal would later become renowned for their technical football, his 1997/98 double winners were more celebrated for their physical power, especially in the centre of the pitch. While the defence and strike partnerships from Rioch's reign remained in place, Wenger overhauled the midfield almost completely, recruiting French defensive midfielders Emmanuel Petit and Patrick Vieira, plus left-winger Marc Overmars from Ajax, while Parlour improved and played on the right. This quartet epitomised Wenger's Arsenal at this stage; while boasting technical quality, there was no outright playmaker – that was Bergkamp's role. Vieira and Petit were renowned for their tenacity, Overmars for his acceleration, Parlour for his energy. Strength, speed and stamina.

Vieira, who arrived at Arsenal upon Wenger's request while serving his notice in Japan, later outlined the difference. 'It wasn't based on technique or on an attacking strategy,' he says of the 1998 title winners. 'The quality came from individual players such as Bergkamp or sometimes Overmars.' In stark contrast, he describes the Arsenal's 2001/02 champions by saying, 'The way in which we won this second double had been very different from the way we had done it in 1998 … gone was the long-ball game, in came quick, accurate passing to players' feet.' Vieira is exaggerating the difference – the 1997/98 side were noticeably keen to keep the ball on the ground compared with other sides of that era – but Arsenal took time to become renowned as a truly beautiful side.

For example, Wenger's Arsenal were heavily criticised in the early days because of their atrocious disciplinary record, with Vieira and Petit frequently in trouble with referees. Only three clubs received more bookings during 1997/98, and Arsenal's red card tally under

Wenger became a running feature in newspapers. Indeed, Arsenal's shift from primarily physical football to primarily technical football is best summarised by Wenger's attitude towards referees – initially he complained they were too strict, later he'd complain they were too lenient. Many ex-players, like Arsenal's Parlour and Lee Dixon, plus regular opponents Gary Neville and Ryan Giggs of Manchester United, insist the 1997/98 side was the best incarnation of Wenger's Arsenal because they were physically powerful and refused to be bullied.

Wenger has never been a particularly keen tactician, rarely attempting to change matches by making a surprise selection decision or switching formation regularly. In his early days he preferred a 4–4–2, however, and angered Arsenal's players by interfering with team shape before he'd officially taken charge. For a UEFA Cup tie at Borussia Monchengladbach, Wenger travelled with the team but was supposed to be merely observing before officially starting the following week. However, with the half-time score at 1–1, Wenger decided to take charge in the dressing room and ordered Arsenal to switch from the 3–5–2 system they'd played for the last year to 4–4–2. It backfired badly – Arsenal lost 3–2, and Adams was furious with the sudden intervention. He persuaded Wenger that Arsenal were comfortable with a back three, and they remained in that shape for the majority of 1996/97.

Although it was unusual to see Arsenal playing with a three-man defence, they were suited to that system because they had three top-class centre-backs, with Adams alongside Bould and Martin Keown. Indeed, the 3–5–2 enjoyed a sudden wave of popularity during the mid-1990s, with the likes of Liverpool, Newcastle, Tottenham, Aston Villa, Leicester and Coventry all using the system regularly, with varying levels of success. As a general rule, utilising a 3–5–2 worked effectively against opponents playing 4–4–2, which remained the dominant system, as it offered a spare man in defence against two centre-forwards, and an extra midfielder to overload the centre. The wing-backs were forced to cover a huge amount of ground, providing attacking width yet retreating to form a five-man defence. Although that allowed the opposition full-backs freedom, this wasn't a significant problem during the mid-90s, before most full-backs had become speedy attacking weapons.

Contests between two sides playing 3–5–2 were often hopelessly dull, however – both teams had a spare man at the back, while the midfield was congested and the wing-backs simply chased one another up and down the touchlines. Arsenal's consecutive goalless draws in February 1997 against Leeds and Tottenham, for example, were both matches between two 3–5–2s. 'It's quite ironic,' said Wenger, 'that while the rest of Europe are moving to the flat back four, more and more sides in England are adopting the old continental approach using sweepers and wing-backs.' England was, as ever, out of step tactically, and Arsenal's evolution into title winners came after Wenger switched to 4–4–2 for 1997/98.

He started the season asking his players to press in advanced positions, which wasn't particularly effective, and it's interesting that the crucial tactical change came at the request of the players rather than the manager. In the first half of the season Arsenal defended poorly by their exceptionally high standards, and after a 1–0 home defeat by Liverpool a team meeting was called. Wenger suggested that the problem was a lack of desire, with players not working hard enough. But Adams, Bould and Platt intervened with a more specific suggestion, saying that Petit and Vieira needed to position themselves deeper in order to shield the defence properly. It didn't work immediately – there was to be a 3–1 defeat at home to Blackburn, which convinced Wenger that Adams required six weeks' rest to recover from an ankle injury – but Arsenal's defence was superb in the second half of the campaign, at one stage going 13 hours without conceding, which included a run of 1–0, 0–0, 1–0, 1–0, 1–0, 1–0. '1–0 to the Arsenal' still applied, although they hit 12 goals in the next three games, prompting Arsenal fans to ironically adopt opposition fans' 'boring, boring Arsenal'. They became the first Premier League side to win ten consecutive matches.

Vieira and Petit were outstanding in the second half of the 1997/98 title-winning campaign as a tight partnership that concentrated on ball-winning, although Vieira surged forward sporadically and Petit offered a wonderful passing range with his left foot. With Bergkamp and Wright often injured in the second half of the campaign, Arsenal would depend upon crucial contributions from young reserve strikers Christopher Wreh and Nicolas Anelka, the latter becoming a significant player in the Premier League's tactical evolution. But the crucial attacker throughout the title run-in was Overmars. Although Arsenal's formation was 4–4–2, Overmars was allowed freedom to push forward down the left, while Parlour played a narrower, shuttling role on the right. In later days it would be termed a 4–2–3–1, although at the time it was considered a lopsided 4–3–3 in the attacking phase, with Petit shifting across slightly to cover and Parlour tucking inside. Overmars was happy on either foot but primarily right-footed, a goal-scoring threat more than a creator.

Overmars's attack-minded positioning helped him provide a truly magnificent performance in the 1–0 victory over Manchester United in mid-March that swung the title race in Arsenal's favour. Almost all Arsenal's attacking play went through the Dutchman, who handed young United right-back John Curtis, then a promising prospect, an afternoon so difficult that his career never really recovered. In the early stages Overmars collected a through-ball from Bergkamp, rounded Peter Schmeichel and fired narrowly wide from a difficult angle. Shortly afterwards he made another run in behind, and was astonished not to be awarded a penalty after Curtis clearly tripped him. Next he stabbed the ball into the side netting having evaded Curtis and Gary Neville, who started as a right-sided centre-back. Finally, Overmars provided the decisive moment ten minutes from time, when both Bergkamp and Anelka flicked on a long ball, allowing the winger to race through and slip the ball between Schmeichel's legs.

Considering this was the decisive game of Arsenal's title-winning campaign, Overmars's one-man show is among the greatest individual performances that the Premier League has seen. He followed this by scoring two brilliant solo goals in the title-clinching 4–0 victory over Everton at Highbury, then opened the scoring in the 2–0 FA Cup Final win over Newcastle, as Arsenal clinched the double in Wenger's first full campaign. That victory at Wembley also showed how Wenger was not remotely a reactive manager – he didn't mention the opposition once before the game, an approach he maintained throughout the majority of the Premier League era.

Such tactical naivety would cost Arsenal in European competition over the following seasons – they didn't qualify from the group stage during their first two Champions League attempts, and Wenger's side would later struggle in the Premier League against more tactically astute opposition. Like so many other revolutionaries in the Premier League, the Frenchman was something of a victim of his own success. Other managers soon replicated his approach, particularly in the three areas where he significantly changed English football: improved physical conditioning, recruiting players from abroad and greater emphasis upon technical football. Gradually Wenger's uniqueness was diminished, but his initial impact was hugely influential, and he summarised it best himself. 'I felt like I was opening the door to the rest of the world,' he said. This was the start of the Premier League becoming the world's most international division.

6

Speed

*'Owen was doing things that made me think, "Hang on, if
so-and-so was in that position, would he have done that?"
And the answer was, "No, he wouldn't have had the pace."'*

Glenn Hoddle

Number 9s during the Premier League's formative years were stereotypically tall, strong target men who stationed themselves inside the penalty box and thrived on crosses. Dion Dublin, Duncan Ferguson and Chris Sutton were the classic examples; they could out-muscle and out-jump opposition centre-backs, but rarely threatened to outrun them.

The Premier League's newfound love of technical football, and its new breed of deep-lying, creative forwards, necessitated a different mould of striker. Increasingly, managers wanted strikers who could sprint in behind the opposition defence to reach clever through-balls between opponents. Gradually, speed replaced aerial power as the most revered attribute up front.

Two of the most memorable Premier League goals in 1997 were solo runs by quick strikers dribbling through the Manchester United defence: Derby County's Paulo Wanchope in April and Coventry's Darren Huckerby in December, both in surprise 3–2 wins for the underdogs over the Premier League champions. These goals epitomised the change in the nature of centre-forwards, but the most revolutionary individuals were two teenage prodigies: Arsenal's Nicolas Anelka and Liverpool's Michael Owen.

The similarities between Anelka and Owen are striking. Both were born in 1979, made their debuts in the second half of 1996/97, before making a serious impact in 1997/98. That season Anelka lifted the title with Arsenal, while Owen won the Premier League Golden Boot and the PFA Young Player of the Year. The following season Owen retained the Golden Boot, while Anelka finished just one goal behind and succeeded Owen as the Young Player winner – although he courted controversy by going nightclubbing rather than attending the awards ceremony.

When both strikers left the Premier League it was for Real Madrid; Anelka in 1999, Owen five years later, although both lasted just a season in the Spanish capital and played the majority of their career in England. Anelka eventually hit 125 Premier League goals, Owen 150. Both were rather distant, aloof characters, and despite all their achievements, neither are remembered as a legend at any one particular club. The main similarity, though, is simple: they were astonishingly quick. Pace had always been a dangerous weapon in a striker's armoury. The likes of Andy Cole and Ian Wright – 187 and 113 Premier League goals respectively – were prolific in the Premier League's first half-decade, and clearly weren't traditional target men. However, they were primarily finishers who happened to boast a turn of speed. Anelka and Owen were essentially sprinters also capable of scoring, and in an era where centre-backs were built for battles in the air, scored easy goals by exploiting their sluggishness on the ground.

* * *

Anelka was a wonderful talent, boasting a sensational mix of speed, trickery and coolness when one-on-one with the goalkeeper. In Premier League terms the Frenchman was a forerunner of compatriot Thierry Henry, a more celebrated player who became an inspiration for the likes of Theo Walcott, Daniel Sturridge, Danny Welbeck and Anthony Martial. That mould of athletic, lightning-quick striker can essentially be traced back to Anelka's initial impact for Arsenal.

Anelka started his first full season, 1997/98, behind Wright in Arsène Wenger's pecking order, but had a crucial impact in Arsenal's double-winning campaign. His first Arsenal goal was the opener against title rivals Manchester United in November 1997, a crucial 3–2 victory, and he ended the season by scoring the second in the 2–0 FA Cup Final triumph over Newcastle. His most typical goal came in a 4–1 victory away at Blackburn Rovers on Easter Monday, when he collected a long chip from Nigel Winterburn, streaked away from the opposition defence, then dummied a shot to put goalkeeper Alan Fettis on the ground, took the ball around him and lifted it past the despairing lunge of a defender into the net. That made it 4–0 before half-time, a typical example of Arsenal's ability to blitz opponents through speed in the opening stages, and produced a round of applause from mesmerised Blackburn supporters.

Signed for just £500,000 from Paris Saint-Germain when Wenger exploited a loophole in France's system of contracting youngsters, Anelka impressed on the pitch but struggled to make friends. Despite his sensational speed he possessed a curious running style in his early years: head down, shoulders slumped awkwardly, barely aware of anything around him. It reflected his introverted nature and his inability to communicate with teammates, who struggled to understand him. He wasn't an entertainer and suggested he'd happily play matches in deserted stadiums. 'I'm bored in London – I don't know anyone here and I don't want to,' he once said. Anelka never smiled, even after scoring or when lifting a trophy, and lasted just two complete seasons with Arsenal before leaving for £23m, a sensational return on Wenger's investment two years earlier.

Arsenal effectively spent the proceeds of Anelka's sale on Henry – and a new training ground. Anelka's transfer was the culmination of a summer-long story that arguably set the tone for long-running transfer sagas of later years, with Anelka pledging allegiance to Lazio, Juventus and Real Madrid at various points. Some aspects were ludicrous; one of his brothers, also acting as his agent, once claimed that Anelka had settled on Lazio because their shirt colour was a perfect blend of the white of Real Madrid, his ideal destination, and the blue of France. He eventually ended up at Real anyway, with Sven-Göran Eriksson's Lazio unsuccessfully switching their attentions to Owen, showing how the two teenage sensations were viewed almost interchangeably.

Meanwhile, Anelka's brothers became pantomime villains for their determination to move him around Europe regularly, collecting signing-on fees in the process. Anelka eventually made 12 transfers, his globetrotting career taking in France, Spain, Italy, Turkey, China and India. Despite his initial dislike of England, however, Anelka always returned, subsequently representing Liverpool, Manchester City, Bolton, Chelsea and West Bromwich Albion. His final Premier League goal was scored 16 years after his first, and was his most infamous – he celebrated with the 'quenelle' gesture, described by experts as an 'inverted Nazi salute'. The FA banned him for five games, Anelka promptly declaring that he was leaving West Brom, who announced they were sacking him anyway. It was a fitting end to an incredibly strange Premier League career.

In his early days, one of Anelka's most impressive displays came for France in a 2–0 victory over England at Wembley in February 1999. He scored both goals, and had another shot hit the bar and cross the goal line, not spotted by the linesman. Bizarrely, Anelka wore goalkeeper gloves throughout that game on a bitterly cold February evening in London, and thrived on playing ahead of World Player of the Year Zinedine Zidane, running in behind to reach his through-balls. It was also significant that Anelka outplayed an England defence featuring Lee Dixon, Tony Adams and Martin Keown ahead of David Seaman, with Chelsea's Graeme Le Saux the only man breaking up the Arsenal connection at the back. Even when his opponents knew his game perfectly, they simply couldn't stop him. 'We've found our Ronaldo,' said France captain Didier Deschamps – a significant remark. France had won the World Cup the previous year despite their lack of a clinical striker, while the rest of the world despaired at Ronaldo's pre-final breakdown, which evidently affected his Brazilian teammates. Anelka was so good that he had improved the world champions.

At club level, Anelka proved the ideal partner for Dennis Bergkamp. Although the Dutchman formed fine relationships with both Wright and Henry either side of Anelka, he considered the young Frenchman ideal for his style. 'As a strike partner, Nicolas was probably the best I've had at Highbury in terms of understanding,' Bergkamp once said, even when playing up front alongside Henry. 'The way Nicolas played suited me perfectly because he was always looking to run forward on goal. That made it easy for me to predict what he wanted and to know instinctively where he would be on the pitch. That directness was just right. Thierry tends to want the ball to come to him or to drift towards the flanks more. Nicolas was focused on heading for goal and scoring. He loved having the ball played for him to run on to and going one-on-one with the keeper.'

The best example of their combination play came in a 5–0 victory over Leicester City in February 1999, which featured an Anelka hat-trick before half-time. Leicester's defence, and in particular towering, old-school centre-back Matt Elliott, were completely unable to cope with his speed. Martin O'Neill's changes at the interval involved switching Elliott to a centre-forward role, underlining both his struggles at the back and the fact that many Premier League sides still based attacking play around a tall, strong aerial threat. Bergkamp collected four assists at Highbury that day: two for Anelka, and two for the onrushing Ray Parlour. Anelka's opener demonstrated how easily Bergkamp and Anelka linked by stretching the defence in different directions. Bergkamp collected a bouncing ball 15 yards inside his own half, glanced over his shoulder to check Anelka was making a run into the inside-right channel before casually lobbing a 40-yard pass in the Frenchman's general direction. Anelka roared past the Leicester defence, chested the ball onto his right foot and finished into the far corner.

It looked so simple. At this stage many defences still concentrated on pushing up the pitch to keep strikers away from goal, a logical approach when dealing with aerial threats. In later years they would learn to defend deeper against quick strikers, while goalkeepers would sweep up proactively to intercept passes in behind when the defence took a more aggressive starting position. On that day, however, Arsenal simply had so much behind Leicester's back line, which was ideal for Anelka. His second was similar, albeit from a neater, toe-poked Bergkamp through-ball. Anelka instinctively celebrated by throwing his arm out to point at Bergkamp, acknowledging the assist, although there would be no such celebration when Marc Overmars teed him up for his hat-trick goal. There was little acknowledgement between them, and only a half-hearted group hug between the two and Bergkamp, who was fittingly playing the link role in the celebration. Overmars and Anelka weren't on good terms.

Earlier in the season, Anelka had complained his teammates weren't passing to him, believing Overmars exclusively looked for his fellow Dutchman Bergkamp. 'I'm not getting enough of the ball,' he muttered to the French press. 'I'm going to see the manager soon because Overmars is too selfish.' Wenger resolved the dispute in a fantastically cunning manner, calling both players into his office for showdown talks. The complication, however, was that Anelka barely spoke English and Overmars didn't understand French, so Wenger was not only moderator but also interpreter, and played the situation beautifully. He asked the two players to spell out their issues; Anelka repeated his complaint to Wenger in their native tongue, while in English, Overmars claimed he always looked out for Anelka's runs and didn't understand his problem. Rather than translating their comments accurately, Wenger simply told Overmars that Anelka had said he no longer had a problem, then told Anelka that Overmars was promising to pass more. Both were lies, but it temporarily resolved the situation.

But Anelka had another major issue with Arsenal's system, which wasn't apparent at the time – he didn't actually like playing up front. 'I played as a centre-forward at Arsenal and scored lots of goals, so people think that's my best position, but I don't,' he complained later in his career. 'I feel more comfortable playing a deeper role, like Bergkamp.' He described France manager Raymond Domenech's decision to play him as an out-and-out striker 'a casting mistake', while on another occasion he outlined his thoughts in blunter terms – 'My main aim is to play well, which is where I differ from real strikers.' Anelka's understanding of a 'real striker', presumably, was a player who concentrated solely upon scoring goals – the likes of Cole and Wright.

Just as Anelka didn't consider himself a 'real striker', Owen was once described by then-England manager Hoddle as 'not a natural goalscorer', a remark that was greeted with astonishment across the country. Hoddle, in typically clumsy fashion, had actually been attempting to compliment Owen. He phoned Owen and clarified his comment, explaining that to him, a 'natural goalscorer' was someone who simply stands in the box and waits for the ball. Owen, however, could pounce from deeper positions, usually by running in behind the opposition defence onto through-balls. It was true. He was a sprinter first, a finisher second.

There was an air of revolution around Britain in early May 1997, as Tony Blair entered Number 10 for the first time. Three days later, English football supporters watched their future number 10 for the first time, as Owen made his professional debut, netting the consolation in Liverpool's 2–1 defeat at Wimbledon.

The goal was typical Owen. Stig Inge Bjørnebye played a through-ball into the inside-left channel, Owen raced onto it, opened up his body then finished into the far corner. It was a run – and a finish – we would witness repeatedly over coming seasons. 'He started making decent runs off people, getting in behind them,' said Liverpool manager Roy Evans, who had begun the match using Patrik Berger behind Stan Collymore, with Fowler suspended. Astonishingly, just 18 months after his professional debut, Owen would finish fourth in the World Player of the Year vote, behind Zinedine Zidane, Davor Šuker and Ronaldo, largely because of his famous goal against Argentina at the 1998 World Cup, when he sprinted past two flat-footed defenders before lifting the ball into the far corner. At this stage, with TV coverage of foreign football relatively rare across the world, one massive moment at a major tournament could elevate your reputation significantly.

There was a youthful exuberance about Owen's early Liverpool performances because he essentially played Premier League matches like they were U11s games. He recalled that, during his schoolboy days, 'all my goals at that time were virtually identical: a ball over the top, followed by a sprint and a finish. I was quicker than everyone else at that time, so it was always a one-on-one with a finish to the side. You don't get many crosses or diving headers in Under-11 football, you're always running onto through-balls.' Little had changed by the time Owen reached Liverpool's first team. The best example of his terrifying pace was the equaliser in a 1–1 draw away at Old Trafford in 1997/98, when he latched onto a hopeful flick-on to poke the ball past Peter Schmeichel. At one stage he appeared third favourite to reach the loose ball, behind Schmeichel and centre-back Gary Pallister (whom Alex Ferguson once surprisingly named the quickest player he'd ever worked with at Manchester United), but Owen's pace was electric. Shortly afterwards, however, he was dismissed for a terrible tackle on Ronny Johnsen, and it's often forgotten that Owen's ill-discipline was considered a serious problem in his early days. He'd already been sent off for England U18s after headbutting a Yugoslavian defender.

In that first complete season, 1997/98, Owen converted a penalty on the opening day and eventually won the Premier League's Golden Boot jointly with Dion Dublin and Chris Sutton, on 18 goals. Owen couldn't have been a more different player; Dublin and Sutton started their careers as centre-backs – both with Norwich, coincidentally – before becoming centre-forwards, and they could play either role because of their aerial power. But Owen was all about speed, and 50 per cent of his 1997/98 non-penalty goals came from him darting in behind the opposition defence. At this point Owen was, understandably for a 17-year-old, somewhat simple in a technical sense. In his autobiography, in a passage about Manchester United's rivalry with Liverpool, Sir Alex Ferguson observes that being forced to play so many matches so early didn't simply harm Owen's physical condition but also his technical development. 'There was no opportunity to take him aside and work on him from a technical point of view,' Ferguson claims.

In 1997/98 Owen scored only once with his left foot, sliding in at the far post to convert into an empty net against Coventry, and only once with his head, a rebound from two yards out against Southampton. 16 of the 18 were scored with his right. Noticeably, Owen generally attempted to work the ball onto his favoured side, even if it meant making the goalscoring opportunity more difficult, and when forced to go left, would still shoot with his right. His first hat-trick, on Valentine's Day 1998 away at Sheffield Wednesday, featured two goals stabbed unconventionally with the outside of his right foot. Gradually, defenders deduced his limitations – Manchester United's Jaap Stam openly admitted his primary approach was to force him onto his left – so Owen was forced to improve his all-round game.

Over the next couple of years, Owen spent hours concentrating on improving his finishing with his left foot and his head. The improvement was drastic. By 2000/01, Owen was an all-round finisher and determined to let everyone know it when celebrating goals. He scored two left-footed goals in a 3–3 draw at Southampton in August, and following the second, ran away with two fingers showing on one hand, the other pointing at his left foot. A month later against Sunderland, Owen beat six-foot-four Niall Quinn to Christian Ziege's whipped left-footed free-kick and powered home a bullet header. This time, he slapped his head in celebration. He almost single-handedly won the FA Cup with two late goals after Liverpool had been outplayed by Arsenal, the winner a fantastic demonstration of his astonishing pace, before yet another left-footed finish into the far corner.

Liverpool also won the League Cup and UEFA Cup that season, then lifted the Charity Shield and European Super Cup at the start of 2001/02. These successes, and Owen's hat-trick in England's famous 5–1 victory over Germany that autumn, helped him win the Ballon d'Or in 2001, one of only two Premier League-based recipients of the award, alongside Cristiano Ronaldo in 2008. Owen, however, says he had played better in the couple of years before 2001.

It's peculiar that Owen wore the number 10 shirt throughout his Liverpool and England career when he was really a number 9, although it's obvious why when one considers who his strike partners were. He broke into the Liverpool side when Fowler dominated; when Owen was rising through the ranks Fowler had been his idol, but they were too similar to function together properly. Owen later offered an Anelka-esque complaint that Steve McManaman, Liverpool's chief creator, always looked to pass to his best mate Fowler. At international level, Alan Shearer was the captain, the main man and the number 9. As Sutton had discovered at Blackburn Rovers, Shearer didn't like playing alongside a fellow goalscorer, and preferred working ahead of a link man. Shearer's relationship with Teddy Sheringham was excellent, which is partly why Hoddle initially ignored Owen in favour of a tried-and-tested combination at the 1998 World Cup.

Hoddle's successor, Kevin Keegan, was also a huge Shearer fan, having broken the world transfer record to take him to Newcastle, and asked Owen to play a deeper role while Shearer remained on the shoulder of the last defender. It didn't suit him, and Owen later said that the Keegan era 'made me question my footballing ability for the first time'. Owen became more consistent for England after 2000, when Shearer retired from international football and Keegan resigned, replaced by Sven-Göran Eriksson.

That year Liverpool signed Emile Heskey, who became Owen's most famous strike partner, a classic little-and-large relationship. 'When he's firing, he's special, and when we fired together it was a really powerful partnership,' Owen once said. 'But Emile's form tended to be in peaks and troughs, and I had the odd injury, so I wouldn't call ours a massively successful or consistent combination.' Intriguingly, though, Owen says he preferred playing alongside a proper striker, rather than with a withdrawn, deep-lying forward. That's a surprising revelation, because what Owen surely lacked at Liverpool, compared with Anelka at Arsenal, was the luxury of playing ahead of a genius deep-lying forward in the mould of Bergkamp. Indeed, his Liverpool teammates found the absence of a number 10 a source of frustration.

Fowler, Owen's forerunner at Liverpool, complained that he never played alongside a creative forward and speaks of his disappointment that Liverpool didn't push for the signing of Sheringham in the late 1990s or offer Ajax's Jari Litmanen better terms at that stage, which meant that the wonderful Finnish forward joined Barcelona instead, despite growing up as a Liverpool fan. The Finn eventually joined Liverpool in 2001. 'Jari was the type of player we'd been crying out for, slotting in behind a more advanced striker,' said Liverpool defender Jamie Carragher. 'All the greatest sides have such players. United began to win titles when they bought Eric Cantona, Arsenal had Dennis Bergkamp. Every summer I hoped Liverpool were going to be in the market for a similar forward.' By this stage, however, injury problems meant Litmanen wasn't able replicate their impact. Had he joined Liverpool four years earlier, things might have been very different.

Owen's best relationship was with Steven Gerrard, who was capable of playing pinpoint through-balls. Owen's last goal for Liverpool, in a 1–1 draw against Newcastle on the final day of 2003/04, was assisted by a brilliant curled Gerrard pass, acknowledged immediately by Owen in his celebration. But at this point Gerrard played relatively deep in midfield and was unable to form a direct partnership with Owen, and wouldn't be pushed up the pitch behind the striker for a couple of years. If Owen had stuck around at Liverpool or had Gerrard moved forward earlier, they might have formed the perfect combination. Owen briefly linked effectively with Wayne Rooney for England, albeit in the days when Rooney's directness made him the greater goal threat.

But Owen's most intriguing strike partner for Liverpool was the forward you would least expect – Anelka. Although the two emerged simultaneously and seemingly played the same role, Anelka's afore-mentioned dislike of playing up front meant that he was happier in a withdrawn position during a brief, half-season loan spell with Liverpool in 2001/02. 'I played my best football at Liverpool, because I played in my best position there,' said Anelka. 'Owen was the main scorer and you knew he was going to score no matter what. He allowed me to play my best.'

Owen remembers Anelka fondly, too. 'He didn't score a lot of goals for us … but you could see he was a class act with great ability; in training he showed that he had a lovely touch, he could drop deep and link play, and had pace as well.' Anelka would be particularly delighted that Owen mentioned his link play before his pace. The Frenchman wasn't signed permanently, however, and Gérard Houllier replaced him with El-Hadji Diouf, a player with all Anelka's bad habits and few of his qualities. You could say the same about Owen's replacement at Liverpool in 2004, Djibril Cissé, who was the purest speedster of all.

By the time he moved to Real Madrid, Owen had already peaked. He spent much of his career on the sidelines, with fitness problems dating back to a serious hamstring injury sustained in April 1999 at just 19 – typically, when sprinting in behind the Leeds defence onto a through-ball. He returned too quickly, partly through Houllier's insistence, against the wishes of Liverpool physio Mark Leather. When Owen announced his retirement in 2013, his statement felt particularly sad. 'An emotion that lives with me is a sense of "what might have been" had injuries not robbed me of my most lethal weapon – speed. Many of my highlights were early on in my career and I can only wonder what more I would have achieved had my body been able to withstand the demands that I was making of it. I was almost too quick. My hamstring gave way at Leeds at the age of 19 and from that moment on my career as a professional footballer was compromised ... I have no doubt that, had I not suffered those "pace-depriving" injuries, I would be sat here now with a sack full of awards and a long list of records.'

Later, Owen adjusted to his diminished mobility by playing a withdrawn role, and impressed during a spell behind Mark Viduka and Obafemi Martins for Newcastle in 2007/08, managed by the returning Keegan – who, as we know, was never afraid to play forwards in deeper roles. Owen was always unable to replicate those early heights, however. Upon leaving Newcastle on a free transfer his management company sent a 34-page brochure outlining Owen's virtues to potentially interested clubs, using statistics to deny he was injury-prone and dedicating a section to debunk tabloid myths. Who knows whether the brochure helped, but he eventually earned a move to champions Manchester United, replacing Cristiano Ronaldo in the famous number 7 shirt. He finally won a league title in 2010/11, although he described the feeling as 'a bit hollow' because of his minimal contribution. He subsequently spent a single season at Stoke City, where he didn't start or win a league game all season, scoring just once, a 91st-minute headed consolation in a 3–1 defeat at Swansea. It's tough to imagine a less fitting final goal.

It wasn't simply that Owen was now slower, it was that opponents – particularly smaller teams fighting relegation – defended deep. During the 1990s defences were accustomed to pushing up to keep aerially dominant strikers away from the box. Increasingly, strikers' key weapon was pace, and at the start of the century it wasn't unusual to see top teams playing two speedsters up front: Henry alongside Sylvain Wiltord at Arsenal, Owen alongside Diouf at Liverpool. That would have been very unusual earlier, when aerial power was key, or later, when defenders retreated towards their own goal. The defenders who continued to play in a high defensive line, meanwhile, became increasingly fast, which was disastrous for Owen. 'Speed is the key to my battles with the game's best defenders,' he said. 'The tough ones were the quick ones. Size doesn't bother me, because my main weapon is pace, it's the fast ones who negate some of my natural swiftness.'

But defenders had become faster precisely because of players like Owen, as Arsène Wenger outlined much later. 'Football always progresses. The attack creates a new problem, the defence responds. What has happened in the last ten years is that the strikers have become quicker and quicker. What's happened? The defence have responded by creating quicker and quicker defenders.' In that respect, Owen was another victim of his own success.

Part Three

Expansion

7

Euro Progress & Squad Rotation

*'His pre-match team talk seems to get longer and
longer as the seasons go by. He always digs into his
dossier for our European games.'*

Andy Cole

Manchester United's 1998/99 campaign remains the greatest season in the history of English football. No one before or since has achieved the treble: United sealed the Premier League, the FA Cup and the Champions League in three consecutive matches, ensuring their place in history. Less than a month later, Alex Ferguson became Sir Alex Ferguson.

United triumphed in astonishing, often unthinkable circumstances. They came from behind on the final day of the league campaign against Tottenham. They won an all-time classic FA Cup semi-final (which felt more like the final itself) against Arsenal with ten men, courtesy of a legendary Ryan Giggs goal. Most memorably, in the Champions League Final they produced one of the most incredible turnarounds in football history when trailing Bayern Munich 1–0 going into stoppage time by snatching two last-gasp goals to leave their opponents stunned. Pundits rightly lauded United's never-say-die spirit, but Ferguson had evolved tactically to become considerably more sophisticated than his Premier League rivals.

The Champions League success was particularly significant, marking the arrival of the Premier League as a serious European force. Many European performances by top English clubs during the 1990s were embarrassing; United were once eliminated by Rotor Volgograd, Blackburn by Trelleborg, Arsenal by PAOK Salonika. But in 1998/99 United battled past Bayern Munich, Barcelona, Inter Milan, Juventus and then Bayern again to lift the trophy. 'Europe had become a personal crusade,' Ferguson later said. 'I knew I would never be judged a great manager until I won the European Cup.' His adventures throughout the 1990s were essentially a long, gradual learning curve.

In terms of United's default system, relatively little had changed. Ferguson continued to use a 4–4–2 – and arguably more of a classic 4–4–2 than the system dominated by Eric Cantona, who had made it more 4–4–1–1. Cantona had retired in 1997, and after Teddy Sheringham initially proved an underwhelming replacement, United signed Dwight Yorke at the start of the Treble campaign. Alongside Sheringham, Andy Cole and Ole Gunnar Solskjær, United now had four genuinely top-class strikers, with pundits left pondering how Ferguson would satisfy them all. Solskjær had finished as United's top goalscorer in 1996/97, Cole took that honour in 1997/98, while Sheringham had been Tottenham's top goalscorer four times and Yorke was Aston Villa's top scorer three times. These weren't players accustomed to being back-ups.

Although Yorke dropped deep into positions between the lines, he was more of a conventional striker than Cantona and, crucially, struck up a brilliant partnership with Andy Cole. This was a surprise, as many predicted Cole would suffer from Yorke's arrival, and he was heavily linked with a move to Yorke's former club Aston Villa. Ferguson admitted he had no particular partnership in mind when signing Yorke, and his first game alongside Cole, a 0–0 draw at West Ham in the second game of the season, was fruitless. But Cole and Yorke became great friends, with Cole inviting United's club record signing to his house for dinner and helping him adjust to life in Manchester. They became inseparable, even buying identical purple Mercedes with near-matching number plates. 'I remembered my own isolation, the life of the hermit,' said Cole. 'I didn't want anyone else to suffer in the same way; I realised I could help him settle in.'

Strikers don't necessarily need to be friends to strike up a great on-pitch relationship, as Alan Shearer and Chris Sutton had demonstrated, while Cole performed reasonably well with Sheringham, despite them despising one another, refusing to speak for years. But Yorke's friendship with Cole mirrored United's tactical development; Cole had previously been considered a difficult character – moody, quiet, something of a loner – which tallied with concerns about his limitations as a striker. Kevin Keegan had sold Cole because he believed he was a mere goalscorer and unable to bring others into play, but just as the cheerful Yorke connected with him as a friend, he linked play brilliantly and ensured United's system involved Cole regularly. Yorke and Cole insist they never specifically worked on their interplay, but some of it was telepathic. Memorably, there was Cole's legendary goal at the Camp Nou when Yorke came short, dummied the ball to ensure it ran onto Cole, who immediately played a quick one-two with Yorke, bamboozling Barcelona's defenders before he converted smartly. It's difficult to recall a better example of a brilliant strike relationship, and their understanding was typical of United in 1998/99. The 4–4–2 is all about partnerships, and United boasted five balanced, reliable double acts ahead of Peter Schmeichel.

At the back there was Jaap Stam and Ronny Johnsen. After Stam initially encountered difficulties with the pace of English football, they formed a superb centre-back duo – sometimes interrupted by Johnsen's injury problems – with Stam the hardman and Johnsen the cooler, calmer, more intelligent operator. Both were very quick, with Ferguson determined to use defenders comfortable defending one-against-one.

David Beckham and Gary Neville were good friends – Neville was best man at Beckham's wedding – and also linked brilliantly down the right. Beckham was a wide midfielder rather than a speedy winger like predecessor Andrei Kanchelskis; his deeper positioning meant he shielded Neville excellently, his narrower position meant Neville could overlap into crossing positions. But Beckham was the star; no other Premier League player has depended so much upon crossing, and he claimed more assists than any other player in 1998/99, the campaign immediately after he'd been cast as England's villain for his World Cup dismissal against Argentina.

On the opposite flank there was Ryan Giggs and Denis Irwin, a long-standing relationship that worked excellently. Giggs dribbled considerably more than Beckham, so Irwin overlapped less regularly than Neville, was right-footed anyway so less inclined to go down the outside, and was now 33 and happy to play a more reserved role.

Finally, in midfield there was Roy Keane and Paul Scholes. The former now occupied a deeper, more defensive-minded role that gave Scholes licence to push forward, spraying passes to Giggs and Beckham before bombing into the box to become a goalscoring threat. In fact, more than a midfield partnership, this should be assessed as a brilliantly balanced quartet: Beckham, Keane, Scholes, Giggs. A crosser, a tackler, a passer, a dribbler.

While Keane and Giggs had both featured heavily in Ferguson's first great United side of 1993/94, Beckham and Scholes had yet to become regulars. They were different to the usual template for players in a four-man midfield, offering more guile; Scholes was a creator rather than a ball-winner (tackling was his major shortcoming), while Beckham was a ball-player rather than a speedster. This proved crucial in European football, where retaining possession was more important than in the Premier League, simply because, as Ferguson regularly explained in the mid-1990s, once you lose the ball in Europe, you don't get it back quickly. Indeed, while United's 'class of '92' had been inspired by Cantona's professionalism, it was Scholes and Beckham who benefited most from his retirement. Scholes emerged as a deep-lying forward 'in the Cantona mould', to use Ferguson's words, and United's manager explicitly said he'd long earmarked Scholes for a regular role once the Frenchman left United. Beckham, meanwhile, took Cantona's famous number 7 shirt, became United's chief assister and – albeit in a very different manner to Cantona – was the individual who commanded the most attention. Besides, Cantona had often struggled to influence Champions League games, in part because European opposition were more accustomed to dealing with deep-lying forwards. 'I can't recall one important European game that he turned for us,' Keane bluntly stated.

There was also a significant change midway through United's treble-winning campaign, with Ferguson's assistant manager Brian Kidd leaving to take charge of Blackburn. His replacement was Steve McClaren, who had earned a reputation as England's most promising young coach at Derby County. McClaren, like Kidd, took the majority of United's training sessions and the players were hugely impressed by his innovative methods and engaging sessions. He brought in a laptop – then something barely seen in a dressing room – to use ProZone, downloading footage of matches and personally editing clips of specific situations. Keane, Beckham and Giggs all said exactly the same thing about McClaren: he was an innovator, and always keen to try new things. He helped bring United into the modern era in terms of pre-match preparation.

Tactically, United were becoming more intelligent than any other Premier League side, primarily because of their European experiences. Even with the influx of foreign playing talent, English football remained isolated from the rest of Europe during this period – there was little TV coverage of overseas football, few foreign coaches and relatively few European runs. By the time United lifted the European Cup in 1999, it was their fifth Champions League campaign; no other Premier League side had enjoyed more than one. Top-flight European sides were, tactically, on a completely different level to Premier League sides, allowing Ferguson a significant advantage over his rivals. 'I've been fascinated by looking at all the systems,' Ferguson said of his European experiences during the mid-1990s, marvelling at Ajax's use of a sweeper, Milan's compactness and Barcelona's possession play. He regularly travelled abroad to scout upcoming opponents.

Ferguson had been nicknamed 'Tinkerbell' by some Manchester United fans in the early to mid-1990s because of his tendency to make apparently unnecessary changes to his starting XI at key moments – his decision to use a 4–5–1 for the fatal final-day draw at West Ham in 1994/95 was a particular source of frustration – but the meddling became more necessary against superior sides, and more advanced tactics, in the Champions League. Ferguson was always learning lessons from Europe. After the 4–0 thrashing by Barcelona at the Nou Camp in 1994, he realised United needed to catch up. 'You hold your hands up when you are beaten tactically,' he said. 'The problem is that we don't have a tactical game in England ... at United, a lot of the players have their own profile and want to play their own way. It doesn't work in Europe, as we've discovered. There has to be a better tactical discipline … they can't just play their own game.'

This, then, was the start of English football 'getting' tactics in the Premier League era, discovering that adjusting your style for the specific challenge of the opposition was crucial. The Barcelona defeat came just four days after United had defeated Newcastle, whom Ferguson considered United's main title rivals, 2–0 at Old Trafford. It was a superb United performance, but the contrast in performances between those games highlighted the difference between English and European football. The Newcastle game was extremely open, a classic end-to-end match. But Ferguson was struck by how United conceded possession readily against Barca, then couldn't regain it because their opponents kept the ball so effectively. From then on, United concentrated on improving their possession play.

'In Europe they pass to each other in midfield,' Ferguson said, making a simple concept seem like a revelation. 'They play in little triangles and keep it there, they play one-twos against you in midfield, whereas our midfielders service the wide players, the full-backs and the front men.' This sounds simple but it was a crucial point. The next couple of decades of European football would be dominated by the battle for midfield possession, whereas in the Premier League the midfield was a war zone, all about tackling hard to get the ball, then quickly distributing it elsewhere. The concept of midfield creativity was, at this point, almost foreign to English football.

Ferguson also recognised the value of defensive versatility, admiring the use of a spare man across Europe. In 1996/97 he sometimes used Premier League games as preparation for Champions League fixtures, taking the rare decision to deploy a three-man defence against Derby County because he intended to play that system against Juventus. United didn't perform well in the 1–1 draw at the

Baseball Ground, however, and Ferguson turned against that idea. Still, it showed how Ferguson was experimenting, and after United lost 1–0 at Juve with a back four, with Ferguson again concentrating on the strategic side of things, he complained that 'the players need to be aware of the tactical implications'. But United continued to improve. Ferguson became convinced of the need to man-mark opposition number 10s, a tactic essentially reserved for Gianfranco Zola, Juninho and Steve McManaman in the Premier League. But almost every Champions League opponent had a player in that mould, and it was notable that, in 1996/97, Keane did a fine job on Rapid Vienna number 10 Dietmar Kühbauer, while Ronny Johnsen was deployed in midfield and tasked with stopping Fenerbahçe's Jay-Jay Okocha.

To beef up the midfield Ferguson started using only one striker, with mixed success. The use of a three-man defence, meanwhile, rarely worked well for United, a poor performance (albeit in a 2–1 win) at Tottenham Hotspur in January 1997 again dissuading Ferguson from that system in Europe. Most pleasing was the 4–0 thrashing of Porto in the first leg of the quarter-final two months later, a rare occasion when Ferguson used a diamond midfield, with Ryan Giggs tucking inside to produce, in his words, the best performance of his career. United were now tactically flexible, and while they lost 2–0 on aggregate to eventual winners Borussia Dortmund in the semi-final, they dominated both legs and created more chances.

United's 1997/98 European campaign ended tamely with quarter-final elimination at the hands of Monaco, but they had performed impressively in the group stage with a 3–2 victory over Italian champions Juventus. This was an extremely significant result; having failed to beat Barcelona, Juve and Dortmund in previous campaigns, it was the first time Ferguson's United had triumphed over a genuine

European giant. Of all the European sides, it was Marcello Lippi's side whom United held in highest esteem and would come to resemble most closely; Juventus couldn't boast the romance or style of Ajax, Milan or Barca, but they were extremely efficient, professional and tactically adaptable. 'During the mid-1990s when we were growing as a team and learning all about how to succeed in the Champions League, Juventus were the benchmark,' recalled Gary Neville. 'They had everything that I would love to have in my team.' Ferguson was the same. 'I have developed an immense respect for Juventus, a class act from top to bottom,' he purred. 'Lippi is one impressive man.'

Juventus were the most tactically impressive side in European football at this stage, in part because they could always call upon a group of versatile, disciplined and tactically intelligent workhorses to perform a particular role. Their 1997/98 squad contained four players – Moreno Torricelli, Angelo Di Livio, Gianluca Pessotto and Alessandro Birindelli – who could play on either flank, in defence or midfield, while future Chelsea manager Antonio Conte was another highly adaptable player; you saw the names on the team sheet, but had no idea where they'd be deployed. 'It was not just the real quality players like Zidane or Del Piero that captured everyone's imagination,' Keane later said. 'But tough, wily defenders, guys nobody's ever heard of, who closed space down, timed their tackles to perfection, were instinctively in the right cover positions and read the game superbly.' They were entirely functional players, limited technically but perfect when Lippi wanted a player to 'do a job' in a certain game. And that expression is particularly pertinent when looking at Italian footballers during this period. In the aptly named *The Italian Job*, his excellent book about the differences between Italian and English football, one of Gianluca Vialli's main conclusions is, 'To the Italian footballer, football is a job: to the English footballer, it's a game.' Ferguson was clearly in awe of the Italians during this period, remarking on their 'bigger respect for the profession' ('profession' rather than 'game' indicating his stance). To catch up with Juventus, Ferguson needed more of his players to perform disciplined, somewhat joyless tactical roles in major games.

That 3–2 victory over Juventus in 1997 was a perfect example. Ferguson used Johnsen, a natural defender who was also capable of playing a holding midfield role, and he performed a wonderful man-marking job on Europe's most revered playmaker, Zinedine Zidane. Johnsen's tactical discipline epitomised Manchester United during this period, and Ferguson increasingly embraced the functional player – that versatile, disciplined, hard-working and tactically aware squad member who could be trusted to 'do a job'. When United lost key games during the Cantona era, Ferguson often regretted not using Brian McClair, the understated and adaptable 'brainy player', in Ferguson's words, who could play anywhere in midfield or attack. For example, in a Premier League match against Liverpool early in 1994/95, Ferguson wavered over whether to select Mark Hughes or McClair, who could play a more disciplined role to stop John Barnes, Liverpool's danger man. Ferguson eventually chose Hughes, but United lost their shape, Barnes was free to run the game and United were on the back foot. When Ferguson summoned McClair early in the second half at 0–0, he helped to stop Barnes and also made dangerous forward runs against the immobile Jan Molby, which forced Liverpool manager Roy Evans to replace the Dane. United eventually won 2–0, with McClair fittingly scoring the second. Tactically, he had simultaneously helped to nullify an opponent's strength and exposed a weakness. Ferguson needed tactically intelligent players like McClair.

Later, Ferguson became infuriated with Paul Ince's inability to follow tactical instructions and was even angier when Gary Pallister and Paul Parker ignored his request for Parker to man-mark

Barcelona's Romario, with the defenders instead using their usual zonal system. But Ferguson loved Keane during the Irishman's younger years because he could deploy him in various tactical roles. 'He can do anything you ask him to because he has such a disciplined mind. You say to him, "Go and man-mark X," and he'll do it. "Play centre-half," no problem. "Play right-back," no problem.' But Keane became too valuable in the engine room to shift around regularly, and by 1999 Ferguson had others who could 'do a job'. Phil Neville could play in either the full-back role or in midfield; Johnsen could play in the centre of defence or midfield; Nicky Butt could be introduced as a midfield 'spoiler', while Jesper Blomqvist and Jordi Cruyff could play midfield roles that didn't adhere to 4–4–2 principles.

A 2–2 draw at Tottenham in December was particularly interesting. United raced into a 2–0 lead with two early Solskjær strikes, but shortly before half-time Gary Neville was dismissed for tugging back Spurs' left-winger David Ginola, who would later be voted PFA Player of the Year, the only non-United player on the six-man shortlist. The Frenchman was clearly exaggerating fouls to draw the referee's attention, and United ended up being shown no fewer than eight yellow cards, including the two for Neville. Therefore, to prevent United going down to nine men, Ferguson rotated the man deployed to mark Ginola, using Keane, Johnson, Berg and finally Phil Neville against him. United had used five markers against the Frenchman in the space of 90 minutes – which other club could have found so many disciplined tactical players in their side? Ginola was largely shepherded into non-threatening areas, although two Sol Campbell goals meant United dropped two points. Nevertheless, this was the major difference between Arsenal and Manchester United throughout the period of their fierce rivalry. Arsenal could usually offer comparable players to United's superstars: Dennis Bergkamp for

Cantona, David Seaman for Schmeichel, Patrick Vieira for Keane, Tony Adams for Stam, Marc Overmars for Giggs. But United boasted a reliable group of reserves who could be trusted to win games tactically, whereas Arsenal concentrated on a Plan A and their back-ups were stylistically similar to the first-choices. They had no one to do a job.

On the way to their Champions League success Ferguson demonstrated his tactical acumen, in particular, with the two-legged victories over Inter and Juventus. Mircea Lucescu's Inter arrived at Old Trafford in a 3–4–2–1 shape, with Roberto Baggio and Youri Djorkaeff floating behind Iván Zamorano. That's a tough system for a 4–4–2 to cope with: two players between the lines and often an overload in central positions. Ferguson gave his players a complex, hybrid task. 'We had to defend the centre of midfield and at the same time get our crosses in,' he explained. 'We had watched them several times and I felt sure we could score from centres.' Ferguson adjusted admirably. His full-backs, Neville and Irwin, played extremely narrow to contain Inter's two number 10s, while United exploited the space on the outside of Inter's back three ruthlessly, with Beckham pushing into the space between left-wing-back Aron Winter and left-sided centre-back Francesco Colonnese. Ferguson's determination to attack Inter with crosses proved crucial; Yorke twice headed in Beckham's deliveries in a 2–0 victory and should have scored another from the same supply line.

For the return leg Lucescu unsurprisingly changed both his left-sided defensive players and selected a fit-again Ronaldo up front. Although Inter's shape was similar, Ferguson approached the task differently because he wanted United to focus on defence rather than attack. He therefore omitted Scholes and moved Johnsen into midfield alongside Keane, bringing in Henning Berg to partner

Stam. The combination of Johnsen and Keane concentrated on stopping Inter's number 10s, which left the full-backs – narrow in the first leg – able to push wide. 'The key tactically,' Ferguson would later say, 'was to get the ball to our full-backs; that way Gary Neville and Denis Irwin could control the game.' They enjoyed plenty of time on the ball as Inter's forwards showed little interest in defending, and the wing-backs were frightened to push forward and leave their natural zones unoccupied after what happened at Old Trafford. United frustrated Inter, the game finishing 1–1 with Scholes off the bench to score the equaliser. United had controlled the tempo excellently and Ferguson considered that two-legged victory 'the biggest step forward under my management'.

For the first leg of the semi-final against Juventus, United were badly exposed in midfield. Beckham and Giggs pushed forward down the flanks, which left Keane and Scholes overrun against a Juve diamond featuring Didier Deschamps deep, Conte and Edgar Davids shuttling from wider positions, and Zidane as the number 10. Zidane inevitably pulled Keane and Scholes around to create space for the shuttlers to exploit, and Davids teed up Conte for the opener. But Ferguson reshuffled at the break, telling Beckham to move inside and effectively become a third central midfielder, with Neville pushing forward to provide right-sided width. United got a grip of the game, built pressure, and Giggs – who had been excellent after half-time in a more advanced role – smashed in a crucial late equaliser. There was minimal celebration, however; Giggs simply pointed towards the ball and gestured for his teammates to get back into their own half and go for the victory. That attitude would prove particularly crucial later in their Champions League run.

United attempted to start cautiously in the away leg, with Beckham and Blomqvist, in for the injured Giggs, remaining narrow. They actually dominated possession from the outset but found themselves

2–0 down thanks to two typical Pippo Inzaghi strikes: one a poacher's effort from two yards, the other a ludicrously fortunate deflected goal. From then on, United were fantastic, effectively reverting to their Premier League style and producing, in Ferguson's words, 'the best-ever performance from a team under my management'. Keane drove United forward marvellously despite being booked, which ruled him out of the final. His header got United back on track, and he was helped by the fact that Ferguson had again omitted Scholes, using the more disciplined Butt, which allowed the Irishman to play an all-action role. Yorke headed the equaliser, Cole tapped in the winner. This time it felt like United had imposed their game plan on the opposition.

In truth, United were battered by Bayern in the final. Ferguson's tactics were questionable; without Scholes and Keane, he used Beckham centrally, where he performed well in terms of dictating the tempo of the game, but United desperately missed his crossing quality. Bayern had been particularly scared of United's width, persuading UEFA to reduce the width of the large Camp Nou pitch by four yards. But Giggs was fielded on the right where he struggled against Bayern's Michael Tarnat, while Blomqvist couldn't influence the game on the left. Bayern went quickly 1–0 up, hit the woodwork twice and should have had the game wrapped up long before United's extraordinary late comeback. United made inroads when Beckham returned to the right, his combinations with Neville pushing them up the pitch. But it was somehow fitting that the goals came from two substitutes: Sheringham, turning home Giggs's scuffed shot, and Solskjær, converting Sheringham's flick-on from Beckham's in-swinging corner. Ferguson's revolutionary approach of assembling four genuinely top-class centre-forwards had paid off, and this was classic Manchester United 1998/99, those deemed not good enough for the first-choice XI providing the crucial contributions.

Solskjær had become renowned as a supersub rather than a starter, and earlier that season had scored four goals in a single game as a substitute against Nottingham Forest. Solskjær actually disliked his supersub reputation but, as an intelligent, studious player, analysed the opposition from the sidelines before exploiting weaknesses in the second half. In fact, almost all of United's crucial victories that season involved the introduction of a supersub or rotation. In the famous 2–1 FA Cup semi-final replay victory over Arsenal, Ferguson made the shock decision to rest Yorke and Cole, fielding Sheringham and Solskjær up front instead. Giggs was also left out, before being introduced as a substitute when Ferguson saw Arsenal's ageing defence was fatiguing. His extra energy proved crucial and he scored the best goal of his career.

In the final Premier League victory over Tottenham, Ferguson used Sheringham from the outset, but then introduced Cole at half-time, asking him to target John Scales, recently returned after injury and not moving comfortably, with his speed. United went 1–0 down, but after Beckham whipped in a brilliant equaliser, Cole scored the winner.

In the FA Cup Final, United's plans took an early blow when Keane departed through injury. Surprisingly, Ferguson opted to introduce Teddy Sheringham in his place, but his logic was sound. He knew both Keane and Scholes were suspended from the Champions League Final four days later, so didn't want to use Butt – now a certain starter against Bayern – for an extended period at Wembley. Instead he introduced Sheringham, with Solskaer dropping back from his centre-forward position to the right of midfield and Beckham tucking inside. Sheringham scored with his first touch, then created the second for Scholes. Another key substitution.

Ferguson also rested Stam and Yorke – his best defender and best attacker – at Wembley in preparation for the Champions League

Final, merely giving them a quick second-half runout to stay sharp. 'Some of the directors have given up trying to understand some of my selections,' Ferguson admitted. 'It's written on their faces – "What on earth is he doing now?"' The idea that a manager could rest two key players for the most important match of the domestic football calendar was incredible, but then Ferguson was always one step ahead. A few years earlier he was the first manager to consider the League Cup as an opportunity to rest key players and blood youngsters, which would later become established practice for big sides.

Squad rotation was generally linked to foreign managers like Chelsea's Claudio Ranieri and later Rafael Benítez at Liverpool. There remained a belief within English football that managers should 'keep a settled side' and, in particular, 'never change a winning side' – Aston Villa famously won the title in 1980/81 by using only 14 players, including seven ever-presents. But in 1998/99 Ferguson was the only Premier League manager who didn't name an unchanged side all season, eternally freshening up things to allow first-teamers a breather and to keep reserves involved. While other title challengers often faded in the last month of the season, United's 1998/99 side kept on going. This was largely attributed to 'bottle', typically the most revered attribute in English football, but it was also simply about fitness. United's players shared the workload, and Ferguson possessed substitutes of comparable ability to his first-choices. 'You can't expect the same players to play in so many games,' said Ferguson. 'At least, you can't if you want them to keep winning.'

The emphasis upon rotation represented an enormous transformation from United's first Premier League title six years earlier. In 1992/93 eight players started at least 40 of United's 42 Premier League games. By 1998/99, in a 38-game season, no one started more than 34. Ferguson's use of the squad was fantastic: Phil Neville, Butt and

Blomqvist weren't considered regulars, but all three started more than half of United's Premier League matches. Centre-back David May, who made just seven starts all season, is often mocked for taking an unreasonably prominent role in the Champions League celebrations. But that was United's treble-winning squad all over, the back-ups always heavily involved.

Slowly, other top Premier League clubs started to embrace rotation. It was particularly evident up front, with title rivals looking to emulate United's four-man strike options. When winning the double in 1997/98, Arsenal's back-ups were the relatively unknown Nicolas Anelka and Christopher Wreh, but immediately after United's treble success they found themselves with experienced internationals Nwankwo Kanu and Davor Šuker in reserve to Thierry Henry and Dennis Bergkamp. The next time they won the league, at Old Trafford in 2001/02, Wenger started his two back-up strikers, two-time African Footballer of the Year Kanu playing alongside Euro 2000 final goalscorer Sylvain Wiltord, who netted the winner. Big clubs started to stockpile top-class players, which increased the gap between them and the also-rans. Established first-teamers, however, generally didn't like rotation – Bergkamp described the concept as 'bullshit'.

Crucially, Ferguson wasn't simply rotating for the sake of it; this wasn't a revolving door policy, as critical pundits often implied. He was often introducing specific players for specific roles against specific opponents, and United's strategic improvement and European progress convinced his players. The fact Ferguson successfully introduced rotation was, in part, because he had successfully embraced tactics.

8

The Foreign Revolution

'Ninety-nine per cent of the innovations you see in the Premier League come from abroad.'

Michael Owen

On the Premier League's first-ever weekend, 15 August 1992, only 11 foreign players started in the entire division. Just over seven years later, on Boxing Day 1999, 11 foreign players started for a single team.

With Chris Sutton and Dennis Wise both injured, Chelsea's starting XI for their 2–1 victory over Southampton consisted of Ed de Goey (Netherlands), Albert Ferrer (Spain), Frank Leboeuf (France), Emerson Thome (Brazil), Celestine Babayaro (Nigeria), Dan Petrescu (Romania), Didier Deschamps (France), Roberto Di Matteo (Italy), Gabriele Ambrosetti (Italy), Gus Poyet (Uruguay) and Tore André Flo (Norway), who scored both goals. Chelsea's manager, meanwhile, was Italian Gianluca Vialli – there had been no foreign managers back in 1992/93.

To Vialli and his players, it felt entirely natural. None of them had noticed anything unusual about the team selection, but when they emerged from the dressing room to be confronted with an unusual number of photographers, the story became obvious. 'I never thought about it,' said Vialli afterwards. 'It makes no difference as long as we talk the same language on the pitch. We had a few players out – and unfortunately a few of them were English – but nationality is not important.'

For the British press, though, it was a momentous occasion, and the story was deemed significant enough to graduate from the sports pages to the main sections of newspapers. The *Guardian* published a leader article discussing the cultural significance of this development, inevitably attempting to find a wider meaning. 'It is not very many years since Chelsea was one of the most xenophobic of football clubs, with supporters booing foreign players when they came onto the field – even on occasion their own players,' it read. 'It is curious how Britain, so reluctant to share a single currency with the rest of Europe, has welcomed continental and non-European players to its bosom.'

When Chelsea again fielded no British players for a 2–1 defeat to Lazio three months later, the *Independent* described a photo of the starting XI as 'a picture that humiliates English football'. If that sounds extreme, it's worth remembering that just a few years earlier, fielding just four foreign players wouldn't simply have been frowned upon – it would have been against the rules.

English football's deep-rooted suspicion of foreign football tactics is notorious, although the extent it ignored foreigners themselves throughout the 20th century is often overlooked. After Herbert Chapman's Arsenal signed Dutch goalkeeper Gerrit Keizer in 1930, the Football Association reacted by introducing a two-year 'residency rule' on foreign players, effectively preventing English clubs from signing footballers from abroad. This rule remained in place until the 1970s, when Britain's entry into the European Economic Community meant such a ban was impossible. This was accepted by the FA in 1976, although the Football League attempted to stand its ground – 'I cannot stop a manager signing an overseas player, but I can stop him playing in our competition,' said league secretary Alan Hardaker. The European Economic Community specifically ruled on the issue two years later, clarifying that discrimination against the employment of other EEC citizens was in breach of the Treaty of Rome, although leagues were surprisingly able to maintain restrictions on the number of players fielded in a starting XI, a situation that lasted the best part of two decades. For the opening years of the Premier League, teams could employ as many foreigners as they liked, but could only field three together at any time.

There was a further complication, however, owing to England and Britain's somewhat complex political and footballing status. In the Premier League, Welsh, Scottish and Northern Irish players were not considered foreign by the FA, because they were all British citizens, while Ireland's long-standing agreement with Britain concerning freedom of movement meant they were not considered foreign either (which is why, in a British footballing context, 'foreign' generally referred to players from outside the UK and Ireland, even though the Republic of Ireland is a separate country).

UEFA's rules were different. In their eyes, England was a separate country to Wales, Scotland, Northern Ireland and Ireland because they competed separately at international level and had separate leagues that all provided teams for UEFA competitions. In Europe, therefore, clubs were only allowed to name three 'foreign' players plus two 'assimilated' players (who had earned residency in a country) in their matchday squad, which caused Manchester United particular problems during their formative Champions League adventures. Peter Schmeichel was once omitted from a 1994 trip to Barcelona because Alex Ferguson felt he needed to use his foreign quota on Welsh and Irish outfielders, and reserve goalkeeper Gary Walsh conceded four goals.

Surprisingly, at this stage the FA were giving serious consideration to falling in line with UEFA by maintaining English football's three-foreigner rule, but classifying anyone other than Englishmen as foreigners, as FA chief executive Graham Kelly confirmed. 'We believe there is a need to examine current regulations to determine if it would be advantageous to the English game, and the production and progress of our own players, to apply a similar classification to Europe,' he said. Ferguson, predictably, was fuming. 'It would effectively close the door to some great talents. Where would the game have been without people like George Best, Danny Blanchflower and Denis Law?'

He didn't need to worry, however, because restrictions upon foreign players in both domestic and European competition were scrapped in 1995, when a journeyman Belgian player named Jean-Marc Bosman blew the system wide open. Bosman was a midfielder for RFC Liège in the Belgian First Division, and upon the expiry of his contract in 1990, he wanted to move to French side Dunkerque. But at this stage, players didn't have freedom of movement at the end of their contract. Dunkerque refused to pay the inflated transfer fee Liège demanded, so Liège refused to let him go. Rules differed across Europe at this stage, and had Bosman been attempting to transfer between two English clubs, for example, he would have moved, with the fee being decided by a tribunal. But Belgian clubs could prevent their players moving abroad if a fee wasn't agreed, so Bosman was essentially trapped and his wages at Liege reduced because he was no longer a first-teamer.

Unsurprisingly, the European Court of Justice ruled that this was against the free movement of workers across European Union countries. It was a landmark case and had two major impacts. First, players could move on a free transfer when their contract expired. Second, leagues were no longer able to enforce any quotas on foreign players from other EU countries (although they could maintain quotas for non-EU players). English football's top brass were not impressed, and talk inevitably turned to the possibility of what Chelsea eventually did four years later. 'Whether the day will come where we see 11 non-British players in a single team, we'll have to wait and see,' said a rueful Kelly. Bosman's legal team, incidentally, had downplayed suggestions this could ever happen, claiming teams would need to field local players to retain supporters' affections. How wrong they were.

In hindsight it's astonishing it took so long before such an obviously unfair system was overhauled; football associations were claiming to be above the law, but couldn't explain precisely why. The changes to football were profound and the entire transfer market was seemingly at risk. Headlines uniformly described football as being 'plunged into crisis', and there were particular concerns about lower-league clubs' ability to survive, as they depended upon selling key players higher up the leagues. Would players ever transfer before the end of their contract, or simply let their deals run down and move for free, in the knowledge their new club would save money on transfer fees, and have more to spend on wages? The power had shifted dramatically from clubs to players.

The greatest impact, though, wasn't on contracts but on freedom of movement – teams could now field an unlimited number of foreigners. The ECJ ruling was made in December and took effect immediately, which meant leagues were forced to change their rules midway through the season, inevitably causing controversy. In Germany Bundesliga clubs formulated a gentleman's agreement not to exceed the previous three-foreigner limit for the rest of the campaign, but in England things changed immediately.

Less than a fortnight after the ruling Manchester City became the first English side to field four foreigners in the same team, using midfielders Georgi Kinkladze and Ronnie Ekelund from Georgia and Denmark respectively, plus two Germans – goalkeeper Eike Immel and striker Uwe Rösler – in a 2–0 defeat at champions Blackburn Rovers on 26 December. Indeed, Boxing Day proved a significant day in the history of foreign players in the Premier League, as it was exactly four years between the first time a Premier League team fielded four foreigners, in 1995, and the first time a Premier League team fielded 11 foreigners, in 1999, as if British players' tendency to overload on turkey and stuffing meant they were more likely to miss the following day's action.

Not everyone fully adjusted. Former Nottingham Forest manager Frank Clark recalls a scene ahead of a UEFA Cup tie against Lyon, when captain Stuart Pearce was delivering a pre-match rallying cry. Psycho was inevitably punching the air while roaring at his teammates, 'We're going to win, because we're English!' 'The factual inaccuracy of the statement didn't seem to occur to Stuart,' Clark said. 'I'm not sure if it occurred to his Norwegian, Dutch, Italian, Scottish, Welsh and Irish teammates, but if it did, none of them seemed in much of a hurry to point out his mistake.'

The sudden introduction of foreign players, more than any other single factor, changed English football. The introduction of Italian, French and Dutch players, in particular, throughout the 1990s enabled English football to embrace different roles, positions and styles, encouraging managers to think outside boxy 4–4–2 formations. The introduction of continental number 10s had provided more attacking flair, but now teams were evolving stylistically all over the pitch.

Certain countries simply produced an entirely different type of player in particular positions. Brazil, for example, was renowned for its attack-minded full-backs, and there was a dramatic change when the tough-tackling, old-school Arsenal left-back Nigel Winterburn was replaced by the dynamic, overlapping Silvinho, who was briefly fantastic and voted into the PFA Team of the Year before departing under a cloud following speculation about an illegitimate passport. He proved his quality in Spain, however, enjoying a successful spell with Barcelona.

The best examples of elegant centre-backs in the 1990s, too, were foreign. There was Belgian Philippe Albert, who starred in Newcastle's 1995/96 title challenge and famously rounded off the 5–0 victory over Manchester United in 1996 with a stupendous chip over Schmeichel. There was also Gheorghe Popescu, who enjoyed a sole season at Tottenham. He was a centre-back but also capable of playing in midfield, and stormed forward into attack when required, scoring the winner in a north London derby against Arsenal when popping up as a centre-forward. He also scored a fine goal against Newcastle, showing tremendous composure in possession, shuffling past a challenge and playing a one-two before firing home. He spent only a year in England, but was another who left for Barcelona.

One of the first genuine deep-lying playmakers was Emerson, the Brazilian who played for Middlesbrough at the same time as Juninho. Emerson was hugely talented, boasting great authority in possession, and was capable of spreading play to the flanks with long diagonal balls. He had a troubled time in England, mainly because his wife flew back to Brazil and refused to return to the north-east, which led to a bizarre stand-off when Emerson remained in Rio de Janeiro mid-season, saying he would happily quit football to remain with his wife. He eventually returned and was yet another who interested Barcelona – their coach, Bobby Robson, had worked with him at

Porto – although he went on to join Tenerife and then La Liga champions Deportivo La Coruña. He played just 41 times and offered little lasting legacy, but his passing range was unlike anything else in English football at the time.

But the best example of a foreign import offering something completely new was the Dutchman Ruud Gullit. Unquestionably one of the greatest players of his generation, having won the Ballon d'Or in 1987 and captained the Netherlands to European Championships glory the following year, Gullit was only the second fully formed superstar to join the Premier League when he signed for Chelsea in 1995, after Jürgen Klinsmann's year-long spell at Tottenham the previous season. Gullit was an incredibly versatile player, comfortable operating in defence, midfield or attack. While that's not entirely unusual for a Dutchman, considering the Netherlands' love of total football that redefined tactical responsibilities, few were truly masters of every position like Gullit.

During his early teenage years Gullit was fielded in defence for DWS, a small club in the west of Amsterdam. He was renowned for his unusual approach to playing as a sweeper, receiving the ball at the back and charging forward on solo runs to turn defence into attack swiftly, which contradicted the short-passing principles that dominated youth football across Amsterdam thanks to Ajax's dominance. Indeed, Gullit was always something of an outsider, not merely because he was an Amsterdamer who never represented Ajax. A tall, dreadlocked figure of Surinamese descent, he endured racism throughout his career, and upon accepting his Ballon d'Or trophy dedicated the award to the imprisoned Nelson Mandela.

He turned professional at Haarlem in 1979 and initially played centre-back before moving up front in his second season, then moved to Feyenoord in 1982, where he was generally fielded on the right wing. Here he was briefly in the same team as the visionary

Johan Cruyff, who was not officially manager but effectively decided the tactics and coached his teammates. On one away trip Gullit and Cruyff started talking about football in the lift up to their hotel rooms, then continued the discussion long into the night. Cruyff – whose niece Gullit later married – advised his pupil that when he inevitably left Feyenoord and moved to a bigger club he needed to dominate the side, ensuring that it was built around him in order to suit his incredible, unique talents. 'He gave me a new insight into tactics through his coaching and his way of talking about football,' Gullit said.

Upon joining PSV in 1985, Gullit therefore became something of a Cruyff figure. He personally persuaded the club to change their kit, saying their red shirts looked uninspiring alongside black shorts and red socks, insisting upon white shorts and white socks instead. When he realised right-back Eric Gerets and right-winger René van der Gijp had no relationship, he personally concentrated upon improving their combination play, away from the manager. But more than anything, Gullit felt his best position was as a rampaging, attack-minded sweeper, with experienced midfielder Willy van de Kerkhof dropping back to cover. 'As a central defender I could move into midfield and would dash from there into an attacking position,' he explained. PSV won the league in both seasons that Gullit was at the club, and while he sometimes switched to a more attack-minded position, 46 league goals in two seasons is an extraordinary tally for a player generally deployed at the back.

Gullit spent his peak years, between 25 and 33, playing in Serie A, chiefly with AC Milan, where he won three league titles and two European Cups. Arrigo Sacchi had created the greatest four-man defence of all-time: Mauro Tassotti, Franco Baresi, Alessandro Costacurta and Paolo Maldini, so there was no place in defence for Gullit, who instead became a world-renowned attacking midfielder or forward, playing the same role in the Dutch national side. But Gullit always wanted to return to his old sweeper position.

In 1995 Glenn Hoddle came calling. Hoddle had been Chelsea's player-manager for the past two seasons, often deploying himself as a sweeper, but realised his playing career was over and wanted to focus on management. Hoddle was a progressive manager who looked outside England for innovations and, recalling Gullit's performances at the back for PSV earlier in his career, convinced the Dutchman to join the Premier League to reprise his old role. To Gullit it was that prospect, as much as anything else, that convinced him to join Chelsea. 'My skills come out better as a sweeper,' Gullit said at his unveiling, which stunned English journalists, who had witnessed Gullit dominating European football from an attacking midfield position, and were accustomed to centre-backs being limited, straightforward destroyers. In the official Premier League sticker album that season, every other player in the division was listed as 'goalkeeper', 'defender', 'midfielder' or 'forward'. Gullit, however, was classified as a 'libero'. He was considered unique.

Gullit started his Chelsea career in that sweeper role, but his technically and tactically limited teammates struggled to comprehend his attacking instincts. He remembers challenging for an aerial ball inside his own box, bringing it down on his chest, then laying it sideways to Michael Duberry. He heard two noises: first a gasp of astonishment from the Chelsea fans, and then Duberry screaming 'What the fuck are you doing?' as he thumped the ball into the stands. In among all that mayhem Gullit was a revelation – head and shoulders above any other Premier League centre-back in possession, as one of the world's outstanding technicians playing in a role previously played primarily by cloggers. Gullit would receive the ball at the back, bring it forward, play a one-two with a midfielder and then find himself between the lines, acting as a number 10. 'It was like watching an 18-year-old play among 12-year-olds,' Hoddle marvelled. Opponents simply weren't accustomed to the idea of treating opposition defenders as attacking threats, and Gullit always had such time on the ball, with one of Chelsea's midfielders, often Nigel Spackman, playing the 'Van de Kerkhof role' and dropping back.

Match reports from Gullit's debut, a 0–0 home draw with Everton, demonstrate the extent to which he was a revelation. 'Ruud Gullit brought skills taken for granted in Holland and Italy to the Premiership, where the radar-controlled pass has yet to see off the longbow,' said David Lacey's enthusiastic *Guardian* report. 'There were moments when Gullit laid the ball off at angles his new teammates didn't realise existed … he has come to English football as a sweeper, but this is plainly not what he is about.'

Frank McGhee's *Observer* report explored Gullit's position a little further. 'He scotched forever the public's image of a sweeper's job,' it read. 'Too often in the English game, any seasoned defender who can tackle a bit and whack the ball hard gets the job. Gullit proved it demands the most accomplished player in a team.'

In truth, 1995/96 wasn't particularly successful for Chelsea. They finished in 11th place, although they reached the FA Cup semi-finals. Gullit was restricted to 21 appearances in all competitions because of injury, and after three months was usually operating in a midfield role, partly because his teammates simply couldn't understand his game. 'I would take a difficult ball, control it, make space and play a good ball in front of the right back,' Gullit later recalled. 'Except that he didn't want that pass. Eventually Glenn said to me, "Ruud, it would be better if you do these things in midfield."'

Hoddle left Stamford Bridge to take the England job after Euro 96, and chairman Ken Bates decided his replacement should be Gullit, who became the Premier League's only foreign manager for a couple of months until Arsène Wenger arrived, and followed in Hoddle's footsteps by acting as player-manager. One of Gullit's first signings was skilled French defender Frank Leboeuf, who had recently been crowned *La Gazzetta dello Sport*'s 'Libero of the Year' – a marvellously niche and brilliantly Italian award – to continue the emphasis upon building from the back. During Gullit's 18-month spell in charge he led Chelsea to the FA Cup in 1997, becoming the first foreign manager and the first black manager to win a major trophy in England. Some of Gullit's tactical acumen during that FA Cup run was highly impressive – in the fourth round, against Liverpool, Chelsea found themselves 2–0 down at the break. But Gullit introduced striker Mark Hughes for left-back Scott Minto at half-time, switched formation to a radical 3–3–1–3, and Chelsea won 4–2. Their tactics in the semi-final against Wimbledon were also impressive, with an extremely aggressive offside trap disrupting Wimbledon's long-ball approach.

Gullit was dismissed the following February in somewhat confusing circumstances, supposedly due to a personality clash with Bates rather than for on-field failings; Chelsea were second in the league, and making progress in the League Cup and Cup Winners' Cup. They would eventually win both under Gullit's successor as player-manager – Vialli, the man who later named that first all-foreign starting XI. Vialli was one of three crucial Italian signings by Gullit, who inevitably boasted tremendous knowledge of Serie A. The other two were Gianfranco Zola, the most important player in Chelsea's development into a technical side, and Roberto Di Matteo, who not only netted in the FA Cup Final victories of 1997 and 2000, but like Vialli would later manage Chelsea, leading them to win the FA Cup and the Champions League in 2012.

As a manager Gullit reacted more quickly than anyone to the lifting of quotas on foreign imports. Just two of Gullit's 14 Chelsea signings were British, and in a subsequent unhappy stint in charge of Newcastle just five of his 23 signings were British. He was strongly criticised in some quarters for his dependence upon foreigners but he tackled the critics head-on, almost introducing a new definition for the term. 'I see that England is still not thinking in a European way,' he complained. 'Because someone from France is not a foreigner any more. You have to get used to that on this island.' It was a brave statement. Indeed, it was Gullit, as much as Vialli, who contributed to Chelsea playing that all-foreign XI. Gullit recruited six of the 11 players, while Petrescu was a survivor from the Hoddle era. Only four were Vialli signings.

But amid the growing internationalism at Chelsea, Gullit – much like Wenger – was an Anglophile. He loved the variety in the Premier League, preaching the importance of passing football while also marvelling at Wimbledon's effective long-ball game, which he considered typically English. 'What the English must not do is play the European way,' he said. 'But I can feel something is changing at Chelsea and in the whole English game.'

Gullit particularly admired captain Dennis Wise, the throwback to the old days who, after a period of uncertainty, embraced Gullit's regime while emphasising the need for an 'English' mentality. Wise handed a book of cockney rhyming slang to the new recruits upon their arrival. 'There was still very much an English feeling in the dressing room and that was mainly down to Dennis, who was as English as you can get,' Di Matteo later said. 'He was very much the leader of the team and he let the others know what it meant to play in the Premier League.' But during this period the dressing rooms at Chelsea's training ground were peculiar: separate rooms, big enough for six players each. There was an English dressing room, an Italian dressing room, a French dressing room and a 'rest of the world' dressing room – the players later agreed it was terrible for team spirit.

It's interesting that both Gullit and Wenger – the first two foreign managers to win silverware in England, and the managers who did the most to introduce foreign players to the Premier League – later became more sceptical about the increasing internationalism. 'Only the really major players were ever transferred to foreign countries [pre-Bosman],' Gullit said. 'Since then, anyone can go anywhere, with a real over-abundance of average players as a result ... but you can't roll back the Bosman case – and even if you could, you would have to totally rewrite European legislation.'

Wenger – who, shortly before joining in 1996, had asked Arsenal's board whether the supporters would accept two foreigners in the same side – felt similarly. In 2001 he surprisingly signed Everton striker Francis Jeffers and Ipswich goalkeeper Richard Wright alongside the earth-shattering capture of Sol Campbell from Tottenham. While Campbell was among Europe's best centre-backs, neither Jeffers nor Wright had demonstrated the requisite quality, and started just 16 Arsenal league games between them. Why did the master of unearthing talented youngsters from obscure European leagues target substandard players? In Wenger's words, it was to 're-Anglicise' Arsenal, 'so that English would remain the first, and only, language spoken in the dressing room'. Even foreign managers worried the Premier League was losing its English identity.

9

Big Sam & Long Balls

*'I remembered watching Wimbledon on television
during the 1980s, so I can't say I was surprised by
this style of football. I knew there would be a
lot of long balls in England.'*

Rafael Benítez

In the decade immediately preceding the Premier League, English football specialised in direct football. While the most successful side of the 1980s, Liverpool, developed a passing game admired across Europe, English football gradually eschewed this philosophy and concentrated on route one football. Goalkeepers and defenders would thump the ball downfield towards a big centre-forward who specialised in aerial battles, while his strike partner and the midfielders would hunt for scraps, attempting to win the 'second ball'. Patient build-up play was considered a waste of time.

England's love of direct football was summarised by the beliefs of Charles Hughes, the FA's director of coaching for much of the 1980s. Hughes also worked with Charles Reep, a former RAF wing commander who was famously among football's first statistical analysts. Reep attempted to prove – with figures that were generally misleading, sometimes illogical and occasionally entirely selective – that the optimum attacking approach was about direct play and hitting long balls. Hughes's most famous coaching manual, *The Winning Formula*, was dismissive of possession football, stating that 85 per cent of goals were scored from moves of five or fewer passes, and he advocated launching the ball into the 'positions of maximum opportunity' (POMO) immediately.

Few managers associate themselves with Hughes and many more are determined to distance themselves from him. But throughout the 1980s long-ball football was common across England and various underdogs enjoyed incredible success with direct play. Wimbledon and Watford both rose from the fourth tier to the top flight in the space of five seasons, with Wimbledon winning the FA Cup and Watford finishing as runners-up in both league and FA Cup. Both were renowned as straightforward, uncompromising long-ball sides. Watford's manager, Graham Taylor, would later be appointed England manager and was in charge at the formation of the Premier League.

The Premier League's early years, however, witnessed a major decline in the popularity of route one football. Rule changes made passing football more viable – the back-pass revision was an obvious factor, while rules governing tackling became much stricter, with the challenge from behind now completely outlawed, ensuring forwards could receive passes into feet without being instantly clattered. A significant improvement in the quality of pitches shouldn't be underestimated, either; it's difficult to pass the ball across a mud bath, much easier on a bowling green.

The route one poster boys during the 1990s were still Wimbledon. The 'Crazy Gang', renowned for their macho behaviour and somewhat amateurish approach, punched above their weight under the no-nonsense Joe Kinnear, courtesy of incessant long balls. They continued that philosophy by appointing Egil Olsen, who had taken Norway to second in the FIFA World Rankings with a particularly direct style of football. Olsen had also become close friends with Reep, who offered to act as Olsen's statistical analyst at Wimbledon despite being 95 years old – this was not modern, progressive football. Wimbledon's relegation in 2001 – coincidentally the same year as Watford's, during Taylor's second spell at the club – seemingly marked the death of direct football at the highest level. But then along came Sam Allardyce's Bolton Wanderers.

Upon their arrival in the Premier League Bolton were almost ignored. They'd been promoted alongside two rather more exciting clubs: former Premier League champions Blackburn, who returned after two seasons away, and the intriguing proposition of Fulham, whose chairman Mohamed Al-Fayed was investing big money and promising to build 'the Manchester United of the south'. Bolton, meanwhile, had suffered immediate relegation from their previous two Premier League experiences and were favourites to finish bottom. But this trio would create history, the first time in the Premier League era that all three promoted teams avoided relegation, with Bolton making the greatest immediate impact.

Bolton's first game of 2001/02 was a trip to Leicester City, where they started sensationally and raced into a 4–0 lead by half-time, eventually winning 5–0. They followed that shock victory with two more wins, against Middlesbrough and Liverpool, and three games into the season found themselves top of the top flight for the first time since 1891. They were unsurprisingly unable to sustain such outstanding form, but over the next six seasons Bolton would establish themselves as the Premier League's most impressive small club, challenging for the Champions League places, routinely upsetting bigger sides and demonstrating that direct football could still succeed in the Premier League.

Among the increasingly studious foreign managers in the Premier League, Allardyce was a distinctly old-school character. As a player he'd risen through the ranks at Bolton, spending nine years at the club as a physical, one-footed centre-back. Playing until the age of 39, Allardyce featured in all four divisions and was renowned for his aerial dominance. His continual heading of the ball for two decades meant he was taking two pre-match aspirins during his twilight years, and he has suffered from neck problems since his retirement.

His leadership qualities were obvious from an early age. He was, amazingly, offered the Millwall manager's job as a 28-year-old player, refusing the offer because he felt he was too young. George Graham was appointed instead and, while the two quickly fell out, Allardyce learned from the Scot's defensive drills. Intriguingly, early in his coaching career at Preston Allardyce also worked under John Beck, probably the most blatant follower of Hughes's methods – here was a man who brought in statisticians to educate players on how few passes were needed to score goals and who ordered his groundsman to keep the grass unmown near the corner flags so that long balls into wide areas would stay in play. Players resented his incredibly strict instructions about knocking the ball into certain zones, but Beck had enjoyed great success with Cambridge, taking them from the fourth tier to the play-offs of the second tier in under three seasons, nearly following Watford and Wimbledon's rise. He was less successful at Preston, however, and Allardyce hated working with him, rebuking his 'brain-dead' football. But while Allardyce's style was more refined, he was considered the modern, Premier League equivalent of Beck.

From the outset Allardyce cast himself as an outsider in the Premier League, refusing to follow the template set by continental rivals. 'I have never seen myself being offered a job by a top Premiership club for the simple reason that I'm not high-profile enough and I don't speak with a foreign accent,' he complained as early as 2000, a year before Bolton's promotion. This would become a familiar theme, although it felt somewhat premature considering that only four Premier League sides – admittedly including three of the top five – employed a foreign manager at this stage. He wound up high-profile managers deliberately, almost as a pantomime villain, but Allardyce was clearly frustrated by his depiction. 'A lot of the job today is about how you hold and portray yourself, about how people perceive you to be, not how you are,' he would later complain. 'Unfortunately I cannot help the way I were born and the way I look.' Allardyce suffers badly from dyslexia, admitting he struggles to write, and he's an extremely slow reader, but believes he compensates with excellent listening skills, remembering aural information instantly.

Beyond the brash persona, Allardyce was a genuinely innovative manager; only Arsène Wenger did more to evolve the Premier League behind the scenes during the Premier League's first decade. Wenger was so progressive because he'd spent time in Japan, which was behind the times in a footballing sense but ahead of the game in terms of physical preparation. Similarly, Allardyce's forward-thinking approach came from an unlikely source: American football.

During the summer of 1983 Allardyce enjoyed a brief spell in the North American Soccer League, playing 11 games for the Tampa Bay Rowdies. Although the football itself was of a relatively low standard, the side's physical preparation was light years ahead of anything witnessed in England, because the Rowdies shared facilities and backroom staff with the Tampa Bay Buccaneers. The soccer players stayed in a complex alongside the NFL players, used their training ground and home stadium, and were completely attuned to the demands and procedures of a physiologically advanced sport. 'The way they prepared during the week opened my eyes and was one of those life-changing experiences,' Allardyce said. 'I learned there was so much more to conditioning than what we did in England; their attention to detail for every player was staggering.'

Allardyce was amazed by the mobile scanners to check immediately for injuries, the presence of masseurs, nutritionists and psychiatrists, as well as the great emphasis upon statisticians and analysts. This was all completely alien to English football, and while it would be some years before Allardyce became a manager, his American experience was crucial – when in charge of Notts County in the late 1990s he regarded his most important signing as a new physio. More than anything, it broadened his horizons, encouraging him to follow developments in other sports to search for innovations. At Bolton, Allardyce employed Dave Alred, the coach who had turned Jonny Wilkinson into rugby union's outstanding kicker, with the fly-half almost single-handedly (or perhaps that should be double-footedly, considering that Alred's methods made Wilkinson ambidextrous, an extremely rare quality in that sport) winning the Rugby World Cup for England in 2003. Allardyce later met both Billy Beane, who revolutionised baseball with his 'moneyball' statistical approach, and Dave Brailsford, who transformed British cycling through his philosophy of 'marginal gains'.

At Bolton, where Allardyce was handed a ten-year contract to encourage long-term thinking, he expanded his backroom team to the point where there were more coaching staff than players, which was extremely unusual at this stage, especially for a club of Bolton's modest stature. When awarded an honorary doctorate by the University of Bolton, a satisfying moment for a keen learner who struggled academically because of his dyslexia, Allardyce remarked upon his pride at 'what we achieved at Bolton, and the work I did to bring in a "team behind the team"'.

There were also developments in terms of diet and physiology: the increased use of energy drinks and electrolytes, of dieticians and physiologists. He particularly cared about statistics involving recovery time. On Boxing Day 2003 Bolton travelled to Liverpool, going 2–0 down after 47 minutes. Allardyce reacted by immediately withdrawing his best three players: Youri Djorkaeff, Jay-Jay Okocha and Iván Campo, in the knowledge that Bolton had a game two days later against Leicester. He knew two full matches in such a short space of time was impossible for players of their age, so effectively gave up on the match at Anfield and concentrated on the winnable game – although Bolton would only draw 2–2 against the Foxes.

But while Wenger was the true revolutionary in terms of introducing scientific methods into the English game, Allardyce brought in more specific footballing innovations. Allardyce was, quite literally, seeing the game from a different perspective; rather than standing in the technical area and bellowing instructions, the accepted practice, Allardyce sat high in the stands to afford himself the best possible view of the tactical battle, and any changes were communicated via radio to his assistants in the dugout. It's peculiar that more managers haven't copied this practice, although Allardyce has since reverted to sitting in the dugout, feeling his presence on the touchline – and in the ear of the fourth official – is valuable.

When Sir Alex Ferguson visited Allardyce's office at the Reebok Stadium for the customary post-match glass of wine he was stunned to discover how many 'boffins' were sitting behind computers, pouring over statistics. Numbers were a crucial part of Allardyce's approach; he provided his players with pre-season targets in terms of clean sheets and goals from each department of the side, and was an early adopter of ProZone, advanced statistical software that allowed him to analyse players and matches in depth. In the dressing room at half-time, Allardyce would screen video clips from the opening 45 minutes to illustrate his instructions.

His analytics staff created statistical profiles for individual positions in Bolton's side, discovering precisely what would be required from, for example, a right-back. Allardyce then used this information to convert players into different roles, in the knowledge they were capable of the appropriate statistical output. This became something of a specialism; he converted strikers Henrik Pedersen and Kevin Davies to left-back and right-midfield respectively, shifted Ricardo Gardner from left-wing to left-back, and played traditional centre-backs Iván Campo and Fernando Hierro as ball-playing midfielders. Allardyce examined statistics concerning dead-ball situations, working out precisely where his players should position themselves. It was a new spin on that old cliché of 'percentage football'.

Sometimes Allardyce went against the statistics; the purchase of Campo was unpopular among his analytics team but proved a success, while towards the end of 2003/04 his improvised policy of allowing the squad four days off after every victory enraged his sports-science team but helped Bolton win five consecutive games. He studied the stats but wasn't a slave to them.

The most fascinating part of Allardyce's statistical obsession was building the 'War Room' at Bolton's training ground. Inside, Allardyce and his confidants would surround themselves with plasma screens displaying charts on players' fitness levels and statistics on pass completion, distance covered, number of sprints, tackles and interceptions. It proved vital for both tactical preparation and physical conditioning, with Allardyce excellent at resting players before they suffered serious injury. And while other Premier League clubs were employing similar methods, Allardyce believed that Bolton's was the most advanced set-up in Europe. Much of the credit goes to Mike

Forde, Allardyce's performance director at the club, who became so revered he was poached by Chelsea, and then worked as a consultant in cycling, the NBA and, most significantly, the NFL. Allardyce had taken inspiration from the NFL – now, an NFL team was taking inspiration from his old performance director.

However, these were all behind-the-scenes features. Supporters didn't see the War Room or Allardyce's statistical models, they simply observed what happened on the pitch, and while Allardyce was unquestionably an innovator in some respects, he prescribed a style of football that was distinctly old-fashioned. The concept of playing out from the back was alien to Bolton, with goalkeeper Jussi Jääskeläinen booting huge balls down towards the strikers and every free-kick being launched into the opposition penalty box. Long throw-ins were frequently used, Allardyce having set Bolton's pitch size to the minimum allowed under the regulations, which made the throws more dangerous and hampered the opposition's ability to play passing football.

The player who most epitomised Bolton during this period was Kevin Nolan, initially an average centre-back in Bolton's academy whom Allardyce wasn't convinced would make it as a professional because he 'couldn't head or tackle'. Nolan was redeployed as a midfielder and became a useful goalscoring weapon, purely on account of his incredible ability to reach the 'second ball', latching onto flick-ons and knock-downs to convert from close range. And that was what Bolton's game was all about – for their first couple of seasons in the Premier League they were brilliant at the simple, Sunday league concept of second balls.

After their flying start in the Premier League, Bolton struggled in their debut campaign, flirting with relegation and only surviving thanks to a sudden upturn in form during the spring. The signings of two international attackers proved crucial; German striker Fredi

Bobic arrived on loan and scored a hat-trick against Ipswich in April, but more important was the man Allardyce considers his all-time best signing: Youri Djorkaeff, the brilliant creative forward who contributed heavily to France's World Cup and European Championships successes. Allardyce ignored his disciplinary problems at former club Kaiserslautern. 'I'm not worried about Youri's character and the reputation he has from his time in Germany,' he said upon his signing. 'I have always enjoyed signing players who have had a bad reputation or have been disruptive elsewhere because I find them a challenge. I'm a good judge of character.' This would prove to be the first in a succession of similar signings – foreign, technical, experienced, risky.

Allardyce offered an intriguing explanation for favouring experienced players, outlining that he could examine years' worth of ProZone data so he knew exactly what players would do when he played them. Experience is often considered in relation to a player's knowledge, but Allardyce considered it in relation to his knowledge of a player. He jokingly referred to Djorkaeff as the club's 'worldwide ambassador' because his arrival put Bolton on the map, and the Trotters were later blessed with the trickery of Okocha, the most gifted African playmaker of his generation and an entertaining showboater, as well as the guile of Hierro and Campo, who provided Spanish passing quality some years before it became so revered. Allardyce took a chance on speedy wide forward El-Hadji Diouf, who had proved incredibly unpopular at Liverpool, and was rewarded with some fine performances. His man-management skills were excellent; Diouf referred to Allardyce as 'Dad' for the trust he'd placed in him, and Allardyce later rescued the similarly difficult Nicolas Anelka from Turkey, rejuvenating the Frenchman's career and doubling his money when selling him on to Chelsea, where he won the Golden Boot.

There were some flops, however. Mário Jardel, astonishingly prolific in Portugal, couldn't get himself in shape and was moved on, while Hidetoshi Nakata, the first big-name Japanese footballer, was more style than substance and retired from football at 29 after a quiet season at the Reebok. But these players were generally signed for free on short-term contracts, and the successes outweighed the flops. Allardyce's main policy when signing a player was simply concentrating on his strengths and ensuring he constantly found himself in situations to demonstrate them, which might sound simple, but in a period when progressive managers were encouraging their defenders to start the attacking – and their attackers to start the defending – Allardyce's back-to-basics approach proved popular with veterans who had become frustrated by being handed unfamiliar duties at bigger clubs.

Finishes of 16th and 17th in Bolton's first two Premier League seasons satisfied their natural target, survival, but they subsequently came 8th, 6th, 8th and 7th, the only club aside from the 'Big Four' of Arsenal, Chelsea, Liverpool and Manchester United to finish in the top half in all four seasons, a considerable achievement. In 2004/05 Bolton finished level on points with that season's Champions League winners, Liverpool, qualifying for Europe for the first time in their history. Two years later, in 2006/07, they were third at the turn of the year and appeared set to challenge for the Champions League places.

Bolton improved not only by increasing their number of technical players but also by perfecting their direct-approach play. This was partly inspired by a switch to a 4–5–1 formation, previously used by Allardyce as an occasional alternative to his 4–4–2 but which became his first-choice system at the start of 2003/04. He would often crowbar in a second striker by deploying him out wide, a trademark of the aforementioned route one ideologues Taylor and Olsen. This gave

Bolton two aerial targets as well as a numerical advantage in central midfield, at a time when few sides had switched to a one-striker formation. It's peculiar that Bolton, a side unashamedly uninterested in the midfield possession battle, were an early adopter of 4–5–1.

Despite his route one approach, Allardyce hadn't been able to count upon a proper target man in those first two seasons spent battling relegation. Michael Ricketts, who made a tremendous impact in his first half-season, possessed the requisite physique but preferred to run in behind. He frustrated Allardyce with his lack of professionalism, while Henrik Pedersen worked hard but wasn't particularly effective at winning aerial balls. So, in 2003, Allardyce picked up Kevin Davies on a free transfer, and if Nolan had previously been Bolton's defining player because of his ability to win second balls, Davies became their main man because of his ability to win first balls. He was a classic Allardyce signing – a talented forward who had once cost Blackburn a club record fee but who seemingly found himself on the scrapheap after a couple of poor campaigns, starting only once in his final season at Southampton.

Davies arrived at Bolton's pre-season training camp a stone overweight and was immediately put on a strict fitness regime that included the Atkins diet. As Davies later recalled, a concerned Allardyce called Davies into his hotel room one evening, telling the striker he had a reputation for not looking after himself and that he was nicknamed 'the Budweiser King', even though Allardyce, while imploring the striker to change his ways, was sitting on his bed in a dressing gown, smoking a cigar and drinking red wine. He referred to Davies and other unfit players as 'the Fat Club', sending them on 70km morning bike rides in the mountains, but upon their return they'd find him tucking into a full English breakfast. The contrast with Wenger, who followed the same diet as his players to set an example, sums up Allardyce's contradictory character.

The fitness regime clearly worked, however. In his first season at Bolton Davies started all 38 league matches – sometimes up front, sometimes wide-right – and eventually spent a decade at the club. He was never prolific, averaging eight goals a season, but was excellent at battling for aerial balls despite being only six foot tall, relatively short for a Premier League target man. Davies would regularly end campaigns as the Premier League player who had both suffered – and committed – the most fouls, with almost all the offences committed when battling for high balls. He essentially turned matches into a stop-start scrap based around dead-ball situations, which suited Bolton perfectly. Allardyce wasn't remotely concerned with ball possession, much more with ball position. The initial route into Davies was rudimentary, but he was nodding the ball down towards some of the Premier League's most exciting footballers, initially the likes of Djorkaeff and Okocha, then later Diouf and Anelka. With veteran Gary Speed a dependable midfield operator and Euro 2004 winner Stelios Giannakopoulos excellent at arriving in goal-scoring positions unmarked, Bolton had the perfect blend of technical players to provide moments of magic and straightforward footballers who helped Bolton play direct and occasionally upset the big boys.

Allardyce was always trying to gain an advantage over opponents. In 2003/04, after the offside law had been tweaked slightly so 'inactive' players in an offside position could play an active part in an attacking move after they'd retreated into an onside position, Bolton changed their free-kick strategy. Allardyce ordered two players to stand in offside positions, not attempting to win the first ball, but dropping back into the goalmouth scramble to latch on to the second ball. Allardyce's reasoning was that their runs originated from a position where defenders wouldn't be able to mark them. It was a tactic most notably deployed at Leicester; Nolan, inevitably one of the 'passive offside' players, hit the post from a second ball, then Bolton equalised when Foxes goalkeeper Ian Walker was distracted by the offside Nolan, fumbling a Davies attempt over his own goal line. Allardyce, however, vehemently opposed the new interpretation. 'I think they have got it wrong. There is nothing I can do about it apart from try use it to my advantage,' he said. 'I don't like it, I don't think it adds anything to the game whatsoever ... it caused some confusion and gave us some good opportunities.' Leicester manager Micky Adams was similarly dismissive. 'How can anyone say players are not interfering with play when they are running across the keeper's eye line?'

Allardyce took it further. Once he realised there was nothing to stop these 'passive offside' players deliberately blocking the view of opposition goalkeepers at free-kicks, he started 2005/06 with an even bolder approach. In Bolton's first home game, a 1–0 defeat to Everton, Allardyce placed Nolan in front of opposition goalkeeper Nigel Martyn, standing face to face with him. When the goalkeeper moved to get a better view, Nolan shifted with him. Allardyce's reaction was familiar. 'I don't like what I've done,' he admitted. 'I don't think it's a good regulation, I think the interpretation is wrong and by doing what I did, I've shown it up to be wrong, even though we've tried to take full advantage of it. But while the regulations are there, we will try to use them to our benefit.'

That was Allardyce, always trying to steal a march on his rivals – and he had plenty of them. A long-running spat with Liverpool manager Rafael Benítez was particularly petty. 'I think it is a model for all the managers around the world, their style of football and his behaviour,' Benítez sarcastically once said. 'It is the perfect model for all the kids and I'm sure all parents will enjoy this model and encourage their kids to be the same. The style of football, I think, Barcelona are thinking of copying.'

Most famously, Bolton's upsets were against Arsenal, the Premier League's symbol of technically proficient football. While there were similarities between Allardyce and Wenger in terms of physiological innovations, their football couldn't have been more different, and these head-to-head meetings ensured Bolton became renowned as the most direct side in the division. They started in April 2003, when Arsenal were 2–0 up at the Reebok Stadium but collapsed in the final 20 minutes, unable to cope with Okocha's skill or Bolton's aerial bombardment, the perfect illustration of their hybrid threat. With Djorkaeff getting a goal back and Arsenal struggling to defend crosses, Martin Keown nodded into his own net to seal a draw for Bolton, which effectively ended Arsenal's title hopes.

Later, between January 2005 and November 2006 – a period during which Arsenal won the FA Cup and reached the Champions League Final – Bolton played the Gunners four times at the Reebok Stadium and won all four games, with every opener a header. The first occasion saw Arsenal goalkeeper Manuel Almunia subjected to a relentless aerial bombardment he appeared completely unprepared for, with Wenger uncharacteristically criticising his goalkeeper's decision-making afterwards. Bolton's goal arrived when Jääskeläinen kicked long, Bolton won the second ball and Diouf crossed for Giannakopoulos to head in. But in addition to their attacking threat, Bolton were also secure at the back. 'We sussed their formation, we forced them into making basic errors,' boasted Allardyce.

While Wenger would complain about Bolton's physicality after subsequent meetings, on this occasion he admitted his players were tactically outwitted. 'We allowed Bolton to play the game that suits them; we gave them their ideal conditions and let them play,' he said. 'They sucked us in and played the long ball, but that's the way Bolton play.' It seemed Arsenal were completely flummoxed by a side using old-school tactics.

Bolton's 2–0 victory in December 2005, when Allardyce targeted the unconvincing Pascal Cygan in an unfamiliar left-back role, again left Wenger acknowledging Arsenal weren't suited to Bolton's approach. 'It was a tentative and frail performance from us. The way they played beat us; that is credit to Bolton and it is down to our weakness ... they showed the type of game you need to beat us,' Wenger admitted, alongside complaints about Bolton's physicality. 'They kicked us as much as we kicked them,' responded Bolton midfielder Nolan. 'But if they want to complain about that, then everybody knows how to beat Arsenal now, don't they?'

They did, but few knew better than Bolton. A 1–0 FA Cup victory a month later saw Bolton again target a centre-back out of position at left-back, this time Philippe Senderos, with Giannakopoulos heading the winner from within the defender's zone. The 3–1 win in November 2006 was slightly more fortunate, with Arsenal hitting the woodwork three times. But at the Reebok it was four defeats in a row for Arsenal, and their physical weakness, not previously considered a particular problem, was ruthlessly exposed by Allardyce.

'Wenger seemed to want a rule where Arsenal should be allowed to do what they wanted with the ball, without us being allowed to tackle them,' Allardyce said. 'There was no credit [from the media] for the fact we'd spent all week studying how to nullify their skilful players and not let them have a second on the ball. It was a skill finding their weakness and how to exploit them.' This is the crucial thing about Allardyce's game plan; he's a studious manager who scouts the opposition in depth before formulating his strategy, making him among the most reactive tacticians the Premier League has seen. He particularly loves playing against managers with a defined, inflexible philosophy – it simply makes his tactical task easier, as he outlined in a 2014 interview.

'There are two types of coaches. There's coaches like me who weigh up the opposition and ask the team to adjust. Fergie was similar. José

[Mourinho] is similar. Then there's Arsène, who won't adjust. There's Brendan [Rodgers], who looks like he won't adjust. There's Manuel Pellegrini, who looks like he won't adjust … their philosophy is different to ours. Ours is more about who are we playing against. Their philosophy is more, "We always play this way," and they won't change, they carry on doing the same thing. That's why you can beat them.'

Allardyce was a master of finding balance – between physicality and flair, between his old-school persona and his innovative methods, between a consistent approach and tactics that took account of the opposition. Few neutrals admired his Bolton side from an aesthetic perspective, but Allardyce's teams always contained exciting players; he also provided tactical variety, challenging the big sides with a completely different threat. Always the outsider, Allardyce reintroduced traditional English football into an increasingly continental Premier League.

Part Four
Universality

10

One Up Front

'You see Thierry, and it's beautiful.
You see me, and it's not classic.'

Ruud van Nistelrooy

Formation changes during the Premier League's early years were primarily player-based evolutions, usually modifications to 4–4–2 in response to a foreign import's unorthodox characteristics and positioning. The start of the 21st century, however, was dominated by the shift from two-striker systems to one-striker systems, and it's significant that Sir Alex Ferguson, this movement's trendsetter, decided to change formation first, then identified players who would fit into the new system. His switch from a player-first to a system-first mentality highlighted the increased emphasis upon tactics.

In keeping with Ferguson's ever-improving tactical acumen throughout the 1990s, his inspiration came from European competition. United's 3–2 defeat to Real Madrid in the European Cup quarter-final of 2000 is sometimes cited as the match when Ferguson decided to shift away from 4–4–2, but United had performed impressively, creating chances but constantly being foiled by young Real goalkeeper Iker Casillas. Besides, there was no shame in being defeated by the eventual European champions. Two losses in the following season's competition, to PSV and Anderlecht, proved more crucial in changing Ferguson's mentality. The Dutch side overcame United 3–1 with a conservative version of the classic Dutch 4–3–3 formation, while the Belgian champions utilised a flexible diamond system in a 2–1 win.

In both matches United struggled to keep possession for long periods, were exposed on the counter-attack and only scored from the penalty spot. 'We were battered,' Ferguson later recalled of those two defeats. 'We played the traditional United way, 4–4–2, and were thumped. I told the players and staff that if we could not keep the ball better and stay solid in midfield we were going to suffer more that way, because opponents had sussed us out. So we switched to playing three in the centre of the park.' With a winger on either flank, that inevitably meant room for only one centre-forward. Ferguson experimented with a 4–5–1 midway through 2000/01, primarily because of injuries, but at the start of the following campaign it had become his default system.

This was a very deliberate move, with Ferguson sacrificing attacking resources to ensure United had the upper hand in midfield, helping them to dominate matches. This proved controversial among Manchester United fans, many of whom considered 4–4–2 part of the club's tradition. The comfortable title victories of 1999/2000 and 2000/01 were achieved with that formation, still with a squad-rotation system incorporating treble-winners Dwight Yorke, Andy Cole, Teddy Sheringham and Ole Gunnar Solskjær.

By this stage, the star man was Sheringham, who top-scored for United from his withdrawn forward role in 2000/01 and was voted both PFA and FWA Player of the Year. Surprisingly, Ferguson allowed Sheringham to rejoin former club Tottenham immediately afterwards. Officially this was because United were only offering Sheringham a one-year deal when the 35-year-old wanted two, but it seemed strange United lost the Premier League's best player purely over contract length, especially when Sheringham was the classic type of player who had never depended on pace, so could easily play into his late 30s. The fact Ferguson intended to move to a 4–5–1, a system that wouldn't suit a second striker like Sheringham, surely contributed to his departure.

The 4–5–1 required different types of players to 4–4–2, and Ferguson therefore made two significant purchases. He broke the British transfer record by signing centre-forward Ruud van Nistelrooy from PSV, then smashed that record shortly afterwards with the purchase of Lazio's Argentine midfielder Juan Sebastián Verón. 'I never thought I'd spend this much money on a player,' Ferguson said about the latter. 'But this is something United had to do.' His intentions were obvious; Van Nistelrooy was a striker capable of playing up front alone, while Verón was a third top-class central midfielder to play alongside Roy Keane and Paul Scholes. Ferguson, incidentally, had announced his intention to retire in a year's time, at the end of 2001/02. That season's Champions League Final was to be played in Ferguson's home city of Glasgow – he'd identified success at Hampden Park as the ideal farewell, and 4–5–1 the best system for winning a second Champions League.

United's experience with the 4–5–1, however, didn't start well. There were various factors; Jaap Stam's shock departure after falling out with Ferguson and his replacement Laurent Blanc struggling wasn't helpful, while Ferguson later admitted that pre-announcing his retirement was a huge mistake, as his players switched off. But the system inevitably attracted plenty of criticism, with United's build-up play being noticeably slower. The scapegoat was Verón, which was slightly unfair considering that he was adapting to a different league. Besides, the change of system had prompted a decline in performance from team-mates boasting considerably more Premier League experience.

There was always confusion about Verón's optimum role, however; he was neither a classic Argentine number 10, nor a deep-lying play-maker, while he was too languid to be considered a box-to-box player. 'I played with him, and I couldn't tell you his best position,' admitted Ryan Giggs. Verón drifted around providing occasional brilliant long-range passes but was rarely decisive. His teammates spoke about his quality in training – and Ferguson called him 'a fucking great player' and lambasted critical journalists as 'fucking idiots' for not appreciating his talent in a press-conference rant – but Verón was ultimately underwhelming considering he was the most expensive – and the highest-paid – Premier League player at that point. It's arguable that Verón arrived a couple of years ahead of his time, when English football hadn't yet embraced silky midfielders and three-man midfields, but then other foreign talents, such as Eric Cantona, fought against the tide and effectively re-educated support-ers. Verón was unable to replicate that influence and was happier with the slower pace of football in Italy and Argentina.

Having found themselves as low as ninth in early December 2001, United improved dramatically and won 14 of their next 16 games, taking them to the top of the league, by which time Ferguson had reversed his decision to retire. Notably, while Ferguson continued with 4–5–1 in Europe, he reverted to 4–4–2 in the Premier League, which suited United's natural style and prompted their sudden improvement. In March, however, they were surprisingly defeated 1–0 at home by Middlesbrough, now coached by their former assis-tant Steve McClaren, courtesy of an Alen Bokšić goal that stemmed from Verón losing the ball unnecessarily in front of the defence. United were leapfrogged by Arsenal that weekend, and the Gunners never conceded first position on their way to the title.

More pertinent than Verón's performances, however, were the displays of Van Nistelrooy, as the Premier League attempted to work out precisely what was required from a lone centre-forward. Previously, playing with one up front was considered a defensive move, usually utilised by smaller clubs away from home. Now, it was a viable attacking strategy.

Van Nistelrooy had, slightly surprisingly, risen through the ranks at Dutch second division side Den Bosch as an attacking midfielder, before being converted to a centre-forward role in the Eredivisie by Heerenveen coach Foppe de Haan. After his move to Manchester United, De Haan recalled that a young Van Nistelrooy 'wasn't a real team player, and had no sense of what it means to play in a technical way – he wanted to have each ball, and he was very good on the ball, but he was playing for himself'. De Haan recognised Van Nistelrooy's limitations, pushing him up front while instructing him to chase the ball less and wait for it more. He thereby created the purest goal poacher the Premier League has witnessed.

Ferguson nearly signed Van Nistelrooy in the summer of 2000, but the striker failed a medical when United detected a problem with his cruciate ligament. PSV insisted any injury was minor and Van Nistelrooy returned to Eindhoven to train, with the club filming him to provide evidence of his fitness. But midway through that training session Van Nistelrooy suddenly collapsed screaming, holding his knee in agony. He'd ruptured the ligament, justifying United's concern. Ferguson visited the striker to assure him the transfer would go through next summer if he recovered properly, and he kept to his word.

Ferguson's faith was justified, as van Nistelrooy proved an instant hit. He netted twice on his home debut against Fulham, and ended on 23 goals from his first Premier League campaign, being voted PFA Player of the Year. Throughout his five-year spell in English football

Van Nistelrooy scored prolifically – and indiscriminately; of his 95 Premier League goals, 48 were scored at home and 47 away. Forty-eight were scored in the first half and 47 in the second half. Most strikers score more at home when their side is dominant, and more in the second half, when games become stretched; but Van Nistelrooy banged in goals whenever, wherever, invariably accompanied by the booming sound of United fans bellowing 'Ruuuud'.

Another statistic underlines Van Nistelrooy's role at Manchester United – of his 95 Premier League goals, only one was scored from outside the penalty area. In fact, extend the sample to Van Nistelrooy's 150 United goals in all competitions and the figure is still only one, away at Charlton in his final campaign. Even for an unashamed goal-hanger like Van Nistelrooy, it's a remarkable statistic considering pure target men such as Emile Heskey (11 of his 111 Premier League goals), Chris Sutton (9 of 83) or Kevin Davies (7 of 83) scored many more from outside the box.

When Wayne Rooney made his debut for Manchester United in a Champions League tie against Fenerbahçe in 2004, he scored a hat-trick comprising three goals from outside the box. Three in 54 minutes; Van Nistelrooy managed just one in five seasons. But the Dutchman was a fantastic poacher, thriving on crosses, predicting where rebounds would fall, sensing when the goalkeeper was advancing and rounding him. While his goals were uniformly from close range, some of them were spectacular, particularly when he received the ball at an awkward height. Then he'd show an incredible ability to cushion the ball into a shooting position before pivoting swiftly and crashing the ball home. The ultimate purpose of football is putting the ball in the net, and of the thousands of footballers who have played in the Premier League no one has been better at that simple task than Van Nistelrooy.

* * *

But Van Nistelrooy also proved problematic. Before his arrival Manchester United won three consecutive Premier League titles. During his period at Old Trafford they triumphed just once in five seasons. When he departed in 2006 they immediately won three consecutive titles again. Van Nistelrooy isn't solely to blame – Chelsea's sudden wealth, Arsenal's improvement and some questionable Ferguson signings are equally responsible – but Van Nistelrooy was impressive individually rather than a great team player.

While Van Nistelrooy's teammates routinely described him as the best finisher they'd played alongside, his one-dimensional nature was obvious. 'If we'd won 3–0 and he'd missed a decent chance, afterwards he'd sit in the corner of the dressing room looking miserable,' said Ryan Giggs. He recalls an incident from a 4–0 win away at Bolton in Van Nistelrooy's first season when Solskjær had upstaged him by bagging a hat-trick and putting the game to bed. With a couple of minutes remaining and the game already won, Giggs teed up Van Nistelrooy for a simple tap-in and was taken aback when Van Nistelrooy ran towards him shouting 'Thank you, thank you!' because he was so delighted not to finish the game without a goal.

His partnership with Solskjær was productive, but overall Van Nistelrooy wasn't adept at linking with others, and fellow strikers found him particularly frustrating. At international level he and Patrick Kluivert disliked one another personally and rarely combined effectively, and for United his dominance partly explains why future European Golden Boot winner Diego Forlán found it so difficult at United, going 27 games – albeit many as a substitute – before finding the net. 'Diego just didn't register on Ruud's radar,' admitted Ferguson.

The most pertinent criticism, however, came from Louis Saha, who joined United in 2004 and was asked about the differences between Van Nistelrooy and his international teammate Thierry Henry. Saha clearly preferred playing alongside his compatriot.

'Ruud never scores from outside the 18-yard area and never takes free-kicks,' Saha said, before more damningly adding, 'Ruud doesn't take much of a part in the team's collective play. His game is all about finishing.' Later, Saha would describe playing alongside Henry as 'like getting swept along by the yellow jersey', a beautiful analogy that could only be uttered by one Frenchman about another.

Henry, more than anything else, was Van Nistelrooy's problem. In the 1990s the Dutchman's relative lack of all-round footballing skill wouldn't have been mentioned, but Van Nistelrooy was inevitably being compared to the Premier League's other top-class goalscorer, who was taking centre-forward play in a different direction. Their apparent rivalry dominated discussion during this period, almost like a Premier League version of the Cristiano Ronaldo v Lionel Messi debate a few years later. Henry outscored Van Nistelrooy, but was also capable of doing so much more. Henry was the Messi figure, Van Nistelrooy was the Ronaldo – and it's fitting, therefore, that both would later play alongside their equivalents.

Paul Scholes confirms that Van Nistelrooy was overly concerned by his rivalry with Henry. 'If he didn't score, he'd sit on the back of the bus and sulk, even if we'd won the game,' he said. 'Then if he'd look at the other results and if, say, Henry had scored then Ruud would be fuming even more. He perceived Henry as a personal rival and Ruud was adamant that he was going to get the most goals.'

During Van Nistelrooy's five-year Premier League career he and Henry won the Golden Boot every year, but it was 4–1 to Henry: 24–23, 24–25, 30–20, 25–6, 27–21. 2002/03 was the only season when Van Nistelrooy prevailed, the only season he lifted the title – and yet Henry somehow still managed to overshadow him, winning the PFA and FWA Player of the Year awards.

On the final day, with United already confirmed as champions, focus turned to Henry and Van Nistelrooy's battle for the Golden

Boot. Henry scored after seven minutes of Arsenal's game at Sunderland to draw level on 24 goals, then Van Nistelrooy netted a late penalty at Everton to move onto 25, admitting he was thinking solely about the Golden Boot while waiting to take the spot-kick. Tellingly, however, Henry showed little interest in boosting his own tally, and in the second half at Sunderland created no fewer than three goals, all for Freddie Ljungberg – one of only three assister-goalscorer Premier League hat-tricks. Henry was a provider as much as a goalscorer, ending the season with 20 assists, a Premier League record that stands today. 'Without the work of the last passer of the ball, the goalscorer is nothing,' Henry once said. 'Besides, I am not one of those players who suffers when he doesn't score.'

One example of that type of player was obvious, and it was notable that while Van Nistelrooy used to celebrate simple tap-ins with tremendous ferocity, Henry reacted to goals with a nonchalant expression borrowed from one of his heroes, basketball legend Michael Jordan. He even suggested that goals he scored in matches Arsenal lost shouldn't count towards his tally – those strikes, to him, were worthless. He was a true team player; when teammates overhit passes intended for him he was keen to applaud the idea. There was a period around the time of the Invincibles season of 2003/4 where, after rare moments when he lost possession, he would determinedly charge after the ball, closing down two or three opponents solo. It was a spectacular, unusual sight; the Premier League's most athletic player tearing across the pitch to start the defensive pressure, setting the example for his teammates – if Henry can work hard, why shouldn't they?

Henry didn't simply dominate the goalscoring charts during this period, he came to define the entire era of English football. He boasted a rare mixture of artistry and athleticism, and unlike Van Nistelrooy was also an entertainer, a crowd pleaser, 'a showman', in the words of the late George Best. His 'greatest goal' highlights reel is remarkable for the sheer variety of strikes – the long-range thunderbolts, the mazy runs, the finishing touches to Arsenal's team play. Henry was cheeky; he scored from backheels, he scored Panenka penalties, he scored quickly taken free-kicks when the goalkeeper was still assembling his wall.

No one has risen to a position of such widespread acclaim in the Premier League – in 2004 Arsenal played an FA Cup tie away at Portsmouth, producing a scintillating display of football to win 5–1. The atmosphere at Fratton Park was wonderful, a relentless wall of noise despite Pompey's heavy defeat, and the home supporters generously applauded Arsenal's attacking play. 'I've never seen that in my whole life,' Henry said, while Arsène Wenger was delighted. 'The result is wonderful,' he said. 'But it is even more enjoyable to hear opposition fans cheering our team.' When Arsenal returned later that season in the Premier League, having already confirmed their title, Portsmouth fans spent much of the second half singing Henry's name. He swapped shirts with an opponent and conducted a mini lap of honour in a Portsmouth shirt, applauding the Portsmouth fans as he left the Fratton Park pitch. It felt like Henry belonged to the Premier League as a whole, not simply to Arsenal.

If Van Nistelrooy was the purest striker imaginable, Henry wasn't really a striker at all. Much has been made of Wenger's decision to convert Henry from a wide player to an outright centre-forward, although realistically, with Wenger still very much committed to a 4–4–2 system, it was the obvious approach – and Henry had played as a forward throughout his youth-team days. The confusion stems, inevitably, from English observers not appreciating the nuances of systems that weren't 4–4–2.

While Wenger handed Henry his professional debut at Monaco in August 1994, he was dismissed from his post the following month, and Henry became accustomed to playing wide in a 4–3–3. Henry played that role during France's victorious 1998 World Cup campaign on home soil; it was a natural fit for a player blessed with tremendous speed but who didn't thrive on crosses. His brief, half-season spell with Juventus was peculiar – Juve didn't play with wide forwards and sometimes used a 3–5–2 system. Henry had chances up front but was also forced to fulfil a wing-back role on occasion, effectively becoming a full-back when his team weren't in possession. This was clearly a complete waste of his talents, although Henry bristles at suggestions that his period in Serie A was a failure – insisting, with some justification, that he played perfectly well and simply recognised that a move to Arsenal was best for his career.

In Arsenal's 4–4–2 Henry had two potential roles: left-midfield or up front, and it's often forgotten that he initially played the former more than the latter. In the first 15 league games of 1999/2000 he was deployed on the left flank five times, up front only three times and was omitted from the starting XI on seven occasions. In fact he was Wenger's fourth-choice centre-forward during this period, with Dennis Bergkamp starting 12 times up front, Nwankwo Kanu ten times and Davor Šuker five times. Henry was forced to bide his time, and while there's little doubt that Wenger had high expectations, Henry's conversion into a centre-forward wasn't a *fait accompli*. When Marc Overmars returned to full fitness and re-took his left-wing slot, things fell into place with Henry moving up front, and he, crucially, credits Wenger for 'giving me the belief that I could play where I always played before', rather than for moving him to an entirely new position.

Henry opened his Premier League account in September 1999 with the only goal as a substitute against Southampton, but it wasn't until late November, when he struck twice against Derby (to turn a 0–1 into a 2–1, with both goals assisted by Overmars), that he showed the goalscoring potential that would eventually make him Arsenal's all-time top goalscorer. From then on he exploded; after a solitary goal in his first eight league appearances, Henry then hit 16 in his subsequent 19 – only once starting on the wing during that spell, and even then remaining there for only 45 minutes before shifting up front. Henry was now a forward.

He was, however, an unorthodox forward. His history as a wide-left player was obvious throughout his Arsenal career because he consistently took up positions on the outside of opposition right-backs before cutting inside and bending the ball into the far corner with his right foot. This became Henry's trademark and owed much to constant work on the training ground as a teenager, repeating the same exercise again and again: receiving the ball near the touchline, cutting inside past a mannequin then shooting inside the far post. When he netted a trademark strike in a 2006 World Cup qualifier away at Ireland, he dedicated the goal to his youth-team coach at Monaco, Claude Puel – who would later take charge of Southampton – because Puel had encouraged him to work on that finish every day after training. 'I wasn't born with a gift for goals,' Henry said in his later years. 'I was quick. I had to have ten chances to convert one into a goal – but at the same time, I kept creating these chances. Then I told myself: "You won't have these chances all the time. You must stick them into the net."'

Henry's positioning made life difficult for opponents. Ferguson admitted that when United faced Arsenal, he instructed his right-back – usually Gary Neville – to remain in position at all times. Henry took inspiration from three players: initially George Weah, who had also worked with Wenger at Monaco, but also Romario and Ronaldo. These three, said Henry, 'reinvented the centre-forward position, they were the first to drop from the box to pick up the ball in midfield, switch to the flanks, attract and disorientate the central defenders with their runs, their accelerations, their dribbling'.

But Henry arguably took things further; that trio were highly mobile but fundamentally were number 9s. Henry didn't feel like a striker at all, and with Bergkamp dropping into his usual positions between the lines, opposition centre-backs found themselves without anyone to mark. Playing with a false nine became fashionable a few years later, but Arsenal were effectively playing a strikerless formation at this stage, fielding only a number 10 and a left-sided attacker. Therefore, while Ferguson had made a very deliberate shift to a one-striker system from a basic 4–4–2, Arsenal had subtly shifted to a no-striker system *within* a basic 4–4–2.

Even though Henry was able to outscore Van Nistelrooy, Arsenal's goals arrived from a variety of sources. Freddie Ljungberg hit 12 goals from just 25 appearances in Arsenal's title-winning campaign of 2001/02, while on the opposite flank Robert Pirès – who won the FWA Player of the Year that season despite missing the last couple of months with a serious knee injury – recovered to hit exactly 14 goals in three consecutive seasons from 2002/03 to 2004/05, a sensational return from a wide midfielder. There was often a role reversal: the forwards were creative, the wide midfielders were goalscorers.

While Bergkamp and Henry's partnership is remembered fondly – and they were unquestionably two brilliant forwards on the same wavelength – Arsenal's peculiar system meant Henry's best relationship was with Pirès, playing lightning-quick one-twos to escape defenders down the left, while Bergkamp combined best with Ljungberg, whose darting runs met the Dutchman's through-balls. 'The most beautiful thing is making the pass when you are in a position to score yourself,' Henry said. 'You know you're good enough to score but you give the ball. You share. And you see that joy in the eyes of the other guy. You know, he knows, everyone knows.' This couldn't have been further from the outlook of Van Nistelrooy – Scholes once converted a tap-in from inside the six-yard box against Aston Villa and then felt compelled to apologise to the Dutchman, who had been waiting just behind, ready to pounce.

When Wenger celebrated his 20th anniversary at Arsenal in 2016, Henry conducted a TV interview with his old manager, quizzing him about the system. 'We played 4–4–2 with Dennis Bergkamp, who was a striker, but when he played with you it became a little bit of a 4–2–3–1,' said Wenger. 'As well, at the time we had players like Freddie Ljungberg, who could make runs from deep, so on occasions it was like playing with two or three strikers.' The shift away from two-striker formations didn't mean the lone striker should dominate goalscoring; it meant goals had to come from a variety of sources.

Ferguson became increasingly aware United came up short in this department, and at the start of Van Nistelrooy's second campaign was surprisingly critical of the Dutchman in public. 'Sometimes I think Ruud's a bit too selfish,' Ferguson told the media. 'Obviously he wouldn't have scored 36 goals last season if he hasn't been a wee bit selfish, but there are times when he could release the ball better and I've told him that. Ruud thinks that if he is not scoring then he is not contributing, and I have spoken to him about that. And when he doesn't score he comes off angry with himself and he gets himself down. Ruud's still only young, and if he can add these things to his game then it will turn him into a truly great player.'

That campaign saw Van Nistelrooy win both the title and the Golden Boot playing up front alone ahead of Scholes, who embraced his more advanced position and enjoyed his best-ever goalscoring return, although Van Nistelrooy saw him as a 'provider' who enabled him to concentrate on banging in the goals. It was difficult to argue with Van Nistelrooy's performances that season, although he never stopped worrying about his lack of all-round ability. 'If I look at [former Germany striker] Gerd Müller, he was only a goalscorer – I didn't like that, although he scored so many goals,' Van Nistelrooy said in late 2003. 'I've always tried to be more complete. My ambition is to combine the best of number 9 and number 10, as a striker who is also a team player and creator.'

But aside from his literal shirt number there were few signs of a number 10 in Van Nistelrooy's game. He averaged fewer than three league assists a season during his five years in English football, whereas Henry averaged over ten. It increasingly appeared that United were simply too predictable with the Dutchman up front, which was the complete opposite of Ferguson's intention when switching to a 4–5–1, and he later admitted that 'at first I believed Ruud's range of attributes was wider than it turned out to be.' Van Nistelrooy was more like a 1990s striker in the manner of Robbie Fowler or Andy Cole – a pure poacher – whereas in the new millennium managers demanded a broader range of attributes.

It's worth remembering, however, that while Henry's legacy has certainly stood the test of time, many pundits during this period thought Van Nistelrooy the better striker. Centre-forwards were still considered in traditional terms, and Van Nistelrooy's superior ability in the air was often cited as the attribute that made him the more potent goal threat. Alan Smith, the former Arsenal striker turned *Telegraph* journalist, wrote that 'in terms of all-round ability, the Dutchman might narrowly pip it,' which seems crazy in hindsight, in a world where passing ability has become so revered. But Henry's lack of headed goals was thought to be a major flaw, and it was considered outrageous that he regularly took corners rather than waiting in the middle to convert them, as well as allowing teammates to take penalties, particularly when he'd been the player fouled.

Van Nistelrooy, having grown accustomed to being the main man at Manchester United, became frustrated when Ferguson signed attackers who challenged his status. In 2003 Ferguson sold David Beckham, the wide midfielder who provided the type of cross Van Nistelrooy demanded, and replaced him with Cristiano Ronaldo, an individualist who frustrated the Dutchman with his reluctance to cross. A year later Wayne Rooney joined – and United started to look better without Van Nistelrooy. He started 2004/05 slowly, scoring just once from open play in nine matches, in addition to three penalties. Then, when the Dutchman was out injured from the end of November until mid-February, United produced their best run of the campaign, winning 32 points from a possible 36, including impressive away wins at Liverpool and Arsenal. They were now based around Rooney and Ronaldo.

Clashes with these two proved decisive in Van Nistelrooy's downfall at United. He never worked particularly well with Rooney, who was critical of Van Nistelrooy after his departure. 'I think he knows the style of football we're playing isn't suited to him,' Rooney said. 'He's still an amazing goalscorer, but the players that the manager has brought in like Ronaldo, Louis [Saha] and myself are more geared to playing quick, counter-attacking football. We play with pace, Ruud likes to slow the play down … I've had the feeling that he's been unhappy since the minute I signed for United … I get on with Ruud, but I don't think he and Ronnie are the best of pals. There's been one or two arguments on the training ground and Ruud's become dead annoyed when Ronnie hasn't released the ball as quickly as he'd like.' This became a common complaint, with Van Nistelrooy openly protesting that he couldn't play with Ronaldo because the winger held onto the ball for too long and never crossed – which, in fairness, was a legitimate complaint at that stage.

But the bust-up became serious. Van Nistelrooy constantly complained about Ronaldo to United's Portuguese assistant manager Carlos Queiroz, complaints that fell on deaf ears because, in part, Queiroz was always likely to protect his young compatriot. This frustrated Van Nistelrooy even more, and resulted in an regrettable training-ground incident after Van Nistelrooy fouled Ronaldo. When the winger typically made the most of the challenge, Van Nistelrooy shouted at him, 'What are you going to do, complain to your daddy?' He was sarcastically referring to Queiroz, but Ronaldo's actual father had recently died after a long struggle with alcoholism. He was understandably upset.

This incident was unfortunate for Van Nistelrooy, who continually struggled to develop good relationships with other attackers, on and off the pitch. He spoke to Ferguson and announced his desire to leave the club in 2005, saying he didn't want to wait for Ronaldo and Rooney to mature into Champions League-winning players, which stunned his manager, who suggested Van Nistelrooy should be acting as their leader.

Things got worse the following season. United again looked better without Van Nistelrooy, and when he realised he wasn't going to get off the bench in the 2006 League Cup Final, an easy 4–0 victory over Wigan, he called Ferguson a swear word that appeared in various publications, mysteriously, as both '****' and '******'. Ahead of United's last game of the 2005/06 season – against Charlton – Van Nistelrooy booted Ronaldo in training, which prompted Rio Ferdinand to get revenge by kicking Van Nistelrooy, who responded by swinging at Ferdinand, narrowly missing. Such incidents aren't uncommon in training, but this was the final straw. Upon his arrival for the Charlton game Ferguson told him in no uncertain terms to go home, and he departed for Real Madrid that summer.

Van Nistelrooy might have been trying to force a move to Spain – the Dutchman had demanded a clause in his contract specifically mentioning Real – but it was an incredibly undignified ending for one of the Premier League's most prolific goalscorers. He linked up effectively with his old pal Beckham in Madrid, although when Ronaldo followed him there in 2009 it was notable that Van Nistelrooy only played one further game, even if the two patched up their differences. Van Nistelrooy later wholeheartedly praised Ronaldo's incredible improvement, and phoned Ferguson to apologise for his behaviour during that final campaign with United.

But Ferguson was right to sell him. After Van Nistelrooy's departure in 2006 United became the Premier League's dominant force again, winning three straight titles and the Champions League. Rooney inherited the number 10 shirt, while Ronaldo exploded and became United's main goalscorer. Most pertinently, Ferguson didn't even seek a replacement for Van Nistelrooy, not signing another centre-forward for two years, as he had learned a crucial lesson about strikers: scoring goals was, in itself, no longer enough.

11

Invincibles & Convincibles

'When you start off, everyone wants to be a centre-forward – but some of us end up having to defend.'

Martin Keown

Arsenal's Invincibles, who achieved the historic feat of going the entire 2003/04 league campaign undefeated, are the most celebrated side of the Premier League era. That season, however, was simply the final move in a three-card trick.

Two years beforehand Arsenal won the Premier League in similarly impressive fashion, setting two extraordinary records in the process. First, they foreshadowed the Invincibles campaign by becoming the first top-flight side in over a century to go the entire campaign undefeated away from home. At this stage they appeared more fearsome on their travels; their home ground Highbury had the smallest pitch in the league, so Arsenal found more space away from home, where the opposition felt the onus to attack and left gaps that Arsenal could exploit in counter-attacks. Second, and even more impressively, they became the first side in top-flight history to score in every league game, a record that's been unfairly – if understandably – overshadowed by the Invincibles campaign. If anything, it typified Arsenal better, underlining the consistency of their attacking threat.

Ahead of the following campaign, 2002/03, Arsène Wenger made an incredible forecast. 'Nobody will finish above us in the league,' he told reporters. 'And it wouldn't surprise me if we were to go unbeaten for the whole of the season.' The reaction was a mixture of scepticism and astonishment at Wenger's arrogance. But he went back for more. 'I am still hopeful we can go through the season unbeaten,' he repeated after a 4–1 thrashing of Leeds in early September 2002. It was a very specific objective, which had no precedent since the Preston North End side of 1888/89. Wenger was left embarrassed the following month at Everton when Arsenal's 30-game unbeaten run was ended by Wayne Rooney's debut Premier League goal, a 90th-minute, 25-yard strike in off the crossbar. 'He's supposed to be 16,' Wenger sighed afterwards, devastated that his dream of an unbeaten campaign was over.

The psychological blow clearly affected Arsenal, as they contrived to lose four consecutive matches, their worst run since 1983. By April, with Manchester United favourites for the title, Wenger's 'unbeaten' prediction was widely mocked. 'I'm sure they would love to turn the clock back six months,' Sir Alex Ferguson said. 'It might come back to haunt them.' Arsenal eventually limped home in second place behind Ferguson's side, their fate sealed by a shock 3–2 home defeat to Leeds, who simultaneously confirmed their Premier League survival and denied Arsenal the title. Martin Keown, the veteran centre-back, blamed Wenger for the failure, saying his pre-season forecast had piled pressure upon the players.

But, incredibly, that Leeds setback was Arsenal's final league loss before another staggering unbeaten run, this time of 49 games, which included the entirety of that 2003/04 campaign. Wenger's seemingly ludicrous prediction came true – simply a year later than he'd anticipated.

Arsenal's 2001/02 and 2003/04 title-winning sides were extremely similar in terms of personnel. There were only two changes to Wenger's first XI: Gilberto Silva played alongside Patrick Vieira in midfield, with Ray Parlour and Edu demoted to deputies, while Kolo Touré had displaced Martin Keown at centre-back. In fact the 2003/04 side was structurally similar to Wenger's first title-winning Arsenal side of 1997/98 – still essentially 4–4–2, featuring two holding midfielders and a deep-lying forward, in a shape that would eventually be considered 4–2–3–1. Vieira remained in midfield, Dennis Bergkamp was still the number 10. Up front, Thierry Henry was a refined version of Ian Wright or Nicolas Anelka, Robert Pirès was a goalscoring left-midfielder in the mould of Marc Overmars, and Freddie Ljungberg a hard-working, onrushing right-sided midfielder in place of Parlour. Gilberto was the Emmanuel Petit figure – both solid, World Cup-winning defensive midfielders who allowed Vieira to charge forward. In midfield and attack, the Invincibles were not revolutionary themselves, simply a continuation of Wenger's initial revolution.

Defensively, however, everything had changed. For 1997/98 Wenger had stuck with the old back four developed by George Graham: Lee Dixon, Keown or Steve Bould, Tony Adams and Nigel Winterburn. They were proper, old-school defenders: tacklers, tight markers and a famously cohesive unit, particularly in terms of catching opponents offside. They could play, too, as Arsenal's legendary title-clinching goal in 1997/98 proved, with Bould chipping the ball over the opposition defence for Adams, who burst forward from centre-back before smashing the ball home with his weaker left foot. With his first title-winners, Wenger encouraged his defenders to attack. The Invincibles back line, however, were natural attackers whom Wenger had convinced to play in defence.

As Jamie Carragher once said, all full-backs can be broken down into two types: failed centre-backs and failed wingers. But the latter are a relatively modern phenomenon, and the development of attacking full-backs was among the most noticeable tactical shifts at the start of the 21st century. At this point, with 4–4–2 the dominant formation, it was often the full-backs who had most space ahead of them, as the opposition's wide players dropped back alongside their midfield colleagues. The full-backs, therefore, could push forward to become vital attacking weapons.

Ashley Cole was a perfect example. A promising forward in Arsenal's youth team, Cole switched to a defensive position in his late teenage years. He would develop into the world's outstanding left-back, but his first couple of seasons were characterised by frequent positional errors. Wenger, however, loved his acceleration, stamina and quality in possession, and correctly believed that Cole had the right attitude to improve his defensive attributes. 'I didn't really want to be a defender; I never really liked defenders or defending,' Cole admitted after Euro 2004, the tournament in which he confirmed his status as one of the world's best full-backs. 'I always liked scoring goals and attacking, and when I was asked to go to left-back for the Arsenal youth team I had to just take it. I know now I wouldn't have made it as a striker and I'm not disappointed that I'm a left-back, but initially I suppose I was. I always wanted the glory of going up front scoring goals for the team.'

Arsenal right-back Lauren wasn't a natural full-back either and was initially sceptical about the positional switch. 'When I first came I was playing as a right-winger. Wenger thought I was capable of playing as a right-back, but at first I didn't know it. It was something progressive; at the beginning it was a bit difficult ... Arsène gave you the confidence in yourself to realise you could play in a new position.' Most remarkable, however, is the fact Wenger included a third unnatural defender in his regular back line. Centre-back Kolo Touré joined Arsenal as an energetic, slightly clumsy all-rounder who deputised effectively in midfield but looked uncomfortable when given opportunities at full-back, being dismissed before half-time in a goalless Champions League game against PSV in late 2002. He had never played centre-back until pre-season 2003/04, when Wenger paired him with Sol Campbell for a 1–0 friendly victory over Beşiktaş in Austria. Opposition manager Mircea Lucescu praised the power of Arsenal's centre-back combination, convincing Wenger that Touré could play there permanently.

Even Campbell, unquestionably the most solid of Arsenal's four defenders, had played higher up the pitch during his formative years. As a teenager at the FA's School of Excellence at Lilleshall he was often fielded on the right of midfield, and when breaking through at Tottenham was considered a potential centre-forward. He eventually became a settled defender, admitting he was forced to overcome initial problems with his heading ability, which is incredible when you consider his aerial dominance by the time he controversially crossed the north London divide in 2001. Arsenal's back four all developed with an emphasis upon attacking.

'I changed every player into a more technical player,' Wenger later said of his defence. 'First by improving existing players. After, when they had to be replaced, by a player who could contribute more to offensive quality, to build up the game from the back, like Kolo Touré, Lauren, Ashley Cole.' Wenger had done the same at Monaco, converting youngster Lillian Thuram from a right-winger to a right-back, in which position he would later be considered Europe's best. Maybe it was a personal mission – Wenger was a midfielder himself, then moved to defence towards the end of his modest playing career. But he wasn't a defensive driller in the mould of Graham, and plenty of coaching came from the experienced defenders; Cole thrived thanks to Adams's instructions, Touré improved because Keown took him under his wing, Lauren had Dixon as a role model. This was the crucial difference between Wenger's Arsenal defence full of attackers and Kevin Keegan's Newcastle rearguard; the Arsenal brigade were actually taught how to defend.

'People always speak of the defence I inherited when I arrived here, and it was an exceptional defence,' said Wenger in 2013. 'But people forget a lot about the defence that was unbeaten. They never speak about that and it's unbelievable that that defence never gets any credit. It was Lauren, Kolo Touré, Sol Campbell and Ashley Cole, and they were absolutely exceptional. They didn't lose a game and yet no one speaks about them ... Kolo and Sol were both very pacey players with unbelievable physical power. When a striker went beyond any of them you knew they would come back and catch them up, they were less calculating but much more physical. On the flanks we had two more footballing players, because Lauren was a midfielder and Cole has made a fantastic career.'

The idea that defenders could base their game around pace and 'catching up' with forwards, rather than nullifying their threat proactively, would have infuriated the old Arsenal back four – but then they would have loved to have possessed enough speed to catch up with Michael Owen, whose pace won Liverpool the 2001 FA Cup Final against Arsenal. As Wenger acknowledged, increasingly quick strikers necessitated increasingly quick defenders. Other defensive imports around the turn of the millennium, like Frenchmen Mikaël Silvestre at Manchester United and Chelsea's William Gallas, weren't imposing aerially, six foot and five foot 11 respectively, but were astonishingly fast. Both, incidentally, would later be signed by Wenger.

Meanwhile, their compatriot Laurent Blanc struggled at Manchester United because he desperately lacked speed. The World

Cup-winning centre-back, who started as an attacking midfielder and once scored 18 goals in a season for Montpellier, was hugely intelligent and a talented technician, but by the time he reached United at the age of 35 his lack of mobility was repeatedly exposed and he proved a disastrous replacement for Jaap Stam. United suffered a mini-crisis at the start of 2001/02, slipping into mid-table shortly before Christmas, and the first letter of the five clubs who had defeated them highlighted United's problem: Bolton, Liverpool, Arsenal, Newcastle, Chelsea. Ferguson's solution, the following summer, was dramatic – breaking the British transfer record to sign Leeds's Rio Ferdinand.

Ferdinand was considered a potential world-class performer from his days in West Ham's academy, playing alongside Frank Lampard in midfield. They took West Ham to the 1996 FA Youth Cup Final, where they lost to a Liverpool side featuring Michael Owen and Jamie Carragher, but Ferdinand was nevertheless named man of the match. That summer, a select group of promising youngsters was asked to train with the full England side ahead of Euro 96, where manager Terry Venables, with great foresight, identified Ferdinand and Lampard as the two players with the brightest futures. That former West Ham midfield partnership would eventually win a combined 247 England caps and nine Premier League titles, and both would lift the European Cup as captain.

Ferdinand was renowned for his adventurous dribbling and tendency to take risks in possession, having fallen in love with football watching Diego Maradona at the 1986 World Cup. He first dropped back to defence when a West Ham teammate didn't turn up for a game. He impressed in that role, and his coaches gradually convinced him it should be his long-term position. 'I suppose defending came naturally to me but it certainly wasn't a pleasure,' he said later. 'I had a strangely unfulfilled feeling after games, even if we won. I thought, "Yeah, but I didn't do anything" … Admittedly I did enjoy racing against a forward and beating him for speed, but the art of defending just left me cold. Even playing for England I still wasn't actually enjoying defending.' As with other players at the time, Ferdinand was pushed into the change of position because of his speed and ball-playing abilities rather than traditional defensive attributes.

Dropping back from midfield became a theme among England's emerging centre-backs. Ledley King, who made his debut for Tottenham in 1999 and later became club captain, was similar in style to Ferdinand. 'I never enjoyed calling myself a defender,' King said, recalling his teenage years. 'I hated being pinned at the back; I felt I had too much to offer. I felt I could affect the game more from the midfield … I didn't study or watch defenders either, I loved attacking players, flair players.' King played in the same east London youth side, Senrab FC, as a young John Terry. Sure enough, the future Chelsea centre-back was yet another who started in a more advanced position. 'He played in midfield back then and was quite short, but he had a leap on him and was great in the air,' King said. 'He made a big difference as a midfield general.' While not considered as cultured as King or Ferdinand, Terry's excellent passing skills have always been overlooked, although he lacked the speed of Ferdinand or King and preferred playing in a deeper defensive line.

Ferdinand was particularly fast, capable of running the 100m in 12 seconds, making him perfect for the new generation of defenders happy to 'catch up' with opponents. Ferdinand was always highlighted as a special case, eternally described as being 'prone to lapses in concentration', something of a problem for a centre-back. He was the first central defender in English football whose major weakness was defending, which later wasn't an entirely unusual problem; John

Stones, for example, is a similar case and considers Ferdinand his role model. Widely considered a ball-playing centre-back, Ferdinand was actually more of a ball-carrying centre-back who loved dribbling forward. 'When you create an extra body in midfield the opposition look as if to say, "Where's he come from?", and if other players are being marked there's usually not a spare player to mark you,' he said. But his actual passing ability wasn't particularly outstanding; it was about his calmness in possession, rather than his incision.

Ferdinand has always proudly spoken of his roots, but he had unusual interests for a Peckham council estate boy and attributes his graceful playing style to taking ballet classes four times a week, improving his 'flexibility, movement, coordination and balance'. He also loved drama, at 13 starring in his school's production of *Bugsy Malone*, playing Fizzy, the man who swept the floor of a speakeasy. As it turned out, a sweeper role was peculiarly prescient.

In the mid- to late 1990s English football was desperate to discover a homegrown centre-back boasting guile, intelligence and ball-playing ability to make a 3–5–2 system – then considered the natural alternative to 4–4–2 – work properly, with the spare man stepping forward from defence. The masterful Matthias Sammer's performances as the German sweeper – he was named player of the tournament on English soil at Euro 96 – underlined the value of this type of footballer. In those early days Ferdinand was considered almost purely in terms of the 3–5–2 system, given the uncertainty about whether he possessed the toughness and natural defensive qualities to play as a man-marking centre-back in a 4–4–2.

England manager Glenn Hoddle repeatedly floated the idea of using Jamie Redknapp at sweeper, a position the Liverpool midfielder never played before. As we've seen, Hoddle had tried something similar at Chelsea, briefly using Ruud Gullit there, and repeatedly spoke of his determination 'to play a real sweeper, someone who can come out with the ball like Germany's Sammer', so the emergence of Ferdinand was hugely exciting. 'He can hit it right to left 60 yards, but I'm not sure he can go left to right,' said Hoddle. His defensive attributes were less of a consideration, Hoddle thinking instinctively about Ferdinand's ability in possession.

Around this time Terry Venables, Hoddle's predecessor, high-lighted both Ferdinand and Sol Campbell as thoroughly modern centre-backs. 'I look at Rio and Sol and see a new type of English defender,' he said. 'They are good examples of the way our attitude towards bringing in young defenders is changing for the better. For too long we failed to train players from a young age to bring the ball out of defence … both Rio and Sol were forwards at one time and that is a real help.' But Hoddle's successor, Keegan, was surprisingly not a fan, omitting Ferdinand from his Euro 2000 squad and telling him he'd probably win more caps if he were French, Brazilian or Dutch. The continual theme throughout Ferdinand's career was him appearing entirely un-English, which is curious considering he exclusively played under British managers at club level.

A few months later Ferdinand moved to Leeds for a staggering £18m, becoming both the most expensive defender in the world and Britain's most expensive player, a status usually reserved for midfield-ers or attackers. At his unveiling even Leeds manager David O'Leary appeared stunned by the size of the fee, having expected to pay £12m to £15m. He bizarrely volunteered the fact that his wife considered the figure 'obscene', an unusual line from a manager welcoming a club-record signing. It was a particularly bold move from Leeds, given that the European Union was at this point threatening to rule football's entire transfer system illegal, considering it a restriction of trade, which would have been even more revolutionary than the Bosman ruling. There was a serious possibility that the system would be overhauled, players would be allowed to move clubs for no fee and every footballer's transfer value would be wiped out overnight. Leeds, however, were willing to take a financial gamble, which rather summed up their approach throughout this era.

At this stage Leeds were a serious contender for the Premier League title, having finished third in the previous campaign, and in Ferdinand's first season they reached the semi-finals of the Champions League. They were reaping the rewards of their excellent youth system, partly thanks to Howard Wilkinson's groundwork in the early 1990s, which developed players such as Harry Kewell, Jonathan Woodgate, Ian Harte, Alan Smith and Paul Robinson. O'Leary somewhat irritatingly referred to his players as 'my babies', although if ever a team deserved that nickname it was his Leeds; in 1999/2000 the average age of their starting XI was 24 years and 162 days, the youngest in the Premier League era.

In the early 1960s Don Revie famously changed Leeds's home kit from yellow and blue to all-white in order to imitate Real Madrid, and in the early 2000s they often appeared to be replicating Real's 'galácticos' policy, albeit on a smaller scale. Their rise owed much to copious overspending on superfluous individuals, eventually leaving the club facing financial ruin; at one point, O'Leary could choose from Mark Viduka, Robbie Fowler, Robbie Keane, Michael Bridges, Alan Smith and Harry Kewell as attacking options. But whereas Real stockpiled attackers and ignored defensive problems, Leeds's rise and fall was marked by the recruitment and sale of their centre-backs.

Their purchase of Ferdinand wasn't strictly necessary, but they were guarding against the risk of losing star centre-back Woodgate – another midfielder in his youth-team days – for a significant period of time, as he and teammate Lee Bowyer were on trial over the vicious attack on a student in a late-night street fight in Leeds city centre. Both were charged with causing grievous bodily harm with intent and affray; Bowyer was cleared on both counts but Woodgate convicted on the latter charge. Another centre-back, Michael Duberry, also became entangled in the case and was later found not guilty of perverting the cause of justice. Bowyer played the best football of his career during this period, but Woodgate's form was badly affected, convincing Leeds to sign another centre-back.

Ferdinand was registered too late to play in Leeds's home match against Arsenal, and after being presented to the Elland Road crowd he watched Woodgate and captain Lucas Radebe perform magnificently in an impressive 1–0 victory. He made his debut away at Leicester, and in keeping with the feeling that Ferdinand necessitated a back three, O'Leary ditched his 4–4–2 and fielded 3–5–2 for the first time, with Ferdinand slotting in between Woodgate and Radebe. It backfired spectacularly; Leeds conceded three headed goals in the first half-hour, Woodgate was sacrificed before half-time as Leeds reverted to 4–4–2, then Radebe was sent off. Leeds lost 3–1. For their next game, a Champions League trip to Lazio, Ferdinand was ineligible, and Woodgate and Radebe were again outstanding together in another 1–0 victory. So where did Ferdinand fit in?

O'Leary could hardly leave out Leeds's record signing, and Ferdinand established himself as first-choice centre-back, playing alongside one of Radebe, Woodgate and Dominic Matteo. His positional sense improved immeasurably under O'Leary, who was an outstanding centre-back during his playing days and had worked as assistant under George Graham, the best defensive coach around. He made Ferdinand work hard on his heading ability, while Ferdinand credits sports psychologist Keith Power for improving his concentration skills, encouraging him to visualise his defensive tasks before a game. Ferdinand became the complete defender and, after being explicitly instructed not to dribble forward in possession by new England manager Sven-Göran Eriksson, there was little sign of his attack-minded past at the 2002 World Cup, where he was magnificent. That's when Manchester United pounced for £30m, another British record, and another world record for a defender after Juventus's Lillian Thuram had briefly earned that status.

Ferdinand's departure was the beginning of the end for Leeds, even if he was one of few players they made a profit on. As Matteo, his replacement as skipper, said, 'His departure was a massive moment, not because we didn't have the capability in the squad to replace Rio, but because it sent out a message to all the other top players at the club that Leeds were on the wane.' Leeds were now a selling club. In the midst of the long-running negotiations O'Leary rowed with Leeds chairman Peter Ridsdale about Ferdinand's imminent departure and was sacked, replaced by Terry Venables.

Ridsdale claimed that Ferdinand's departure wasn't a huge blow and that he had simply been a temporary replacement for Woodgate, whom Leeds considered the superior defender. Woodgate was now Leeds's great hope, but he lasted only six months before Leeds sold him to Newcastle in a further effort to raise funds. He was the last player Leeds had wanted to sell, with Ridsdale even approaching Liverpool in a desperate attempt to offload Harry Kewell instead, then considered to be Leeds's outstanding footballer. Liverpool needed to wait until the summer, however, so Woodgate departed.

Venables, who had been assured that Woodgate wouldn't leave, threatened to quit but was convinced to stay for another couple of months before his inevitable departure. At the press conference confirming Woodgate's sale, Venables looked furious alongside Ridsdale, who famously declared, 'Should we have spent so heavily in the past? Probably not. But we lived the dream.' That moment, coming after the departure of Leeds's most valued player – a centre-back – felt like an obituary. Leeds lasted just one more season in the Premier League, and have never returned. The subtext to their decline, however, was that centre-backs were now a prized commodity.

At Manchester United Ferdinand developed into one of Europe's best footballers. There was no longer any suggestion that he required a 3–5–2 to thrive, although he always excelled when playing alongside an old-school stopper: Campbell and John Terry at international level, and particularly Nemanja Vidić at United, the two forming the outstanding centre-back duo of the Premier League era. He was especially admired for the cool, calm manner he regained possession, never jumping into tackles and rarely provoking trouble with referees. Towards the end of his career his disciplinary record was exemplary, and he once went 28 league games without conceding a foul, never mind collecting a yellow card. When asked for the two toughest defenders in the Premier League, Jimmy Floyd Hasselbaink named Martin Keown and Ferdinand, but whereas Keown left him covered in bruises, Ferdinand 'you almost don't notice.'

What was notable about the final years of Ferdinand's career, however, was that he struggled to cope with his loss of pace, a surprising problem for such an intelligent performer. In Manchester United's thrilling 4–3 victory over Manchester City in September 2009, Ferdinand allowed City back into the game with a careless error, playing an unnecessary scooped pass on the halfway line straight to Craig Bellamy, who breezed past him with ease and scored. In fairness almost every other Premier League centre-back would have been unable to keep pace with Bellamy, but it was unusual to see Ferdinand struggling. 'Since he has been with us, he's has been fantastically consistent, top-class,' said Sir Alex Ferguson in 2011. 'He is still one of the best footballers in the country in terms of using the ball, he can still tackle, he can still head and he still has a great presence. But what has changed for Rio is that he has lost that electric yard of pace that he had a few years ago and so he needs to rearrange his game a little bit. He is almost 33, and when you arrive in your 30s you have to tailor your game in a different way. We have all faced that decisive moment when you suddenly realise you can no longer do everything you used to be able to, and you have to change your game. I had to do it myself when I lost my sharpness, other players at this club have had to adapt and Rio will have to do the same.'

Ferguson was frustrated by Ferdinand and Vidić's insistence on sitting back and protecting the space in behind, rather than moving up the pitch to close down Lionel Messi in that year's 3–1 Champions League Final defeat to Barcelona. There was clearly no obvious solution to stopping Pep Guardiola's side, but Ferguson became convinced that the lack of pace in his back line was a serious problem. A couple of months later Ferdinand was worryingly poor in a 3–0 defeat away at Newcastle, often ending up miles behind the rest of the defensive line in an attempt to hide his lack of speed. He was struggling badly against quick attackers and only won one further England cap; this was somewhat unfair, as he seemed to be deliberately overlooked after John Terry was accused – and then banned and fined by the FA, having been cleared in a court of law – of racially abusing Ferdinand's younger brother Anton. Ferdinand recovered to play excellently in 2012/13, although he was generally fielded alongside a younger, quicker centre-back partner like Jonny Evans or Chris Smalling, rather than Vidić.

By now Ferdinand's ability in possession was nothing particularly noteworthy. 'I've heard for a decade how Rio Ferdinand is an elegant passer of the ball who starts attacks from the back,' Jamie Carragher once complained. 'He must have hit a 60-yard pass when he was 17 because I haven't seen much evidence since.' But that underlines the huge transformation in centre-back styles over the course of his career, with Ferdinand the most influential defender in English football during this period. Now, the world's most expensive defenders are John Stones and David Luiz, centre-backs initially considered to be weak defensively. Ferdinand had changed perceptions of what top-class centre-backs needed to be: all-rounders who could be moulded into defenders.

After leaving Manchester United in 2014 Ferdinand considered retiring but was convinced to play one final season at QPR, where he had trained as a ten-year-old. He was managed by Harry Redknapp, Ferdinand's first West Ham manager, who recruited Hoddle, Ferdinand's first England manager, to take training sessions. To complete the feeling Ferdinand's career had come full circle, QPR started their campaign playing 3–5–2 to accommodate Ferdinand at sweeper. That QPR campaign ended in relegation, although Ferdinand played a minimal part, his mind understandably elsewhere as his wife, Rebecca, died towards the end of the season. Ferdinand quietly confirmed his retirement the following month – there was little fanfare amid his personal loss, and his career never received the plaudits it deserved.

But it shouldn't be forgotten that Ferdinand changed perceptions of centre-backs in England: they weren't necessarily unglamorous, functional footballers who simply tackled and headed. They could be fast, intelligent, comfortable in possession and the most valuable players in the country. In a division defined by foreign imports, Ferdinand is the most influential Englishman of the Premier League era.

12

The Makélélé Role

'I didn't invent anything ... I am simply
a more complete footballer.'

Claude Makélélé

A seven-year Premier League period incorporating the turn of the century was dominated by two clubs: Arsenal and Manchester United. It remains the Premier League's most enduring rivalry – the title fight was usually a two-horse race without the league becoming a complete duopoly, and the rivalry itself was the perfect mixture: mostly animosity, with a hint of begrudging respect.

Then, in 2003, things changed with Roman Abramovich's takeover of Chelsea. His wealth and relentless acquisition of new signings meant Chelsea became serious contenders almost overnight, having spent the previous few years on the fringes of the title race. Arsenal and Manchester United have never since finished as the Premier League's top two, and this significant shift from red to blue dominance was mirrored by the period's most revered defensive midfielders.

Arsenal and Manchester United's rivalry was personified by the clashes between Patrick Vieira and Roy Keane, two physical, combative captains. There has never been a more significant personal battle in the Premier League era; their scraps were legendary and played a huge role in dictating the outcome of top-of-the-table clashes. Both relished their battles. 'They made me a better player,' said Keane, while Vieira described the Irishman as his 'favourite enemy'. Then, however a different type of defensive midfielder emerged, with Chelsea's Claude Makélélé, signed from Real Madrid, becoming the Premier League's most celebrated player in that mould. It symbolised the changing of the guard.

Vieira and Keane's most famous encounter didn't even take place on the pitch, occurring in the Highbury tunnel shortly before Manchester United's 4–2 victory over Arsenal in February 2005. It made for tremendous viewing – and it was, effectively, a TV-only event away from the spectators, who remained oblivious. Vieira had confronted Gary Neville shortly beforehand, who went and told Keane. United's captain was seemingly furious Vieira had picked on Neville rather than himself and charged down the narrow Highbury tunnel to confront him, bizarrely complaining that Vieira wasn't the 'nice guy' everyone made out. Their insults were often laughably childish, Keane annoying Vieira by asking him why he banged on about his home country of Senegal when he chose to play for France instead, Vieira responding by mentioning Keane's 2002 World Cup walkout. 'It was grown men, bitching,' as Keane admitted.

But by this stage their rivalry had effectively jumped the shark. The media were portraying Arsenal v Manchester United as purely Vieira v Keane, to the extent many believe Keane's intimidation of Vieira in the tunnel was a crucial factor in United's victory that day. This is a curious reading of events, considering Vieira opened the scoring as Arsenal dominated the first half, leading 2–1 at the break. If 'intimidation' was really a factor, it took an hour to kick in. The less dramatic truth, of course, was that United simply outperformed Arsenal technically and tactically.

Vieira and Keane were now past their best, and this would be their last Premier League meeting: Arsenal sold Vieira in the summer, United released Keane a few months later. The reasons for their demise were similar: although both were considered defensive midfielders when they were actually somewhere between defensive midfielders and box-to-box players at their peak, and preferred playing alongside more cautious partners who allowed them freedom to attack. Vieira played his best football next to Emmanuel Petit from 1997 to 2000 then Gilberto Silva from 2002 to 2005, and during the two-year intermission performed better next to the functional, limited Gilles Grimandi rather than Edu or Ray Parlour, who pushed forward. Similarly, Keane named Paul Ince as his favourite midfield colleague at Manchester United, and after Ince left, some of Keane's outstanding individual performances – in the 3–2 victory at Juventus in 1999, for example – came when Sir Alex Ferguson played the defensive Nicky Butt instead of the more creative Paul Scholes.

Both players' physical attributes had declined, but neither were capable of switching to a pure holding role. Arsène Wenger decided to sell Vieira to Juventus in 2005 following the emergence of a creative midfielder who needed licence to attack. 'I played Cesc Fàbregas in a 4–4–2 with Patrick Vieira and I saw it did not work,' Wenger said. 'Then I had the decision to make about letting Patrick go, because Gilberto and Vieira worked, Gilberto and Fàbregas worked, but I could not play Fàbregas and Vieira.' Fàbregas, Arsenal's future, needed a covering midfielder, and Vieira simply wasn't that man.

Similarly, Ferguson believes his fallout with Keane stemmed from asking the Irishman to play a more restricted role. 'Acting on a conviction that some of his strengths had been stolen from him by injury and age, we tried to change his job description ... we altered his role by discouraging him from charging all over the pitch and making forward runs,' said Ferguson. 'Our solution was to tell him to stay in that same area of central midfield. He could control the game from there. Deep down, I believe, he knew that better than anyone, but he simply could not bring himself to abandon his old talismanic role.' Keane insists he was 'relieved' to be doing less running, but Ferguson's comment about the difference between Keane's true thoughts and his actual performances makes sense.

The deepest midfield role had changed, particularly as managers increasingly used three central midfielders in an attempt to dominate that zone, leaving only one player up front. It meant responsibilities were different, and managers wanted a holding midfielder who never advanced from in front of the defence. 'I would never have been the classic sitting midfielder like Claude Makélélé – he wouldn't budge,' Keane wrote in his autobiography, while Vieira said his teammate Gilberto was 'a holding midfielder like Makélélé ... that enabled me push forward more'. Neither Vieira nor Keane was quite as defensive as Makélélé.

In fact the simple term 'defensive midfielder' didn't do Makélélé's role justice; he was described as a 'holding midfielder', a 'sitting midfielder', a 'screening player', all of which implied his role was based around positioning and protecting rather than simply tackling. And then, eventually, it just became the 'Makélélé role' – a position in itself – an extremely rare honour. The surprising aspect of Makélélé's position, however, is that he started playing the Makélélé role – the sole holding midfielder at the base of a trio or a diamond – very late in his career. Far from it being his natural position, Makélélé essentially dropped deeper and sacrificed himself for the team in the autumn of his career, precisely what Vieira and Keane were unable to do.

* * *

Makélélé started at Nantes, winning Ligue 1 in 1995. He was a winger renowned for regularly slaloming past opposition challenges, and later become an industrious midfielder on the right of a diamond, somewhat reminiscent of future Chelsea midfielder Ramires, being about energy rather than positional discipline. Although not prolific, registering nine goals in 169 games, those strikes were often excellent, slamming the ball home from tight angles. However, future World Cup-winning winger Christian Karembeu played at right-back and pushed forward regularly, so Makélélé would drop back and cover.

After a sole season with Marseille, where he played a similar role, Makélélé moved to Spanish side Celta Vigo in 1998. Here he was deployed in a central role alongside disciplined Brazilian World Cup winner Mazinho. His solid positioning meant Makélélé could break forward more, but he also trained the Frenchman in the art of the holding midfield position. 'It's Mazinho who opened up the spirit of this new role,' Makélélé recalled. 'I spent hours working with Mazinho, him explaining the correct positions to take up, when to play one touch and two touches.' The Brazilian was on his last legs, however, and in Makélélé's second season he generally played along-side Albert Celades. Celta produced some incredible performances in the UEFA Cup that year, recording a staggering 7–0 win over Benfica and thrashing Juventus 4–0, particularly impressive considering both victories were against European Cup-winning managers, Jupp Heynckes and Marcello Lippi. Makélélé scored in both, including after just 27 seconds against Juve; he was clearly not yet a pure holding midfielder.

In 2000 Real Madrid surprisingly sold Fernando Redondo, the outstanding defensive midfielder of his era, to AC Milan and replaced him with Celta's midfield partnership – both Makélélé and Celades – plus Deportivo's defensive midfielder Flávio Conceição. During his three years at Real Makélélé would become renowned as the club's most important player; behind Real's expensively assembled *galácticos* – Zinedine Zidane, Luís Figo, Ronaldo, Raúl – Makélélé was the responsible midfielder who sat deep. Real's manager Vicente del Bosque told Makélélé he had the perfect skill set to be both the 'first defender and the first attacking midfielder', a neat summary of his dual role.

Contrary to popular belief, however, Makélélé wasn't on his own. A false picture has developed of Real attacking with seven players, leaving Makélélé to protect the centre-backs by himself. Realistically, that wasn't remotely true. In Makélélé's 95 league starts for Real Madrid, on 76 occasions he was deployed alongside another disciplined defensive midfielder – Ivan Helguera (36 times), Conceição (19), Esteban Cambiasso (12), Celades (7) or Fernando Hierro (2). Only 17 times was Makélélé the only defensive midfielder, and even then it was often in home matches against inferior opposition where it was natural to play a more creative midfielder, such as Guti or Steve McManaman, alongside him.

It's significant that Makélélé later named Helguera, such a defensive-minded midfielder that he was sometimes deployed at centre-back, as his favourite teammate. 'He knew where I'd move on the pitch, I'd know when he was going to push up and try to score,' Makélélé said. 'We didn't even need to talk, just a look was enough to know what the other was going to do.' Makélélé appreciated playing alongside a similarly minded partner, but was gradually deployed more on his own in front of the defence. Sometimes he was paired with Santi Solari, naturally a left-sided player who would drift wide to cover for Roberto Carlos's forward runs, leaving Makélélé alone in the centre. But Makélélé had not yet defined his eponymous role.

His 2003 transfer to Chelsea was the point at which Real's obsession with superstars spiralled out of control. Makélélé complained he was paid considerably less than his more illustrious teammates, but

President Florentino Pérez had little interest in keeping him at the club, and upon the Frenchman's departure, memorably told the press, 'We will not miss Makélélé. His technique is average; he lacks the speed and skill to take the ball past opponents, and ninety per cent of his distribution either goes backwards or sideways. He wasn't a header of the ball and he rarely passed the ball more than three metres.' Unknowingly, Pérez was describing the Makélélé role, rather than his skill set – those who recalled his Nantes days remembered his all-round ability. His former teammates were bemused at his departure and the arrival of David Beckham. 'Why put another layer of gold paint on the Bentley,' Zidane asked, 'when you are losing the entire engine?'

Real had won La Liga in Makélélé's final campaign, but slumped to fourth without him. Their problem, as much as his departure in itself, was that the club essentially went from playing two holding midfielders, Makélélé alongside Flavio Conceição or Cambiasso in 2002/03, to frequently fielding none in 2003/04, with Beckham deployed alongside the creative Guti. It wouldn't have been so problematic had Real realised Cambiasso's qualities, and it's interesting that Real later tried to sign both Vieira in 2004 and Keane in 2005. Real clearly wanted a combative but energetic midfielder in that mould, and later, bizarrely, ended up signing Everton's Thomas Gravesen. This was peculiar for two reasons: first, Gravesen was well below the standard required for Real Madrid and, second, he wasn't a holding midfielder either, being accustomed to a more advanced role. 'It is totally different to my Everton role,' Gravesen admitted after joining Real and being played in the deepest midfield position. 'Lee Carsley was playing where I do here.' It seemed Real had mixed up their bald Everton central midfielders.

Real's loss was Chelsea's gain, but it's worth reiterating that by this stage Makélélé was already 30 and had played 11 full seasons of top-level football, often as an energetic midfielder forced to get through lots of running. He was now ready to play a more defined, solid, defensive midfield role, which worked particularly well considering the nature of Chelsea's squad. In his first summer Abramovich had already signed attacking midfielders Damien Duff, Joe Cole and Juan Sebastian Verón, plus strikers Adrian Mutu and Hernán Crespo. There were some more functional, defensive players too: Glen Johnson, Geremi and Wayne Bridge, but no proper holding midfielder. Brian Clough summarised the situation neatly. 'I'd love to know who's going to do all the fetching and carrying for all these glamorous, over-priced internationals who love to bomb forward yet can't tackle their dinner, never mind a ball,' he said. 'Verón, Cole and Duff won't get their hands dirty doing the donkey work.'

That, of course, was before the arrival of Makélélé, who effectively solved the problem overnight. 'I have a fantastic watch and Claude is my battery,' said his new manager Claudio Ranieri, before, significantly, referring to him as 'one of the best, if not the best, playmakers in the world'. Ranieri never considered him a purely defensive player.

Makélélé made his first Premier League start in a 5–0 away victory at Wolves, playing in a 4–4–2 system alongside Frank Lampard, with Jesper Grønkjær and Damien Duff out wide. His defensive-minded positioning in this system was obvious, to the extent that, after Chelsea's narrow 2–1 victory over Middlesbrough with the same midfield quartet, one newspaper described it as a 4–1–1–2–2 formation: Makélélé sitting in front of the defence and allowing Lampard to break forward. But this left Lampard overrun, and Makélélé wasn't suited to playing in a flat four-man midfield. The Frenchman looked more comfortable when Ranieri played a diamond, which allowed him to remain in front of the defence but also afforded Lampard a proper midfield partner. When combative central midfielder Scott Parker arrived from Charlton in January 2004, he was often deployed on the right of a notional four-man midfield, but tucked inside to create a midfield trio with Makélélé and Lampard, leaving the right flank bare. This lopsided system worked much better, as Makélélé was allowed to sit deep.

When José Mourinho replaced Ranieri in the summer, he interrupted Makélélé's holiday by phoning him to emphasise his importance to his Chelsea side. Mourinho used the two systems he'd developed at Porto: a midfield diamond and a 4–3–3, which both necessitated a strict holding midfielder in Makélélé's mould. Opposition midfielders struggled to cope with Makélélé's positioning – they couldn't close him down without leaving a more advanced Chelsea midfielder free – and it was the positioning rather than Makélélé's individual brilliance that proved crucial.

Makélélé managed just two goals in 144 Premier League games – one a rebound from his own saved penalty – and only four assists. But he unquestionably played a crucial role in starting Chelsea's attacks. While his Real Madrid role was purely defensive – all about covering for midfield runs and protecting the defence – that was less obvious at Chelsea, a defensive side who got numbers behind the ball quickly and remained compact. Instead he was crucial in possession, which is strange because he was an entirely unfussy, reserved distributor – there were no sudden dribbles into attack, and few diagonal balls or killer passes. He simply held his position, mopped up and then passed the ball sideways. But this was vital, as Mourinho outlined.

'Look, if I have a triangle in midfield – Claude Makélélé behind and two others just in front – I will always have an advantage against a pure 4–4–2 where the central midfielders are side by side,' he explained. 'That's because I will always have an extra man. It starts with Makélélé, who is between the lines. If nobody comes to him he can see the whole pitch and has time. If he gets closed down it means one of the two other central midfielders is open. If they are closed down and the other team's wingers come inside to help, it means there is space now for us on the flank, either for our own wingers or for our full-backs. There is nothing a pure 4–4–2 can do to stop things.' It was as simple as that, and literally about the Makélélé role, rather than Makélélé himself.

Makélélé, though, insists his technical skill set and history as an attacking midfielder ensured he was a different type of deep-lying midfielder. 'As a former winger I know how to make attackers feel confident,' he said, and he also believed the major difference between him and previous holding midfielders was simply that he was better in possession. 'People spoke of the "Makélélé role" to describe the modern, ball-recovering midfielder. But in fact, I didn't invent anything. I am perhaps better technically and tactically than the old defensive midfielders of the 80s and 90s, like Luis Fernández, Franck Sauzée or Didier Deschamps, but I don't do anything radically different to what they did, I am simply a more complete footballer,' Makélélé insisted. 'I think rather that the game has changed and that, to be a top-level player in any position, you now have to know how to keep the ball, give precise passes and contribute to each phase of a move. It is no longer enough to be good in the air or tough in the tackle to carve out a place for yourself as a midfielder. You have to be a multifaceted footballer.'

This is a fascinating analysis, because many would claim Makélélé was, in fact, the complete antithesis of a universal player. Legendary Milan coach Arrigo Sacchi, for example, the great champion of universality, specifically highlighted Makélélé as an anti-universal player. 'In my football, the playmaker is whoever had the ball,' he said. 'But if you have Makélélé, he can't do that. He doesn't have the ideas to do it, although of course he's great at winning the ball. It's become all about specialists.' That underestimated his role. Although

Makélélé wasn't launching pinpoint diagonal passes like Andrea Pirlo or Xabi Alonso, he played between the opposition lines of midfield and attack, found space to pull the strings and delivered crisp, effective passes into attacking players.

Because Makélélé was essentially playing between the opposition lines there's a similarity to the way his compatriot Eric Cantona redefined centre-forward play – even if their level of artistry is significantly different – and teams needed to cope with Makélélé in a similar manner. Conventional wisdom suggested the natural order of things was simple – the defensive midfielder marked the opposition's attacking midfielder. But Makélélé became so influential that a literal role reversal occurred, and managers realised they needed their attacking midfielder to man-mark Chelsea's defensive midfielder. The best example came in March 2006, when Fulham manager Chris Coleman masterminded a 1–0 victory over Chelsea by deploying playmaker Steed Malbranque at the top of a diamond to stop Makélélé. 'Every time we play against Chelsea and every time we've watched them play, everything goes through Makélélé and he starts the attacks,' Coleman said. 'Malbranque loves playing in that position. We told him to go where he liked when he had the ball but, as soon as he didn't have it, Makélélé was his man. We wanted Petr Čech to kick it rather than pass it out, and it worked very well.'

Fulham went ahead early through Luís Boa Morte, and their dominance was so complete that Mourinho made two substitutions, purely for tactical reasons, after just 25 minutes – the Premier League's earliest-ever double change. Wingers Joe Cole and Shaun Wright-Phillips were sacrificed in favour of Damien Duff and Didier Drogba as Chelsea matched Fulham's system. 'José started with 4–3–3 and changed very early,' Coleman continued. 'He gave Crespo a bit of support with Drogba, brought Duff on and matched us up in midfield, which was a compliment. It was going well for us so we didn't need to change.' Chelsea subsequently used a 3–5–2 system in the second half in an attempt to launch a fightback – so it was two dramatic changes of system, almost exclusively because Fulham had successfully stopped Makélélé. Post-match discussion focused on ugly scenes at Craven Cottage, with rival supporters fighting on the pitch after full-time, but Fulham's first win against their local rivals since 1979 was hugely significant. Because it owed so much to a naturally attacking player performing such a strict defensive role, it emphasised the need for footballers to increasingly become all-rounders.

Just as Cantona had prompted a wave of copycats, other top-level Premier League teams started searching for their Makélélé. But it was significant that, having realised how much time in possession the Frenchman enjoyed, they turned to naturally more attack-minded midfielders. A curious phenomenon in the mid-2000s was the so-called Big Four all buying promising young attacking midfielders, but converting them into defensive midfielders.

The classic example was Liverpool's purchase of Lucas Leiva. The Brazilian was signed from Grêmio in 2007 and was renowned as an exciting all-round midfielder with an eye for goal. He was the youngest-ever winner of the Bola de Ouro, for the best player in the Brazilian championship, and helped Brazil to glory at the South American U20 Championships that year, scoring four goals in nine appearances. 'He can play as a holding midfielder but he can also get from box to box,' said Liverpool manager Rafael Benítez upon his arrival. 'So I am looking forward to seeing him score goals for Liverpool in the future.' One goal in over 200 Premier League games underlines the fact he was deployed exclusively in a defensive role.

South American football is played at a slow pace, and it was felt that Lucas lacked the requisite speed to thrive as an attacking midfielder in the Premier League. 'This choice to play more defensively was a way for me to feel more comfortable,' he explained. 'It suits my characteristics and also those of the Premier League. Of course, it's cooler to play closer to the attack, but in a defensive role I believe I can offer more to the team.' Lucas was heavily criticised for his lack of ambition in possession, however, and while there was evidence of his experience as a more attacking player in the way he worked tirelessly finding space to receive the ball, his transformation into a holding midfielder robbed him of his creativity.

Arsenal and Manchester United experienced something extremely similar with the midfield pairing who took Brazil to South American U17 Championships glory in 2005 and reached the World U17 Championships Final later that year. Arsenal signed the captain, Denilson, who was considered 'somewhere between Gilberto and Tomáš Rosický' by Arsène Wenger upon his arrival. Yet after being introduced to the side in an all-round midfield role, Denilson was eventually played in a pure defensive midfield position by Wenger, again frustrating supporters with his unambitious distribution but also receiving criticism for his lack of defensive skills.

Manchester United, meanwhile, later signed his old midfield partner Anderson – a swaggering, powerful playmaker who made driving runs from midfield. FIFA's report from that World U17 tournament described him as 'a playmaker with a seemingly inexhaustible box of tricks', and their Technical Study Group identified him as 'an outstanding individual player, who was fast, could take charge of game, skilfully linked up with teammates and very effective on counter-attacks'. But he was another converted to a deeper position in England, 'a role that no coach in his native land would have considered for a nanosecond,' as the BBC's South American football correspondent Tim Vickery wrote at the time. 'Could it be that in this new role Anderson is forced to sacrifice a bit too much of what he is naturally good at?'

But the most obvious example was Makélélé's successor at Chelsea, John Obi Mikel. There's a very familiar story here; Mikel was a gloriously talented attacking midfielder in his younger days, leading Nigeria to the U20 World Cup Final in 2005, where his side were beaten by Argentina, and Mikel was voted the tournament's second-best player, behind a young Argentine attacker named Lionel Messi. There was an extraordinary tug-of-war between Manchester United and Chelsea for his services, Mikel signing a contract with the former while the latter claimed they'd already arranged his transfer. United eventually received a fee of £12m from Chelsea, despite the fact he'd never officially joined them.

Mikel was almost instantly cast as the new Makélélé, playing the holding role when the Frenchman was rested, and eventually succeeding him permanently when Makélélé returned to France in 2008. But, once again, Mikel was transformed into a scrappy, aggressive defensive midfielder, constantly in trouble with referees for poor tackles and criticised by supporters for his square passes. His goalscoring record, meanwhile, was as bad as Lucas's – one in 249 Premier League games. 'Mikel has lost the creativity that catapulted him onto the world stage,' complained Samson Siasia, who managed him at U20 level and later for the full Nigerian side. 'Chelsea destroyed the player Mikel once was.' Mikel acknowledged that himself. 'I have always said in my time at Chelsea that I am a team player,' he said, as he approached the end of his decade at the club. 'I've gone out of my way to do things to limit my game for the good of the team.'

Premier League managers realised the potential value of playing a creative player in the Makélélé role, but by concentrating upon improving such players' defensive qualities, they effectively turned potentially exciting playmakers into pure scrappers.

Much later, Les Ferdinand – then a coach at Tottenham – was scathing about Makélélé's impact upon the English game. 'I was saying to William Gallas when he was here, the worst thing that happened in this league was Claude Makélélé,' he said in 2014. 'When he came into this country, he wasn't a holding midfield player. He was a player who had the intelligence to say: "Frank [Lampard], you can score more goals than me so I'm going to tuck in here for you and I'll hold. You keep going forward." Then everyone went, "Right, we've got to have a holding midfield player," and what we've done is produce a crop of players who don't want to go over the halfway line, who don't want to pass over the halfway line and are happy to just sit in front of the back four.'

Ferdinand was widely criticised for his comments, but there's an element of truth in his assessment of Makélélé's legacy. The Frenchman himself was a perfectly effective footballer and wasn't the problem. But his tremendous impact in English football was largely because of his role in a 4–3–3, which, as Mourinho outlined, meant he played a basic passing role in a system that outmanoeuvred a 4–4–2. Once other teams reacted and moved away from the 4–4–2 towards 4–3–3 and 4–2–3–1, Makélélé clones were now simply playing a basic passing role in a system that *wasn't* outmanoeuvring the opposition, merely retaining the ball in deep positions without offering penetration. The impact of the Premier League's most influential defensive midfielder was, unsurprisingly, entirely defensive – at a time when the division was becoming more cautious than ever.

Part Five

Reactive Strategy

13

Iberian Influence I

'If you have a Ferrari and I have a small car,
to beat you in a race I have to break your wheel,
or put sugar in your tank.'

José Mourinho

Identifying significant moments and historic turning points is simple in hindsight, but even at the time, 2004 felt like a watershed year in football.

The first four years of the 21st century were largely about attacking football. Euro 2000 was a celebration of creative, technical play, while the 2002 World Cup was won by Brazil's terrifying trio of attackers: Ronaldo, Ronaldinho and Rivaldo. Arsenal had become Manchester United's regular title rivals by playing attacking football, Real Madrid won the European Cup in 2000 and 2002 with their *galácticos*, and Serie A – traditionally considered Europe's most defensive league – was on the decline. Attacking football dominated.

Then came 2004, which featured historic shocks at both club and international level. First, in a brilliant Champions League competition dominated by well-drilled underdogs, José Mourinho's Porto recorded a sensational victory, defeating Monaco 3–0 in the final. Thirty-nine days later, there was an equally improbable triumph at Euro 2004, when 80/1 outsiders Greece shocked Europe by lifting the trophy. Both Porto and Greece, while thoroughly impressive, were unquestionably defensive. Porto's outstanding qualities were their defensive shape and their incredibly effective offside trap. Mourinho had deliberately made a defensive shift – in the Portuguese league, where Porto were champions, Porto both scored and conceded their fewest number of goals in nine seasons, as he realised a more cautious outlook was required to succeed in Europe. Greece, meanwhile, used man-marking at the back, a tactic rarely witnessed in top-level modern football, combined with a reactive formation and a heavy reliance upon set-pieces for goals. They won their knockout games 1–0, 1–0, 1–0 against the holders (France), the best attacking team (Czech Republic) and the hosts (Portugal), each time with a headed goal. Suddenly, it felt like Porto and Greece had shown the way to succeed, particularly for underdogs – play defensively.

The UEFA Cup also proved significant. It was won by Valencia, who also triumphed in La Liga, and they were another side who focused upon defensive structure rather than attacking firepower. Their coach, Rafael Benítez, was famed for his excellent organisational skills, and while his 2003/04 side were perfectly attractive, he'd developed a reputation for defensive football, as his 2001/02 title winners scored just 51 goals in 38 games, an astonishingly low tally for champions. In each of Benítez's three campaigns at Valencia, the team conceded the fewest goals in La Liga.

When both Chelsea and Liverpool found themselves with managerial vacancies that summer, they turned to Mourinho and Benítez respectively. Both could have ended up in either job; a young Mourinho was a huge admirer of Liverpool, and his agent approached the Reds in March, when Gerard Houllier was still in charge, trying to broker a deal for the following season. Liverpool were reluctant to go behind Houllier's back, but Chelsea had fewer reservations, and even their manager Claudio Ranieri was aware of the situation – when Charlton fans sang 'You're getting sacked in the summer' to the Italian, he showed typically good grace by turning around and responding, 'No, I will be sacked in May!' His prediction was correct – he headed to Valencia as Benítez's replacement, and wouldn't reappear in the Premier League for 11 years.

Had Liverpool been bolder and pounced for Mourinho, it's likely that Chelsea would have turned to Benítez – he would join many years later, winning the Europa League in 2013. But regardless of their specific destination in 2004, Mourinho and Benítez's joint arrival was a significant moment; two managers who had triumphed in continental competition through defensive football were about to transform the English game. It made the Premier League more tactically intelligent, more suited to European football – and, almost immediately, more cautious. The goals-per-game rate dropped from 2.66 to 2.57 for 2004/05, before falling further to 2.48 in 2005/06 and then 2.45 in 2006/07, the lowest rate in the Premier League era. It's also the only time that figure has declined in three consecutive campaigns – the three years Mourinho and Benítez were together in the league. Their impact is difficult to ignore.

The more eye-catching appointment was Mourinho. English football had been introduced to the 41-year-old when he sprinted down the Old Trafford touchline to celebrate with his players after Costinha netted a late equaliser against Manchester United, sending Porto into the Champions League quarter-finals. He was unlike anything the Premier League had witnessed before: young, handsome, highly confrontational but also somewhat charming. At his unveiling he pronounced himself 'a special one' – not *the* special one, as is often reported – a quote that would dominate headlines for years. Mourinho, from the outset, provided tremendous excitement in press conferences, but rather less entertainment on the pitch.

His coaching background initially appeared simple – a brief spell with Benfica, then half a campaign with União de Leiria before his success at Porto – but his experiences beforehand proved most fascinating. Mourinho studied for his coaching badges and worked with various small Portuguese clubs, but then received his big break in an unusual fashion, when former England manager Bobby Robson was appointed at Sporting Lisbon and required an interpreter. Mourinho got the job, and he subsequently followed Robson to Porto in 1994 and Barcelona in 1996. Initially Mourinho was literally a mere interpreter, translating Robson's instructions to the squad, but Robson gradually recognised Mourinho's footballing intelligence and his role steadily increased, to the point where he served as an assistant to both Robson and his replacement at Barcelona, Louis van Gaal.

Under Robson, Mourinho was handed the task of planning training sessions, focusing upon the areas Robson tended to ignore – defensive issues. 'If we were to divide the match into three parts, we'd see that Bobby Robson's work concentrates mainly on the final part, finishing and scoring,' Mourinho later explained. 'I tried to take a step back – that is, while maintaining the primacy of attacking football, I tried to organise it better, and this organisation stems directly from the defence.'

More than anything, however, Mourinho impressed both Robson and Van Gaal when scouting upcoming opponents. 'He'd come back and hand me a dossier that was absolutely first class,' said Robson. 'I mean first class, as good as anything I'd ever received. Here he was, in his early thirties, never been a player, never been a coach to speak of either, giving me reports as good as anything I ever got from the top professional people I'd brought in to scout for me at World Cups ... There would be the way the teams played in the match he'd been sent to – both teams – with defence and attack covered very well, patterns of play, nicely set out with diagrams and a different colour for each team, all clear as a bell. I remember telling him, "Well done, son."'

Mourinho thrived at Barcelona, where he worked with a considerably higher standard of players than in Portugal. Although some of Barcelona's attacking superstars paid little attention to him, Mourinho developed particularly good relationships with two players, Laurent Blanc and Pep Guardiola. Both would later become top-level coaches themselves, the latter becoming his major rival. Robson was shifted upstairs after a season to accommodate Van Gaal, and convinced the Dutchman to retain Mourinho's services. Van Gaal tells a familiar tale. 'He was kept on, initially for a year. To start with he was just a translator, but gradually he became as valued as my other assistants – he could read the game and he analysed the opposition so well that, after my first year, when we won the Spanish championship and Cup, I was happy for him to stay for three more years.' Again, an experienced manager was won over by Mourinho's ability to assess the opposition.

This emphasis upon the opposition became Mourinho's defining feature as a coach. Here was no footballing philosopher in the manner of Arsène Wenger, who emphasised the importance of beautiful football and a consistent strategy, but instead a true tactician, someone who would vary his approach every week and concentrate heavily upon stopping the opposition. Ahead of Mourinho's first match in charge of Benfica in 2000/01 he requested a scouting report on the opposition, eventual champions Boavista. But Mourinho was appalled at the amateurish nature of the report from the scouting department, which included a tactical diagram featuring only ten players, omitting Boavista's inspirational midfielder Erwin Sánchez. He didn't request another report, and instead hired an old university colleague at his own expense to scout the opposition.

Mourinho continued to place great emphasis upon the opposition. Later, when at Porto and preparing for a crucial game against his former side Benfica, Mourinho sent a spy to observe Benfica's training sessions because he was unsure whether they would use a tall centre-forward, Edgaras Jankauskas (whom Mourinho later signed), or the speedier Mantorras – his choice of centre-backs would change according to which one his team were facing. Mourinho's opposition scouts went above and beyond the call of duty. By the time Porto had qualified for the Champions League Final against Monaco in 2004, the opposition scouting was even more thorough. Mourinho's staff created a personal DVD for each individual player, showing clips of their direct opponent. Then, after the players had watched the DVDs, Mourinho assembled the squad and chaired a discussion about Monaco's characteristics, effectively transforming opposition scouting into a group activity. It's little surprise that when he arrived at Chelsea a few weeks later, captain John Terry declared that Mourinho 'prepares for the opposition more thoroughly than anything I have ever known.'

At a time when Wenger seldom mentioned the opposition to his players and Sir Alex Ferguson did so primarily for major games against tough opponents, Mourinho was entirely different. A couple of days before each game Chelsea's players would return to the dressing room after training to find a dossier, usually six or seven pages long, next to their peg. It was entirely devoted to the opposition, explaining their team shape and set-pieces, and featured a paragraph on each player. It contained specific information and diagrams for key danger men – the runs they made at corners, the type of passes playmakers attempted. Tellingly, Mourinho handed the job of opposition scout to the most talented member of his coaching staff – a young André Villas-Boas, who would later win the Europa League with Porto before taking charge of Chelsea and Tottenham. Like Mourinho, he became renowned for the quality of his dossiers.

This approach continued in Chelsea's training sessions. Pre-season, which had been heavily dominated by fitness work under Ranieri, was now all about defensive organisation and team shape, and once the season was under way there was a specific focus upon the opposition. Ranieri had introduced this practice, although many Chelsea players felt he simply highlighted the opposition's strengths, which they found demoralising – 'After three years at Real Madrid, where we were never asked the slightest question about our opponents, it was bizarre to me,' complained Claude Makélélé. Mourinho was keener to suggest how weaknesses could be exploited.

Like many other clubs during this period, Chelsea increasingly used ProZone to statistically analyse their performance. But, as Terry said, 'We get the same information about the other team, and that's what we tend to focus on more.' Chelsea had a team meeting the day before a match, when Mourinho would talk through video clips of the opposition, and then the final training session would be specifically geared towards that weekend's task. 'You believe you are playing your opponents in that final training session,' said Terry. 'Everything you are doing is with them in mind. Your whole week has been building up to this point – you've read the dossier the manager has prepared, you've listened to what he has had to say at the team meeting and by Friday afternoon you feel ready.' While opposition scouting was hardly a new innovation, this level of focus was generally considered the preserve of underdogs. Chelsea were no underdog – in Mourinho's first season they won the league with 95 points, the Premier League's highest tally.

This was a defensive side. Chelsea sat deep, with Terry partnered by the excellent Ricardo Carvalho, who boasted a great relationship with right-back Paulo Ferreira, both players having followed Mourinho from Porto. Mourinho chopped and changed at left-back, but the most common starter was William Gallas, a right-footed centre-back who inevitably played more defensively than a natural left-back. Makélélé, of course, sat solidly in front of the defence. The midfielders were under strict instructions to track runners, and the centre-forward was expected to start the defensive work. One of Mourinho's favourite training exercises involved Chelsea playing possession football, but always keeping at least five men behind the ball.

No other Premier League team has recorded such incredible defensive statistics. Only 15 goals conceded in an entire campaign is remarkable, and somehow 25 clean sheets in 38 Premier League games sounds even better. Between mid-December and early March Chelsea didn't concede a single league goal; for 1,025 minutes and ten complete games Čech remained unbeaten until Leon McKenzie – who later quit football to become a professional boxer – headed home for Norwich. McKenzie's header was arguably the first time all season Chelsea conceded a 'preventable' goal from open play. Five of the eight previous strikes were unstoppable long-range efforts from Southampton's James Beattie, West Brom's Zoltán Gera, Fulham's Papa Bouba Diop and two from Arsenal's Thierry Henry, including a quickly taken free-kick. There was also a Nicolas Anelka penalty in Chelsea's first and only defeat of the season – at Manchester City – while two concessions against Bolton came, inevitably, from free-kicks aimed towards the head of Kevin Davies, one he nodded in himself, the other he knocked down for Rahdi Jaïdi to smash home. Clearly, Mourinho would have been annoyed to lose goals from set-pieces. But as far as Chelsea's shape in open play was concerned, it took until March for them to be breached properly. This largely stemmed from their incredible attention to detail in terms of stopping the opposition.

The real story of Chelsea's season – and Mourinho's overall approach – was about the wingers. That's slightly surprising, because for the first few games of the campaign, Mourinho didn't use wingers at all, preferring a diamond midfield. His debut Premier League game was a 1–0 home victory over Manchester United, which foreshadowed Chelsea's performance throughout the season – conceding possession to the opposition, scoring a counter-attacking goal and keeping a clean sheet. Chelsea's diamond was overwhelmingly defensive: Makélélé flanked by Geremi and Alexey Smertin, two hard-working runners, with Frank Lampard higher up. Later, the cultured Portuguese passer Tiago would bring more technical quality, and Joe Cole was sometimes accommodated, but Chelsea were hugely uninspiring in that diamond system. The comparison with title rivals Arsenal, still continuing their unbeaten run from that Invincibles season, didn't flatter Chelsea. By the time Mourinho's side suffered the defeat at Manchester City, their nine games had featured just ten goals: scored eight, conceded two. Arsenal, during that same period, had scored 29.

But the next weekend proved significant, as two major events occurred. First, Arsenal's unbeaten spell finally ended one short of 50 games at Old Trafford, thanks to goals from two old foes: Ruud van Nistelrooy, whose penalty miss the previous year was the closest Arsenal had come to losing their unbeaten season, and Wayne Rooney, whose debut Premier League strike had ended their previous undefeated run. Second, Mourinho handed a Premier League debut to Dutch winger Arjen Robben. Many of the Premier League's greatest foreign imports took time to settle, but Robben was a revelation from the outset.

Mourinho had partly used the diamond shape due to the absences of both Robben and Damien Duff, his two star wingers. He tried Duff and Cole in his diamond midfield, but there was never a chance Robben could follow suit; he was a classic Dutch winger in the Marc Overmars mould who could play on either flank, a 4–3–3 rather than a 4–4–2 player. Chelsea had previously depended heavily upon set-pieces for goals, including a spell during which eight of their ten goals were from corners, free-kicks or penalties. Suddenly they offered a greater threat from open play. Robben's debut against Blackburn coincided with the first big win of Mourinho's tenure, 4–0, and although he only played half an hour as a substitute he made an immediate impact. It neatly symbolised the start of a different type of Chelsea; from eight goals in their first nine games, Chelsea then hit 30 in their subsequent nine. Robben won Player of the Month, and his incredible ability convinced Mourinho to regard the diamond system as an alternative and focus on the 4–3–3 instead.

Robben's second league appearance, this time as a half-time substitute, transformed Chelsea in a 4–1 win away at West Brom. Chelsea went ahead on the stroke of half-time with Gallas's goal from a set-piece, but Mourinho was furious with his team's display, introducing Carvalho for Bridge and, more significantly, Robben for Cole. Chelsea were rampant in the second half, with Robben the star. 'They were two completely different halves and the first was too bad to be true,' said Mourinho. 'The first half was the worst period since I've been manager, but the second was one of the best – it was beautiful. I was really disappointed with the performance of the team and I could have changed five or six players, but Robben was fantastic. He is bringing something special to us.'

Three days later Robben made his first start, away at CSKA Moscow in the Champions League, scoring the winner in a 1–0 victory. This involved a long ball being flicked on by Gudjohnsen, which Robben raced onto down the right. He played the ball into Duff, then continued his run, collected the return pass and fired home with his left foot. It was a simple, long-ball goal and demonstrated the role of Chelsea's centre-forward, to play as a target man, and the job of the wingers, to sprint in behind. Next came Everton – Robben's first league start and his first league goal, again in a 1–0 victory. This time Gudjohnsen dropped deep and lofted a ball over the top for Robben to run onto down the right. The Dutchman declined the option of squaring to Duff, and converted impressively himself. Again, Gudjohnsen was the link man, with Robben and Duff racing through. In Robben's next game, against Fulham, he scored a remarkable goal, his tricky dribbling leaving three defenders on the ground before he fired home, putting Chelsea ahead in an eventual 4–1 win. In total, Robben contributed seven goals and nine assists in just 14 starts and four substitute appearances throughout 2004/05.

Chelsea became defined by the speed, dribbling ability and directness of Robben and Duff, with Cole featuring primarily during Robben's injury lay-offs. Although the Premier League had previously seen plenty of speedsters out wide, the fact that Robben and Duff were playing in a 4–3–3 rather than a 4–4–2 or 4–4–1–1 changed everything. They were proper wingers, taking up more advanced positions when Chelsea had possession, playing high up against the opposition defence and stretching the play on both flanks. The absence of a deep-lying forward, meanwhile, meant the wingers didn't play many passing combinations. They had – literally – a more straightforward job: collect the ball in deep positions and sprint towards goal.

* * *

At this point counter-attacking started to become viewed in a negative sense. For the early Manchester United and Arsenal sides it was a term used in a complimentary manner, referring to their sudden, enthralling ability to break at speed from deep. Chelsea offered that too, but were considerably more blatant in the manner they disregarded possession to create those counter-attacking chances, which inevitably meant long periods defending. It didn't help, either, that Chelsea's key counter-attacking players were constantly evaluated in a primarily defensive sense by their manager.

The 'transition' now started to become a major concept. It was the moment a team went from being in possession to out of possession, or vice-versa. Mourinho placed more emphasis upon the transition than any previous Premier League coach, ordering his players to sprint forward suddenly when the ball was won and retreat immediately when it was lost. 'Mourinho was big on transitions,' said Duff, remembering Mourinho's initial impact upon English football. 'It was probably the first time I heard it. If you lose the ball it is transition from attack to defence, running back quickly, recovery runs or sprints – on the other hand, if you win the ball it's transition from defence, exploding forward quickly … that's when teams are most vulnerable because they're not in a defensive shape, and boom, you're gone. We steamrolled teams that year by having that down to a T; I could go through, off the top of my head, 30 or 40 goals when it was: win the ball back and go, within four or five seconds.'

To Mourinho, defensive transitions were equally important as attacking transitions. At a time when full-backs were becoming attacking weapons and needed to be tracked, Mourinho wanted his wingers to work hard defensively. After the 1–0 Boxing Day victory over Aston Villa, when Robben set up Duff for the winner, Mourinho marvelled: 'They can play left and right, inside and outside, they can shoot and cross, they have all these things in their pocket, they are doing that fantastically – but also their defensive contribution is fantastic. I took Damien off because I know 15 minutes for Damien means about two miles.' Mourinho loved his work rate.

Cole, meanwhile, experienced the most dramatic revolution. A precocious attacking talent who had struggled to channel his incredible skill into efficiency and didn't know his best position, Mourinho turned Cole from a box of tricks into a streamlined, purposeful wide midfielder. Again, the focus was on defence. When Chelsea defeated Benítez's Liverpool 1–0 in a dour game at Stamford Bridge in October, Cole came off the bench to provide the difference, volleying in the winner. Journalists celebrated English football's next big thing showcasing his star quality, but Mourinho was unhappy. 'After he scored, the game finished for Joe,' he complained. 'I need eleven players for defensive organisation and I had just ten.'

That underlined the emphasis upon defending as a team, although Cole's defensive work rate quickly improved. After a routine 3–1 victory over Scunthorpe in the FA Cup third round, Mourinho said Cole 'was fantastic. Now he thinks not as an individual but as one of 11 players. He understands what the team needs, and what he has to do when we don't have the ball. He's improving a lot, a completely different player.' Some despaired at Cole's transformation from a playmaker to a defensive-minded workhorse, but he retained an ability to dazzle opponents, and the following season he would seal Chelsea's second title with a brilliant goal in a 3–0 victory over Manchester United – meaning Chelsea's two titles in Mourinho's first spell were bookended by wins over Sir Alex Ferguson's side.

Chelsea's players shared the goalscoring burden, with Didier Drogba enduring a disappointing first campaign in English football – his form was so patchy that he wasn't a regular, starting only half the Premier League games. He didn't like playing up front alone in the 4–3–3 system, was criticised for going to ground too easily and managed only ten goals. However, he led the line well physically and his defensive effort was commendable, which inevitably pleased Mourinho. Chelsea's top goalscorer was Lampard, a revelation in his left-of-centre midfield role and a player who would help define midfield play during this era. His goalscoring return was sensational, usually finishing powerfully after receiving cut-backs on the edge of the box, and he fittingly scored both goals in the title-clinching 2–0 victory at Bolton in April 2005.

While Mourinho usually used a functional midfielder to complete the trio alongside Makélélé and Lampard, towards the end of the season he became braver and used natural forward Eidur Gudjohnsen – who had previously partnered Drogba in the diamond system or played up front alone – in the right-of-centre midfield role. The Icelander's ability to play there demonstrated his incredible football-ing intelligence, but this was nevertheless a surprisingly adventurous system for Mourinho. He was so confident the defence and Makélélé would remain solid, and the midfielders would get through their defensive work, that he was happy to play Cole, Lampard, Gudjohnsen and Duff behind Drogba during the spring, in Robben's absence, including in a clash against reigning champions Arsenal.

There were sporadic glimpses of genuine all-out-attack football when Chelsea were chasing matches, and Mourinho was quick to change formation dramatically if required. In an FA Cup tie at Newcastle, with Chelsea 1–0 down at the break, Mourinho made a half-time triple change, bringing on Gudjohnsen, Lampard and Duff for Geremi, Cole and Tiago, a gamble that backfired spectacularly when Wayne Bridge departed with a broken leg, meaning Chelsea played almost the entire second half with ten men. There were no further goals. But the gambles often worked. In the League Cup Final against Benítez's Liverpool Chelsea were 1–0 down, so Mourinho brought on forward Gudjohnsen for midfielder Jiří Jarošík, then another forward – Mateja Kežman – for left-back Gallas, moving to something like a 3–1–4–2. Chelsea won 3–2 after extra-time. When drawing 1–1 with Fulham at half-time in April he introduced a midfielder for a defender and moved Duff to left-back, as Chelsea went in search of the win. They triumphed 3–1.

While Mourinho's mid-game switches were dramatic, Chelsea never lacked cohesion. They knew exactly how to rearrange themselves, because Mourinho had specifically worked on different shapes in training, explaining what the approach would be if Chelsea were shutting down the game, what the plan would be if they were chasing it. When he threw on multiple strikers, they never crowded each other, as was often the case with other teams – they'd spread across the pitch and play different roles. Of course, a manager can't plan for every eventuality, and Mourinho often wrote instructions on small pieces of paper and told substitutes to pass the note on to a specific teammate, because he realised some footballers found visual instructions more memorable than aural instructions. These notes ranged from details about formation changes to set-piece responsibilities, although on a couple of occasions the relevant player unfolded the note to reveal a written message simply saying 'Win!'

Mourinho had taken tactical planning to an entirely new level, although his greatest legacy was simply popularising the 4–3–3 system. More teams started playing their own version of the formation, although it often became more like 4–5–1; Aston Villa's Martin O'Neill briefly played Gareth Barry on the left flank in that system, and there's no way Barry can be considered enough of a winger to make the formation a 4–3–3. Unfortunately, few sides boasted proper goalscoring wingers like Robben and Duff. 'Most 4–5–1 schemes in England, with a few exceptions, consist of little more than taking off a striker and inserting a third central ball-winner in midfield,' said former Chelsea boss Gianluca Vialli in 2006. And therefore while the 4–3–3/4–5–1 system does not have to be defensive, in England during the mid-2000s it generally was.

Remarkably, Chelsea found their record-breaking achievements in José Mourinho's debut campaign overshadowed by Rafael Benítez's Liverpool. Chelsea may have been champions of England, but Liverpool became champions of Europe.

Liverpool and Chelsea played five times in Mourinho and Benítez's debut campaign, with Chelsea twice prevailing 1–0 in the league, both thanks to Joe Cole goals, and winning the League Cup Final 3–2 after extra-time, following a 1–1 draw in 90 minutes. Then, most significantly, came Liverpool's aggregate victory over Chelsea in the Champions League semi-final, a typically tight, tactical, two-legged tie that produced just one goal in 180 minutes – and that goal might not even have crossed the line anyway. It was the type of contest Mourinho and Benítez's tactics had encouraged.

Just one instalment of this five-part Mourinho–Benítez battle was needed for it to become obvious that English football had become considerably more cautious. After the first of Chelsea's 1–0 Premier League victories, in October 2004, when many had already remarked upon the defensive nature of the Premier League, the *Guardian*'s Kevin McCarra was moved to suggest that the dreary match 'might have you brooding over the coordinated arrival on these shores of José Mourinho and Rafael Benítez, not to mention Tottenham Hotspur's Jacques Santini. Have they come to carry out a continental plot to drive down the value of the Premier League's worldwide TV rights?' McCarra's comments were tongue in cheek, certainly, but the Premier League was facing its first crisis of confidence; this was a division created for TV entertainment, which boasted of being the most exciting in the world, but was now producing extremely defensive matches.

Santini, incidentally, was another high-profile managerial import, having left the France job to take charge of Spurs. He lasted just three months and therefore had little impact, but he was certainly contributing to the defensive mindset – his 11 games in charge produced results of 1–1, 1–0, 1–1, 1–0, 0–0, 0–0, 0–1, 1–0, 0–1, 1–2 and 0–2. One of these matches was away at Mourinho's Chelsea and is among the most significant goalless draws in the Premier League, as it prompted Mourinho to introduce a new phrase into the English footballing lexicon. 'As we say in Portugal, they brought the bus and they left the bus in front of the goal,' he complained. This became 'parking the bus', and it's ironic that while Mourinho was using the expression to criticise the opposition, he was also heavily associated with that approach. Mourinho, Benítez, Santini – you wait ages for a bus, then three turn up at once.

Santini was replaced by his assistant Martin Jol, who immediately presided over defeats of 3–2 to Charlton and 5–4 to Arsenal. It was quite a contrast in terms of entertainment value – from 14 goals in 11 games under Santini to 14 goals in two games under Jol. The 5–4 north London derby defeat, the only Premier League game to feature nine different goalscorers, was probably the most enthralling game of that Premier League campaign, although one man was unsurprisingly unimpressed.

'5–4 is a hockey score, not a football score,' Mourinho weighed in. 'In a three-against-three training match, if the score reaches 5–4 I send the players back to the dressing rooms as they are not defending properly, so to get a result like that in a game of 11 against 11 is disgraceful.' This was the new world order in the Mourinho and Benítez era; high-scoring matches were not to be celebrated, but ridiculed.

14

Iberian Influence II

*'We have prepared everything perfectly, poring
over DVD footage, practising set-piece routines,
analysing the opponents, passing our knowledge
onto the players. Each game is simply the
culmination of a process lasting days, based
on research going back decades.'*

Rafael Benítez

Rafael Benítez's arrival was less heralded than Mourinho's; he wasn't such an engaging personality and was more reserved with the media. But he was a similarly studious coach who helped to transform English football with his tactical acumen and made a significant contribution to English clubs' massive progress in the Champions League during the mid-2000s. By 2008 the Premier League was ranked as the best league in Europe by UEFA, a sudden rise that owed much to Mourinho and Benítez's continental expertise.

Benítez's appointment prompted immediate excitement among Liverpool supporters, who remembered the way his Valencia side had destroyed them at the Mestalla two years earlier in a dominant performance that deserved more than the eventual 2–0 victory. Particularly memorable was a brilliant passing move featuring the midfield pairing of Rubén Baraja and David Albelda, and finished smartly by the diminutive Argentine number 10 Pablo Aimar – one of the Champions League's best-ever team goals. This was pass-and-move football that would go down very nicely on the Kop. 'I can't remember a European tie when we've been so much on the back foot,' admitted Gérard Houllier, Liverpool's manager at the time. Liverpool's players, meanwhile, remarked upon Valencia's tremendous organisation, a consequence of Benítez's coaching style. Although he spoke about wanting to win 'the right way' at his Liverpool unveiling, Benítez didn't place great emphasis upon entertainment nor did he particularly appreciate flair players. Instead he was a pure strategist.

From his early teenage years Benítez was a great lover of chess and clearly viewed football in a very similar way. 'In football, like chess, you have to think and analyse what's going to happen, to have a plan A, plan B and even a plan C,' he said. 'You have to calmly evaluate action before you put it into practice, and be prepared, foreseeing the different options of the opponent.' That could be an analysis of any sport, but Benítez's outlook on chess and football was more specific. 'You have to control the middle of the park, to wait for the right moments to attack,' he said of chess. 'Some people are very aggressive, very offensive, but in chess it's sometimes dangerous because if the other is good at defending, they can play counter-attack.' That's a perfect summary of Benítez's approach with Liverpool, and particularly the games against Mourinho's Chelsea; his opponents were excellent at attacking transitions, so Liverpool were cautious, refusing to play into their hands. Accounts from his former players suggest Benítez viewed them rather like chess pieces – functional objects who served a purpose, rather than people with personalities who occasionally needed support and encouragement. 'I am not sure he is that interested in players as people,' suggested captain Steven Gerrard.

After Benítez's playing career was compromised when he picked up a knee injury while representing Spain in the World University Games – an apt summary of his academic pedigree – he rose through the coaching ranks at Real Madrid, enjoying a brief spell as assistant manager to future Champions League and World Cup-winning manager Vicente del Bosque. When Del Bosque departed in 1994 and was replaced by Jorge Valdano, a footballing romantic, Benítez was demoted to B-team coach. Valdano and Benítez fell out, particularly over a young midfielder named Sandro, a diminutive, creative, typically Spanish playmaker whom Valdano believed deserved a free role in Benítez's B-team. But Benítez complained about Sandro's lack of tactical awareness and often omitted him from the side. That was Benítez – tactics over talent.

Benítez, who as a player filmed his own matches for self-analysis, was obsessed with creating a footballing video library. At one stage, before he could count upon an analysis team, he owned a TV connected to two video recorders – one to tape the whole match, the other focusing on specific situations. His library grew extensively, and Benítez introduced regular video sessions for his squad ahead of matches, a new practice to many. At Valladolid he suffered a minor car accident, and upon his return to the dressing room was greeted by one of his attackers mocking him with, 'We're glad you're alright – we were worried the video player would miss you.' Benítez was clearly more comfortable studying the tapes and compiling analysis than engaging with his players. He was an early adopter of the ZX Spectrum and Atari to store information, and later dubbed himself – somewhat sadly – as 'a loner with a laptop', which at least proves his technology evolved. His office at Liverpool's training ground was dominated by a huge wall of DVDs, some of which he lent to defender Jamie Carragher, including an example of how his Valencia side defended and how legendary centre-back Franco Baresi commanded AC Milan's back line.

That Milan side, coached by the revolutionary Arrigo Sacchi, was Benítez's main inspiration – they offered 'quality, discipline and intensity', in his words. Although a relentless attacking force, Sacchi's Milan became renowned for their aggressive offside trap and tremendous defensive organisation in a 4–4–2 system, boasting incredible compactness from front to back, denying the opposition space between the lines. 'If we played with 25 metres between the last defender and the centre-forward, given our ability, no one could beat us,' said Sacchi. 'And thus, the team had to move as a unit, up and down the pitch, and also from left to right.'

This was the key characteristic of Benítez's Liverpool. He was fortunate to inherit the team from Gérard Houllier, who believed heavily in lateral compactness to the extent that he often fielded a defence featuring four natural centre-backs, and jettisoned proper wingers to play central midfielders in wide positions. Benítez, however, focused on vertical compactness from front to back. He'd often stand nervously on the edge of the technical area, encouraging the defensive, midfield and attacking lines to squeeze closer together with a hand gesture that looked like he was miming playing the accordion. 'Teams hated playing against us,' Carragher said later. 'The games would be horrible for the opposition because we would not give them any space to breathe. If you asked me to say the one word I heard most during training and games, it would be him shouting "Compact!" After the first year of working with Rafa, we were like robots, we knew exactly what he wanted us to do. This came about through repetition on the training ground, the drills being done over and over again until he was satisfied.'

Benítez, or one of his coaches, would set up Liverpool's XI on the training pitch and walk into different zones with the ball, commanding the nearest player to pressure him, while everyone else shifted positions accordingly, always remaining compact and denying space between the lines. It was a method borrowed from Sacchi, whose training sessions Benítez had observed twice in the 1990s during his spells with Milan and the Italian national side. It will have particularly pleased Benítez that Sacchi later described his Liverpool side as 'exemplary in two ways: their spirit and tactical organisation. Benítez knows what he is doing. His team lacks talent, but they are a true team, compact and modern.' At their best, Liverpool were tactically flexible enough to play a deep defensive line or a very aggressive offside trap – but they always remained highly compact, which included the goalkeeper. Jerzy Dudek was surprised when Benítez immediately placed such emphasis upon him remaining close to the back four. 'It took most of the season to adapt,' he admitted. Meanwhile, Benítez was already lining up Pepe Reina, a more comfortable sweeper-keeper.

Liverpool's players were shocked by the frequency of tactical sessions during Benítez's first pre-season, while Benítez was similarly taken aback by his players' limited tactical understanding. He believed Liverpool played too intuitively and demanded they performed in a more methodical manner, telling Steven Gerrard he ran around too much. He was also surprised by the limitations of the forwards, who played little part in build-up play. Benítez fashioned a considerably more organised, structured Liverpool side.

Benítez considered the opposition as much as his own team, sometimes compiling 30-page dossiers before condensing that information into a 15- or 20-minute talk for his players. He was obsessed with keeping his game plan secret and only announced his starting XI to his squad shortly before matches. This irritated some players, as they found it difficult to prepare mentally, but Benítez was determined to guard against leaks to the opposition. Again, this was very Benítez, concerned more with how the opposition might adjust rather than his own players' mentality.

In his first game at Anfield, a 2–1 victory over Manchester City, Benítez claims he was dismayed by the close proximity between the two benches and was worried that the opposition manager could overhear his instructions. He therefore decided to start shouting in his native language to Josemi, telling the Spaniard to translate the message for his teammates so the opposition manager wouldn't understand. Ironically, the opposition manager was Kevin Keegan, who, unless his mentality had changed drastically since his Newcastle days, paid no attention to the opposition's tactics anyway.

The players initially protested at Benítez's use of zonal marking when defending set-pieces, which involved each player occupying a specific area rather than concentrating upon the runs of opponents, a system that was widely mocked when Liverpool struggled in the early days, and later lent its name to a football tactics website. 'A zone has never scored a goal' became the standard rebuke from pundits. The criticism continued but soon became academic; in Benítez's first season Liverpool conceded 12 set-piece goals, the fourth-best record in the Premier League. Then, in both 2005/06 and 2006/07 they conceded only six goals from dead-ball situations, the best record in the division. Liverpool's players were initially determined to revert to man-to-man, but Benítez insisted a zonal system would work in the long run – and he was right.

'Overall I believe we conceded fewer since Rafa introduced zonal marking,' said Carragher. 'It may seem like more only because if you lose a goal with zonal marking, the system always gets the blame – if you do it with man-to-man, an individual gets the blame.' It was peculiar that it was always considered a 'foreign' idea, however –

George Graham's Arsenal side, the most revered defence of the 1990s, also organised themselves zonally at set-pieces. What it demonstrated, though, was that Benítez had tremendous belief in his principles and wouldn't waver simply because players expressed doubts. Even the nature of zonal marking itself reflected his approach, being about teamwork and structure rather than individuals. Benítez was also criticised for favouring squad rotation, receiving an unreasonable share of the blame for a concept that most top-level coaches had already embraced.

Benítez's debut league campaign was disappointing, with the club slipping to fifth place, and it took until the Champions League knockout stage before Liverpool really impressed. This was Benítez in his element, approaching two-legged matches when Liverpool's main task was stopping superior opponents. In fact, Liverpool's Champions League triumph was remarkably similar to Manchester United's in 1999; they showed tremendous tactical maturity throughout the knockout stage, until the final, when they were completely outclassed before launching an unthinkable comeback.

Liverpool's knockout stage effectively started in their final group game, at home to Olympiakos. Having collected just seven points from their previous five matches, Liverpool required a victory to move onto ten points alongside the Greek side and stand a chance of qualification. They'd lost 1–0 away in Athens, and because teams level on points were separated by their head-to-head record, if Liverpool conceded an away goal they'd need to score three. So when Rivaldo curled in a free-kick, Liverpool required a miracle.

At half-time Benítez went for broke. He switched to a three-man defence by taking off left-back Djimi Traoré and introducing French forward Florent Sinama Pongolle, who took just two minutes to equalise. On 78 minutes Benítez replaced Milan Baroš with youngster

Neil Mellor – and he also took just two minutes to score, meaning Liverpool required one more to progress. The hero, inevitably, was Gerrard, latching onto Mellor's intelligent knock-down just outside the box and thumping a stunning half-volley into the far corner. It was a legendary individual moment from Liverpool's skipper, but behind that was something more significant: a decisive half-time change of system, which allowed Liverpool to score the three second-half goals they required – not for the last time.

In the second round Liverpool faced Bayer Leverkusen. Although a relatively simple draw on paper, this opposition provided painful memories. Two years earlier, when Houllier was in charge, Liverpool took a 1–0 first-leg lead to Leverkusen at the quarter-final stage. After an hour in Germany the score was 1–1 and Liverpool were on course to progress. But then Houllier made a curious change, removing German holding midfielder Dietmar Hamann and introducing the more attack-minded Vladimír Šmicer. Things fell apart dramatically, with Liverpool conceding three goals in half an hour and losing 4–2. They were eliminated, and Houllier called an impromptu meeting at Liverpool's hotel that night, where he explicitly told his players that they were banned from discussing his substitutions with the media. He realised he'd made an error, and that was arguably the beginning of the end for Houllier.

In 2005, Hamann was one of Liverpool's key players against Leverkusen home and away, Liverpool winning 3–1 in both games, with the two Leverkusen goals mere late consolations. Liverpool were narrow and compact, their forwards pressed to disrupt Leverkusen's build-up play, and Hamann protected the back four excellently alongside Igor Bišćan in the absence of Xabi Alonso. Funnily enough, Benítez actually made the same substitution as Houllier after an hour: Šmicer for Hamann. By this point, however, Leverkusen required six goals, the tie was over and Benítez was simply resting Hamann.

Next up were Juventus. At home Benítez selected a 4–4–2 formation, with young Frenchman Anthony Le Tallec playing his best game for the Liverpool up front alongside Baroš. Liverpool went ahead through a set-piece routine from the training ground, scored by Sami Hyypiä and assisted by Luis García, who promptly smashed in a stunning second. Liverpool again played narrow, crowding out Juve's brilliant playmaker Pavel Nedvěd, and while Fabio Cannavaro nodded in a late goal, Liverpool were in control.

Away in Turin, Liverpool produced a classic Benítez performance; they didn't manage a single shot on target but achieved the goalless draw required. Crucially, Benítez demonstrated his determination to keep the opposition guessing. In response to Juventus's narrow system and two-man strike force, he deployed an unusual 3–5–1–1 formation for the first time, and Liverpool inevitably spent all week practising the system in training. But when Dudek was summoned to a UEFA press conference on the eve of the game, Benítez told his goalkeeper to keep repeating that Liverpool would play 4–4–2, tricking Juventus coach Fabio Capello. Sure enough, at kick-off, Liverpool lined up in that 4–4–2 shape but were under instructions to subtly shift to 3–5–1–1 inside the first couple of minutes, outfoxing Juve. Capello's side tried to play through the centre into the feet of Nedvěd, Alessandro Del Piero and Zlatan Ibrahimović, but Liverpool's three centre-backs and three central midfielders dominated that zone.

Then came that famous European semi-final: Mourinho's Chelsea against Benítez's Liverpool, the moment when it felt like Premier League clubs had finally cracked the Champions League, thanks largely to the two foreign managers who had succeeded in Europe the previous season. This was probably the most tactical tie ever contested by two English clubs, with Mourinho and Benítez concentrating almost solely upon stopping each other. It was hyped like a final, but on paper was a complete mismatch; Liverpool would finish an astonishing 37 points behind Chelsea in the Premier League that season, meaning they were considerably closer to bottom-placed Southampton in points' terms than to the champions. 'The only way we could make up for the difference in quality was to focus,' Benítez said later. 'We named a line-up whose emphasis was very much on solidity ... it would be an evening for resilience rather than beauty.' At one stage in the build-up to the game, Benítez worked for 22 hours, non-stop, on his research and game plan.

The first leg was a truly turgid 0–0, with both sides concentrating on preventing the other counter-attacking, a blatant example of the defensive football prospering under the two managers. 'The game was a bit of an anti-climax, really, it never sparked into life; we both played cagey football,' said John Terry. 'They were cautious and we were too ... it felt as if the tie hadn't really started.' But Liverpool were delighted with the goalless draw. 'It was all down to the work we had done the week before,' said Benítez's assistant Pako Ayestarán. 'We spent a great deal of time analysing Chelsea, using a lot of taped material – far beyond the normal extent ... it wasn't a beautiful game, but it was one of those that you'll go back to watch again and again because it involved perfect planning and execution.'

The key incident saw Alonso, the tie's most inventive midfielder, ruled out of the second leg when Eidur Gudjohnsen theatrically collapsed after no contact whatsoever from the Spaniard. Some newspapers reported that Gudjohnsen later told Alonso he deliberately dived because he was aware of his precarious disciplinary situation. That felt grimly appropriate for this tie – an otherwise wonderful footballer given information about an opponent and exploiting it cynically, focusing upon nullifying the opposition's strengths rather than playing to his own. In the Stamford Bridge dressing room afterwards, Alonso was in tears.

In the second leg at Anfield Liverpool triumphed 1–0. In front of a raucous crowd, it was another tight, tense, tactical game, with Hamann the outstanding performer – 'He played a blinder,' said Terry. The German's dominance of midfield prompted Chelsea to play simple long-ball football, with Mourinho remembering how Chelsea had done similar in the League Cup Final against Liverpool, forcing Gerrard into a headed own goal. Centre-back Robert Huth, a considerable aerial force, was introduced up front as Chelsea went route one.

The controversial winner was scored early by Luis García, a goal that might not even have been legitimate, with William Gallas hooking the ball out from on – or possibly just behind – the goal line. Mourinho complained for years about the goal, although he ignored the fact that, had it not been awarded, the referee would probably have given Liverpool a penalty and dismissed Petr Čech for a last-man foul on Baroš seconds earlier. It felt fitting that García was the matchwinner; in a structured, organised, attritional game of football, the diminutive Spaniard was the only player providing unpredictable movement, attempting trickery in tight situations and launching ambitious efforts at goal. He always seemed a peculiarly un-Benítez player; he drifted away from his position and was infuriatingly inconsistent, but was a welcome source of random brilliance in an otherwise frustratingly systemised tie. This winner against Chelsea was his fifth goal in six knockout games; much like Liverpool, he came alive on European nights.

The final against AC Milan featured a truly legendary comeback. Liverpool were 3–0 down at half-time, having been destroyed on the counter-attack, but after a change of system and the introduction of Hamann, Liverpool recovered to 3–3 within 15 minutes. In simple terms it was the most effective, decisive half-time tactical switch in football history. The reality is considerably more complex.

Benítez's initial decision to omit Hamann was hugely surprising. Although he'd sometimes used a two-man central midfield of Alonso and Gerrard in the Premier League, Liverpool's European progress depended upon fielding a holding player. Bišćan, the Croatian defensive midfielder, had started all six knockout matches, three times paired with Hamann to provide a very defensive shield. Besides, Benítez was obsessed with reacting to the opposition, and Carlo Ancelotti's Milan featured three outright playmakers: Andrea Pirlo, Clarence Seedorf and Kaká in a midfield diamond alongside workhorse Gennaro Gattuso. In fact Ancelotti had sometimes gone even further by including Rui Costa in place of a striker and switching to 4–3–2–1. Milan boasted more midfield creativity than any side in Europe.

Although Benítez, as always, didn't tell his players the starting XI until shortly before kick-off, he'd already confided to Gerrard that he intended to deploy a 4–4–2, with Harry Kewell just behind Baroš, leaving Gerrard and Alonso together in midfield. When Gerrard informed Carragher, the centre-back couldn't believe it. 'There was no question in my mind Didi was the man to nullify Kaká's threat. It had never occurred to me, or him, that he wouldn't start the final … I wasn't supposed to know the team until shortly before kick-off, but part of me wanted to speak out and tell the boss he'd got it wrong.' Hamann was similarly shocked, and when Benítez announced the XI in the dressing room and named Gerrard as a deep midfielder, Hamann didn't initially grasp the reality – his first thought was 'I can't believe he's not playing Xabi.'

Benítez hadn't overlooked the threat of Kaká – inevitably he'd watched dozens of Milan's matches, and his pre-match tactical video concentrated upon the Brazilian's movement. But Alonso and Gerrard simply couldn't cope. 'Never in my career had I encountered anyone as fast with the ball at their feet,' Gerrard gasped. 'Kaká was lightning.' Milan went ahead through an early Paolo Maldini set-piece goal, and although Liverpool enjoyed spells of possession, Milan were brilliant on the break. Kaká burst into the space created by the runs of Andrei Shevchenko and Hernán Crespo, who dragged Carragher and Hyypiä into wide areas. Crespo scored the next two goals, with his second particularly magnificent – Kaká received a pass and turned Gerrard beautifully before curling a perfect ball in behind, which allowed Crespo to stab into the far corner, first-time, with the outside of his right foot. 3–0, and goodnight. At half-time Carragher was imploring his teammates to avoid a massacre.

Then came the changes. Benítez wanted to switch to a three-man defence, so immediately told Djimi Traoré to take a shower because he was coming off, and summoned Hamann, explained his role on the chalkboard – stop Kaká – then told him to go out early to warm up. Benítez had planned to make another substitution, bringing on Djibril Cissé, until a colleague reminded him he'd already introduced Šmicer for the injured Kewell midway through the first half, and it would be dangerous to use all three substitutes by half-time. Suddenly, Liverpool's physio announced – much to the player's fury – that right-back Steve Finnan might not last 90 minutes and so should be substituted. This forced Benítez to summon Traoré back from the shower, with the defender frantically trying to find his discarded socks as Benítez explained the new system.

The chalkboard was now a complete mess; a couple of players recall it briefly depicting Liverpool with 12 players for their second-half shape, although Benítez remembers it as ten, having removed Luis García from the right but forgotten to place him in his new central position. As Liverpool filed out onto the pitch, where Hamann was waiting, he was stunned to see Traoré – whom he'd previously seen half-naked on the way to the showers – reprising his defensive role.

Amid this chaos various players suggest Benítez suddenly projected an air of confidence and calmness. Most importantly, he switched to the obvious system to blunt Milan, a 3–4–2–1. This offered a spare man at the back, which meant Shevchenko and Crespo's runs would cause fewer problems; four against four in central midfield, where Liverpool had been overrun; and even the correct wing-back balance, with a natural defender, John Arne Riise, on the left against the attack-minded Cafu, while Šmicer could play a more advanced role against Maldini. Considering Liverpool had played a similar system away at Juventus, it was surely something Benítez had considered beforehand.

The new system was effective at blunting Milan's attacking play, but getting the three goals was all about Gerrard. With Hamann behind him, Gerrard pushed up and embarked upon one of his classic one-man midfield displays, driving Liverpool forward in search of an unlikely fightback. He headed the first goal, briefly took up a right-wing position that allowed Šmicer inside to score a long-range second, and then burst into the box, was fouled by Gattuso, and Alonso scored the rebound having seen his initial penalty saved. It defied logic; Liverpool had scored three times in seven minutes against a Milan defence comprising Cafu, Jaap Stam, Alessandro Nesta and Maldini, possibly the most fearsome defence the Champions League has seen.

The remaining hour, including extra-time, was tense but less eventful, the crucial change involving Ancelotti's introduction of speedy left-winger Serginho in place of Seedorf. Gerrard was therefore switched to right-wing-back, although he was understandably exhausted, and Serginho became the game's most dangerous player, sending in a stream of crosses, including one that resulted in Dudek's extraordinary double save from Shevchenko. The Polish goalkeeper was also the hero in the shoot-out, making saves from both Pirlo and

Shevchenko. Liverpool were, almost inexplicably, European champions.

That Istanbul comeback was peculiarly similar to Liverpool's other trophy success under Benítez, in the following year's FA Cup Final. They again performed poorly, trailing 2–0 and then 3–2 to an average West Ham side, before Gerrard scored a quite incredible stoppage-time equaliser from 35 yards, his second of the game. Liverpool won on penalties. There's something inappropriate about Benítez, the master of research, preparation and control, winning his two Liverpool trophies in such dramatic, improbable and manic circumstances. Neil Mellor, the youth product who provided some crucial goals during 2004/05, summarised it best. 'For all Rafa's tactics – which were important – some of his best results were achieved in chaos.'

Throughout Benítez's six-year period at Liverpool his teams were always extremely solid in central positions, but his tactical demands made it difficult for wide players to thrive; his full-backs were expected to tuck inside, which meant Liverpool lacked the attacking thrust required to break down inferior opponents, while his wide midfielders were allowed little positional freedom and were tasked with joylessly shuttling up and down the touchlines. During his first three months at Liverpool he deployed one of the previous season's full-backs – Finnan or Riise – in a wide midfield role to provide balance and shape. Although he gradually played more attack-minded wingers, that underlined what Benítez wanted.

The story of Dirk Kuyt was typical. Signed in 2006 from Feyenoord as an exciting striker, having smashed in 91 goals in four seasons in the admittedly unreliable barometer that is the Eredivisie, Benítez converted the Dutchman into a functional, hard-working wide midfielder renowned for tracking opposition full-backs diligently.

Benítez and Mourinho shared an obsession with wide midfielders working hard defensively, a direct response to the rise of attacking full-backs. Tellingly, Benítez once wanted to sign Daniel Alves – who would become the world's best right-back at Barcelona – to play on the right of midfield.

The likes of Albert Riera, Jermaine Pennant and Mark González, all considerably below the standard required to win titles, were recruited because they fitted the template of a Benítez wide midfielder: up-and-down players who retained the team's shape. Riera recalls his manager's instructions for a 1–0 victory at Real Madrid in 2009 – Benítez had concluded that if Real's right-winger Arjen Robben wasn't regularly involved, Liverpool would probably keep a clean sheet. So Riera's primary job was to remain solidly in front of Liverpool left-back Fábio Aurélio, denying passes from Real right-back Sergio Ramos into Robben. Riera therefore wasn't allowed to leave his wide-left position at all, effectively being banned from drifting inside. It worked a charm with that memorable victory at Benítez's boyhood club – and few would question his European record – but denying his wide players any spontaneity harmed Liverpool when trying to break down weaker opponents.

Ryan Babel, a speedy wide forward considered 'the next Thierry Henry' upon his arrival in 2007, infuriated Benítez because he eternally cut inside, but that was natural for a right-footed player deployed on the left. Benítez devised a series of one-on-one training exercises with the Dutchman, at one point formulating a drill where Babel had to cut inside or go down the line depending upon which foot he initially controlled the ball with, essentially meaning Babel had no freedom to direct his dribbles in response to the positioning of opponents.

Craig Bellamy, capable of playing wide or up front, experienced something similar. 'Rafa's tactical work was very, very good. I learned a lot from him in that area. But he couldn't come to terms with the idea that some players need an element of freedom and that we express ourselves in different ways,' he said. 'Defensively, Rafa was exceptional. He was very good on the opposition and how to nullify their threat and stifle their forward players. He would use video analysis to go through the opposition's strengths and weaknesses, nothing was left to chance ... but there was no scope for spontaneity. None. Of all the managers I have worked with, he trusted his players the least.' Confusingly, however, despite all these instructions it was difficult to find a genuine identity in Liverpool's attacking approach. They were well defined without possession, organised and compact, but there was no overwhelming philosophy with the ball.

Benítez came closest to winning the title in his fifth season, 2008/09, when Liverpool finished second behind Manchester United. The spine – Reina in goal, Carragher and one of Daniel Agger, Martin Škrtel and Sami Hyypiä at centre-back, a midfield trio of Javier Mascherano, Alonso and Gerrard, with Fernando Torres up front – was arguably the strongest the Premier League has ever seen. Liverpool took all 12 points from the four matches against champions Manchester United and third-placed Chelsea. There wasn't quite enough attacking variety to win the title, however, and although Liverpool finished as the division's top goalscorers, they recorded five goalless draws: at home to Stoke, Fulham and West Ham, plus away at Aston Villa and Stoke again, all comparatively poor sides.

Break down that season's Premier League table and the situation becomes clear – against fellow top seven sides, Liverpool were unbeaten and collected ten more points than champions Manchester United. But against sides who finished 8th and below, United won 14 extra points. Benítez's cautious and reactive approach was perfect against strong opposition, but the Premier League is equally about overpowering minnows, where Liverpool were found wanting.

'We've always done well against the bigger teams,' Steven Gerrard said many years later. 'But we've always struggled against a Fulham at home or a West Brom at home, when they park the bus and we haven't got that bit of magic to open them up.'

Indeed, passages of Benítez's autobiography would suggest he focused too much upon big matches – consider, for example, his approach to set-pieces. 'If you see from the reports of the opposition that they are weak at the near post from corners, then maybe in the preceding two games, you play all your corners to the far post, or deep into the box. Anywhere but to the near post.' There's clearly some logic in this approach, and it's easy to identify Liverpool working clever set-piece routines in big matches, often with surprise scorers – Agger against Chelsea in 2007, Yossi Benayoun against Real Madrid in 2009. But the emphasis upon surprising major opponents surely harmed them in those preceding matches against smaller teams, who presumably found Liverpool's routines somewhat predictable.

Interestingly, upon his arrival in 2004 Benítez had been given a three-year 'rebuilding' window by the board, reflecting the enormity of the change required at Anfield. Once over, Liverpool would be expected to compete. But Benítez's three major achievements came in cup competitions during those first three seasons: the Champions League and FA Cup successes in 2005 and 2006, then reaching the Champions League Final against Milan again in 2007, when Liverpool performed considerably better than in 2005 and were unfortunate to lose to two Pippo Inzaghi goals.

During this reactive era – the three seasons Mourinho and Benítez were together in the Premier League – they battled it out no fewer than 15 times, five each season. Nine of these matches produced no goals or one goal. As they regularly met in European competition, foreign observers noticed the significant shift towards defensive, physical, heavily systemised football, epitomised by both teams. The aforementioned Valdano – the Argentine World Cup winner who coached Real Madrid, where he fell out with Benítez – had become a respected football writer in Spain and delivered an astonishingly strong, almost unprecedented rebuke after the 15th meeting between Mourinho's Chelsea and Benítez's Liverpool – the Reds came out on top that night, although Mourinho got the better of Benítez 7–5 overall.

'Put a shit hanging from a stick in the middle of this passionate, crazy stadium [Anfield] and there are people who will tell you it's a work of art. It's not: it's a shit hanging from a stick,' Valdano blasted. 'Chelsea and Liverpool are the clearest, most exaggerated example of the way football is going: very intense, very collective, very tactical, very physical, and very direct. But, a short pass? Noooo. A feint? Noooo. A change of pace? Noooo. A one-two? A nutmeg? A back-heel? Don't be ridiculous. None of that. The extreme control and seriousness with which both teams played the semi-final neutralised any creative licence, any moments of exquisite skill.

'If Didier Drogba was the best player it was purely because he was the one who ran the fastest, jumped the highest and crashed into people the hardest. Such extreme intensity wipes away talent, even leaving a player of Joe Cole's class disoriented. If football is going the way Chelsea and Liverpool are taking it, we had better be ready to wave goodbye to any expression of the cleverness and talent we have enjoyed for a century.

'[Mourinho and Benítez] have two things in common: a previously denied, hitherto unsatisfied hunger for glory, and a desire to have everything under control. Both of these things stem from one key factor: neither Mourinho nor Benítez made it as a player. That has made them channel all their vanity into coaching. Those who did not have the talent to make it as players do not believe in the talent of players, they do not believe in the ability to improvise in order to win football matches. In short, Mourinho and Benítez are exactly the kind of coaches that Mourinho and Benítez would have needed to have made it as players.'

It's a particularly strong rant, but Valdano's final conclusion is genuinely intriguing: Mourinho and Benítez appeared entirely distrustful of flair, spontaneity and individual brilliance. Interestingly, Valdano later became a Real Madrid director but was dismissed in 2011 after falling out badly with the club's manager – Mourinho. 'He's a figure who is perfectly suited to these bombastic, shallow times,' Valdano complained. 'I've never heard him say a single thing about football worth remembering, whether in public or in private.' Neither of the two key coaches in the Premier League's reactive era satisfied the demands of this footballing romantic.

But to merely blame Mourinho and Benítez for making the Premier League more cautious would be ignoring their role in the division's greatest tactical leap forward. This duo studied the opposition in greater depth, they emphasised defensive shape – to the extent their teams were defined by their appearance without possession – and they attempted to dominate the centre of midfield with 4–3–3 and 4–2–3–1 systems that often outwitted the English 4–4–2. They showed the importance of being both compact and quick at transitions.

More than anything it felt like their sides' shape was 'top-down' rather than 'bottom-up'. Whereas the successful Manchester United and Arsenal systems of the 1990s were largely dictated by the particular characteristics of individuals, Chelsea and Liverpool throughout the mid-2000s were essentially a reflection of their manager's strategic vision. For the first time, managerial philosophy had become more important than the style of players.

15

The Midfield Trio

*'Gerrard and Lampard were both intelligent
footballers. If one player went forward, the other had
to stay back. It was not more difficult than that.'*

Sven-Göran Eriksson

The most significant tactical change during the first few years of the
21st century was the shift towards one-striker formations, essentially
started by Sir Alex Ferguson's decision to switch from 4–4–2 to
4–5–1 in 2001. Although the initial focus was on the striker, suddenly
forced to cope alone against two centre-backs, the midfield zone
experienced an equally significant revolution.

After all, the reason for this shift was to beef up midfield with an
extra man. As English clubs increasingly realised the importance of
keeping possession in the centre – or, looking at it from a more reactive perspective, not being overrun in that zone – managers increasingly needed three central midfielders. It's worth remembering Sir
Alex Ferguson's assessment of this zone in the 1990s. 'In Europe they
pass to each other in midfield,' he said. 'They play in little triangles
and keep it there, they play one-twos against you in midfield, whereas

our midfielders service the wide players, the full-backs and the front-men.' In the 1990s the primary instinct was to get the ball out of the midfield zone. In the 2000s it was all about keeping it there.

English football essentially embraced the European model, thanks to a variety of factors, including more foreign players, stricter laws about tackling – which benefited technical talents – and, crucially, a dramatic improvement in the quality of pitches. As late as the 1990s winter matches were often played on horrendous mud baths, which made good football almost impossible. Now, with slick bowling greens up and down the country, teams could trust the pitch and pass the ball.

In the days of two-man central midfields there were basically three types of combination. You could have two box-to-box midfielders, like a young Roy Keane and Paul Ince at Manchester United, you could have one player sitting in front of the defence and the other scampering forward into attack, like Lee Clark and Robert Lee at Newcastle, or you could have two defensive midfielders, like Patrick Vieira and Emmanuel Petit at Arsenal.

The three-man midfield made everything considerably more complex. For a start, the positioning of the midfielders took two different forms: always a triangle, but arranged in completely oppo-site ways. The 4–3–3, as popularised by José Mourinho, featured one holding player with the two others broadly playing box-to-box roles, whereas the 4–2–3–1 favoured by Rafael Benítez meant two players sharing defensive midfield responsibilities, often with some freedom to advance, and a proper number 10. That's just the positioning of the players, too; their actual styles could vary wildly. The deepest midfielder could be a pure ball-winner like Javier Mascherano or a deep-lying creator like Michael Carrick, the 'second' midfielder could be a pure passer like Xabi Alonso or an enegetic all-rounder like Michael Essien, and the most attacking midfielder could be a driving, powerful player like Steven Gerrard or a playmaker like Tomáš Rosický. Forming a cohesive midfield became more difficult, and traditional midfield roles were crucially altered.

During this period English football observers didn't often appreciate the variation in the different midfield roles, in part because English football vocabulary is somewhat lacking in tactical terms. An Italian, for example, can instantly pinpoint the difference between a *regista* like Andrea Pirlo, a deep-lying midfielder, and a *trequartista* like Francesco Totti, who plays behind the forwards. But in England they were all 'midfielders', and the addition of 'defensive' and 'attacking' as prefixes didn't differentiate between roles in a 4–4–2, a 4–3–3 or a 4–2–3–1. These terms also failed to appreciate that, as football became more universal, deep-lying midfielders could play creative roles and advanced midfielders could play defensive roles.

Such changes are best explained by the tactical development of three outstanding English midfielders during this period: Manchester United's Paul Scholes, Chelsea's Frank Lampard and Liverpool's Steven Gerrard. This trio were among the most revered players of their generation and represented the three most dominant sides during the mid-2000s. But, more significantly, they learned their trade in 4–4–2 systems before thriving in three-man midfields, and all played multiple roles throughout their career, because of personal development and the changing nature of the Premier League. Of course, they also played together at international level, which posed a tricky tactical conundrum never entirely solved, and England's tactical inadequacy throughout the 2000s was particularly obvious when juxtaposed with increasingly sophisticated Premier League strategies.

* * *

The first to emerge was Scholes, who is considered part of two 'golden generations', but was actually slightly separated from both. At international level he's often remembered alongside Lampard and Gerrard, but was nearly four years older than the former and six older than the latter. At club level he belonged to the 'class of '92', but it's significant that while Nicky Butt, David Beckham, Gary Neville and Ryan Giggs all played regularly throughout United's famous Youth Cup victory that year, Scholes didn't play a single minute, and also made his first-team breakthrough later.

Although a prodigiously talented youngster, there were major concerns about Scholes's lack of physicality. He played alongside future teammates Butt and Neville even before joining Manchester United, in the all-conquering Boundary Park youth side. 'He might have stood out to the trained eye for his lovely skills, but as a 15-year-old my first thought was that he was too small,' remembered Neville. Mike Walsh, Boundary Park's manager at the time, described Scholes as 'like a baby' in terms of stature, and tried to protect him against physical opposition, which included playing him on the right flank, although Scholes was 'always drifting into the middle because he wanted to play centre-forward'.

Upon joining Manchester United, Scholes suffered from knee problems and bronchitis, while youth coach Eric Harrison, responsible for developing the class of '92, admitted Scholes had 'no real pace, no strength' and needed to convince him that this wasn't a barrier to success. Ferguson was also unconvinced by Scholes's physical capabilities. One day in training he turned to his assistant Jim Ryan and said of Scholes, 'He's got no chance, he's a midget.' But the more he watched Scholes, the more he appreciated his technical quality.

When breaking through, Scholes was a deep-lying forward rather than a midfielder. Harrison said he reminded him of Kenny Dalglish, while Ferguson expressed concerns about playing him in the same side as Cantona because they were too similar. 'When Eric goes, that's when he will really emerge as a really key player,' Ferguson said. 'They play in similar positions, and I have him marked down as Eric's successor.' Scholes made his debut up front in a 2–0 League Cup victory over Port Vale in 1994, wearing the number 10 shirt and scoring both goals, a calm dink over the goalkeeper, then a powerful near-post header. But physical concerns remained a problem. 'There was no getting away from the fact that Paul was small for a centre-forward,' Ferguson later recalled, 'And it was also clear that he didn't have the requisite pace for that role.'

After initially playing him in various positions, more in midfield than attack, Ferguson stuck to his word after Cantona's retirement in 1997 and used Scholes in the Frenchman's role. He was a classic number 10, and his first six starts of 1997/98 saw him playing just behind Teddy Sheringham or Andy Cole, with Butt and Roy Keane the two central midfielders. However, Keane's season-ending knee injury in September meant United suddenly lacked options in midfield, so Scholes retreated to a position alongside Butt, with Beckham and Giggs either side. That became his default role – at least at club level.

Scholes made his England debut that summer against South Africa, introduced in place of Sheringham to play off Ian Wright. He assisted England's winner within ten minutes, a classic strike partnership goal, with Scholes's flicked header finding Wright, who finished first-time. England's manager at the time, Glenn Hoddle, was perfect for a cultured, un-English footballer like Scholes, who was all about technical skills rather than physicality, and he also starred in the Tournoi de France, a World Cup warm-up event, again combining brilliantly with Wright as they assisted one another in England's 2–0 win over Italy. He quickly became a first-team regular, partly because of Paul Gascoigne's sudden decline, and by the 1998 World Cup, only a year after his debut, was handed the number 10 role behind Alan Shearer and Michael Owen in a 3–4–1–2 system largely based around him. He scored seven goals in his first 16 games, including a hat-trick in a 3–1 victory over Poland in 1999, Kevin Keegan's first game in charge, then hit two in the crucial Euro 2000 play-off away at Scotland.

Before that two-legged play-off, Scholes was rested for a friendly against Belgium. The man who took his place was debutant Frank Lampard, and this is where the rivalry for England's attacking midfield slot began.

Lampard was a very different player to Scholes. He'd enjoyed the perfect footballing upbringing; his dad, also named Frank, was a West Ham legend, playing 660 games at left-back, and was twice capped by England. By the mid-1990s Frank Snr was West Ham's assistant manager under Harry Redknapp, who was also his brother-in-law – that, of course, meant Redknapp was Lampard Jr's uncle, and England international Jamie Redknapp was his cousin. Lampard also remembers Bobby Moore dropping around for cups of tea and chats about West Ham – he was immersed in football from an early age.

Lampard lacked the natural ability of a player like Scholes, however, admitting that other West Ham youth products such as Joe Cole, Rio Ferdinand and Michael Carrick had more technical quality, and his defining feature was his incredible dedication and commitment. More than anything, this was about improving his physical qualities. Often mocked for being chubby in his younger days, Lampard spent hours sprinting the length of his back garden in running spikes, and stayed behind at West Ham's training ground for solo shuttle runs, charging repeatedly from box to box. At one point a teammate caught him performing a drill on a wet pitch that involved running a short distance between two cones, then sliding across the ground at the end, simulating a slide tackle, then getting up and doing the same in the opposite direction. There was no ball, no opponent; Lampard was purely concerned with the physical aspect of the skill. He unexpectedly made his first start for West Ham in late 1996, for a League Cup game against Stockport when John Moncur came down with flu. Typically, when he received the call from his dad informing him of the selection, Lampard was at the park doing sprint exercises.

Lampard faced constant accusations of nepotism from West Ham supporters during his early years, and retains genuine antipathy towards their fan base. At a 1996 fans' forum, which featured a panel including Harry Redknapp, Lampard Jnr and other members of the coaching and playing staff, a supporter implied that Redknapp had given special treatment to his nephew, releasing 'better' midfielders like Matt Holland, who enjoyed a fine Premier League career, and Scott Canham, who spent his career in the lower leagues. 'He will go right to the very top,' Redknapp hit back. 'He's got everything that's needed to become a top-class midfield player; his attitude is first-class, he's got strength, he can play, he can pass it and he can score goals.'

Lampard was always a box-to-box midfielder who prided himself on making constant runs and getting into goalscoring positions, hitting a hat-trick in a League Cup tie against Walsall in 1997/98, his first season as a regular. He was annoyed when England U21 manager Peter Taylor took him aside and suggested his long-term future was as a holding player, but also rejected the idea that he was a mere goalscorer. 'I didn't want to be a goalscoring midfielder in the mould of Robert Pirès or Gus Poyet,' he said. 'I wanted to be a midfielder who scored goals – someone who was involved in all aspects of the play, from defending to making the final pass, as well as hitting the back of the net regularly.'

Lampard's England debut in late 1999 – when he started alongside his cousin, Jamie Redknapp – probably came a little early. His second appearance was in Sven-Göran Eriksson's first game in charge, 18 months later, his next start was two and a half years later, and his first international goal nearly four years later, in August 2003. He wasn't involved at Euro 2000 or the 2002 World Cup, by which time he'd moved to Chelsea. In the meantime someone else had established himself as Scholes's midfield partner in Eriksson's 4–4–2 system: Steven Gerrard.

Born and raised in Liverpool, Gerrard joined the club's academy when he was nine and played in youth teams alongside Michael Owen from the age of 11. There was, however, something unique about Gerrard's young football experience. His cousin Jon-Paul Gilhooley – a couple of years older and a huge Liverpool fan – was the youngest person killed at the Hillsborough disaster in 1989. They regularly played football together in the street outside Gerrard's house in Huyton, and Gerrard spoke about the impact Jon-Paul's death had on his football career. 'Whenever I saw his parents during my trainee days, it gave me an extra determination to succeed.'

Gerrard was an excellent passer from a young age, although his football career was nearly over at the age of ten because of a freak accident. When playing football near his house the ball bounced into a patch of nettles. In an attempt to retrieve it Gerrard launched a big kick at the undergrowth, only to plough his foot straight into an upturned garden fork, which became embedded in his big toe. At the hospital there was serious talk of having to amputate the toe, which prompted Gerrard's father to phone Steve Heighway, Liverpool's academy director, who rushed to the hospital to convince the doctors not to. Whether his impact made any difference is questionable, but the toe survived.

Like Lampard, Gerrard was rejected by the FA's Centre of Excellence in his teenage years and therefore continued at Liverpool, and like Scholes, there was concern about his lack of physicality. In 1998 he made his first-team debut at the age of 18 as a substitute right-back, while his first start was as a right-wing-back against Tottenham, marking David Ginola. But Gerrard was clearly a central midfielder, and his first game in that position, against a Celta Vigo team featuring Claude Makélélé, saw him named man of the match.

Opportunities were limited for the next couple of years and Gerrard was often forced to play on the right, but he became a regular in early 2000 alongside the defensive-minded Didi Hamann. Gerrard played a role comparable to Patrick Vieira at that time; although he had licence to storm forward into attack and scored some fine long-range goals, he was essentially a defensive midfielder charged with breaking up the opposition's play. During his early years the most distinctive feature of Gerrard's game was his aggressive tackling, something that prompted concerns. At one stage Heighway called Gerrard's father to ask if his home life was alright because he showed such aggression in training, and at 16 Gerrard was sent to a sports psychologist, Bill Beswick, in an attempt to stop him lunging into tackles. He was twice dismissed in Merseyside derbies for awful tackles on Kevin Campbell and Gary Naysmith, once left Arsène Wenger fuming after a challenge on Vieira in a Community Shield game, and was dismissed for a tackle on Aston Villa's George Boateng that was so bad he felt compelled to phone the Dutchman and apologise. 'The physical nature of the Premiership suits my style,' he said. 'Tackle and be tackled, get up and get on with it.'

Gerrard was fast-tracked into the England squad, where he was blown away by Scholes's ability in training. 'He was just so sharp, so

clever,' he remembered. 'He was banging goals in from everywhere
– crossing, finishing, volleys, the power on his shots, the dip and the
movement.' His debut came in May 2000, a 2–0 victory over Ukraine
playing holding midfield in a 3–5–2 behind Scholes and Steve
McManaman, and was so impressive that he was included in the
squad for Euro 2000 as an understudy for Paul Ince, playing half an
hour in England's 1–0 win over Germany. That performance was
memorable for a trademark crunching tackle on Hamann, his club
teammate. 'I don't think he deserved that tackle,' said Gerrard, ahead
of another meeting between the countries later that year. 'But he
shouldn't have squealed like a girl, should he?'

Ince retired from internationals after Euro 2000, and with limited
competition for the defensive-minded midfield slot – centre-backs
Gareth Southgate and Jamie Carragher occasionally being used there
– Gerrard became a regular under Eriksson. He was outstanding on
his sixth appearance, scoring the goal that put England ahead in the
famous 5–1 victory away at Germany.

However, this is where England's compromise in the centre of
midfield started. 'My job was to break everything up, smash the
Germans before they got going. I'd prefer to be more attack-minded,
but this was still good, banging into Germans,' recalled Gerrard, who
generally wore the number 4 shirt for England but took 8 at Liverpool,
underlining the difference in roles. It was notable, too, that he
remembers Scholes 'playing more defensive than normal' against
Germany, partly because of the tactical performance required, but
also because Gerrard was less disciplined than Scholes's usual
midfield partners, the likes of Ince, Nicky Butt and David Batty.

So while England recorded a significant victory, generally by
counter-attacking through Michael Owen and Emile Heskey rather
than outpassing Germany, they'd subtly started deploying neither
central midfielder in their optimum position. Both were playing

more defensively than they liked. There was little sign of Eriksson ditching the 4–4–2 system for an alternative shape – indeed, for all the controversy about England appointing their first-ever foreign boss, Eriksson was much more of an 'English' 4–4–2 man than Terry Venables, Hoddle or Keegan, in part because two Englishmen, Bob Houghton and Roy Hodgson, had introduced the 4–4–2 system to Eriksson's native Sweden in the 1970s.

Around this point, Scholes's performances for England dipped. His goalscoring rate slowed dramatically, partly because of this change in role; from seven goals in his first 16 internationals, he only managed seven more in his subsequent 50. He wasn't offering particularly authoritative passing displays, either; he was particularly poor in the famous 2–2 draw against Greece, when David Beckham's last-gasp free-kick sealed qualification to the 2002 World Cup, then was outperformed by Manchester United colleague Butt at the tournament itself, with Gerrard absent through injury.

Gerrard and Scholes became England's first-choice midfield partnership throughout qualification for Euro 2004, although Scholes's lack of goals had become a major talking point. At club level he'd been pushed forward to an attacking midfield position in a 4–4–1–1 formation behind Ruud van Nistelrooy, scoring a career-high 14 league goals in 2002/03. But going into Euro 2004 Scholes hadn't scored for England in three years. 'I'm in the team to score goals, and if I'm not doing that, I know there's a chance I won't be picked,' he admitted. 'I am expected to score. If that's not happening, I'm not contributing as much as I should be to the team. It's not just about me, either. When there are players like Frank Lampard having a great season, they probably deserve to be given a place in the starting line-up. If the manager were to pick him instead of me, I'd wish him all the best because I know I haven't done what I should have been doing.'

Lampard was thriving at Chelsea, partly thanks to Roman Abramovich's wealth turning them into title contenders, and partly because Claudio Ranieri changed Lampard's game, ordering him to become more conservative with his running in a 4–4–2 system. Upon signing Lampard, Ranieri said his game at West Ham had been 70:30 in terms of attacking and defending, whereas at Chelsea he wanted it to be 50:50. 'He wanted to balance my play by coaching me to be more aware of when to make runs forward, how to time them better,' Lampard said. Until then he had been so determined to showcase his stamina by outrunning opponents that he turned up inside the box and waited for service, almost as a bonus striker. Ranieri would constantly shout 'Stay!' to Lampard in training matches, wanting him to advance as attacks were developing, delaying his runs to the edge of the box. 'I learned how to react to play in individual situations, to sense when I might have the best chance of a goal,' he said. He became more tactically responsible.

Then came Euro 2004, which is unfairly remembered as the tournament when England underlined their distrust of creativity by deploying Scholes on the left flank. The reality was very different. Eriksson found himself with four outstanding central midfielders: Beckham, Lampard, Gerrard and Scholes. Beckham was captain and often England's saviour, Lampard had enjoyed the most impressive club season of the quartet, while Gerrard provided all-round midfield qualities and was undroppable. But Scholes, for all his incredible talent, simply wasn't playing well for England. All four were naturally creative, attack-minded midfielders, and Eriksson should probably have introduced a more functional holding player to provide some balance – Butt and Owen Hargreaves were also in the squad. If so, Scholes would have been the natural player to drop out. Eriksson's decision to keep him in the side, potentially compromising England's shape, underlined his faith in Scholes's talent.

Indeed, far from banishing him to the fringes, Eriksson tried to play a diamond midfield with Scholes, whom he later described as 'England's best player', at the top, the side effectively built around him. The diamond made sense. Gary Neville and Ashley Cole would overlap to provide the width, allowing the four midfielders to play centrally. It's significant that in this diamond system Lampard was deployed in front of the defence, underlining the extent to which he was considered England's most disciplined player, even if he disliked that deep role. Gerrard, meanwhile, was frustrated playing on the left of a diamond. He and Lampard wanted the advanced role, but Eriksson entrusted this to Scholes.

At Euro 2004 England tried the diamond system in a training session with disastrous consequences, the first XI finding themselves 3–0 down to a second-string side. Eriksson subsequently gathered the midfielders together and asked them which system they liked best. Scholes preferred the diamond, but the other three favoured the four-man midfield, so Eriksson reverted to 4–4–2. Scholes was disappointed, but it would have been ludicrous to ignore the majority to placate the one midfielder who, by his own admission, simply wasn't playing well enough. Furthermore, Scholes wasn't likely to last the duration of matches. Eriksson says that when England practised penalties in training during that tournament, Scholes didn't bother. When the Swede asked why, Scholes replied that he'd do well to make it past 60 minutes, let alone 120.

Playing Scholes centrally in a flat, attack-minded midfield would have been unwise. At this point, screening the defence was still widely considered to involve plenty of tackling, and this was unquestionably Scholes's weakness; each of his four managers – Ferguson, Hoddle, Keegan and Eriksson – highlighted tackling as a significant shortcoming in an otherwise flawless skill set. Scholes simply couldn't master the art of dispossessing opponents, wildly mistiming challenges and being punished particularly severely by continental referees; he is the most booked player in Champions League history. Eriksson simply couldn't risk a poor tackler who lacked stamina in a two-man central midfield.

Meanwhile, Gerrard was still renowned as a predominantly defensive midfielder, with Beckham specifically saying England were 'so much better balanced with him in the side', while Lampard had become more disciplined at Chelsea thanks to Ranieri's tutelage. Those two, at this stage, made the most sense as a central midfield partnership, and Scholes's left-sided positioning didn't prevent him from coming inside, especially with Cole overlapping. Indeed, Eriksson deploying a creator drifting inside from the left was a significant improvement upon the previous situation, when England had worried for years about their 'left-sided problem' solely because there was a dearth of talented left-footers around. It's notable that the three subsequent World Cup winners, Italy, Spain and Germany, featured natural central midfielders playing from the left: Simone Perrotta, Andrés Iniesta and Mesut Özil. There's no reason Scholes couldn't have played there successfully.

England broadly played well at Euro 2004, courtesy of a gung-ho approach that depended upon the precocious Wayne Rooney. His tournament-ending injury at the quarter-final stage, rather than Eriksson's system, was England's major problem. Scholes retired from international football afterwards, and repeatedly said his positioning wasn't the reason for his decision. 'A lot of people blamed Sven for me quitting England, but the truth is I played on the wing for Man United too and scored a lot of goals,' he said. It just wasn't working out with England, and Scholes admits he simply didn't enjoy international duty, particularly being away from his family for extended periods. However, much later he criticised England players for being too selfish. 'We have some of the best players,' he said, 'but maybe some of them are out there for personal glory.' Scholes's most significant contribution to the tactical development of English football would actually occur much later, in a considerably deeper role, which has seemingly convinced many he'd always played that position.

After Euro 2004 things changed dramatically in England's midfield zone. First, there was no more Scholes. Second, José Mourinho took charge of Chelsea and deployed Lampard in the left-centre position of a 4–3–3, giving him the most attacking role in Chelsea's midfield triangle. Third, Rafael Benítez arrived at Liverpool, and while he initially used Gerrard in the centre or the right of a 4–4–2, it became apparent that Gerrard's optimum position was at the top of midfield in a 4–2–3–1, with two holding midfielders behind him. It's worth underlining how brilliant Lampard and Gerrard were at this stage – in the 2005 Ballon d'Or they finished second and third respectively, behind Brazilian forward Ronaldinho. England therefore officially had Europe's best two footballers – and the world's best two midfielders – at their disposal.

Lampard was fundamentally a basic footballer. He had three primary strengths: he was excellent physically, timed his runs to the edge of the box perfectly and was superb at firing home from around 25 yards. As a youngster his dad's favourite motto was 'Simplicity is genius,' and Lampard proved this perfectly – few players reach his level, the world's second-best player, with such a straightforward game. Lampard's frequently scored from long-range, hitting the most Premier League goals from outside the box, but genuine thunderbolts were relatively rare. Instead, he possessed an uncanny knack of scoring slightly scuffy efforts from that range, often catching a favourable deflection or benefiting from a goalkeeping fumble. Interestingly, he says that this stemmed from a deliberate change.

'The increase in goals was in part due to changing my technique in hitting the ball,' he explained. 'I used to strike it much more true, which is fine if you can direct the ball into the corner at power. The modern football is lighter, though, and if you hit across it you can make it move around in flight, which makes it much harder for a keeper to save. Even Petr Čech ends up palming a shot that is coming straight at him into the net if you catch it right and it suddenly changes direction.' That summarises Lampard, efficient rather than beautiful.

Incidentally, the change in footballs themselves is often underestimated as a factor in the development of the game. Surprisingly, it took the Premier League until the late 1990s to insist upon a standard football – until that point, teams often had their own preferences. While the Mitre football dominated, Chelsea used an Umbro ball that goalkeepers considered unpredictable, while Liverpool's Adidas ball was faster through the air. It provided an extra dimension to the concept of home advantage.

Gerrard's tactical history, meanwhile, was more complex. Although Benítez often played 4–2–3–1, with Gerrard behind the main striker in big games, the Spaniard spent much of 2005/06 and 2006/07 convincing the media – and Gerrard himself – that he could play effectively on the right of a 4–4–2, pointing to his increased goalscoring return. However, Gerrard thrived when switched to a permanent position at the top of a 4–2–3–1, driving forward and becoming a regular goal threat. He credits Xabi Alonso for his ability to play that role. 'I didn't think I could play as a number 10,' Gerrard admitted. 'But I could, because of the amount of time Xabi gave me on the ball with his speed of thought.'

His tactical deployment could have been very different, however, because Gerrard came extremely close to leaving Liverpool to join Lampard at Chelsea. There were initial rumours about the switch in

2004, but a year later, shortly after Gerrard led Liverpool to the Champions League, he handed in a transfer request when Liverpool rejected a British record fee from Chelsea. Gerrard later insisted he never wanted to leave, blaming Liverpool's poor handling of contract negotiations, but had the transfer materialised – as briefly seemed inevitable – Gerrard and Lampard would have played together week in, week out, in Mourinho's 4–3–3, and Eriksson would have felt compelled to replicate that template. Instead, the transfer never materialised, Gerrard withdrew his transfer request and Chelsea turned to Michael Essien instead.

The opening game of the 2006 World Cup qualifiers, away at Austria, set the tone for what followed. Without Scholes to worry about, Eriksson provided some midfield balance by using Wayne Bridge on the left flank. Beckham was still on the right, and Lampard and Gerrard again started centrally. Lampard and Gerrard both underlined their attacking capabilities by scoring to put England 2–0 ahead, but then both showed defensive lapses to allow Austria to snatch a point. First, Lampard conceded a free-kick that was fired home by Roland Kollmann, then Gerrard got caught ahead of play and desperately tried to recover and block Andreas Ivanschitz's shot, only managing a deflection that helped the ball squirm under David James. This was the start of a debate that dominated much of the ensuing decade: could Gerrard and Lampard play together?

Really, of course, the question was whether they could play together in the centre of a 4–4–2. Although the obvious move was switching to a 4–3–3 to get the best from both, Eriksson was dissuaded because three other key players were all more suited to a 4–4–2: Beckham, a right-sided crossing midfielder; Rooney, a second striker; and Michael Owen, a quick goalpoacher who needed a partner. Eriksson continued to shift between the diamond, which England never looked comfortable in, and 4–4–2, with Gerrard and

Lampard together in midfield, a system that worked against minnows in qualifiers but seemed unworkable against major opposition. There was a brief experiment with 4–3–3 away at Northern Ireland, when David Beckham played the holding role behind Gerrard and Lampard, with Shaun Wright-Phillips and Rooney either side of Owen. That failed miserably in a 1–0 defeat, as Beckham, in Eriksson's words, 'kept hitting long passes that seldom found their target'. It was interesting, though, that Eriksson believed that Owen could play up front and Rooney could play on the left of a 4–3–3, but didn't think that Beckham was suited to the right in that system. Beckham, therefore, was the barrier to playing 4–3–3, especially after underperforming in the deep role.

By the 2006 World Cup, Eriksson's final tournament, the situation had become entirely confused. For a pre-tournament friendly against Hungary, Gerrard was stunned when handed the number 9 shirt and instructed to play just behind lone striker Michael Owen. It was a 4–1–3–1–1 system, with Carragher in the holding role and Beckham, Lampard and Joe Cole across midfield. This seemingly suited everyone nicely and England won 3–1, but then Eriksson used 4–4–2 with Gerrard and Lampard together for an inevitable thrashing of Jamaica, and stuck with that system throughout the group stage. Peculiarly, though, Gerrard was asked to play the more defensive of the two central midfield roles; in one system he was deployed significantly in advance of Lampard, in the other he was slightly deeper. It's no wonder they never developed any understanding.

Owen sustained a serious knee injury in the final group game against Sweden, and for the knockout stages England switched to a 4–1–4–1 system: Rooney was up front alone, and Eriksson introduced a holding midfielder, allowing Gerrard and Lampard freedom to attack. In the second-round win over Ecuador, Michael Carrick played the holding role and was absolutely outstanding, controlling the tempo and playing penetrative passes. He was harshly dropped for the quarter-final against Portugal, with Hargreaves switching from right-back to the holding role. The Portugal game, where England were eliminated on penalties, was when everyone realised the importance of a holding midfielder.

Hargreaves had been the subject of sustained, unreasonable criticism going into the tournament, primarily because he was a rare England player who had never, at that stage, played his football in England. Few in English football watched the Bundesliga, although it was obvious Hargreaves offered quality, purely from the fact that he'd won four Bundesliga titles and the Champions League as a regular in Bayern Munich's midfield. Still, large sections of the English press were oblivious to Hargreaves's quality before the tournament, to the extent that one journalist asked Lampard at a press conference: 'What is the point of Owen Hargreaves?' A month later Hargreaves was widely acknowledged to have been England's best performer in the quarter-final, and was subsequently voted England fans' player of the year. Gerrard and Lampard remained England's best midfielders, but it was obvious they required a holding player behind them. Combined with two seasons of Makélélé-inspired Chelsea success in the Premier League, the holding player had never been so popular.

This was evident throughout England's ultimately disastrous Euro 2008 qualifying campaign under Steve McClaren, who at least understood the requirement for a holding player, fielding at least one of Hargreaves, Carrick or Gareth Barry in 11 of the 12 matches. The partnership between Barry and Gerrard worked well, partly because they'd become close friends as the youngest squad members at Euro 2000. England were largely very disciplined, keeping a clean sheet in nine of the 12 qualification games, and the real problem was attack, as England suffered two goalless draws against Macedonia and Israel.

Then came that infamous home defeat against Croatia. An improbable series of events meant England only required a draw at Wembley against a team who had already qualified and therefore had nothing to play for. Barry, Lampard and Gerrard were the midfield trio in a 4-3-3, but England started nervously, epitomised by the awful performance of goalkeeper Scott Carson, making his competitive debut. England found themselves 2-0 down at half-time. McClaren sacrificed Barry and switched to 4-4-2, England went all-out-attack and recovered to 2-2. They were on course for qualification. But then, crucially, McClaren didn't seek control by introducing an extra holding midfielder; Hargreaves remained on the bench, and Gerrard and Lampard were overrun. It would be unfair to suggest a holding midfielder would have entirely solved the problem – England had conceded twice with Barry on the pitch – but it was the obvious approach when England simply needed to see out 25 minutes without conceding.

England, despite not needing a third goal, seemingly felt their natural attacking game was working better and kept on pushing forward, but the nature of their concession felt inevitable. Mladen Petrić collected the ball just outside the box in space, exactly where a holding midfielder would have been positioned – Lampard had been dragged towards the flank and Gerrard was slow to close down – and the Croatian forward fired home. England were eliminated, and even Gerrard realised England's tactical naivety. 'When you are 2-0 down you have to take risks, and there was a big improvement in the second half. We got back into the game,' he said. 'We should have shut up shop then. When you get back into it, you've got to see it out and take a draw. But we took risks and got done on the counter-attack.'

2008 was the year in which the Premier League became UEFA's top-ranked league for the first time. But it was also the year in which

England failed to qualify for the European Championships. England boasted the best league in Europe but weren't among its best 16 international sides. The difference, more than anything else, was about tactical intelligence, underlining the Premier League's reliance on foreign influences for strategic nous.

Part Six

Direct Attacking

16

Roonaldo

*'All the premeditated tactical theories I had learned
about getting and staying in your shape and tracking
back with your runner, all the things that had been
drummed into me, were thrown out over two years
because we had a player who could make up his own
rules with the blessing of his team-mates. Ronaldo
has helped to redefine the game.'*

Gary Neville

Despite the woes of the national side, by 2008 the Premier League
was officially Europe's best according to UEFA's somewhat complex
coefficient system. You didn't need a full understanding of their
methodology, however, to realise the superiority of the English top
flight.

For three consecutive seasons, 2006/07, 2007/08 and 2008/09, the
Premier League provided three of the four Champions League
semi-finalists, an unprecedented level of dominance. In truth, this
wasn't converted into enough outright success, and in four consecutive years – Arsenal in 2006, Liverpool in 2007, Chelsea in 2008 and

Manchester United in 2009 – each member of the Big Four was a defeated finalist. It took an all-Premier League final, in 2008, for an English club to taste success during these years, when Manchester United defeated Chelsea after a dramatic penalty shoot-out.

Manchester United were unquestionably the Premier League's best side; in this three-year period they won the title every season as Sir Alex Ferguson created his greatest team. The defensive quartet of Gary Neville, Rio Ferdinand, Nemanja Vidić and Patrice Evra was so cohesive that all four were voted into the PFA Team of the Year for 2006/07, the only time this has happened in the Premier League, while Edwin van der Sar was United's best goalkeeper since Peter Schmeichel, keeping an incredible, record-breaking 14 consecutive clean sheets midway through 2008/09. The midfield was boosted by the addition of Michael Carrick and Owen Hargreaves, while Paul Scholes played an increasingly withdrawn role and became an outstanding deep-lying playmaker.

More than anything, however, this side was defined by its attacking flair and versatility. The interchanging of positions between Wayne Rooney, Carlos Tevez and Cristiano Ronaldo was spectacular at times, with the latter producing arguably the best-ever individual Premier League campaign in 2007/08 with 31 goals in 31 starts, realising his ambition of becoming the world's best by winning that year's Ballon d'Or. He represented an entirely new type of Manchester United team, because Ferguson – and assistant Carlos Queiroz – created Europe's most complete side by playing without a genuine striker.

Not since Blackburn's Ray Harford had an assistant exerted such influence upon the tactical approach of the title winners. This was Queiroz's second stint at United – he was Ferguson's assistant in 2002/03 but left to become Real Madrid's manager, before being dismissed after a year and returning to his old job at Old Trafford.

The fact that United's assistant was considered talented enough to manage Real – one of the few clubs in Europe deemed bigger than United and a club who regularly poached United's stars – spoke volumes about his reputation. His four-year spell from 2004 to 2008 helped United revolutionise attacking football.

Ferguson described Queiroz as 'brilliant, just brilliant – outstanding, an intelligent, meticulous man' and deferred to him in terms of tactics. While the process of moving from 4–4–2 to 4–5–1 had started upon Ruud van Nistelrooy's arrival in 2001, with mixed results, this was still a controversial formation for United's supporters. The reputation of José Mourinho's Chelsea meant one-striker systems were considered a sure-fire sign of defensive football, and Queiroz became a target for some fans, who blamed him for the shift away from United's 'traditional' way of playing, even chanting 'four–four–two!' in protest at the new system. Queiroz hit back, somewhat unwisely, midway through 2005/06. 'People have been crying out for us to use a 4–4–2 formation but in the Blackburn game we tried the system and we lost,' he complained. 'That's why football is a game in which imagination and, on many occasions, stupidity has no limits.' He remained convinced that United needed to move away from immobile central strikers. As coach of Portugal's 'golden generation' at both youth and full international level in the early 1990s he created the style of football that country became renowned for: a solid defence, plenty of possession, brilliantly tricky wingers, creative playmakers – and a centre-forward based around movement rather than goals.

United's era of success started immediately after the departure of Ruud van Nistelrooy in 2006. For all the Dutchman's goals, he simply wasn't appropriate for the type of side Ferguson and Queiroz wanted. Van Nistelrooy, as we've established, was nothing more than a penalty-box poacher, whereas this new United team was based around movement, selflessness, cohesion and counter-attacking. After United won the title in 2006/07, Ferguson was asked whether he'd made two big decisions the previous year, sanctioning the departures of Van Nistelrooy and Roy Keane. 'Well … Roy was, certainly, because he was such an influence on the club,' Ferguson replied. 'But I'm not sure about Van Nistelrooy being a big decision at all.' That spoke volumes. Now it was all about Ronaldo and Rooney – although Ferguson's intention of building the team around them nearly proved fatal after an incident at the 2006 World Cup.

Midway through England and Portugal's quarter-final – which England went on to lose on penalties – Rooney battled Ricardo Carvalho for the ball. Both fell to the ground and, upon getting to his feet, Rooney stepped backwards and stamped on Carvalho. Ronaldo immediately raced over to referee Horacio Elizondo, gesturing wildly towards the prostrate Carvalho to draw attention to Rooney's misdemeanor. Rooney reacted by grabbing Ronaldo and pushing him away. Elizondo showed Rooney the red card for his stamp, and England never recovered. Worse was to follow. TV footage caught Ronaldo winking, seemingly towards the Portugal dugout, in the aftermath of the incident, while a pre-match clip showed Ronaldo approaching Rooney from behind, sticking his head into Rooney's, whispering something and then gently headbutting him. These three clips created a narrative that Ronaldo had got Rooney dismissed, which somewhat ignored the fact that Rooney had stamped on an opponent's groin entirely through his own volition. The recently retired Alan Shearer, now a pundit for the BBC, led the fury. 'I think there's every chance Rooney could go back to the Manchester United training ground and stick one on Ronaldo,' he said. This was disastrous for United – their two star players were seemingly at war.

Ultimately, there was little resentment. 'I bear no ill feeling to Cristiano but I am disappointed he chose to get involved,' Rooney said afterwards. Handily, they bumped into one another after the match and agreed to put the incident behind them, and Rooney texted Ronaldo to further clear the air. 'The things that have been said regarding me and my teammate and friend Rooney are incredible,' said Ronaldo. 'He wished me the best of luck in the World Cup. He wasn't angry and told me to completely ignore what the English press has said, that all they wanted was to create confusion, but we are already used to that.' Rooney was even intelligent enough to realise Ronaldo's antics worked in his favour. 'I was happy I didn't get the stick Becks got [in 1998] and even Phil Neville did after Euro 2000,' he admitted. 'I didn't really get any stick – Ronaldo took a lot of it and I'm pleased with that.'

Upon Ronaldo and Rooney's return to training, Ferguson sat them down together for a pep talk but both agreed there was no need – they'd sorted things out themselves. There was, disappointingly, no call for the boxing gloves a teammate had brought into training. It would have been a good fight; what Rooney gave away in height and reach he made up in experience, having trained in his uncle's boxing gym throughout his early teenage years. No wonder Ronaldo spent his summer bulking up and improving his upper body, arriving back in Manchester a completely different beast.

Crucially, Ferguson flew to Portugal in the aftermath of the World Cup to dissuade Ronaldo from his rumoured switch to Real Madrid, assuring him United's post-Van Nistelrooy side would be based primarily around him. Although this seems an obvious move in hindsight, with Ronaldo's ludicrous goalscoring figures and multiple Ballons d'Or, it's worth remembering that he was briefly considered something of a laughing stock in English football. Although sensational on a memorable debut against Bolton Wanderers in 2003, Ronaldo struggled badly at points during his first couple of seasons, and his tendency to make multiple stepovers prompted considerable derision. On more than one occasion opponents got sick of his show-boating and simply kicked him off the park – although he gradually become accustomed to this treatment, as something similar happened in training. 'We all saw the huge potential he had,' said Rio Ferdinand. 'When he came over here, his first thought was to enter-tain. We wanted to win. We knew that if we had an end product, we had a far better chance of being successful. For want of a better word, we were kicking it out of him, the entertainment factor, to get goals and assists.' Ronaldo became a different type of player, about effi-ciency and directness rather than skills, and United's other attackers – including Rooney – played a backseat role.

United didn't suffer from Ronaldo and Rooney's squabble. In their opening game of 2006/07, they were 4–0 up against Fulham within 19 minutes when Rooney crossed for a fine Ronaldo half-volley. United eventually won 5–1. 'With Ruud gone, the manager wants us to work on a style of football that will blow everyone away,' outlined Rooney. 'He sets up the team to have bags of pace with myself, Ronaldo and Louis Saha up front. We're being told to counter-attack at speed. He reckons teams will find it impossible to play against us.'

Two games in early autumn away at north-west rivals showed United's quality. First, they battered Bolton 4–0 with a quite wonder-ful display, featuring a Rooney hat-trick and one for Ronaldo, assisted by a selfless square pass from Saha. There was movement, interplay and unpredictability. 'The best we have played for years,' marvelled Ferguson. At Blackburn they only won 1–0, but it was another hugely impressive attacking performance, with Ronaldo so brilliant that although the Blackburn Rovers fans started the match by booing him for his World Cup transgression, they ended the night giving him a standing ovation when he was substituted in the 90th minute. The highlight came when he was flattened by an awful tackle from Blackburn winger Sergio Peter – whereas once he would have rolled around for ages, Ronaldo simply got up and carried on. He, Rooney, Giggs and Saha buzzed around almost uncontrollably. 'It's as good as I've seen United for a good few seasons,' said Blackburn manager Mark Hughes, who likened them to the United title-winners of 1992/93, when he played up front. 'The angles of their passing, their rotation of movement, the interchanging, they just pick you off … This side, without Van Nistelrooy, is more dynamic.' United were top after 37 of the Premier League's 38 matchdays, on their way to their first title in four years.

Manchester United were not quite strikerless yet, however. Van Nistelrooy had departed, but Saha, Ole Gunnar Solskjær and Alan Smith remained. All three found themselves compromised by injury but played important roles in 2006/07, while United also benefited from Henrik Larsson's brief mid-season loan spell. In the vast majority of matches, therefore, United used a conventional striker – but all four contributed heavily to interplay: Saha's movement was sensational, Solskjær always linked well, Smith held up the ball effectively, while Larsson was an intelligent all-round forward. Nevertheless, United's joint-top goalscorers that season were Ronaldo and Rooney, both managing 23 in all competitions. United generally used a proper striker, but he wasn't the major goal threat.

United's most significant encounter that season was a two-legged Champions League tie against Roma. The second leg, an outstanding 7–1 victory Ferguson described as United's greatest European performance during his tenure, was notable for brilliant performances from Carrick in his deep-lying playmaking role and Smith as an old-fashioned battering ram up front. But the first leg, a 2–1 defeat in Rome, was surprisingly more significant. Ferguson always learned his greatest lessons from European competition, and Roma boss Luciano Spalletti defeated United with an unusual system often described as 4–6–0. Their most advanced player was legendary captain Francesco Totti, considerably more of a number 10 than a number 9. He dropped deep, peeling off into midfield and creating space for teammates to exploit. While Ferguson had ditched the pure goalpoacher, Spalletti had ditched strikers entirely. Ferguson, as always, would adjust his side to keep pace with tactical innovations.

That summer Solskjær retired and Smith moved to Newcastle, while Saha's injury problems restricted him to just six league starts in 2007/08. Meanwhile, Ferguson signed Carlos Tevez, a surprising move considering the Argentine was, like Rooney, considered a second striker rather than a pure goalscorer. But the Scot had a plan. 'I've read all these opinions about the two of them being identical,' he said. 'I don't think they are at all. What you can say is they both have a similar physique, they are both two-footed, they are both quick-ish, they can both beat a man. I don't think it's a bad thing in terms of the similarities. When they get playing with each other they will hopefully get an understanding about where they are playing.' It's an intriguing quote. Ferguson didn't suggest one would permanently play behind the other, or that one would be shifted wide. He instead envisaged them working out positional responsibilities naturally, gradually developing the understanding to dovetail and rotate. That's precisely what happened.

Initially things weren't promising. United stumbled to a goalless draw at home to Reading on the opening weekend; the lack of a penalty-box threat was so obvious that Ferguson deployed substitute John O'Shea as an emergency centre-forward. The Irishman was renowned for his versatility, but a striking role was somewhat out of his comfort zone. After a 1–1 draw at Portsmouth and a 1–0 defeat at Manchester City there were serious questions about United's approach, with just two points from three matches. But injuries and suspensions meant United hadn't yet fielded their three attackers in tandem, and when Rooney, Ronaldo and Tevez started together for the first time, against Chelsea, United won 2–0. This, incidentally, was Chelsea's first game after Mourinho's sudden departure, and it felt poetic that the debut of United's revolutionary new system came immediately after the Premier League's previous innovator had left. It was the start of something special, and United's reward would eventually come eight months later, after another meeting with Avram Grant's Chelsea.

During 2007/08 it was impossible to define Manchester United's system. The rotation between the attackers – generally including Ronaldo, Rooney and Tevez but sometimes one of Nani, Park Ji-sung and Ryan Giggs too – was exceptional. At times United's basic shape looked like a 4–3–3, on other occasions it was 4–4–2, but ultimately it was fluid, flexible and fantastic to watch. In some matches, particularly at home to weaker sides, the attackers had no set positions and simply had responsibility to cover the wide areas between them when possession was lost. Tevez and Rooney struck up a fine relationship, helped by the fact that Rooney drove the Argentine into training most mornings, despite admitting that they rarely talked because Tevez spoke such little English. They sacrificed their own abilities to get the best from Ronaldo, and while they were among the Premier League's most talented footballers, they received most praise for their energy and work rate.

At this stage such attacking fluidity was extremely rare in the Premier League, with the division still based around the structured systems that became popular when Mourinho and Rafael Benítez joined the league in 2004. Chelsea still played a Mourinho-esque system under Grant, who changed little. Benítez still asked his wide players to play linear roles, not allowing his attackers any freedom of movement. Even Arsène Wenger's Arsenal were at their most structured during this period; for their two away Champions League knockout matches at AC Milan and Liverpool in 2007/08, Wenger used an uncharacteristically defensive-minded wide midfield combination: box-to-box midfielder Abou Diaby and natural right-back Emmanuel Eboué. That – considering Wenger had used Robert Pirès and Freddie Ljungberg a couple of seasons earlier – was quite remarkable. Of course, Ferguson's continued use of Park was almost exclusively because the Korean was hard-working defensively and nullified opposition full-backs, but United's level of attacking rotation was nevertheless completely different to anything else in the Premier League and effectively marked the return of exciting, free-flowing attacking play after a period of defensive, cautious football. It's worth remembering the age of United's attackers, too; at the start of 2007/08 Rooney and Ronaldo were 22, Tevez 23. This felt like something genuinely new.

Ronaldo thrived with this freedom. He'd play on the right, the left and through the middle at different points in the same match, with the likes of Rooney, Tevez and Park expected to fill in wherever necessary. Ronaldo was absolutely ruthless, simply positioning himself in the appropriate position to get goals. 'He sniffs blood, he will find the weakness in the back four,' Gary Neville recalled a few years later. 'If he's not getting the left-back in the first 15 minutes, he'll switch to the right-back. If he's not getting the right-back, he'll switch to the left-centre-back. He'll find someone in your back four who is weak and doesn't like defending one on one, and against pace and power.'

Ronaldo enjoyed a perfect combination: Ferguson's trust, Queiroz's tactics and individual training sessions with René Meulensteen. The highly rated Dutchman worked with Ronaldo for hours, turning him into a ruthless goalscoring machine by getting him to finish in an efficient rather than a spectacular manner. It was a holistic process, involving drawing diagrams, visualising goalscoring situations, splitting the final third into zones to help his decision-making, and assigning different colours to the four corners of the goal. Meulensteen encouraged Ronaldo to be more like Alan Shearer, Gary Lineker, Solskjær – and Van Nistelrooy – when in front of goal. It proved transformative, and Ronaldo became only the fifth player (after Shearer, Andy Cole, Kevin Phillips and Thierry Henry) to hit 30 goals in a Premier League season. But whereas three of those were traditional number 9s, and Henry a roving attacker, Ronaldo wasn't a striker at all.

Or was he? Ferguson used United's attacking versatility in a more clinical manner for big matches, particularly in Europe. His attackers stuck to positions with greater discipline within games – but not always the same positions from game to game. For example, in United's 2–0 victory away against old foes Roma in the Champions League quarter-final first leg, Ronaldo was deployed up front, with Park and Rooney playing functional, hard-working roles on the flanks in a 4–3–3 that became 4–5–1 for long periods. Ferguson wanted Ronaldo to use his searing pace in behind, and he showed traditional centre-forward qualities too, with a towering header to put United ahead. But Ronaldo spent long periods drifting to the flanks and leaving the Roma centre-backs without anyone to mark; the most significant aspect of his header was that he started his run-up from extremely deep – he was only United's sixth most-advanced player as the attack developed. For most of the game he played as a false nine, the most advanced players being Park or Rooney. United were strikerless, yet had a towering aerial threat and the Premier League's top goalscorer as their most advanced attacker.

In the return leg, with Ronaldo unavailable and Rooney only on the bench, Ferguson used a more defensive-minded 4–5–1; Tevez was up front, continually dropping deep with sporadic support from Park and Giggs out wide. 'They're even more Italian than we are,' grumbled a frustrated Roma boss Spalletti afterwards. He was presumably commenting on United's defence-first approach, but probably knew that United's inspiration had come from his own team.

In the 1-0 aggregate victory over Barcelona in the semi-finals, Ronaldo was again deployed up front, but this time Ferguson used Tevez in the number 10 role, giving United two points of attack in a 4-4-1-1 both home and away. Park and either Rooney or Nani were deployed wide. United won the contest in the second leg thanks to a Paul Scholes long-range drive – his first goal for eight months, demonstrating his increasingly deep role. The key, though, was United's brilliant organisation without the ball, which owed much to Queiroz's tactical work. One afternoon he laid out mats on the floor in United's gym prescribing the exact shape he wanted, surprising United's players by placing Scholes and Carrick's mats almost together. The key, he insisted, was ensuring Barcelona didn't play penetrative passes between them. The Catalans barely created a chance.

Then came the final in Moscow, which felt like the Premier League's high-water mark – England's two best teams competing for the right to be considered the best in Europe. It was a historic occasion for both. For United it was the 50th anniversary of the Munich air disaster and the 40th anniversary of their first European Cup victory, while Chelsea were determined to lift club football's greatest prize in the home country of owner Roman Abramovich. It was also a slightly surreal match; the time difference between Russia and Western Europe meant that the game kicked off at 10.45 pm local time and didn't finish until 1.30 am, by which time a biblical downpour meant the game was played in horrendous conditions.

For this game United's system was more 4-4-2. Rooney and Tevez were up front together, and Ronaldo was switched to the left specifically because Ferguson wanted him up against Michael Essien, a midfielder out of position at right-back. Sure enough, Ronaldo towered over Essien to meet Wes Brown's right-wing cross and nod United into the lead. Although United failed to defeat Chelsea in 120 minutes, they were the better side for the majority of the game, Ferguson's two major tactical decisions giving them the upper hand. The decision to use Ronaldo wide-left was vindicated by his opener, while Tevez and Rooney both dropped deep from their centre-forward roles, helping United to dominate possession and create the better chances. Frank Lampard equalised with a fortunate goal on the stroke of half-time, and at the start of the second period Chelsea rallied. But then Ferguson changed system, switching from 4–4–2 to 4–5–1 by putting Rooney on the right and asking Owen Hargreaves to tuck inside and become a third central midfielder alongside Carrick and Scholes. United reasserted their dominance.

It eventually all came down to penalty kicks. And while a decade or so earlier it was customary to refer to this as the 'lottery of a penalty shoot-out', research and opposition scouting had improved considerably, to the point that it was no longer a lottery and more about complex game theory. In a tactical sense the shoot-out was arguably more intriguing than the previous 120 minutes.

As revealed in Simon Kuper and Stefan Szymanski's *Soccernomics*, Chelsea's penalty strategy appears to have been influenced by the work of Ignacio Palacios-Huerta, a Basque economist who had been recording penalty patterns for 13 years. An academic colleague of his happened to be friends with Chelsea manager Grant, and he put them in touch. Palacios-Huerta then sent Grant a report about United's penalty habits.

Along with the revelation that the team taking the first penalty in a shoot-out triumphs 60 per cent of the time, there were two crucial points concerning United. First, goalkeeper Edwin van der Sar anticipated penalty takers would shoot across their body – he usually dived to his right against right-footed takers and to his left against left-footed takers. Shooting the other way, therefore, made sense. Second, Cristiano Ronaldo tended to pause in his run-up, hoping the goalkeeper would dive early, and after his pause he kicked left 85 per cent of the time. This information nearly worked a treat.

United won both tosses before the shoot-out. It meant that the penalties took place in front of their own supporters and that Rio Ferdinand, as captain, had the choice of whether to kick first or second. Ferdinand, however, was unsure about what to do and turned towards United's coaching staff, taking some time to make his decision. At this point Chelsea captain John Terry grabbed Ferdinand's shirt and then pulled at his arm, offering to shoot first. Ferdinand ignored him and, having taken instructions, correctly chose to kick first. The odds were already in United's favour.

Chelsea goalkeeper Petr Čech, whose poor penalty-saving record is his only weakness, made only one save in the shoot-out – from Ronaldo. Sure enough, as he approached the penalty, Ronaldo suddenly froze. Čech froze too. There was a momentary stand-off before Ronaldo, as predicted, went left – and Čech dived correctly, beating away the shot.

More fascinating, however, was the direction of Chelsea's kicks. Four of the initial five penalty takers – Michael Ballack, Juliano Belletti, Frank Lampard and John Terry – were right-footers and seemingly followed Palacios-Huerta's advice, going right rather than shooting across their body. The only player who did shoot across his body was also the only left-footer, Ashley Cole. That's what Van der Sar expected and he nearly saved the shot, the wet ball squirming under his body. It meant all five of Chelsea's penalties were kicked to the same corner.

One of these penalties, however, was off-target. After Ronaldo's failure, Chelsea would have triumphed had Terry converted Chelsea's fifth penalty. He approached the kick confidently and chose the correct side, as Van der Sar anticipated him shooting across his body and dived the wrong way. But Terry's standing foot slipped, he toppled to the floor and his kick bounced back off the post. This was considered nothing more than an unfortunate moment, but the truth was entirely different – Terry had a fatal tendency to slip.

Two years before this penalty shoot-out, Frank Lampard wrote an autobiography, *Totally Frank*. Lampard recalled England's penalty shoot-out defeat to Portugal at Euro 2004, which featured both Lampard and Terry scoring. But Terry's penalty, according to Lampard, didn't go smoothly. 'He didn't seem too bothered as he ran towards the ball and then he slipped, and for a split-second it seemed our chance of winning had gone, but it was a goal. At Chelsea, John will occasionally re-enact that kick, complete with the sliding foot – sometimes it goes in, sometimes not.'

This is a crucial revelation. Interestingly, video footage of that penalty against Portugal doesn't show Terry slipping. It's a curious technique, certainly – his standing foot was close to the ball, his body more angled than a textbook would advise – but no one, without Lampard's passage above, would notice that Terry had slightly slipped. Lampard's recollection is probably based upon Terry's own account, but either way, the fact that Terry 're-enacts that kick, complete with the sliding foot' is crucial. You suspect this passage wouldn't have been included had Lampard's autobiography been released post-Moscow; it reveals that Terry wasn't unlucky, he simply had a technical weakness when taking penalties.

Terry's miss forced the shoot-out into sudden death. Anderson and Ryan Giggs scored for Manchester United, as did Chelsea's Salomon Kalou, who followed instructions and kicked right. This meant all six of Chelsea's penalties were struck into the same corner – five by right-footers following the plan, one by the left-footed Cole disobeying instructions and only just squeezing the ball home.

Next came Nicolas Anelka, another right-footer. By this stage, Manchester United thought they'd deduced Chelsea's approach – kicking right every time. That wasn't quite correct, but Cole's decision to go against the plan gave that impression. On the halfway line, captain Ferdinand was frantically pointing and screaming for Van der Sar to dive that way. The Dutchman, meanwhile, seemed to have deduced the pattern too, and as Anelka waited for the whistle, Van der Sar made a crucial gesture. For the previous six kicks he'd spread both arms high and wide, as if he was about to start the 'YMCA' dance, but this time he pointed towards the corner where Chelsea had sent their previous six kicks, the direction Anelka was meant to be choosing. Did this cause Anelka to change his mind, suspecting Van der Sar had worked out his intentions? He unconvincingly shot across his body and Van der Sar dived that way, making his first save of the shoot-out. United were European champions.

Anelka, inevitably, was made the villain of the piece, but blame should be shared. Terry's miss was about technique rather than misfortune. Cole going against the supposed plan may have unwittingly caused United to suspect a pattern, even if not quite correctly, enabling Van der Sar to psych out Anelka. Meanwhile, Didier Drogba's dismissal five minutes from the end of extra-time for slapping Vidić meant Chelsea were without a key penalty taker. Had he remained on the pitch then Terry would have been spared from taking one of the first five penalties. Indeed, four years later Drogba took the fifth, triumphant kick when Chelsea finally won the Champions League on penalties against Bayern Munich. Somehow everything about this Moscow shoot-out encapsulated football tactics: research, planning, devising a strategy, players not quite sticking to the strategy, a bit of technique, a bit of luck, a bit of psychology. Chelsea's tactics were fascinating and entirely logical, yet they still lost.

Manchester United's dramatic triumph was slightly inappropriate. That type of win was more the 1999-era United – always finding a way – but during this period Manchester United were hugely dominant, and Ferguson must regret the fact he never won a European Cup by absolutely playing the opposition off the park. This United were the most tactically flexible side of the Premier League era, capable of playing pure defensive football, possession football or thrilling counter-attacking football. This last style was most obvious in big games and provided some of their most memorable moments with brilliant goals on the break, generally finished by Ronaldo or Rooney.

Even after Ronaldo and Tevez's departure in 2009, Manchester United played in a similar way, with Nani and Park playing more important roles and Rooney becoming the Ronaldo equivalent in big games – the number 9 who was sometimes very false, and sometimes very true. Antonio Valencia and Dimitar Berbatov also played important roles at points, but Nani, Park and Rooney were United's most thrilling front trio. Indeed, the finest counter-attacking goal of the Premier League era was scored the season after Ronaldo's departure, with all three involved.

United had struck a brilliant counter-attacking goal at the Emirates in the Champions League semi-final of 2009, when Park, Rooney and Ronaldo combined majestically to finish off Arsenal. But a goal the following season in a 3–1 Premier League victory at the same ground was even better. It started with United having nine outfielders in their own penalty box, crowding out Arsenal's passing moves. The ball fell to Park inside his own box – and, in a situation where many players would have simply cleared their lines, Park realised the possibility for an attacking transition, looked up and chipped the ball into the path of Rooney, coming short from his number 9 position. Rooney was United's most advanced attacker, but was midway inside his own half; his movement opened up space for others to break into. Nani, on the right, was already on his bike, while Park tore down the left. Rooney controlled the ball, moved short and fired a pass into Nani, who controlled the ball perfectly and sprinted towards goal. Even better than that initial burst, however, was the fact that Nani slightly slowed his dribble as he approached the box, waiting for Rooney to catch up and storm into a goalscoring position. But the best part of the move was that Park, last seen in his own penalty box, has darted 80 yards down the left, a decoy run that distracted Arsenal centre-back Thomas Vermaelen and created space for Rooney to burst into. It was classic Park – clever, hard-working, selfless. Nani's pass was perfect, and Rooney swept in the finish first-time. It was a truly outstanding goal that brilliantly epitomised United's big-game approach in this era – except for the fact Ronaldo was now in Madrid. There was also an obvious similarity with United's goals in the 3–1 victory over Norwich 17 years earlier, in the Premier League's inaugural season: a false striker, midfield runners and a quick counter. In that sense, this flexible and direct United side were simultaneously retro and revolutionary.

17

A Wet and Windy Night at Stoke

'It's a man's game.'

Tony Pulis

If the 2007/08 Champions League campaign illustrated the strength of England's top clubs, the 2007/08 Premier League campaign underlined something entirely different. A hapless Derby County side were relegated before the end of March, collecting just one victory and 11 points all season, the worst-ever Premier League campaign. With the Big Four dominance ensuring the same sides gobbled up the Champions League revenue every season, the gap between rich and poor was growing considerably, and it appeared no-hopers might become a regular feature of the division.

Ahead of the following season's campaign, along came another obvious candidate for that status. Tony Pulis's Stoke City were surprisingly promoted with a technically unimpressive side and were widely tipped to finish bottom. Many predicted that they would 'do a Derby' – or repeat their previous top-flight campaign, 1984/85, when they collected just three victories from 42 matches and finished a staggering 33 points from safety.

Stoke's manager, Tony Pulis, had never experienced the top flight as either a player or a manager and seemed entirely unsuited to the demands of modern football. An old-school manager who insisted on wearing a tracksuit and a baseball cap, he was renowned for signing physical, old-fashioned British footballers. In fact Pulis the manager played the type of football Pulis the player would have appreciated – his old bosses were rarely charitable about his skill set. John Rudge said Pulis 'wasn't quite what you would call a technical player', Harry Redknapp described him as 'the toughest tackler I have ever seen' but admitted 'he couldn't actually play, he couldn't pass it more than five yards,' while Bobby Gould called him 'the slowest runner I ever saw – a good tackler, mind, and a fantastic football brain'. The final part of that assessment is the most significant; behind the hard man there was a studious coach, and Pulis earned his UEFA A coaching badge at 21, among the youngest to complete the course at the time.

Pulis was renowned for creating dreadfully defensive, dour and direct teams. He once achieved promotion from the fourth tier with Gillingham despite a goals-scored tally of just 49 in 46 games, largely because their defensive record of 20 goals conceded was nearly twice as good as anyone else. That set the tone for his managerial career. In the last year of an initial three-year spell at Stoke he presided over what supporters refer to as 'the binary season'. In late October Stoke drew 1–1 away at Leicester – the most goals Stoke fans witnessed in a league contest for four months. Subsequent results were 1–0, 0–1, 0–1, 1–0, 0–0, 0–1, 1–0, 1–0, 1–0, 0–0, 0–1, 0–1, 0–1, 0–1, 0–1, 1–0 and 1–0, before this staggering sequence was broken when they faced Leicester again, and recorded a barely believable 3–2 victory. Pulis was dismissed at the end of that campaign, spent a year at Plymouth, but returned to Stoke for 2006/07 after the club's acquisition by the Coates family, who subsequently invested vast sums of money. When Plymouth visited in August, the away fans gleefully chanted 'We're not boring any more' to the Stoke supporters.

Such was the unhappiness at Pulis's return that, two months into the season, a Stoke fan named Richard Grisdale – a former copywriter for Saatchi & Saatchi – spent £200 printing 10,000 'red cards' and planned to hand them out to supporters at an upcoming game, envisaging a protest that would persuade the board to sack Pulis. The cards were printed with horrendous puns: 'Give Pulis His Cards' on one side and 'Time to Get Rolling, Tone' on the other. However, the protest was postponed after the loan signing of Aston Villa's Lee Hendrie, which was deemed the most exciting event to have happened under Pulis. Hendrie was a success, and Stoke's subsequent improvement ensured the red cards remained unused in Grisdale's attic. In 2008, after Stoke's promotion, he tried to sell them to raise money for charity. 'I'm sick of tripping over them,' he complained. 'I certainly don't mind what people do with them. They can burn them if they want.'

'Pulisball', as his approach became known, essentially had two distinct components. Without possession, Stoke remained in a deep, narrow shape thanks to unusually long training sessions based around defensive positioning. Pulis treated the midfield quartet like a secondary defence, referring to his two banks of four as 'the back eight'. One of his favoured training drills involved the midfield shuffling laterally across the pitch, denying any penetrative passes between them and funnelling opposition attacks out wide. From there, if the opposition crossed, Pulis had strong, aerially commanding centre-backs. With the ball, meanwhile, it was route one; Pulis favoured tall centre-forwards who were rarely prolific but won long balls and provided knock-downs to teammates. He sometimes accommodated an extra striker out wide, simply getting more height into the team, and Stoke were always excellent at set-pieces.

It was essentially a lower-league strategy based around physicality and dead balls – the most blatant old-school tactics since Sam Allardyce's Bolton Wanderers – so it was ironic that their opening day defeat came at Bolton, now coached by Gary Megson. They found themselves 3–0 down by half-time, eventually being defeated 3–1; two of Bolton's three goals were headers, the other an over-hit cross that drifted straight in. It felt like Stoke couldn't even cope with the type of contest they wanted, and after that opening-day defeat one bookmaker paid out on Stoke to be relegated immediately. It was a blatant publicity stunt, although few disagreed with the sentiment.

But then, amid speculation about when and how Stoke could possibly collect points, they won their first home Premier League fixture 3–2 against Aston Villa. They played some decent football, and striker Ricardo Fuller scored a sensational Bergkamp-esque strike with a flick and turn past Martin Laursen and a fine low finish. Stoke's injury-time winner, however, came from a more basic source; Rory Delap took a long throw-in from the left, launched the ball into the six-yard box, and Mamady Sidibé nodded in. Stoke were up and running.

This goal defined Stoke's approach, and Delap became the Premier League's most unique tactical weapon with his sensational long throw. The Premier League had witnessed long throws many times before – in fact its first-ever goal was scored by Brian Deane for Sheffield United from a long throw and a flick-on – but there had been nothing quite like Delap. A high-school javelin champion blessed with natural upper-body strength, Delap's throw-in expertise only became significant late in his career. By the time of Stoke's promotion in 2008, Delap was 32 and had already made over 200 Premier League appearances for Derby, Southampton and Sunderland. He'd made his Republic of Ireland debut a decade previously. Yet there was little sign Delap possessed this extraordinary, game-changing quality; he'd been renowned as a talented, efficient and hard-working midfielder capable of the odd spectacular goal, his traditional footballing qualities quite sufficient to make him Southampton's club record signing, a status he retained for 11 years. He had occasionally taken throws elsewhere, but with Stoke he would regularly end matches having taken more throws than he played passes; he was a thrower first, a footballer second. Stoke's approach was simple – stick it in the mixer.

Delap initially joined Stoke on loan in the Championship in October 2006, although after only a week he suffered a broken leg against Sunderland, his parent club. He was ruled out for the rest of the season, but Pulis stuck by him and signed him permanently in the January transfer window, realising he had a unique talent on his hands. Delap's throw-in ability justified his faith. 'At Derby, the emphasis was more on trying to throw the ball in behind defenders for Paulo Wanchope to run on to, and at other clubs it would just be in the last few minutes if we were trying to salvage something from a game,' Delap explained. 'But when I joined Stoke, the manager made no bones about it and made it clear he knew all about my throw-ins and that he intended to make full use of them … it's one thing being able to throw the ball into the heart of the area, but you need players who are good enough and brave enough for it to work. They have to time their runs just right, but we hardly do any practice. Maybe one or two goes at it on a Friday, when we are going through set-plays, but that's about it.' Pulis had assembled an extremely tall side, packing his team with six-footers and sending two or three defenders up into the penalty box simultaneously when Stoke won a throw in a dangerous position.

The distance on Delap's throws was incredible – he could launch the ball up to 40 yards, meaning he could often land the ball between the width of the goalposts. Stoke started basing their entire game around his throws, sending long balls into the channels, hoping the opposition would clear the ball into touch. Interestingly, his throws proved much more effective in the Premier League. Whereas Championship defenders were accustomed to constant defending against crosses and dead balls, top-flight centre-backs were increasingly selected for their speed and technical quality. There was also a significant change in Delap's deliveries at the start of Stoke's Premier League campaign. Previously he arced deliveries into the box, but Pulis requested flatter throws that defenders simply couldn't read.

In a functional side full of hard-working but limited players, Delap became Stoke's star attraction, and his unique talent meant he was forced to perform some curious publicity stunts. Stoke being in the Potteries ensured that these often involved throwing balls at plates and jugs, although Delap objected when asked to chuck a Christmas pudding over a double-decker bus, which sounds like a challenge set by Finchy from *The Office*. But he was a likeable character who enjoyed a great career, taking him from the fourth tier to the Premier League and back down to the fourth tier again. 'I'd like to think I've done a half-decent job with the ball at my feet down the years,' he said. 'But if people want to remember me for my long throw, that's fine. It's better than not being remembered at all.'

In their debut Premier League campaign Stoke were seemingly only dangerous at the Britannia Stadium. Only six sides in the division collected more points at home, but only two – the bottom two – collected fewer points on their travels. There was something particularly intimidating about the Britannia, and Pulis used a few old tricks to give his side an extra advantage. He set Stoke's pitch to the minimum possible dimensions under the regulations, suiting Delap's throws and hampering the passing game of technical visitors. The grass was noticeably longer than at most grounds, disrupting the possession play of passing sides but barely affecting Stoke's route one football. Pulis sometimes went even further against top teams, holding training at the Britannia the day before matches and playing a short-sided game in the midfield zone between the penalty boxes. This scuffed up the midfield but didn't affect the wings or penalty boxes, the areas Stoke's direct play concentrated upon.

The atmosphere played a part, too. The Britannia was a new ground, built in 1997, but retained an old-school feel, complete with advertising hoardings displaying the logos of local building and plumbing firms rather than investment banks or insurance companies. During Stoke's first couple of Premier League seasons the corners of the ground were open, meaning some supporters could stand outside on a nearby hill and watch the action for free. Perhaps that openness contributed to the sheer windiness inside the stadium. At home to Spurs, Danny Higginbotham stepped up to take a penalty, eventually smashing it home, but was forced to place the ball on the spot three separate times because it kept blowing away. Then there was the crowd – at a time when Premier League grounds were becoming noticeably quieter, Stoke fans were loud. They contributed to the aura surrounding Delap's throws by gesticulating wildly with a throw-in gesture whenever appropriate, then providing menacing sound effects as he commenced his run-up. They were baffled why West Bromwich Albion, who had beaten them to the Championship title the previous season, received plaudits for their slick, possession-based football, considering they were on course for immediate relegation and eventually finished bottom. Stoke did the double over them that season, Potters fans celebrating with a rendition of 'Long ball! You should have played long ball …'

After Aston Villa, the next visitors to the Britannia were Everton, who conceded two second-half goals from Delap's throws, with a particularly strong wind adding a couple of extra yards to his deliveries. The first arrived when his throw from the left-wing was punched away by Tim Howard, the ball falling to Seyi Olofinjana loitering on the edge of the box and the midfielder smashing it home. Next, Delap's right-wing throw skimmed off the head of Everton defender Phil Jagielka and flew straight past Howard. Everton won 3–2, but they'd been given a serious test at the back. 'He's like a human sling,' said Everton boss David Moyes of Delap. 'It was strange today; we had new players, a couple don't speak English, and explaining what game they'll have against Stoke wasn't easy.'

Next up at home was Chelsea, whose manager Luiz Felipe Scolari sounded genuinely excited by the prospect of facing Delap. 'I think he puts the ball in better with his hands than his foot – it's fantastic,' he said. 'Maybe it's not beautiful football but it's effective ... they put the touchline inside because they are intelligent. I like this coach, I like this because it's different.' This was a World Cup-winning manager marvelling at Stoke's basic approach. As it happened, Delap missed that game through injury – he had, unsurprisingly, picked up a shoulder problem.

He returned for the trip to Portsmouth, where his throw brought another headed goal for Fuller via a Dave Kitson flick-on. Then there was a 1–0 home win over Sunderland; Delap throw, Fuller header. The next home game brought a 2–1 win over Arsenal, with Delap's throws creating goals for both Fuller and Olofinjana. By mid-November more than half of Stoke's goals had been scored from throws, and they continued to score in their classic manner throughout the season. 'A wet and windy night at Stoke' became shorthand for questioning whether a foreign player possessed the requisite toughness for the Premier League, and was already a frequently mocked cliché by the time Sky Sports commentator Andy Gray pondered whether two-time Ballon d'Or winner Lionel Messi would be capable of performing in these conditions.

The deliveries themselves were problematic enough, but Stoke also benefited from the knock-on effects. For example, at throw-ins the offside law doesn't apply. Whereas teams can defend wide free-kicks with an aggressive defensive line and push opponents away from goal, that approach wasn't possible with Delap's throws. Even if the throw was 30 yards from the corner flag, Stoke could crowd the goal-keeper and create mayhem inside the box. Furthermore, if Stoke had a throw midway inside their own half, Delap could turn the opposition by launching the ball in behind, which was perfect for a manager like Pulis, concerned with territory rather than possession. The threat also meant opposition defenders desperately attempted to play out of trouble in tight situations rather than conceding throws, which inevitably resulted in errors and Stoke winning the ball close to the opposition goal.

It was fascinating to observe opponents' tactics when defending these throws. Some were desperate not to crowd their own goal-keeper, so broke the number one rule of defensive play and let Stoke's players move goalside. A couple of sides dropped onto the goal line, almost like a hockey side defending a short corner, while others pushed three men forward, trying to force Stoke to leave players back. Part of the problem, of course, was that it was simply impossible to practise defending against Delap's throws in training; Middlesbrough manager Gareth Southgate worked on defending throws ahead of his side's trip to Stoke but was forced to bring his thrower in from the touchline to the edge of the penalty area to replicate the distance Delap could achieve. Even then it served as poor preparation. Middlesbrough supporters spent much of the game chanting that Stoke's fans were 'only here for the throw-ins', and sure enough, Ryan Shawcross powered home the winner from Delap's delivery. Against Wigan, Delap managed to throw the ball with such force that it sailed straight into the top corner – the goal, of course, didn't stand.

While there was a comedy element to Stoke's approach, it forced opposition managers and players to think about the game, reconsidering sacrosanct concepts. Stoke's meeting against Hull, a fellow newly promoted side who had previously faced Delap's throws, was remarkable for two unique incidents. First, Hull goalkeeper Boaz Myhill found himself sweeping out of his goal in the left-back zone, but rather than knocking the ball out for a throw, promptly turned around and booted it out for a Stoke corner instead. No one had ever previously considered the idea a throw-in could be more dangerous than a corner, but Delap changed the situation entirely.

Second, and even more bizarrely, Hull manager Phil Brown was so worried by Delap's deliveries that when Stoke won a throw-in midway inside Hull's half, he instructed substitute Dean Windass to trot along the touchline and warm-up directly in front of Delap as he prepared his run-up. It's remarkable that Brown thought that this was a legitimate tactic, and the veteran striker was inevitably booked for his blocking. But this was surely another first – the positioning of a substitute relevant to the action, the tactical battle including a 12th player. In the return meeting Hull tried another underhand tactic, bringing in the pitchside advertising hoardings to disrupt Delap's run-up, forcing him to bend his run like a high-jumper. That wasn't a problem at the Britannia Stadium, of course, thanks to the small pitch.

It was surprising that the Premier League didn't have regulations about these situations, and Delap prompted further questions about the subtleties of the laws. Should the considerable periods Delap spent jogging across to the touchlines count towards stoppage time? Should Delap be allowed to use pitch-side towels provided by Stoke's ball boys – who mysteriously vanished when the opposition had throws of their own – to dry the ball? These towels weren't available away from home, which forced Delap to wear a peculiar ball-drying bib under his shirt, prompting speculation about its material. It was actually nothing more than a simple vest with the back cut out for reasons of comfort, as Delap wore it even when the weather was unsuited to an extra layer.

It felt inevitable that Arsène Wenger's Arsenal would become the most consistent victims of the fabled 'wet and windy night at Stoke' – much as they became the fall guys against Allardyce's Bolton – and Stoke versus Arsenal became a major Premier League rivalry. In fact the stylistic contrast goes back much further. In 1980/81 Stoke manager Alan Durban, a no-nonsense Welshman like Pulis, played an almost unheard-of 4–5–1 formation in a 2–0 defeat away at Arsenal, and when criticised for the lack of entertainment value, famously replied, 'If you want entertainment, go and watch a bunch of clowns.' Pulis had a similar philosophy. In six league and cup visits to Pulis's Stoke, Arsenal lost three times, drew twice and won only once – and even that was overshadowed by the broken leg suffered by Aaron Ramsey. In stark contrast, Arsenal won all five contests at the Emirates. It really was the trip to Stoke's ground, rather than Stoke themselves, that intimidated Arsenal.

Wenger once criticised the way that Stoke crowded goalkeepers at set-pieces, complaining, 'You cannot say any more it is football; it is rugby on the goalkeepers.' Stoke supporters reacted, to their immense credit, by bellowing out 'Swing Low, Sweet Chariot' throughout Arsenal's next visit. This story effectively came full circle many years later, when, in a bizarre twist, England rugby coach Eddie Jones distanced his coaching philosophy from Pulisball. 'If you want to play like the old Stoke City, then that is the safest way to play,' he explained. 'Just stick the ball in the air, chase hard and get everyone to clap … Rugby is exactly the same; every time you run with the ball, you take a greater risk than if you kick. We don't want to be reckless, but we don't want to be like Stoke City of old either.' Stoke captain Ryan Shawcross hit back by suggesting Jones 'should stick to talking about the sport he's paid to work in, rather than dipping his toe in football'. He had a point – look at Sir Clive Woodward.

Throughout Pulis's five top-flight seasons with Stoke his approach wasn't always about throw-ins – Delap's delivieries became less of a novelty, and opponents started to cope better – but it *was* largely about route one, with only subtle upgrades in terms of technical quality. Pulis's choice of centre-forward was always based more around height than goalscoring return, and he struggled to accommodate flair players. He signed the talented Turkish forward Tuncay Şanlı after he'd played excellently against Stoke for Middlesbrough, but he used him sparingly. There was an extraordinary incident away at Hull, when Tuncay was introduced as an 81st-minute substitute in place of the misfiring Kitson. Five minutes later Stoke midfielder Amdy Faye was sent off, which prompted Pulis to desperately search for height on his bench to compensate. Defender Andy Wilkinson was quickly summoned in place of Tuncay, who stormed straight down the tunnel after his five-minute cameo. That underlined how much Pulis prioritised height, although it didn't prevent Hull scoring a stoppage-time winner. This somewhat contradicted Pulis's repeated assertions, amid criticism of his approach, that Stoke would play better football if he had better players – and Eidur Gudjohnsen endured a similarly frustrating experience.

Pulis presented Stoke as underdogs – once literally, when he marvellously referred to his squad as being 'from Battersea Dogs Home rather than Cruft's' – and emphasised the wealth of bigger clubs. After a narrow 1–0 defeat away at old foes Arsenal in 2013, Pulis directly mentioned the difference in spending power. 'You have a look at Arsenal's resources, what they've got, what they've spent, the players they've got … They spent, was it £12m? On a left-back [Nacho Monreal]? We're not in their league in a lot of respects.' At face value – looking at Stoke's side – you wouldn't have questioned that assertion. But, astonishingly, over the previous five years Stoke had the third-highest 'net spend' figure in the Premier League behind the expected duo, Manchester City and Chelsea. Pulis had simply purchased run-of-the-mill players who played basic football, the odd technical talent who was underused and a stream of target men who furthered Pulis's obsession with route one. There were clear limitations to his approach, and he was sacked later that year. His finishes of 12th, 11th, 13th, 14th and 13th – plus reaching the FA Cup Final in 2011, where they lost 1–0 to Manchester City – should be commended, considering how Stoke were initially written off.

Pulis's approach at Stoke was back to basics rather than progressive, but few other managers have forced their opposite numbers to reconsider fundamental principles so extensively. Scolari's simple assessment of Stoke's play – 'I like it because it's different' – is particularly appropriate. When it comes to strategy, heterogeneity is crucial, and Pulis, more than anyone else, ensured that there was unrivalled tactical variety in the Premier League. The 'wet and windy night' line was probably overplayed, although Pulis once said he'd omitted Honduras international Wilson Palacios from his starting XI because 'it was too windy'. No one was entirely sure if he was joking.

18

Inverted Wingers

'Bale can cross, his left foot is great on the run, he can shoot, dribble, head it – he's got everything.'

Harry Redknapp

By 2010, the dominance of the Big Four had become suffocating. The Premier League might have been Europe's best division according to UEFA coefficients, but it was also among its least competitive.

In the four seasons from 2005/06 to 2008/09 the same sides always finished in the top four; Manchester United, Chelsea, Liverpool and Arsenal seemingly boasted an unbreakable stranglehold on the Champions League places. In fact, you can backdate this sequence even further. While Everton finished in fourth – and therefore ahead of city rivals Liverpool – in 2004/05, the Toffees failed to progress through the Champions League play-off round. Meanwhile Liverpool lifted the European Cup and, after a late intervention by UEFA, whose rules at this stage hadn't stipulated that the holders would re-qualify if they finished outside their domestic qualifying positions, were allowed back into the competition. It was therefore the same four sides earning Champions League revenue from 2003/04 to 2009/10, strengthening their squads and thereby maintaining their advantage over the Premier League's also-rans. This was the antithesis of how the Premier League marketed itself, as a division where anyone could beat anyone.

For a major league this quadopoly was unprecedented. Four clubs had never monopolised the top places for four consecutive campaigns in England, France, Germany, Holland, Italy or Spain, although it had occurred in less respected leagues such as Portugal, Scotland and Turkey. It became impossible to imagine anyone breaking through, as Kevin Keegan suggested in 2008 during a brief spell back at Newcastle United, having just made the natural transition from his previous job, funding a 'soccer circus' in Scotland. 'This league is in danger of becoming one of the most boring but great leagues in the world,' he complained. 'The top four next year will be the same top four as this year. I thought, "What can I do next year to get near them?" – and the truth is there's nothing I can do at all. What I can say to the Newcastle fans is that we will be trying to get fifth and we will be trying to win the "other league" that's going on within the Premier League.' It was troubling to hear the divide described in such a stark manner, especially by a manager who had, in his previous spell, taken Newcastle from the bottom of the second tier to second place in the Premier League.

Early May 2010, however, proved transformative for English football, which fitted the mood of the country. On 5 May 2010 Tottenham's 1–0 victory at Manchester City confirmed Spurs' Champions League qualification, effectively ending the Big Four era. The following day's election resulted in a hung parliament, and prompted the formation of the first coalition government in Britain since the Second World War. This was a brave new world – things had opened up, and everything was suddenly more complex.

The decline of the Big Four was primarily about Liverpool's sudden decline. They'd slumped from runners-up in 2008/09 to seventh in 2009/10, resulting in Rafael Benítez's dismissal, and so the last Champions League place was a fight between Tottenham and Manchester City. They'd originally been scheduled to meet in early March, but the fixture was postponed because of Spurs' FA Cup commitments and handily rearranged for the penultimate game of the season, effectively turning the contest into a straight play-off for fourth place. With City boosted by a significant influx of money from the deputy prime minister of the United Arab Emirates – the extraordinarily wealthy Sheikh Mansour – and set to challenge for the title long-term, they were considered the obvious contenders to take Liverpool's place, which might have simply created a new Big Four. Harry Redknapp's Tottenham, however, had other ideas.

Redknapp had been appointed early in 2008/09, replacing Juande Ramos. The Spaniard was a high-profile appointment, having won consecutive UEFA Cups with Sevilla, and he took Spurs to the League Cup in 2008, but his start to the following campaign was disastrous, collecting just two points from eight matches – as his successor constantly reminded everyone. Redknapp was a surprise choice, but he'd recently won the FA Cup with Portsmouth and his back-to-basics approach proved effective. After hauling Spurs away from the relegation zone and into the top half, he turned the club into top four challengers in his first full season.

2009/10 was an eventful campaign for Tottenham. They were top after four matches, and in October became only the second Premier League side to score nine times in a match, thrashing Wigan 9–1. They started the new year poorly, and dropped to seventh after a 1–0 defeat at Wolves in February. Then, however, they won nine of their following 11 matches, culminating in that decisive 1–0 victory at City. It was their highest-ever Premier League finish, and owed much to the sudden impact of emerging left-winger Gareth Bale.

The Welshman's contribution was entirely unexpected, because he'd previously been considered a figure of fun. Bale was a highly rated teenager at Southampton, where he roomed with Theo Walcott, before joining Tottenham in 2007. But amid injury problems and bad luck, Bale didn't win any of his first 24 Premier League matches, the longest winless start by a player in the competition's history. His technical and physical qualities were undeniable but some considered him a jinx, and it wasn't until 26 September 2009 that he finally tasted victory. Even then he only appeared for the final five minutes of a 5–0 victory over Burnley, with Redknapp introducing him specifically to disprove the notion of a curse. It took another four months before Bale started in a Premier League victory.

Bale wore number 3 because he was initially a left-back, in keeping with the tendency to convert young, dynamic crossers into overlapping full-backs. But Benoît Assou-Ekotto was impressing in that position, and Niko Kranjčar, a Redknapp favourite, was providing creativity from the left of midfield. In the first 20 matches of 2009/10 Bale didn't make a single start and only made five substitute appearances, of which three saw him introduced after the 85th minute. Redknapp, determined to afford the Welshman some playing time, seriously considered loaning him out in January. But then, with three minutes remaining of Spurs' 2–0 win over West Ham, their final game of 2009, Assou-Ekotto collected a groin strain that sidelined him for two months. Bale started the next game, and then didn't miss a single minute of Premier League action in 2010. This was the definition of a breakthrough year.

Bale's initial eight starts were at left-back, where he was particularly impressive in a 2–0 victory over Fulham, and he scampered forward to create the opener for Jermain Defoe in a 3–0 win at Wigan. When Assou-Ekotto returned, Bale pushed forward and became Spurs' regular left-sided midfielder, and from that advanced position he was sensational, collecting the man-of-the-match award in 2–1 victories over both Arsenal and Chelsea within the space of four days in April, then picking up Player of the Month too. Almost overnight, Bale had gone from a bad-luck charm to the Premier League's most dangerous winger.

At this stage, 4–4–2 was considered almost dead at the highest level, with the Big Four all playing either 4–2–3–1 or 4–3–3 in big matches. But Tottenham's victories over Arsenal and Chelsea demonstrated that the system was perfectly viable when used correctly – they didn't engage their opponents in a possession battle, and instead played on the counter-attack. Their defending, meanwhile, was impressively flexible: against Arsenal they played deep and narrow to prevent their north London rivals playing through-balls, while against Chelsea they played higher up the pitch to force Didier Drogba away from goal. They compensated for their numerical disadvantage in midfield with strikers Jermain Defoe and Roman Pavlyuchenko dropping onto the opposition's holding player. Going forward, it was classic 4–4–2: attack directly, get the ball wide, cross.

That approach was particularly obvious in the victory over Arsenal, who lived up to the cliché of 'trying to walk the ball into the net', their wide players Samir Nasri and Tomáš Rosický unable to thread the ball between defenders. Debutant Danny Rose's stunning volleyed opener meant Arsenal had to take the game to Spurs, and Bale proved a constant counter-attacking threat, adding the crucial second goal. He was even better against Chelsea, with Tottenham constantly finding him on the run and also sending goal-kicks towards him to take advantage of his aerial power. After Defoe opened the scoring from the spot, Bale surprised Chelsea right-back Paulo Ferreira by cutting inside before firing home with his right foot to put Spurs 2–0 ahead. Ferreira had a nightmare afternoon and was replaced by Branislav Ivanović at half-time. Bale continued to threaten, however, and John Terry was later dismissed for scything down the Welshman.

A few weeks later Tottenham's memorable victory at Manchester City secured fourth place, in what was essentially a 4–4–2 versus 4–4–2 battle. Roberto Mancini used Carlos Tevez dropping off Emmanuel Adebayor, while Redknapp used a classic little-and-large partnership of Defoe and Peter Crouch. But whereas Mancini's wingers drifted in-field with right-footed Craig Bellamy on the left and left-footed Adam Johnson on the right, Spurs stretched the play with Bale and Aaron Lennon hugging the touchlines. 'That's one of my defining matches as a manager, because of the way we played,' Redknapp recalled. 'I decided that it didn't matter that we were the away team. This was a Cup Final, one-off, and we were going to go for it.'

Bale and Lennon were both outstanding – they were better than City's wide pairing at protecting their full-backs and also more dangerous in possession. Assou-Ekotto and Bale were rampant down the left, and twice their combination play should have put Spurs ahead; first Bale released Assou-Ekotto on the overlap and the Cameroonian delivered a teasing ball across the six-yard box that Defoe and Crouch couldn't quite reach, before Bale crossed from a similar position and Crouch headed straight at the goalkeeper. Eventually Crouch headed the winner, after a deflected cross from makeshift right-back Younès Kaboul. But the major difference was the nature of the wingers. Both Adebayor and Crouch were target men who thrived on crosses, but only Spurs' pairing provided them. 'As a striker, it's a dream to have Bale on the left and Lennon on the right,' Crouch said. 'You just have to get yourself in the box and you know, nine times out of ten, they will get the right cross in for you.' It was reminiscent of Les Ferdinand talking about David Ginola and Keith Gillespie – Tottenham were the new Entertainers.

* * *

2009/10 proved a particularly successful season for London clubs. Chelsea, Arsenal and Tottenham all finished in the top four, while most impressively, Roy Hodgson's Fulham defied expectations by reaching the Europa League Final. They were defeated 2–1 in extra-time by Atlético Madrid, but their achievements in progressing past holders Shakhtar Donetsk, Italian giants Juventus and German champions Wolfsburg shouldn't be underestimated.

When Hodgson took change of Fulham in December 2007 the Cottagers were in the relegation zone, having won just twice all season. It took a while for him to transform Fulham's fortunes – at one point, when 2–0 down at Manchester City, they were set for relegation, but a fantastic late comeback meant they won 3–2, and they confirmed their survival with a 1–0 victory over Portsmouth on the final day. 2008/09 was a huge success – their finish of 7th was the highest in the club's history and meant they qualified for the Europa League.

Like Redknapp, Hodgson was a 4–4–2 man, although the two were opposites in almost every other respect. Redknapp had never managed outside the south of England, while Hodgson had worked in Sweden, Finland, Norway, Denmark, Italy, Switzerland and the UAE. Redknapp delegated training to his assistants, Hodgson was a tracksuit coach. Redknapp often dismissed the importance of tactics, Hodgson was all about shape and structure. It was notable that the Football Association were effectively choosing between them for the vacant England manager's job two years later, with Hodgson preferred.

Hodgson was a studious and intelligent man who emphasised the importance of collective organisation, and his success at Fulham owed much to constantly drilling his side in a solid shape on the training ground. When asked how he prepared players for a game, Hodgson responded simply: 'You do it in the day-to-day training work. You don't do it with a Churchillian talk 15 minutes before a game ... the team talk should be nothing more than flagging up the most important things you've been working on all week.' His training regime had a defined pattern – Monday was recovery work, Tuesday was defending, Wednesday was off, Thursday was attacking and Friday was based around the opposition. The drills were 11 v 11, 11 v 8 or 11 v 6, and always focused on shape and structure. The training sessions were, most players agreed, incredibly boring – about repetition and following pre-determined instructions. It's funny that Hodgson later proved such an unpopular replacement for Rafael Benítez at Liverpool, because there were many similarities in their way of operating.

'Every day in training is geared towards team shape in the match coming up,' explained midfielder Simon Davies. 'Every day is about team shape, and it shows. We have a laugh about it now and again, but when he came in we were fighting relegation and now we're in the Europa League, so you take it. I don't want to give any secrets away, but he gets the 11 that he wants on a matchday and he drills everything in that he wants. There are no diagrams. It's all on the pitch with the ball, nothing unopposed.'

Hodgson didn't appreciate players who struggled to play within a system – he was happy to sell a maverick like Jimmy Bullard – but more functional players were fulsome in their praise. 'I have a lot to thank Roy Hodgson for, because he helped me a lot,' said holding midfielder Dickson Etuhu. 'He almost coached me from the beginning again, and I understand football better now because of him.'

The most impressive aspect of Fulham's system, however, was Hodgson fitting four creative players into an otherwise highly structured team. With Etuhu the holding midfielder and Bobby Zamora a traditional targetman, Hodgson used Zoltán Gera just off the front, Danny Murphy as the deep-lying creator, plus Davies and Damien Duff out wide. But a major difference between Redknapp's Spurs and

Hodgson's Fulham was the nature of the wingers. Whereas Bale and Lennon were fielded on their natural sides and hugged the touch-lines, Hodgson used inverted wingers. Davies started on the left and cut inside onto his preferred right foot, while Duff started on the right and cut inside onto his left, although the Irishman became a well-rounded, two-footed winger when moved to that flank.

'I probably left it too late. I wish I'd started when I was 15: just right foot, right foot, right foot, and now I prefer kicking the ball with my right rather than my left,' Duff said. That's a surprising revelation, although practising your weaker side sometimes means you 'unlearn' using your stronger foot – Blackburn winger Morten Gamst Pedersen and Gaël Clichy of Arsenal and Manchester City were right-footed as youngsters, but their fathers encouraged them to exclusively use their weaker foot in training and they became left-footed. 'When I hit 30 I could play on the right and cut in, but I was happy getting down the wing and crossing as well, which I couldn't have done ten years before when I was at Chelsea and Blackburn,' Duff continued. 'I didn't look back. I became a right-winger, which is amazing after 15 or 20 years as a left-winger.' This was, of course, further evidence that attackers were becoming all-rounders.

Inverted wingers were becoming increasingly common, and in the semi-final against Hamburg and in the final against Atlético, Fulham faced opponents who also deployed wide players cutting inside. A contest between traditional wingers and inverted wingers often proved fascinating, as the aforementioned Manchester City versus Spurs match underlined. But games between two sides playing 4–4–2 (or 4–4–1–1) with all four wingers determined to cut inside were generally frustrating; the centre became congested, and if the full-backs were limited in possession there was little excitement out wide. Fulham's goalless draw away in Hamburg was a particularly poor game.

Nevertheless, Fulham were entirely happy to shepherd dangerous wingers into the crowded midfield zone, and in the final, Atletico's right-footed left-winger Simão Sabrosa and left-footed right-winger José Antonio Reyes were the first two players substituted by future Watford manager Quique Sánchez Flores. In a 2–1 victory sealed two minutes from the end of extra-time, Atletico's goals were both assisted by Sergio Agüero and scored by Diego Forlán, an indication of the quality Fulham were up against. Davies had equalised for Hodgson's side, but they were badly affected by Zamora's obvious lack of match fitness and inability to play his target-man role properly. His replacement, Clint Dempsey, was less comfortable battling for aerial balls, and Fulham's attacking game plan simply didn't work.

It was notable that the 2010 Champions League Final, like the Europa League Final, also featured two teams playing inverted wingers. José Mourinho's Inter Milan, with right-footed Samuel Eto'o on the left and left-footed Goran Pandev on the right (granted, both were converted forwards rather than proper wingers), triumphed 2–0 against Bayern Munich, who used left-footed Arjen Robben on the right and right-footed Franck Ribéry on the left. Of course, there have been many wingers fielded on the 'wrong' flank before, but this generally happened when a manager had two star wingers who preferred the same foot, meaning that one was inevitably fielded out of position. Famously, in the 1950s England used Tom Finney on the left because Stanley Matthews was on the right, while in the Premier League era Mourinho's Chelsea had two left-footers, Duff and Robben. The use of both wingers on their unnatural flank, however, was a deliberate ploy and a significant tactical development, marking the decline of the traditional winger.

This arose because of two factors. First, it was effectively a response to the rise of the attacking full-back. The traditional winger's job was stretching the play and crossing, but as those responsibilities were increasingly covered by the full-backs, wingers needed to provide something different. Besides, attacking full-backs needed space to overlap into, and a wide player drifting in and pulling the opposition full-back inside proved useful.

Second, top teams now played intricate football based around passing combinations. With fewer traditional targetmen – and more centre-forwards who thrived on through-balls – there was less reason for playing wingers who would naturally go wide. Inverted wingers offered more; they could drift inside and overload the midfield zone, they could play through-balls with their stronger foot and – most obviously – they could shoot. This was particularly crucial. Since strikers were expected to do more than simply score goals, that burden needed to be shared around, and wingers had a big responsibility to get onto the scoresheet. The debate was essentially 'crossing versus through-balls and shooting', and the latter roles were considered more important in the modern game. The Inter v Bayern Champions League Final demonstrated that top clubs had generally moved away from traditional wingers by this stage, while right-footed Cristiano Ronaldo and left-footed Lionel Messi had become the world's most revered players by cutting inside onto their strongest foot, before the Argentine switched to a central position.

Most top Premier League sides weren't set up around crossing, and therefore wingers – either traditional or inverted – weren't always used. Arsenal fielded natural number 10s like Nasri, Rosický and Andrey Arshavin drifting infield to create, while Chelsea boasted powerful goalscorers like Florent Malouda and Nicolas Anelka. Manchester United were a slight exception, with Antonio Valencia an old-fashioned winger who regularly crossed for Wayne Rooney, but it was significant that Sir Alex Ferguson omitted him from the Champions League quarter-final trip to Bayern Munich in March 2010, explaining that he selected Nani and Park Ji-sung because they had the versatility to play on either flank and could be switched mid-game to give him tactical options. This was another body blow for the traditional, one-dimensional winger.

The second tier of Premier League sides, however, were still very much based around wing play. As well as Tottenham and Fulham, both Everton and Aston Villa – regular challengers for Europa League places – depended heavily upon their wide players for chances.

David Moyes's Everton, for example, boasted the Premier League's best left-sided partnership, with South African Steven Pienaar drifting inside to allow Leighton Baines, probably the most dangerous crosser in the division, forward on the overlap. They had a telepathic understanding, and Baines also struck up a good relationship with Australian midfielder Tim Cahill, who was technically limited but among the most effective penalty-box poachers around, and fantastic in the air despite being only five foot ten. Indeed, Everton's dependence upon width and crossing is reflected by the fact that Moyes fielded both Cahill and Marouane Fellaini, two unusual midfielders whose strength wasn't silky passing but getting on the end of crosses.

Moyes's training sessions were often based around creating overloads in wide positions, forming two-against-one or three-against-two situations to outnumber the opposition, and he particularly liked a small-sided drill that involved teams attacking into three mini-goals placed across the width of the pitch. This encouraged players to attack towards a mini-goal down one flank, find opponents blocking the path and then switch play suddenly to the opposite wing. That was Everton's game plan: switches of play and using the flanks.

Aston Villa, meanwhile, were managed by Martin O'Neill, who had enjoyed success at both Leicester and Celtic with a crossing-based approach, often in a 3–5–2. At Villa he played 4–4–2 or

4–5–1, usually with two good crossers in Stewart Downing and Ashley Young. Although initially deployed on their traditional flanks, both became more dangerous as inverted wingers. Right-footed Young became a top-class performer from the left, where he had a peculiar tendency to cut inside onto his right foot, trick the defender by shaping to go outside on his left, before cutting inside onto his right for a second time. Downing, meanwhile, excelled when moved to the right by O'Neill's replacement Gérard Houllier, who famously disliked traditional wingers at Liverpool. In 2011 Young and Downing earned major transfers to Manchester United and Liverpool respectively, but found their crossing abilities less valued at bigger clubs.

This newfound emphasis upon inverted wingers meant it was unusual to see a speedy, dangerous left-footer like Bale on the flank in 2010/11. 'I believe in putting the best players in the position where they feel most comfortable, and Bale is a lightning-quick, left-footed player, so I used him on the left throughout that season,' Redknapp recalled. 'The fashion was for right-footed players on the left at the time, like Ashley Young, so they could cut inside and get to goal – but I saw Gareth needed to build confidence, and he felt best playing in his natural position.'

Bale had become a Premier League star in the second half of 2009/10, then turned into a Champions League star in the first half of 2010/11, with two staggering performances against European champions Inter in his left-wing role. The first display came in peculiar circumstances, Spurs finding themselves down to ten men and 4–0 down by half-time in the San Siro. Bale proceeded to launch a one-man fightback with two stunning goals on the run, then sealed his hat-trick to prove that wingers remained a major goal threat when deployed on their traditional flank. All three goals were arrowed into the far corner with his left foot, and each celebrated by nothing more than a gesture for teammates to retrieve the ball and restart the game quickly. Bale terrorised Maicon, then considered the world's best right-back, who later insisted he was suffering from a 24-hour bug, rendering him unable to cope with Bale's speed. He did, at least, keep apologising whenever he fouled the Welshman.

It must have been a two-week bug, however, because when the sides reconvened at White Hart Lane Maicon was again destroyed by Bale. Redknapp had happily outlined his strategy before the game. 'Their two wide men do not really defend,' he said at a press conference. 'Inter attack with three forwards and Wesley Sneijder behind, and they have two holding midfielders. The key will be ripping into them on the flanks – we need Bale to get the better of Maicon again.' That's exactly what happened, as Bale produced a performance that topped his hat-trick of the previous fortnight. New Inter boss Rafael Benítez's tactics appeared somewhat naive, as neither right-sided attacker Jonathan Biabiany nor right-centre holding midfielder Javier Zanetti offered Maicon any assistance. Bale didn't get on the scoresheet, but motored forward and crossed for two tap-ins for Crouch and his replacement, Pavlyuchenko. 'Inter didn't really operate with a wide-right midfielder offering protection,' said an amazed Redknapp. 'Maicon was hung out to dry.'

It was a curious oversight from Benítez, considering that Bale had been quiet since the San Siro – precisely because domestic opponents had doubled up against him. 'How to stop Bale' became the Premier League's major tactical question. Moyes's Everton held Tottenham to a 1–1 draw at White Hart Lane, with Bale inefffective as Moyes used two right-backs, with Seamus Coleman just ahead of Phil Neville. 'It wasn't only Neville that made it hard for me; he had two or three players helping him,' Bale observed. 'The right-winger was right on my toes all the time so I couldn't get the ball.' Redknapp eventually instructed Bale to switch flanks, and he played from the right for the first time.

The pattern continued. In a 2–0 defeat at Manchester United, Ferguson instructed Darren Fletcher to sprint across to support right-back Rafael da Silva whenever Bale received possession on the left. Next, Sunderland's tough-tackling central midfielder Lee Cattermole effectively replicated Fletcher's role to assist Nedum Onuoha, while Bolton's right-winger Lee Chung-yong dropped deep to protect Grétar Steinsson – although the Icelandic right-back seemed entirely nonplussed about the Welshman's threat. 'I've never received so many texts before a game' said Steinsson. 'Bale is a fantastic player, but facing him was just the same as facing anyone else. Friday was Bonfire Night, and I just relaxed and had a really good chicken korma.'

Spurs now had a problem. In four Premier League matches since Bale's incredible San Siro hat-trick all four opponents used two players against him, and the results were clear – Bale had no space to work in and had no assists or goals, with Spurs collecting just two points. 'It's what you get in front of you that helps you,' explained ex-Tottenham right-back Stephen Carr, now captaining Birmingham, who also nullified Bale. 'I thought I did OK, but I had a lot of help from in front.'

However, Bale provided a fine performance in a 4–2 win over Blackburn, notable because he twice turned home right-wing crosses, the first a near-post header, the second a scruffy poacher's effort. There was also a classic dribble and cross for Pavlyuchenko's towering far-post header, but Bale had demonstrated a different side to his game. 'It has been difficult for me recently when teams have had two players marking me,' he said. 'I've got to find another way to get past them. I did that against Blackburn and I was delighted.' Even so, this performance was the exception to the rule in 2010/11 – that cross for

Pavlyuchenko proved Bale's only assist in the entire league campaign. He scored nine goals but was rather flattered by his PFA Player of the Year award, in a season without any standout candidates. Nevertheless, Balemania was under way, largely fuelled by those two performances against Inter.

But both Bale and Redknapp recognised that he needed to evolve to exert a consistent influence upon matches, and so in 2011/12 Bale increasingly wandered inside from the left, with mixed results. He'd previously only ever played wide, and had been a regular for just 18 months – at that stage most players are attempting to improve in their primary position, never mind learning an entirely new role because they're being double-marked.

Playing centrally required a different skill set, and Bale struggled to receive the ball in dangerous zones, with the correct body position to take the ball in his stride. When it worked, however, the results were sometimes spectacular. He scored both goals in a 2–0 victory at Norwich just after Christmas from a free role, the second after an extraordinary dribble from his own half through the centre of the pitch. At the start of the new year Spurs appeared set for a genuine title challenge, but their form – and Bale's – dipped dramatically, and his final Premier League goal of the campaign came in January. More elaborate positional experiments didn't work. Away at Everton, Redknapp realised that Moyes had again fielded Coleman and Neville together to stop Bale, so switched him to the right. He was hugely underwhelming, however, and the travelling Tottenham fans chanted 'Gareth Bale, he plays on the left' in frustration at his positioning. Spurs eventually slipped to fourth, and were denied a Champions League place when sixth-place Chelsea defeated Bayern Munich in the Champions League Final, taking the final slot – UEFA's qualification rules having been revised after the Liverpool debacle seven years beforehand. Redknapp was harshly dismissed.

Redknapp's replacement, André Villas-Boas, outlined his intention to build the side around Bale, and the Welshman's final campaign at Spurs was intriguing in a tactical sense. Now wearing the number 11 shirt in recognition of his advanced positioning, he started the season on the left with licence to drift inside. But he was most effective in the second half of the campaign, when fielded as the number 10 in a 4–2–3–1. Again, he was allowed to roam with the likes of Lewis Holtby and Gylfi Sigurdsson making reverse runs to ensure Bale's drifts didn't undermine Spurs' shape. He scored 21 league goals that season – none of them penalties – the same number he'd managed in his previous five campaigns combined. When he found the centre crowded, he naturally drifted wide – but rarely to his former home on the left, and instead to the right. From there, he regularly cut inside, and scored stunning goals against both West Brom and Southampton. Then, in his final game for Spurs, against Sunderland, Bale spent the entire second half on the right flank, eternally trying to cut inside and shoot. With a minute of his Spurs career remaining, he finally managed it, collecting the ball in an inside-right position, stopping dead, then shifting the ball inside young substitute Adam Mitchell (who played just three minutes in his Premier League career and found himself the fall-guy in a Bale blockbuster) and firing into the top corner. It was a fitting finale.

Bale's expertise in cutting inside from the right convinced Real Madrid to make him the world's most expensive footballer that summer, beating their own record from four years beforehand when they'd signed Cristiano Ronaldo. There was an obvious similarity between them; positionally, they both started as a traditional winger, increasingly drifted into central zones and eventually became an inverted winger. Superstar wingers were now about shooting rather than crossing, and therefore had become even more direct.

Part Seven

Possession

19

The Italian Job

*'To find a clear identity for the team – this is what
I was told should be my goal.'*

Carlo Ancelotti

In five of Sir Alex Ferguson's final seven seasons before his retirement
in 2013, Manchester United claimed the Premier League title. The
exceptions came in 2009/10 and 2011/12, when Chelsea and
Manchester City triumphed respectively. There were obvious similarities between the two. Both sides had beaten Manchester United
home and away, both sides clinched the title on the final day, and
both sides were managed by Italians, Carlo Ancelotti and Roberto
Mancini. Italian managers typically valued the importance of
controlling matches, traditionally with cagey, defensive football – but
increasingly by dominating possession.

While Serie A was no longer Europe's best league, Italian managers were still considered the most astute tacticians – thoughtful,
flexible strategists who viewed football matches like a game of chess,
methodically moving their pieces to nullify the opposition's strengths.

There had been precious little Italian influence upon the Premier League, however. Gianluca Vialli lifted the FA Cup with Chelsea in 2000, but was hardly offering Serie A expertise having been suddenly been promoted from player to player-manager, and he relied heavily upon assistant Graham Rix. His successor, Claudio Ranieri, was more typically Italian, being nicknamed 'the Tinkerman' for his regular tactical changes, but having coached Napoli and Fiorentina rather than genuine title-challengers he wasn't considered a world-class manager. Ranieri would later prove himself in the most unexpected manner imaginable, but the arrival of Ancelotti and Mancini in 2009 was the first time that revered Italian coaches had touched down in England. Ancelotti had won the Champions League twice as manager at AC Milan and Mancini had won Serie A three years running at Inter. With four-time Serie A winner Fabio Capello now in charge of the England side, English football suddenly experienced an Italian invasion.

Ancelotti was a hugely respected coach, and Chelsea owner Roman Abramovich appointed him for two primary reasons. First, the Russian remained desperate for European success, and Ancelotti had an enviable Champions League record. Second, and more intriguingly, Abramovich was determined for Chelsea to embrace a grander footballing philosophy, and realised Ancelotti's Milan were considered the classiest footballing side in Europe – until Barcelona appointed Pep Guardiola in 2008 – by accommodating three or four playmakers in their starting XI. 'I want to find a manager that gives my team an identity,' Ancelotti recalls Abramovich explaining. 'When I see Barcelona or Manchester United, I find an identity in the team, but when I watch Chelsea, I cannot.'

That was unsurprising considering Chelsea had worked their way through four coaches – José Mourinho, Avram Grant, Luiz Felipe Scolari and Guus Hiddink – during the previous two seasons, and were a watered-down, individualistic version of Mourinho's defensive-minded side. Ancelotti promised he would embrace a possession-based approach, and was desperate to sign an old favourite, Milan's Andrea Pirlo – the most artistic deep-lying playmaker in Europe.

But Abramovich misunderstood Ancelotti. Of all the top-class managers of his generation, Ancelotti was the most player-centric coach, moulding a formation and style around his best footballers. That's a perfectly reasonable approach, but in an era where coaching ideologies are considered paramount, Ancelotti's personal philosophy is difficult to define. More than anything he's an outstanding man-manager, embracing and encouraging star players, with even tempestuous talents like Zlatan Ibrahimović and Cristiano Ronaldo declaring him their favourite coach. But his playmaker-dependent, possession-based Milan side wasn't really about Ancelotti's vision, simply a natural consequence of a squad overloaded with number 10s. 'I was struggling to fit them all into the team and keep them happy,' Ancelotti admits, 'but then we stumbled upon a beautiful accident, the Christmas tree formation.' Ancelotti often favoured that 4–3–2–1 formation, despite the 4–3–1–2 producing better results, because it placated more of Milan's star players.

His Chelsea dressing room boasted experienced leaders, including Petr Čech, John Terry, Frank Lampard and Didier Drogba. In typically flexible fashion, Ancelotti consulted them about training patterns and consequently completely changed his coaching style. Previously he had separated technical, physical and tactical sessions, but he discovered that Chelsea's players preferred combined sessions – technical drills that were also physically demanding. In terms of tactics, Ancelotti attempted to introduce these elements two days before matches, but Chelsea's players expressed their dissatisfaction, so again Ancelotti adjusted and effectively aligned himself with the approach introduced by Mourinho, looking at tactics the day before a match.

Ancelotti's Chelsea started 2009/10 in astonishing form, winning 12 of their first 14 matches. Ancelotti used a diamond midfield: Drogba and Nicolas Anelka up front together, Lampard pushed forward to the top of the diamond, Florent Malouda in a roaming, left-of-centre role, with Michael Essien used in either the right-sided or defensive midfield role, and holding midfielder John Obi Mikel or the more forward-thinking Michael Ballack used accordingly. Meanwhile, Ashley Cole and José Bosingwa provided width from full-back. The star performers were Malouda, who embraced his unusual role and produced his most decisive performances in a Chelsea shirt, and Drogba, who crashed in 13 goals in his first 15 matches. Lampard, however, was never comfortable at the top of the diamond, and Anelka appeared marginalised. There were surprise defeats against Aston Villa and Wigan, but Ancelotti's use of an unusual system – at least in Premier League terms – was justified. That is, until November's home meeting with Manchester United, a game Chelsea actually won.

By this point, a knee injury had ruled out Bosingwa for the remainder of the season, and while he was the least celebrated member of Chelsea's starting XI, he was crucial for providing right-sided width. In his absence Ancelotti deployed Branislav Ivanović, who would later become comfortable at right-back but at this point was an awkward converted centre-back who contributed little in possession. At Stamford Bridge, Ferguson's tactics exposed this weakness; right-winger Antonio Valencia pinned back Cole, but left-sided Ryan Giggs drifted inside to become a fourth central midfielder, matching Chelsea's diamond in the engine room. Chelsea's quartet of midfielders continually came extremely deep to collect possession, discovered there were limited forward passing options, so reluctantly knocked out-balls to the hapless Ivanović, prompting audible moans from around Stamford Bridge. United, on the other hand, attacked dangerously by pushing their full-backs forward to overload their opposite numbers. Ferguson's side dominated possession – which shouldn't be considered a victory in itself, but was significant considering Ancelotti's promise about identity – and led 12–8 in terms of shots and 7–0 on corners. United couldn't find the breakthrough, however, and against the run of play Terry nodded home the only goal from a controversially awarded free-kick. Chelsea won the season's first title showdown – but despite their system, rather than because of it.

Ferguson's approach set the template for playing against Ancelotti's diamond, because Chelsea struggled badly when teams exposed their lack of width throughout December. They lost to Manchester City and dropped points to Everton, West Ham and Birmingham, only recording unconvincing 2–1 victories over Portsmouth and Fulham. January, meanwhile, offered an entirely different challenge, because Chelsea were without Drogba, away at the Africa Cup of Nations. However, as Ancelotti had acknowledged about his Milan system overloaded with playmakers, 'the best ideas often come from constraints.' Without Drogba, Chelsea played their best football.

Chelsea's first game of 2010 – and their first without Drogba – was an astonishing 7–2 thrashing of Sunderland. They were 4–0 up after 35 minutes and so comfortable that Ancelotti substituted both Terry and Ashley Cole at half-time. Ancelotti had, typically, changed his formation and created something entirely new to reflect the individuals at his disposal, playing Anelka up front alone, and asking Malouda and Joe Cole to drift inside from the flanks, in a hybrid between 4–3–3 and 4–3–2–1. Anelka – who preferred linking play rather than sprinting in behind – came short and created space, exploited not simply by Malouda and Cole, but also by Ballack and

Lampard, who both scored headed goals following trademark late runs of the sort they'd rarely made in the diamond system with two strikers in the box. Lampard had been particularly below-par in the first half of the campaign, managing only one goal from open play. Here, he managed two in one match. Chelsea were slick, cohesive and ruthless.

Ancelotti continued with this formation for Chelsea's next two fixtures, defeating Birmingham and Burnley. But then Drogba returned, and Ancelotti opted for an awkward compromise between old and new systems, with Anelka shifted into Cole's right-sided roaming role. Drogba was individually magnificent, scoring ten goals in an eight-game spell, but Chelsea's attacking play was predictable and they collected just 13 points from those matches, short of title-winning form.

Next, there was a significant incident ahead of the home fixture against Aston Villa towards the end of March – Drogba was left on the bench, which was initially blamed upon a groin strain. Six years later, however, Ancelotti revealed it was actually because Drogba had turned up late for a team meeting. 'Drogba arrived 30 minutes late, so for this reason he didn't play,' the Italian explained. 'Not because I was upset, but because he needed to be present at the meeting, as I had presented the tactical plan for the game, explaining it all to the players, and I couldn't allow Drogba special consideration.' Drogba was therefore not simply making Chelsea's approach less cohesive, but – unwittingly or otherwise – not involving himself in Ancelotti's tactical plans. Incredibly, for the second time in 2010 – and for the second time without Drogba – Chelsea smashed in seven goals. Lampard scored four times, Malouda managed two, and Anelka was again magnificent as the elusive lone striker. 'Anelka didn't score, but he played a fantastic game, he killed Aston Villa with movement,' raved Ancelotti. Again, Chelsea looked better without Drogba.

That 7–1 victory came just a week before Chelsea's crucial trip to Old Trafford in April, which was inevitably billed as a title decider with Chelsea just one point behind United. Ancelotti had a major decision to make: would he omit the Premier League's top goalscorer Drogba, in the belief his attacking midfielders were performing better with Anelka upfront alone? The answer was yes, with Drogba left on the bench. 'This time it wasn't because he was late, but because Anelka played so brilliantly against Aston Villa,' Ancelotti recalled.

While Chelsea had been outpassed by United at Stamford Bridge, at Old Trafford they were magnificent, with Anelka coming short to link play and allowing Malouda and Joe Cole forward. That duo combined for the opener when Malouda drove to the byline and crossed into the six-yard box, prompting Cole's marvellous back-heeled finish. Ferguson tried to replicate the lopsided system he'd successfully used in the reverse fixture, but Chelsea's 4–3–2–1 approach proved superior; Malouda and Cole dragged the United full-backs out of position, while it was crucial that Ancelotti used Paulo Ferreira, a natural attacking right-back, rather than Ivanović. Now, Chelsea could exploit Giggs's narrowness, and Ferreira was outstanding, nearly putting Chelsea 2–0 ahead when running in behind. It was significant that Ferguson eventually switched Giggs with Park Ji-sung, who specialised in nullifying dangerous attacking full-backs.

Drogba's contribution should not be overlooked, however. When United rallied in the second half, Ancelotti introduced him in place of the tired Anelka, and the Ivorian scored the crucial second goal, albeit from an offside position. Nevertheless, it was significant that in Chelsea's biggest game of the season, Drogba was only a Plan B, despite being the division's top goalscorer, because Ancelotti had stumbled upon a more cohesive system without him. Indeed, other Chelsea managers often found themselves building without Drogba.

He only started half the matches in Mourinho's 2004/05 campaign because Eidur Gudjohnsen linked play better, while Scolari primarily used him as a substitute, and later André Villas-Boas built around Fernando Torres. The Ivorian is arguably the greatest 'big game' player in English football history, scoring four times in FA Cup finals, four times in League Cup finals and, most crucially, the late equaliser for Chelsea in the 2012 Champions League Final. But in pure Premier League terms, he was either sensational or frustrating – he won two Golden Boots with 20 goals in 2006/07 and 29 in this 2009/10 campaign, but tallies of 10, 12, 8, 5, 11 and 5 in his other six campaigns illustrate his inconsistency.

Drogba regained his place for the run-in. While his link-up play was noticeably poor, he made crucial contributions to Chelsea's final three victories, including a hugely dominant 7–0 win against Stoke, a nervy 2–0 win at Anfield and then the title celebration, the relentless 8–0 thrashing of Wigan, the joint second-biggest Premier League victory. In a very peculiar match, however, Chelsea spent the opening period chasing shadows, overrun by Wigan's unusual 3–3–1–3 formation, and only dominated after their opponents went down to ten men.

Chelsea completed the double the following weekend, with a 1–0 victory over Portsmouth, who had finished bottom of the Premier League. This game was most significant for Ancelotti's laissez-faire tactical approach; he allowed his players complete responsibility for devising Chelsea's strategy, with assistant manager Paul Clement standing at the front of a team meeting and writing their suggestions on the whiteboard. This stream of contributions served as the team talk, and was the perfect illustration of Ancelotti's managerial approach.

The postscript to Chelsea's 2009/10 campaign involves the aftermath of their opening match of 2010/11, when Ancelotti was summoned to Abramovich's house, given a dressing-down and asked to explain his side's poor performance. The extraordinary aspect of this tale, however, is that Chelsea had just defeated Roberto Di Matteo's West Bromwich Albion 6–0.

Clearly, Abramovich was being entirely unreasonable. That said, the display hadn't been particularly impressive – the BBC's match report, for example, described it as 'far from a complete performance by Chelsea, who at times seemed to be going through the motions before suddenly raising the tempo', which neatly summarises a couple of heavy victories towards the end of the title-winning season, particularly the Wigan game on the final day. It's remarkable that poor performances often produced such dominant victories, but Abramovich was still concerned about the team's style: Chelsea, particularly when Drogba played, were still a predominantly physical side based around individual power rather than collective interplay. Ancelotti hadn't given Chelsea the identity Abramovich desperately wanted, which probably explains why he was sacked the following summer, despite a perfectly respectable second-place finish.

Six months after Ancelotti's appointment at Chelsea, Manchester City appointed Roberto Mancini. The two had played together for Italy and regularly faced one another as coaches in the Milan derby; their relationship was warm and cordial, but they were very different managers. Ancelotti was the master man-manager and permanently relaxed, whereas Mancini was a spikey character, with his City tenure defined by fallouts with two star strikers, Carlos Tevez and Mario Balotelli.

Mancini dearly loved English football. Even prior to his appointment shortly before Christmas 2009 he spoke warmly about his fascination with the English game, the birthplace of football, explaining why he'd surprisingly elected to come out of retirement at 37 to play four matches for Peter Taylor's Leicester in 2001. After his dismissal from Inter in 2008, Mancini spent a 'gap year' learning English and watching Premier League football, and was linked with every half-decent job that emerged – including, almost inevitably, Chelsea. But Abramovich chose Ancelotti, and therefore Mancini needed to wait for Mark Hughes's dismissal at Manchester City before realising his dream of managing in the Premier League.

City had undergone two high-profile takeovers in the preceding years, bought first by Thaksin Shinawatra, then by Sheikh Mansour; both had invested significant sums of money, although the latter had the greater long-term ambitions. Upon Mancini's arrival, City were essentially a halfway house between mid-table also-rans and title challengers. His first game in charge, on Boxing Day 2009, featured Robinho and Carlos Tevez up front, but the likes of Stephen Ireland and Martin Petrov in midfield. He needed time – and further signings – to turn City into serious contenders.

Whereas Ancelotti promised possession play at Chelsea, Mancini unashamedly focused upon the defence. In addition to plenty of work on the training ground with his back four, he often protected them with no fewer than three defensive midfielders. He signed Patrick Vieira from his old club Inter, and often fielded the now-immobile Frenchman alongside two other holding midfielders, the tough-tackling Nigel de Jong and the ultra-reliable Gareth Barry. Unsurprisingly, City had an infuriating habit of playing out goalless draws in big matches. In Mancini's first half-season there were 0–0s at home to Liverpool and away at Arsenal, and by the time he'd been in charge for just over a year, there had been four more, against Tottenham, Manchester United, Birmingham and Arsenal, with City recording no shots on target in a particularly negative display at the Emirates. It wasn't simply that City recorded plenty of 0–0s, more that Mancini often seemed absolutely delighted with them. In that goalless draw at home to Birmingham, he stunned supporters by making a bizarre substitution with ten minutes remaining – Barry replaced Tevez, a holding midfielder for a forward. Mancini seemed content with a home goalless draw against a side who were eventually relegated. It felt like a parody of an Italian manager.

Things improved ahead of 2010/11 – David Silva was recruited to create from between the lines, Balotelli provided unpredictability up front, while Yaya Touré was signed from Barcelona. However, at this point the Ivorian was considered a defensive midfielder, and Mancini's use of him at the top of midfield was considered another sign of his defensiveness. City boasted the joint-best defensive record alongside Chelsea and controlled matches through possession, with Silva drifting infield and Tevez dropping deep, but offered little penetration. Nevertheless, they achieved a landmark FA Cup semi-final victory over Manchester United at Wembley, courtesy of an aggressive, physical and high-tempo approach, with Balotelli and Touré as the attacking partnership. Touré scored the only goal, which felt typical of the tactical battle – he intercepted a wayward sideways pass from Michael Carrick intended for Paul Scholes, roared forward and crashed the ball home. It was power over precision. Touré also netted the winner in the 1–0 final victory against Stoke City, when City's pressing disrupted Stoke's long-ball tactics – although this success was overshadowed by Manchester United clinching the league title on the same day, their fierce rivals somehow always managing to upstage them.

By 2011/12 Mancini had no excuses for not attacking. Edin Džeko had arrived the previous January and, after half a season adjusting to the pace of the Premier League, started City's title-winning campaign in great form, while Samir Nasri was signed from Arsenal to provide ball-retention skills. Most crucially, Sergio Agüero arrived from Atlético Madrid to play upfront. With Tevez and Balotelli in reserve,

Touré developing his attacking game and James Milner providing balance out wide, City had the most impressive offensive options in the Premier League.

Mancini's system was peculiar. Agüero preferred playing just behind a classic number 9 like Džeko or Balotelli, but continually sprinted in behind rather than drifting between the lines. This meant that City's system often looked like 4-4-2, but with Silva and Nasri moving inside there was plenty of creativity. Touré broke forward from his partnership with Barry, although in big matches Mancini would beef up his midfield, introducing De Jong and moving Touré higher. There were similarities with Ancelotti's Chelsea: a solid defence, dominance of the centre thanks to the wide players coming inside – Italian coaches rarely trust natural wingers – but an uncertainty about the best attacking combination. It was surprising Mancini didn't install Džeko and Agüero as his permanent centre-forward duo; they boasted a fine relationship, and Džeko hit six goals in the first three games of 2011/12, including four in a 5–1 victory at Tottenham. On the same day, Manchester United demolished Arsenal 8–2. Clearly, the two Manchester clubs were going head to head for the title.

Džeko was in and out of the side, however. Mancini handed plenty of opportunities to the volatile Balotelli, who was highly inconsistent, and Tevez, who vanished for the majority of the season. The Argentine had a blazing row with Mancini during a 2–0 Champions League defeat at Bayern Munich, when Tevez refused to warm up. Mancini supposedly told Tevez to 'go back to Argentina'; his striker followed those orders, seemingly spent a few months playing golf, and didn't reappear for several months. Džeko was fit for the entire campaign but started only 16 times, becoming regarded as a Plan B.

At times Mancini's tremendous faith in Balotelli, whom he had brought through at Inter, was justified – most obviously in the historic 6–1 victory over Manchester United at Old Trafford in October, although Balotelli prepared for this game in typically unprofessional fashion. In the early hours of Saturday morning he was forced to escape from a 'substantial fire' in his house after he and his friends had tried to let off fireworks from inside the house through the bathroom window, with predictable consequences. Yet the Italian reported for training as normal, and started the following day's Manchester derby. He opened the scoring with a precise finish from Milner's low cross, before brilliantly turning to the TV camera and revealing a T-shirt that simply read: 'Why always me?' After that morning's headlines, it was another genuinely laugh-out-loud moment from a player who had previously refused to celebrate goals.

Balotelli's speed subsequently got United centre-back Jonny Evans dismissed shortly after half-time, before the Italian doubled City's lead from another Milner assist. Tactically, City relied on the movement of Silva and Milner, who drifted towards the opposite flank in turn, creating overloads and playing one-twos before looking for cut-backs. In a City side otherwise lacking dependable partnerships, Milner and Silva were always on the same wavelength.

Agüero put City 3–0 ahead, before Darren Fletcher scored a magnificent goal with ten minutes remaining, prompting United to pile forward in desperate search of another famous comeback. In doing so they left themselves understaffed at the back, and City counter-attacked to extend the scoring through Džeko in the 89th minute and Silva in the 91st, before Silva's outrageous volleyed assist allowed Džeko to slam home the sixth. 'It's the biggest defeat of my career,' said a shocked Ferguson afterwards. 6–1 was an exaggerated reflection of the contest, but City had unquestionably been superior. They'd tactically outclassed United, recorded a historic victory, and went five points clear at the top.

Shortly afterwards, Balotelli became an ambassador for firework safety ahead of Bonfire Night. 'They can be very dangerous if they are not used in the right way,' he confirmed. 'People should follow the firework code.' Balotelli proved one of English football's most compelling characters, also receiving attention for his inability to put on a training bib, for being substituted after attempting a backheeled finish when through one on one in a friendly, and for being arrested back in Italy for breaking into a women's prison to have a look around. For all the viral moments, however, Balotelli was sometimes devastatingly effective on the pitch – never more so than in that famous 6–1.

City were top for the majority of the campaign, but appeared to have blown their title chances with a run of one victory from five matches in spring. But then United slipped up with a shock 1–0 loss at Wigan, followed by an extraordinary 4–4 draw with Everton, when they'd led 4–2 with seven minutes remaining. With three games left, City were three points behind United but had a superior goal difference – and the next game was the Manchester derby at the Etihad. A City victory would make them title favourites, while United could play for a draw.

It showed. In the closest thing the Premier League has witnessed to a genuine title decider, United were astonishingly negative. Park Ji-sung was fielded centrally to nullify Touré but performed poorly and kept losing his balance, while Nasri and Silva drifted in behind Carrick and Scholes to ensure City dominated the centre along with Agüero and Tevez – who had suddenly reappeared after burying the hatchet with Mancini. Ryan Giggs's narrowness on United's left opened up space for City right-back Pablo Zabaleta to force spells of pressure, and from Nasri's corner from that flank, captain Vincent Kompany powered home the crucial winner. It finished 1–0, a slender victory, but United performed considerably worse than in the 6–1.

City's penultimate victory was a 2–0 win at Newcastle, sealed after Mancini surprisingly introduced De Jong for Nasri, freeing Touré to push forward and score both goals. Then came the Premier League's most dramatic day. City and United were level on 86 points, but City boasted a considerably better goal difference, and were at home to relegation-threatened QPR. City had the best home record in the division, QPR the worst away record. An easy home win seemed inevitable.

At Sunderland Wayne Rooney headed United into an early lead, so United had done their part and were relying upon QPR. City's display was extremely nervy and they took nearly 45 minutes to go ahead through Zabaleta. But shortly into the second half Djibril Cissé equalised for QPR, who were still desperately fighting for survival. Their prospects of beating the drop took a significant hit, however, when their captain Joey Barton got himself dismissed for elbowing Tevez, and reacted with typically good grace by kicking Agüero and headbutting Kompany on his way off the pitch. QPR were surely doomed, with 35 minutes remaining, a numerical deficit and knowing a single concession could condemn them to relegation. But, remarkably, ten minutes later they counter-attacked through Shaun Wright-Phillips, who crossed for Jamie Mackie's precise headed goal. QPR were 2–1 ahead, and suddenly City required two goals in 25 minutes.

By this stage, the home side were panicking, but Mancini introduced Džeko in place of Barry, and then Balotelli – who had recently been dismissed against Arsenal, with Mancini promising he'd never play for City again – in place of Tevez. These changes proved crucial.

As the clocked ticked past 90 minutes, Manchester City still trailed 2–1. Manchester United had won 1–0 and were ready to celebrate on the Sunderland pitch. But equally crucial was what had happened at the Britannia, where Stoke's Jon Walters scored his second goal of the game to equalise against former club Bolton Wanderers. This is a hugely underrated goal in terms of its probable bearing upon what followed; it meant Bolton, who needed to win to stay up, were relegated. On hearing that result, a member of QPR's coaching staff shouted across to his players, 'We're safe! We're safe!' While it's impossible to be certain of the significance of that call, it surely affected QPR's concentration.

Still, City still needed two goals and attacked with incredible force. Their tally of 44 shots against QPR is the most in Premier League history, and, brilliantly, they scored with their 43rd and 44th attempts. First, supersub Džeko powered home Silva's corner, and then almost immediately City attacked once again. The ball found its way to Balotelli, who recorded his first and only Premier League assist by finding the composure to slip in Agüero. The Argentine took a touch, steadied himself and then crashed home the winning goal to send the entire Etihad wild. And it was literally the entire Etihad – QPR supporters, now assured of their team's survival, decided to celebrate the goal for the sheer lunacy of it all. City were champions because their goal difference was 12 better than United's – and, with 6–1 and 1–0 victories over their city rivals, that exact goal difference had come from those two Manchester derbies. In the dying seconds of the Premier League's 20th season, the division now had an undisputable greatest-ever moment.

Yet just like Ancelotti, Mancini was fired after a second-place finish the following season. Was his problem the same as Ancelotti's, a lack of a clear identity? Quite possibly. In a confusing statement confirming his sacking, City said Mancini had failed to meet targets and, intriguingly, 'combined with an identified need to develop a holistic approach to all aspects of football at the club, has meant that the decision has been taken to find a new manager'. That implied that

City wanted an overarching ideology, which Mancini never truly provided.

There was also another Italian success that season, one almost as dramatic as Mancini's. In March Abramovich decided to sack Ancelotti's replacement, André Villas-Boas, a young coach whose approach to football certainly possessed a very clear identity – it just didn't suit Chelsea's players. He was replaced on a caretaker basis by his assistant Roberto Di Matteo, the former Chelsea midfielder who had taken West Bromwich Albion to the Premier League before being dismissed because of his team's defensive shortcomings. Somehow, he turned Chelsea into an extraordinarily solid defensive side that produced an astonishingly unlikely Champions League victory.

After turning around a two-goal deficit to Napoli and easing past Benfica, there came an extraordinary two-legged semi-final against Pep Guardiola's all-conquering Barcelona side, who were European champions and overwhelming favourites. Pep Guardiola's Barca played some astonishing football in the first leg at Stamford Bridge, but Chelsea produced a classic counter-attacking performance and scored on the stroke of half-time. Frank Lampard played a long, diagonal ball to the energetic Ramires, who crossed for Didier Drogba to convert. Somehow, and thanks partly to excellent midfield positioning from Lampard, Jon Obi Mikel and Raul Meireles, Chelsea saw out the game 1–0.

The away leg was even crazier. Barcelona went into a 2–0 lead thanks to goals from Sergio Busquets and Andrés Iniesta, while Chelsea had captain John Terry dismissed for needlessly kneeing Alexis Sánchez. But then, again on the stroke of half-time, Chelsea scored another crucial goal. Again it involved a long diagonal from Lampard into Ramires, who this time didn't look for Drogba and instead produced a wonderful, entirely uncharacteristic chip to put Chelsea ahead on away goals. It was still an uphill struggle. With Terry dismissed and Gary Cahill off injured, Chelsea were forced to play Branislav Ivanović and José Bosingwa as their centre-back pairing, with Ramires at right-back, while Drogba spent most of the game on the left wing. Chelsea played extremely deep and extremely narrow, defended brilliantly and were fortunate Lionel Messi missed a penalty. Somehow, Chelsea actually ended up winning the tie thanks to a breakaway goal from the comically out-of-sorts Fernando Torres.

Most miraculously, Chelsea repeated that performance against Bayern in the final – which was effectively an away game, at Munich's Allianz Arena. This was another backs-to-the-wall defensive effort, with Bayern battering Chelsea throughout and going ahead late through Thomas Müller. But then the ultimate big-game player, Drogba, produced a thumping near-post header to equalise with Chelsea's first shot on target in the 88th minute. Extra-time was even more one-sided, and again the opposition's star player wasted a penalty, with ex-Chelsea winger Arjen Robben's effort foiled by Petr Čech. It came down to a shootout, something Chelsea had bad memories of. But, for once, the Germans didn't win on penalties – and Drogba converted the final spot-kick to seal a barely believable victory.

Just like Manchester United's triumph in 1999 and Liverpool's in 2005, this was an entirely bonkers Champions League success for an English side – Chelsea had been completely dominated, 35 shots to 9, and required an improbable comeback to win. These three victories supported the old cliché about English sides: lacking in technical and tactical quality, but full of hunger, determination and never-say-die spirit. Chelsea, like Liverpool in 2005, had actually slipped outside the Premier League's qualifying spots for the following season's competition, although they sealed their requalification as holders.

Yet like Ancelotti and Mancini, Di Matteo didn't last long. Despite this Champions League success – and also guiding Chelsea to the FA Cup just beforehand – Di Matteo was dismissed six months later following a Champions League defeat to Juventus, which left Chelsea on the brink of an early exit. 'The team's recent performances and results have not been good enough and the owner and board felt a change was necessary to keep the club moving in the right direction,' read a Chelsea statement. Di Matteo had embraced more positive football for the new season, incorporating recent signings Eden Hazard and Oscar in the same side as Juan Mata, creating the most technically impressive Chelsea team of the Abramovich era. In the league they were just four points behind leaders Manchester City, who they were hosting that weekend. It was, among stiff competition, Abramovich's harshest sacking considering Di Matteo's tremendous success in such a short period.

2012 also saw the departure of another Italian manager. England boss Fabio Capello, who had achieved impressive qualifying results but whose tactics proved unsuccessful at the 2010 World Cup, resigned in February. It happened in quite extraordinary circumstances and was linked to the fallout from John Terry being charged with racially abusing QPR's Anton Ferdinand. Terry was stripped of the England captaincy pending his trial in the summer, a decision Capello disagreed with, and the Italian resigned in protest. 'I cannot permit interference from the FA in my work,' he explained. That was a perfectly honourable stance, although the FA's decision was surely more justifiable than Capello's own decision to strip Terry of the captain's armband two years earlier over allegations he'd had an affair with the ex-partner of former Chelsea teammate Wayne Bridge.

Whatever the rights and wrongs of the tiresome debate about whether Terry should wear an armband, Capello had little impact upon English football. Players disliked his stern disciplinarian manner, but more crucially found his tactics alarmingly simple. England usually played a flat, boxy 4–4–2, while Capello continued with immobile target man Emile Heskey up front at the World Cup, despite the Aston Villa striker hitting just three goals in the preceding Premier League campaign. It's notable that England's two foreign coaches, Eriksson and Capello, have both been wedded to 4–4–2 and traditional English centre-forwards more than any homegrown England managers during the Premier League era.

Meanwhile it was difficult to pinpoint any particular legacy from the reigns of Ancelotti, Mancini and Di Matteo – despite the fact that, between 2010 and 2012 they won two league titles, the Champions League and all three FA Cups. The impact of French coaches Arsène Wenger and Gérard Houllier in the late 1990s was clear, as was the transformative effect of Iberian managers José Mourinho and Rafael Benítez in the mid-2000s. The early 2010s, then, should have been about Italians re-educating the English about tactics – but teams wanted a positive identity, and Italian coaches weren't famed for that. Top teams now elsewhere for tactical inspiration: Spain.

20

Tiki-Taka

'If you are better than the opponent with the ball,
you have a 79 per cent chance of winning the game.'

Brendan Rodgers

The overwhelming majority of the Premier League's significant tactical influences have been foreign, but there's been a shift through three completely different forms of foreign revolutionaries.

In the division's formative years it was largely about the arrival of foreign players, with the likes of Eric Cantona, Dennis Bergkamp and Gianfranco Zola particularly pivotal. Then, it became about foreign managers, with Arsène Wenger, José Mourinho and Rafael Benítez offering obvious legacies: better physical conditioning, new formations, more attention paid to opposition tactics. Later, however, it became about foreign teams. As English football broadened its horizons, actually participating in the Premier League was no longer a prequisitite for becoming a major influence on it.

Around the turn of the decade, world football's dominant club side and its dominant international side were effectively the same thing. Barcelona won the Champions League in both 2009 and 2011 with a ground-breaking system featuring Lionel Messi as a false nine and a remarkable commitment to the dominance of possession. Barcelona's players, albeit without Messi, also comprised the majority of Spain's starting XI during this period, and the national side achieved the historic feat of winning three consecutive major international tournaments: Euro 2008, the 2010 World Cup and Euro 2012. That four-year period, also the four years when Barcelona were coached by Pep Guardiola, saw possession football popularised like never before.

This was a hugely significant development. As a player, Guardiola was a gifted deep playmaker who held his position and spread possession reliably from flank to flank, the symbol of Barcelona's ideals. But his top-level career was effectively over at the age of just 32, and he moved to Qatar and Mexico because no major European clubs wanted him. Guardiola, entirely reasonably, blamed the shifting demands upon central midfielders. 'I haven't changed ... my skills haven't declined,' he claimed in a 2004 interview published in *The Times*. 'It's just that football now is different, it's played at a higher pace and it's a lot more physical. The tactics are different now, you have to be a ball-winner, a tackler, like Patrick Vieira or Edgar Davids. If you can pass too, well, that's a bonus. But the emphasis, as far as central midfielders are concerned, is all on defensive work ... players like me have become extinct.'

A look across the Premier League demonstrated that nicely, as there were very few genuine deep-lying playmakers. The likes of Vieira, Claude Makélélé, Didi Hamann and Roy Keane dominated, although in 2004 Liverpool signed Xabi Alonso, a creative rather than destructive deep midfielder. Other exceptions could be found at mid-table clubs: Manchester City's American deep-lying playmaker Claudio Reyna was hugely underrated, while Blackburn's Tugay Kerimoğlu also deserved to play for a bigger side. 'He's a one-off, he's creative and a different type of player to the holding player most teams employ,' said his manager Mark Hughes. That was a prescient comment – there simply weren't many deep-lying playmakers around. 'People say to me, "Don't you wish he was 10 years younger?" My answer is "No," because if he was, he would be at Barcelona.'

During their joint spell of success, Barcelona and Spain both featured, at various points, the likes of Carles Puyol, Gerard Piqué, Jordi Alba, Cesc Fàbregas, Pedro Rodríguez and David Villa. But the most important link was the wonderful midfield trio of Sergio Busquets, Xavi Hernández and Andrés Iniesta. All three grew up in Barcelona's La Masia academy, where they were schooled in the importance of possession football thanks to the legacy of Total Football architects Rinus Michels and Johan Cruyff, and told to learn from the playmaking skills of Guardiola. In Barcelona's midfield trio, Busquets sat deep and protected the defence, Xavi played to the right, orchestrating play, while Iniesta slalomed forward into attack. Spain were even more dependent upon midfield passers; their midfield and attack were similar to Barcelona's, but they couldn't count upon Messi and therefore utilised another deep-lying play-maker, Xabi Alonso, with Iniesta moving into the forward trio along-side Villa and Pedro.

Barcelona and Spain's greatest legacy wasn't their astonishing run of trophies, but in convincing the rest of Europe to play possession football. No one else, however, could depend upon an overarching philosophy that had been in place for decades, and only Barcelona had the five-foot-seven trio who were, according to the 2010 Ballon d'Or results, the world's three greatest footballers: Messi, Iniesta and Xavi. The two Spanish midfielders were particularly militant about their footballing principles. Iniesta recalled his footballing education with the simple phrase: 'Receive, pass, offer. Receive, pass, offer.' That's what he did, again and again and again, while Xavi outlined something similar. 'I get the ball, I pass the ball. I get the ball, I pass the ball. I get the ball, I pass the ball.' The repetition should be infuriating, but it perfectly replicated the feeling of watching their endless passing moves.

This overwhelming focus upon short passing became widely referred to as 'tiki-taka'. The phrase was intended as a term of derision when coined by Javier Clemente, who won two league titles with Athletic Bilbao – traditionally Spanish football's most direct major side – in the 1980s, and who later coached Spain. Clemente was effectively a Spanish Tony Pulis, renowned for favouring direct and physical football, and it's amusing how similar 'tiki-taka' is to the dismissive English phrase for unnecessary short passing. When Pulis took charge of West Brom he vowed not to copy previous managers who had 'played tippy-tappy football, and not winning football'.

Tiki-taka, tippy-tappy – it came to dominate football. Still, it's notable that Spain's World Cup-winning manager Vicente del Bosque referred to tiki-taka as 'a simplification' while Guardiola was even more dismissive. 'I loathe all that passing for the sake of it, all that tiki-taka. It's so much rubbish,' he said. 'I hate tiki-taka. Tiki-taka means passing the ball for the sake of it, with no clear intention, and it's pointless. Don't believe what people say, Barça didn't do tiki-taka!' This felt like a musician unsuccessfully claiming their output didn't conform to any particular genre, and the term stuck. Barcelona played, by common consent, tiki-taka.

Messi was unquestionably Barcelona's best player, but he was a classic superstar, an attacker who could dribble past opponents repeatedly and score relentlessly. Xavi, however, was doing something entirely different – playing short, safe, sideways balls, but dominating big matches and ensuring his team were always in control. Football history is littered with solid, reliable midfielders who allowed talented attackers to shine, but Xavi was always building play subtly and methodically, slowly carving opponents apart.

Predictably, however, his style wasn't initially appreciated in England. When Xavi appeared in a photo alongside Messi, Kaká, Fernando Torres and Cristiano Ronaldo at a ceremony to crown Ronaldo 2008 FIFA World Player of the Year, the *Daily Mail*'s pitiful headline was: 'The best players in the world (and Xavi)'. Over the next couple of years Xavi completely dominated almost every big match he participated in, and the *Mail* was forced into a grovelling apology. 'In a previous edition, we may have given the impression that Xavi wasn't up to it,' it read. 'Now he is King Xavi, pass master of Barcelona … for proving us wrong, we salute you.' We were suddenly all living in a Xavi world.

Newcastle midfielder Yohan Cabaye, who considered Xavi the greatest player around, once heard him say he wanted 100 touches of the ball per game. Cabaye adopted that approach, seeking out his passing number after every match – just one small example of Xavi's huge influence upon European football. Simply keeping the ball, rather than attempting to do anything spectacular, was considered more important than ever, and Xavi was the most influential player of his generation. He, like Messi and Iniesta, was noticeably diminutive – so much for Guardiola's previous declaration that football had become all about physicality. Xavi changed football. 'He helped us to build, or to see, a new player profile that ended up running through all levels of the national team,' said future Spain manager Julen Lopetegui. 'He killed off the myth of physicality being above all else and opened people's eyes to the qualities of small, technical players, proving that you can attack and also defend with the ball.'

England mercifully avoided Spain at international tournaments during this period, but Barcelona regularly defeated English opposition in the Champions League, eliminating Chelsea in 2009 and Arsenal in both 2010 and 2011. Most influential, however, were their two victories in the 2009 and 2011 finals of this competition against Manchester United.

The first success came after Guardiola surprised Sir Alex Ferguson with his use of Messi, previously considered a right-winger, in a false nine role. Barca went ahead against the run of play, but when United chased the game and ended up in a 4–2–4 shape with Wayne Rooney, Cristiano Ronaldo, Carlos Tevez and Dimitar Berbatov across the frontline, they were completely overwhelmed in midfield and well beaten 2–0. Two years later, with Messi established as a false nine, Rooney not marking Busquets properly and United using the immobile central midfield duo of Michael Carrick and Ryan Giggs, they were again overrun in midfield. 3–1 didn't accurately reflect Barça's dominance. Incredibly, Barcelona's most frequent passing combination was Xavi passing to Iniesta 33 times, while United's was Nemanja Vidić passing sideways to centre-back partner Rio Ferdinand 10 times. The three Barça midfielders, Busquets, Xavi and Iniesta, all claimed an assist. The three forwards, Messi, Pedro and Villa, all scored. Guardiola had created a beautifully balanced side that took possession football to new levels.

In that second final defeat, United attempted to engage Barcelona too high up the pitch, with Vidić and Ferdinand instructed to hold a relatively high defensive line. Neither were happy with that approach, with the latter infuriating Ferguson by openly questioning his tactics. But ahead of a 2013 meeting with Real Madrid, Ferguson's last European tie, he admitted to his players that his tactics against Barcelona in these finals had been wrong. A simple passage from his autobiography speaks volumes. Discussing the way United defended extremely deep in the 2008 semi-final victory over Barça, Ferguson says simply: 'We might have done that again in the 2009 and 2011 finals, had I not been determined to win those games our way.' Ferguson let his heart rule his head and, having clinched the

Champions League in somewhat fortunate circumstances in both 1999 and 2008, was determined to triumph in a manner that accurately reflected United's footballing principles.

Barcelona's 2011 victory was also notable for Paul Scholes getting a 13-minute run-out when the contest was effectively dead. At fulltime he swapped shirts with Iniesta, paraded around the Wembley pitch in a Barcelona shirt and later announced his retirement from professional football. There was a gushing stream of tributes for his possession play, led by the Barcelona players who had just defeated him. 'If he'd been Spanish,' said Xavi, 'he might have been rated more highly.' But Scholes was only considered a true world-class performer once Xavi and his fellow Spaniards had popularised the type of possession football he epitomised during his final few seasons.

Scholes was a wonderfully talented footballer, but the incredible explosion in his reputation upon retirement demonstrates this entirely new perception of midfielders. He was now cast as a midfielder revered across Europe but cruelly unappreciated in his homeland, resulting in a completely revisionist account of his left-sided positioning at Euro 2004, as outlined in Chapter 15. For all the glowing tributes offered by the likes of Xavi, Iniesta and Zinedine Zidane, Ballon d'Or voting figures suggest Scholes was never considered a truly elite player throughout his supposed peak years. While nominated for the 50-man shortlist in 2000, 2001, 2003, 2004 and 2007, he never received a vote – not a single vote from any member of the judging panel in any year – which puts him behind somewhat forgettable Premier League players like Adrian Mutu, Karel Poborský and Papa Bouba Diop in the all-time Ballon d'Or voting stakes.

The modest, shy midfielder wasn't the type to worry about awards and he accepted his lack of individual honours with good grace.

After his retirement, when asked whether he was disappointed never to have won the Ballon d'Or, he was typically droll. 'I wasn't even the best player in the dressing room at Manchester United,' he admitted. 'So it would have been pushing it to make a claim to be the best footballer in the world.' Of course, the very fact that Scholes was asked about not winning the award – when he never even received a single vote – says much about how his status soared.

While Scholes enjoyed several fine seasons – 1998/99, 2002/03 and 2006/07 were particularly impressive – his best Manchester United form was arguably around 2010, by which time he'd retreated into a withdrawn role directly in front of the defence. He won Player of the Month in August 2010 following some outstanding displays packed with brilliant diagonal balls, prompting bizarre discussion – because it was seven months early – about whether he should win Footballer of the Year, underlining how his lack of individual awards suddenly become an issue. Possession football was in vogue, it suited Scholes's footballing intelligence wonderfully, and during the first few weeks of 2010/11 he exerted an influence greater than any deep-lying playmaker in Premier League history, with the arguable exception of Xabi Alonso at Liverpool.

This was wrongly inferred to have been Scholes's style throughout his career, however. Beforehand he couldn't play so deep because that role was considered to be about tackling, and a couple of years later the rise of heavy pressing would have affected his ability to dominate matches. But around 2010 came the perfect storm of Scholes at his most experienced and football at its most possession-based. 'People associate me with with starting attacks by knocking long balls,' Scholes said. 'It became something of a trademark over the last few years when I wasn't scoring so many goals.' It's worth remembering, of course, that he initially played in such an advanced position that United fans sang 'Paul Scholes, he scores goals'. By the time Scholes became universally celebrated towards the end of his career he didn't score goals at all – although admittedly 'he assists goals' doesn't scan particularly well.

After initially quitting football after the Champions League Final, showered with praise by world-renowned opponents, Scholes was only away for half a season before returning for another 18-month stint with United. While reversing a retirement decision is common in other sports, it's difficult to think of another top-level footballer in the modern era who has made such a comeback. Scholes's shock return was surely because he realised his talents were more in demand than ever, despite the fact that he was now 37. Considering Guardiola was in charge of Barcelona by that age, after his top-level playing career ended at 31, there had been a quite extraordinary change over the course of a decade, a shift to technical rather than physical qualities. Scholes excelled throughout 2012 before retiring for a second time at the end of 2012/13, again as a league champion. This coincided with Ferguson's retirement – and English football's most successful manager used his retirement speech to pay particular tribute to Scholes.

Compare Scholes's departure to the manner other 'golden generation' players left English football, and there's an enormous contrast. David Beckham was sold having been dropped by Ferguson, Steven Gerrard was awkwardly shifted aside amid talk of his famous slip against Chelsea, Frank Lampard had an ill-advised, controversial loan spell at Manchester City, Ashley Cole found himself on Chelsea's bench, Michael Owen barely got a game for Stoke, Rio Ferdinand was relegated with QPR, Gary Neville retired after a poor performance at West Brom having realised he could no longer compete at the top, Sol Campbell was completely unfit throughout a short spell at Newcastle, Owen Hargreaves spent entire seasons on the treatment table and Joe Cole ended up at third-tier Coventry City. These were once world-class players, but they suffered entirely undignified endings to their career. By virtue of Scholes twice bowing out on a high, at a time when English football had learned to appreciate players in his mould, his legacy wasn't simply preserved, but actually enhanced. Scholes was always a fine player, but only in a tiki-taka, Xavified world was he considered a true great.

A similar, if less spectacular, late-career renaissance was enjoyed by Mikel Arteta. The Spanish central midfielder, a childhood friend of Xabi Alonso in San Sebastián, was educated at Barcelona between the ages of 15 and 20 and was another who based his game around passing, idolising Guardiola. After spells in Scotland and France he joined Everton, where he was considered a forward-thinking midfielder and sometimes fielded on the right flank. His move to Arsenal in 2011, in the wake of Cesc Fàbregas decamping to Guardiola's Barcelona, meant Arteta became appreciated like never before. He wasn't a world-class player and was never capped by Spain, but his impact upon Arsenal shouldn't be underestimated. He signed shortly after their lowest point in the Premier League era, their astonishing 8–2 loss to Manchester United in August 2011, when they were a shambles and huge outsiders for a Champions League place. But Arteta's footballing intelligence, his passing quality and methodical, patient, Xavi-esque use of the ball meant Arsenal became solid, steadily improved and eventually confirmed their top-four place at the expense of Tottenham. Arsenal had averted their first genuine crisis under Arsène Wenger, largely thanks to the footballing intelligence of a Spanish passing midfielder. Like Scholes, Arteta initially played alongside a sturdier holding player, before eventually becoming his side's deepest midfielder. He became Arsenal's club captain, before announcing his retirement in 2016 after receiving a coaching offer he couldn't turn down – fittingly, from Guardiola.

This period of possession play wasn't all about midfielders becoming ball-hoarders, however – it was about entire teams holding onto the ball for longer periods and attacking in a considerably more patient manner. This shift must be considered alongside the increasing dependence upon club analysts, who revered Barça's dominance and ended up focusing too much upon passing figures. 'It is important not to get too carried away with the numbers. They are a tool – they shouldn't become an obsession,' warned Carlo Ancelotti. 'At one time it was all about possession, with all the analysts concentrating upon that. Why? Because it was something they could measure. But as Albert Einstein said, "Not everything that can be counted counts, and not everything that counts can be counted." Possession alone doesn't win the game.'

That might sound obvious, but during this period it became common for managers to cite passing statistics and possession percentages. Manager of West Bromwich Albion Roberto Di Matteo once raved about the number of passes Barça had played in a recent match, before promising his team was working towards improving their tally. Before this possession era such numbers would have been considered irrelevant; who knew how many passes per game Barcelona – or anyone – played? Now, every Premier League manager did. When David Moyes replaced Ferguson at Manchester United he specifically focused upon passing figures, as Rio Ferdinand recalled with some bemusement. 'He'd say, "Today I want us to have 600 passes in the game. Last week it was only 400." Who cares? I'd rather score five goals from 10 passes.'

While passing statistics concerning individual teams proved problematic, passing statistics for the Premier League overall emphasised the significant shift towards a possession-based style. From 2003/04 to 2013/14 the pass-completion rate in the Premier League improved from 70 per cent to 81 per cent, a huge rise in a decade. That obviously translates to around 1 per cent each year, but a further breakdown reveals a particular period of progression. In the three years from 2003/04 to 2006/07 it rose just 1 per cent in total, whereas in the two years from 2009/10 to 2011/12 it jumped 6 per cent.

While the Premier League's tactical development is usually about the top clubs, that 6 per cent jump owed much to the division's lesser lights. In 2009/10, eight sides – Stoke, Bolton, Blackburn, Sunderland, Hull, Birmingham, Wolves and Burnley – recorded a pass completion rate of less than 70 per cent. By 2011/12 only one was under that figure – Stoke – and even Pulis's side had improved their figure by an above-average 7 per cent. This was a league-wide strategic shift towards the Spanish model, and in those two seasons of rapid pass completion progress, two Premier League newcomers proved particularly fascinating.

The first example was Ian Holloway's Blackpool, who surprisingly achieved promotion through the play-offs in 2010 and started their inaugural Premier League campaign as favourites for relegation. 'After watching the World Cup, I've realised that we need to get more like Spain,' Holloway declared before 2010/11. 'I wouldn't like to try and get the ball off them, and we want to be more like that ... you have to caress the ball, you have to love it and you must not give it to anyone else.' The charismatic, slightly bonkers Holloway wanted Blackpool to dominate possession, and his references to Spanish football became a common theme. After an impressive 2–0 victory at Newcastle in early September he returned to the subject. 'You've got to look at tiki-taka, you've got to look at Spain, how they pass the ball, how they keep the ball,' he said. 'They are little guys who run around passing and they are quite brilliant. What's wrong with us, why can't we do it? I want my team to be more like Spain!'

Holloway always used three central midfielders, either in a 4–3–3 or a 4–2–3–1 formation, and stretched the play on both flanks. His wide forwards were located by the laser-sharp, long-range diagonal balls of Charlie Adam, Blackpool's star man. The Scottish midfielder was a curious player; he boasted an absolutely wonderful left foot and an extensive passing range, but lacked athleticism and struggled to get around the pitch. Holloway, therefore, constructed a system that allowed him to exhibit his strengths without exposing his weaknesses. When Adam collected the ball from deep, his midfield colleagues would push forward into attack. When he found himself in an advanced position, the other two would provide defensive balance. He had free rein to move wherever he liked, in the knowledge that two teammates would act as the counterweight.

Constructing a side unashamedly around one player seems alarmingly simple, but in the first half of 2010/11 this worked brilliantly for Blackpool. At the turn of the year they were seventh, a hugely impressive position for such a small club – who had, for example, a total of one full-time scout on the lookout for new players. Adam was briefly among the most revered players in the league, launching a succession of diagonal passes towards Blackpool's wide men and providing a great set-piece threat. On a windy January evening at Bloomfield Road Blackpool led eventual champions Manchester United 2–0 at half-time, with Adam pinging brilliant diagonal balls towards the touchlines and fizzing in set-pieces. United recovered to win 3–2, but Ferguson was taken aback by Adam's quality. 'The first half we were battered, and we couldn't handle Charlie Adam,' he said, before mischievously adding, amid reports that Blackpool had turned down an offer from Liverpool, 'His corner kicks are worth £10m alone'. Adam eventually moved to Liverpool that summer, somewhat optimistically billed as a belated replacement for Xabi Alonso.

In the second half of that campaign at Blackpool, however, Adam and Blackpool's form dipped alarmingly. Adam's concentration was clearly affected by rumours of his departure, and he became carried away with his privileged role in Blackpool's side. Weirdly, he started to regularly shoot from the halfway line. He certainly had the range for these Beckham-esque attempts, and netted for Stoke City in precisely that manner away at Chelsea four years later, but at Blackpool he was trying it every other week. In terms of his passing, opponents got wise to Blackpool's dependence upon one man, concentrated upon nullifying him, and after Christmas Holloway's side won just three games. Their defensive shortcomings were impossible to ignore – they conceded, on average, more than two goals per game and were eventually relegated after a final-day defeat at Old Trafford. 'The fat lady has finished singing and unfortunately I don't like her tune,' Holloway mused. 'That's it in football – you're famous for two seconds and then you're gone.' This was particularly true in the case of Blackpool, who found themselves in the fourth tier by 2016/17 after despicable financial management by their owners.

Another north-west club who received rave reviews for their possession play in 2010/11 were Owen Coyle's Bolton Wanderers – largely on the basis of one excellent team goal against Blackpool, rounded off by midfielder Mark Davies. Coyle was largely credited with overhauling the long-ball legacy of Sam Allardyce, briefly being spoken about as a potential successor to Arsène Wenger. But statistics suggested this supposed revolution was a mirage; Bolton had the fourth-lowest possession share and the third-lowest pass completion rate in the division. They played the third-fewest number of short passes, but the fourth-highest number of long balls. They were still based around physical football – they made the most tackles, committed the most fouls and had the joint-best aerial success rate. It was essentially still Allardyce-esque football, and Coyle was unhappy when presented with these facts, simultaneously questioning the validity of statistics while claiming his statistics showed something entirely different. But Bolton evidently hadn't embraced a possession-based model, this spell of praise was short-lived and they were relegated the following season.

2011/12, however, featured an excellent passing side with a genuinely promising, upwardly mobile young manager. Succeeding Blackpool as Championship play-off winners were Swansea City, who had risen through the divisions impressively, having narrowly avoided relegation from the entire Football League with a final-day victory over Hull City in 2002/03. Nine seasons later they were in the Premier League. Their defining feature throughout this rise was an unwavering commitment to technical, positive possession football, which began with Kenny Jackett between 2004 and 2007, before he was replaced by Roberto Martínez, who had spent three seasons playing central midfield for the club. Swansea was Martínez's first managerial role, and the Catalan was appointed because he perfectly understood the footballing culture Swansea were trying to create. Martínez left for Wigan in 2009, bringing his open, attack-minded football to the Premier League. Meanwhile, his successor Brendan Rodgers took Swansea's emphasis on possession to an entirely new level.

Stylistically, Rodgers is the most 'foreign' British manager the Premier League has seen. His professional playing career ended at 20 because of a congenital knee condition, but Rodgers was determined to make a serious impact on British football. 'My ideology was, "OK, I'm not going to have an influence on the game as a player, technically or tactically. Can I do it as a coach?" My objective was to show that British players could play football.' Rodgers particularly admired the Spanish model, long before their dominance at international level, and spent extended periods in that country furthering his coaching education. His ideal weekend involved flying into Barcelona on a Saturday evening, spending the Sunday watching Barça's youth matches, heading to the Nou Camp to observe the first team, then flying home. He visited the training grounds of Valencia, Sevilla and Betis, always pinpointing clubs who emphasised a long-term, possession-based, collective football style and regularly promoted youth products – in other words, he didn't bother with Real Madrid. He took Spanish lessons for seven years, conscious that a move to Spain might suit his coaching career, and he also paid close attention to the likes of Ajax and FC Twente in the Netherlands.

Rodgers' big break, however, came when José Mourinho recruited him as Chelsea's youth team coach in 2004. Although possessing very different footballing philosophies, Rodgers was particularly delighted to be working under a man who learnt the ropes from Louis van Gaal at Barça. 'Barcelona has been my inspiration, I never run away from that,' he says. 'I spent many years travelling there, learning about the model of Louis van Gaal and Johan Cruyff.' Rodgers, therefore, was the perfect Premier League manager at a point when the Barcelona model was overwhelmingly celebrated – and he, like Holloway, used the phrase 'tiki-taka' to refer to his footballing approach. You didn't need to know about Rodgers' love of Spain, however, to grasp Swansea's commitment to possession.

The season before Swansea's promotion, 2010/11, there was a strong correlation between possession statistics and league position. The top six – Manchester United, Chelsea, Manchester City, Arsenal, Tottenham and Liverpool – were also the six teams who enjoyed the longest periods on the ball. But Swansea completely smashed this link; in their debut campaign, 2011/12, their possession average of 56 per cent was the third-highest in the league, behind Arsenal and Manchester City – and they both outpassed, and outscored, those two sides at the Liberty Stadium, winning 3–2 and 1–0 respectively. Swansea offered little physical threat – they won the fewest aerial duels in the Premier League and committed the fewest fouls. It was all about passing, and Swansea stamped their authority upon matches in remarkable fashion. They finished the season in 11th place, a considerably impressive achievement for a small club boasting little top-flight experience and somewhat modest resources. Swansea didn't even have their own training ground, sharing the facilities of Glamorgan Health and Racquets Club.

Like Blackpool, Swansea played 4–3–3 or 4–2–3–1, always packing three technical midfielders into the centre of the pitch, while Nathan Dyer and Scott Sinclair stayed wide, stretching the play rather than running in behind. Their passing started from the back. Dutchman Michel Vorm was shorter than most Premier League goalkeepers – just six foot – but was recruited because he was extremely comfortable in possession. Centre-back Ashley Williams usually played the most passes, but one of their key passers was, surprisingly, right-back Àngel Rangel. The Spaniard was a thoughtful, intelligent distributor of the ball, often holding his position and dictating play rather than continually overlapping. But there were inevitably mistakes at the back, with Rangel guilty of the most glaring example when Swansea lost 1–0 to Manchester United in November. Javier Hernández's winner came directly from a mistake by the right-back, who played a weak pass in a dangerous position, allowing Ryan Giggs to intercept. Rodgers refused to criticise him. 'Àngel Rangel was terrific, there's no blame attached to him for giving the ball away because I ask my players to play football,' he declared. 'If there is any blame, it is to me. I ask my players to play and pass the ball out rather than kick it up the field.' Rodgers accepted the odd mistake, believing Swansea's overall control of matches made the risk worthwhile.

While Blackpool's star player, Adam, was all about spraying ambitious diagonal balls towards the flanks, Swansea's key man was Leon Britton, the division's shortest player and the safest passer around.

His pass completion rate of 93.4 per cent was the highest in the Premier League, and a further breakdown of his contributions reveals precisely how committed he was to keeping passing moves flowing. He played 2,258 passes in 2011/12, but only one successful through-ball, and only ten of those passes resulted in the recipient attempting a shot. Britton ended the season without an assist, and also failed to score, which was unsurprising considering he only shot four times in 36 games. He had one job: short, sideways passing.

Swansea's style was misunderstood, however, as they were frequently praised for their 'attacking football'. Technical football? Yes. Possession football? Yes. But attacking football? Far from it. Further statistics revealed Swansea's complete lack of attacking; despite such impressive figures in terms of ball retention, they had the fifth-fewest shots (and shots on target) in the Premier League, and no side scored in fewer matches – Swansea failed to net in 15 of their 38 games. Instead, Swansea's football was better as a defensive tool, as only three sides kept more clean sheets.

'Our way of defending is to have the ball,' explained Rodgers. Swansea would keep the ball for extraordinarily long periods in deep positions, simply passing between their defenders and midfielders without seeking to penetrate the opposition. 'My template for everything is organisation,' Rodgers continued. 'With the ball you have to know the movement patterns, the rotation, the fluidity and positioning of the team. Then there's our defensive organisation, so if it is not going well we have a default mechanism which makes us hard to beat and we can pass our way into the game again.' The concept of using possession for defensive purposes wasn't a revelation – holding onto the ball to preserve a lead was an established tactic – but by starting matches with such a conservative approach in possession, Swansea were very different from anything the Premier League had previously witnessed, and the closest thing to Spain.

Shortly after Swansea's debut campaign Spain won their third straight international tournament at Euro 2012, courtesy of even more cautious possession play. This brought critical remarks from Arsène Wenger, the man usually so enthusiastic about possession. 'They have betrayed their philosophy and turned it into something more negative,' he complained. 'Originally they wanted possession in order to attack and win the game; now it seems to be first and foremost a way not to lose. They have become more conservative, and they don't want to give the ball up because they don't want to give you a chance to score.' That's also a perfect description of Swansea's approach under Rodgers, who visited Spain's Euro 2012 training sessions, keen to learn more ideas from his favourite footballing nation.

Swansea's caution, however, only became obvious when witnessing them repeatedly or by comparing their statistics with Premier League rivals, and opposition supporters were rather taken with Swansea's philosophy. After a 3–0 victory at Craven Cottage, for example, their players were enthusiastically applauded off the pitch by Fulham fans, which had become such a regular occurrence that Rodgers occasionally got carried away. 'It is great for the public here at Sunderland to see us,' he beamed after a trip to the Stadium of Light. 'They must have been wondering what this team everyone is talking about are all about – and now they have seen. We were wonderful.' His team had just lost 2–0.

To Rodgers it was about the process as much as the outcome. He was an ambitious young manager who arrived in the Premier League at the perfect time, when possession was revered like never before aesthetically and was considered crucial for winning matches. One of the grounds that Swansea were applauded off was Anfield. 'That was really touching,' said Rodgers, 'because that is such an historic ground.' That ovation would prove particularly prescient.

21

Assisters & False Nines

'I prefer to call myself a "9 and a half"'.

Robin van Persie

The increased emphasis upon passing quality was particularly obvious during this possession-based period, but it was also a long, gradual process that occurred over the course of the Premier League era. Assessing this development in a positional sense suggests it originated at the back, before slowly working its way forward.

The Premier League's first tactical development came from the back-pass rule forcing goalkeepers to participate in passing moves, while the knock-on effect of defenders becoming ball-players quickly became obvious. Later, central midfielders were increasingly considered in ball-playing terms rather than the old-fashioned English ideals of getting around the pitch and battling hard. It was inevitable, therefore, that there was also a shift towards reliable passers among attacking midfielders and centre-forwards.

The evolution of attacking midfielders during this period of Spanish dominance was epitomised by the arrival, in three consecutive summers between 2010 and 2012, of three truly outstanding Spanish playmakers: David Silva joined Manchester City, Juan Mata moved to Chelsea, while Arsenal signed Santi Cazorla. All three participated in their national team's triumphs: Silva played a part in three straight successes, Cazorla missed the 2010 World Cup through injury but won the European Championships in 2008 and 2012, while Mata was involved in both 2010 and 2012. None of the trio was among Spain's most revered midfielders, and only Silva was a regular, but they were nevertheless hugely talented creators and neat technicians who found pockets of space intelligently and slipped through-balls between defenders. This was the Premier League's second 'between the lines' revolution.

The first, of course, had taken place around 15 years beforehand with the arrival of Eric Cantona, Dennis Bergkamp and Gianfranco Zola. There were discernible differences, however; those three were deep-lying forwards who found themselves marginalised in other countries and took refuge in England, and who were all surprisingly physical. Defenders remarked upon Cantona's height, upon Bergkamp's surprising strength, upon Zola's unrivalled ability to shield the ball. Silva, Mata and Cazorla were very different. They were unquestionably midfielders rather than forwards, they considered a move to the Premier League a natural step up from their previous clubs and they were diminutive footballers liable to being outmuscled.

These three weren't identical. Silva was the most effective at playing through-balls, Mata a more prolific goalscorer and Cazorla superior at controlling the game from deeper positions. But there were obvious similarities. All had emerged from a Spanish footballing culture that was – despite Barcelona's insistence upon 4–3–3 – largely based around the 4–2–3–1. Although that had become an established formation in English football, in part thanks to Rafael Benítez, it was often simply a glorified 4-4-1-1, with wide midfielders shuttling up and down the pitch as they'd always done. In Spain the attacking band of three operated with more freedom and interchanged positions fluidly as their team held onto possession for longer periods. Indeed, Silva and Mata played together at Valencia in a perfect example of the Spanish 4-2-3-1, with those two and Pablo Hernández – who later ended up at Swansea, a fitting destination – all occupying right, left and central positions within the same match. David Villa remained the central striker, but the three attacking midfielders simply defended their nearest zone when long passing moves broke down. Cazorla played a similar role at Málaga alongside the wonderful Isco and had done something similar at Villarreal, where he and Cani both drifted inside to turn a 4-4-2 into a 4-2-2-2, almost permanently playing between the central midfielders and the strikers.

Silva, Mata and Cazorla's versatility ensured it was difficult to determine their best role. Instinctively, it felt as if such talented players belonged in the centre, although all three generally found themselves deployed from wide positions. This made sense, considering opponents increasingly played two deep-lying midfielders and protected the space between the lines keenly – these playmakers therefore could pop up unannounced in dangerous zones, rather than remaining there permanently and finding themselves closely marked. 'It offers me the chance to come inside and that way I have a broader field of vision,' Mata explained of his wide role.

Besides, the idea of them having a favoured position was a moot point. Attacking midfielders based around crossing prefer playing on their natural side, and those based around shooting prefer the opposite flank, because their positioning dictates how they can use their stronger foot most effectively. But Silva, Mata and Cazorla were based around short passing, clever movement and pinpoint through-balls, so it didn't really matter where they were deployed, as they always played the same role. This was, of course, another example of universality – players across the pitch becoming similar laterally, from left to right, not simply from back to front.

English football now takes this mould of playmaker for granted, but until recently in the Premier League there were relatively few players like these three: attacking midfielders who could play right, left or centrally with minimal difference to their game. Arsenal were the exception, with Aliaksandr Hleb and Tomáš Rosický in that mould, although Samir Nasri, who later played alongside Silva at Manchester City, spoke about how playing on the right meant he was more likely to sprint in behind whereas from the left he drifted inside more. Joe Cole was another who could play in all three roles, although he never truly excelled in the number 10 position, having been converted to a hard-working wide midfielder by José Mourinho.

Silva, Mata and Cazorla were, however, broadly a new breed. English football didn't quite have an appropriate term to describe them – they certainly weren't wingers or even wide midfielders, while 'playmaker' is too vague and doesn't describe their positioning. Perhaps the simple term 'assisters' explains it best. These weren't proper midfielders but certainly not forwards; they weren't hugely concerned with shooting or dribbling and they weren't crossers. Their job was simply to provide assists.

The assist is now an established concept in English football, but is very much a 'Premier League era' term. Opta, the most established football statistics provider, recruited former Arsenal manager Don Howe in 1996 to establish a precise definition for the concept, arriving at 'the final pass or pass-cum-shot which directly leads to a goal scored by recipient of the ball'. Opta's definition is now largely accepted, and is displayed alongside each player's profile and goals record on the official Premier League website, but it was only around 2010 when reliable assist figures became widely available. Thierry Henry's record 20 assists in a season, for example, came in 2002/03 but was barely mentioned at the time. The presence of these talented assisters coincided with the greater emphasis upon these figures; equally, they became particularly revered because their contribution had become more quantifiable.

Silva was the first of the conquistador assisters to reach England. Although he arrived after Spain's World Cup success in 2010, it had been a difficult tournament for Silva. Vicente del Bosque's side lost their opening match 1–0 to Switzerland, when they appeared a one-dimensional, extremely narrow and predictable side. Playing two playmakers out wide wasn't working. Del Bosque required a player who offered more running in behind – Fernando Torres, Jesús Navas or Pedro Rodríguez at various points – and Silva, another short passer in a team already overloaded with them, was the fall guy, substituted after an hour of the opening match and never reappearing. 'I feel lucky to be part of this great squad, but I also get the feeling that the coach doesn't really need me,' Silva complained the following year. 'When we lost against Switzerland at the World Cup, I was the only one who felt the consequences.' Del Bosque, a manager who concentrated upon squad harmony as much as tactics, was noticeably keen to accommodate Silva over the next couple of years, and he played a key role in the Euro 2012 victory, heading in the opener in the 4–0 final victory over Italy.

Silva had therefore something to prove upon his arrival in England. Before Christmas in his debut campaign he was quiet, managing only one goal – a lovely curled effort following a jinking run against Blackpool – and just three assists. But City's system, which lacked runners in behind the opposition, didn't suit Silva's tendency to play through-balls. He also seemed surprised by the physicality of English football, although he got to grips with things in the second half of the campaign, when he improved significantly.

By the time City started their title-winning 2011/12 campaign Silva was on a different level to anyone else in English football. Opposition defenders simply couldn't cope with his elusive drifts inside from wide positions, and when he played against an old-school English full-back it often made for hilarious viewing. In a 3–2 victory over Bolton in City's second game of the season Silva opened the scoring and completely bamboozled Trotters left-back Paul Robinson, who had absolutely no idea how far inside he should be tracking him. He held his position for too long, only closing down Silva when he received possession, inviting the Spaniard to poke the ball past him for an onrushing teammate.

Eventually, Silva's positioning proved so elusive that he received the ultimate compliment from opposition managers – being man-marked. This wasn't always successful, however. In a trip to City, Everton manager David Moyes instructed Jack Rodwell to follow him across the pitch, but the midfielder was booked after just 20 minutes for fouling the mazy Silva. Moyes immediately handed that role to Phil Neville instead, who lasted just five minutes before being booked himself, which forced Moyes to turn to Rodwell again. Silva still ran the show and teed up James Milner for City's second in a 2–0 victory. Silva was voted Player of the Month for September, enjoyed a run of three goals and 12 assists in 16 starts, and produced one of the greatest individual half-seasons the Premier League has witnessed. With a spate of niggling injuries, however, he only managed one goal and two assists in his final 14 games, as City just about lifted the title.

By this point Silva had been joined in the Premier League by his old Valencia teammate Mata. Whereas Silva initially struggled with English life, Mata adjusted instantly. His sister was living in Brighton and he picked up the language quickly, charming his social media followers with touristy photos of London, his new home city. 'If you want to be anonymous you can go to Soho or Camden and it's not a problem,' he explained. 'There are a lot of Spanish people. If you go to Piccadilly or Oxford Circus you hear lots of Spanish voices but I'm not recognised much. I like Hyde Park and Regent's Park where you can take good pictures, and I have found good tapas in the King's Road.'

More importantly, he started his Chelsea career with a goal on debut against Norwich, and, at precisely the same period as Silva was in his hot streak, Mata managed two goals and six assists in an eight-game spell. Eventually, Silva and Mata finished 2011/12 as the two players who created the most chances in the Premier League, and were also first and joint-second in the assists table. Mata was seemingly the symbol of the new Chelsea, led by André Villas-Boas – although that era lasted less than half the campaign. Nevertheless, Mata proved hugely successful under Villas-Boas, Roberto Di Matteo and Rafael Benítez, three very different managers with very different systems.

He was often played on the left under Villas-Boas, on the right by Di Matteo in big games, and centrally under Benítez. But it simply didn't matter to Mata – 'I can play in any of the three,' he said. He continued to assist with alarming regularity, especially at big moments. He created Ramires's opener in the 2–1 FA Cup victory over Liverpool in 2011, and then Didier Drogba's crucial headed equaliser against Bayern in the Champions League Final. The following season he provided the assists for Fernando Torres and Branislav Ivanović's goals in the 2–1 Europa League Final win over Benfica. He won Chelsea's Player of the Year award in both of his two complete seasons at the club, although he found himself marginalised and then sold to Manchester United after the return of José Mourinho.

Arsenal, meanwhile, signed Cazorla from Málaga in 2012. Although he would later become renowned in a deeper midfield role, initially he was fielded, like Silva and Mata, as an assister drifting inside from wide in a 4–2–3–1, or playing as the number 10. Cazorla described his role as 'playing between the lines, between a defence and the midfielders, and taking up a position where you can do damage to the opposition defence … playing a bit behind the forward and giving assists'. The eternally cheerful Cazorla was a stocky figure who lacked speed over long distances, but was tremendously quick at slaloming away from opposition challenges in tight zones. He was superb in his third Premier League match, Arsenal's controlled 2–0 victory over Liverpool at Anfield, creating the opener for Lukas Podolski and then slamming in the second himself. It was a superb first individual campaign, and in May he managed the extremely rare feat of assisting four goals in the same game, in Arsenal's 4–1 thrashing of Wigan. Only one player achieved more assists than Cazorla that season – Mata. Meanwhile, if you discount Everton's set-piece specialist Leighton Baines, it was Silva, Mata and Cazorla who created the most chances in 2012/13.

Within the next couple of seasons, meanwhile, English football was blessed with the arrival of several more comparable assisters. The players who created the most goals in 2015/16, for example, were Mesut Özil, Christian Eriksen, Dimitri Payet and Dušan Tadić, all in this mould. There was a noticeable shift towards technical playmakers, and the hugely impressive displays of Silva, Mata and Cazorla helped to change what Premier League teams required from attacking midfielders, popularising the concept of the assister.

A more significant story than attacking midfielders becoming more based around ball retention, however, was a similar development for centre-forwards. The use of the term 'false nine' – an unconventional centre-forward being deployed as his side's most advanced attacker but dropping deep into midfield – would have baffled football fans as recently as 2008. A couple of years later it was an accepted tactic.

The popularity of the false nine was another of Barcelona's legacies. Lionel Messi's rise to become the best player of his generation – and arguably the best of all time – owes much to his repositioning at the centre of Barcelona's attacking trio. He was naturally a number 10 rather than a number 9, and at times played extraordinarily deep to ensure Barça dominated midfield, while also achieving record-breaking goalscoring figures.

The term 'false nine' has often been misused in English football, however. While it certainly refers to a player not generally considered an out-and-out striker, it's about the role rather than the individual. For example, at one point an injury crisis meant Liverpool were forced to deploy midfielder Jonjo Shelvey up front for an away trip to West Ham. But Shelvey didn't drop deep and link play in midfield; he simply played as a makeshift centre-forward. This wasn't a false nine. Spain's Euro 2012, success, meanwhile, saw Vicente del Bosque struggling to find an appropriate centre-forward. He surprisingly played Cesc Fàbregas for the opening match, and he naturally dropped into his customary midfield role, which meant Spain were playing a false nine. But then, after a spell on the bench, Fàbregas returned to the side for the 4–0 final victory over Italy. Ostensibly he was playing in the same role, but rather than coming short he played on the shoulder of the last defender, making runs in behind. In the first match he was a false nine, in the second he was simply a makeshift striker.

The false nine in its strictest sense has not become a particularly established role in English football. Nevertheless, the concept has unquestionably changed what managers have come to expect from centre-forwards. The old-fashioned Premier League thesis about a classic centre-forward was a tall, strong number 9 who remained in the penalty box and thrived on crosses. The false nine, then, was very much the antithesis.

The synthesis between the two models was the type of centre-forward who dominated between 2011 and 2016. Premier League Golden Boot winners Carlos Tevez, Robin van Persie, Luis Suárez and Sergio Agüero became prolific goalscorers as their club's most advanced forward, despite all arriving in English football as second strikers who played behind a teammate. The fact that they became top-class number 9s rather than number 10s demonstrated the shifting requirements for centre-forwards. Of course, this wasn't the first time Premier League sides had played without conventional strikers – Arsenal's Thierry Henry and Manchester United's Cristiano Ronaldo had done similar things – but their positioning was primarily about allowing themselves more space to break into. Now, it was all about link-up play.

Wayne Rooney was, if not a false nine, certainly a dubious nine. Manchester United's record goalscorer arguably never discovered his optimum position, having often been shifted wide during the Ronaldo era, then alternating between a number 9 and number 10 position in subsequent years, and later being deployed in midfield. In 2009/10, however, Rooney produced his first genuinely sensational spell of goalscoring form and was often fielded up front alone in a 4–3–3. While improving his ability to score classic centre-forward goals, netting many with his head, Rooney sometimes played much deeper, without a strike partner running in behind. The counter-attacking goal he rounded off in a 3–1 victory over Arsenal in 2010 was the classic false nine goal; he came short to drag the opposition centre-backs up the pitch and received a pass from Park Ji-sung midway inside his own half. Then, after laying the ball right to Nani, who dribbled forward 50 yards in possession, and finding space because Park's decoy run distracted Arsenal's defenders, Rooney powered into the box to sweep home the return pass. It was, tactically speaking, one of the Premier League's all-time finest goals, a perfect demonstration of how centre-forwards were expected to both link play and score.

Nicolas Anelka, while always considered a number 9 – much to his disgust – provided the most important false nine Premier League performance in Chelsea's aforementioned 2–1 victory over Manchester United in 2010, but he was rarely fielded in that role because of Didier Drogba. Therefore, the most important false nine in English football is Tevez. As previously outlined, his signing for Manchester United prompted speculation about whether he and Wayne Rooney could play together because both were considered the same sort of player: number 10s. They played backseat roles in Manchester United's sometimes-strikerless Champions League-winning side, but Tevez's controversial transfer to Manchester City ensured he finally became his side's main man.

Initially he was deployed behind Emmanuel Adebayor, a traditional target man, but during 2010/11 – the season when Messi particularly underlined the value of a false nine by taking Barcelona to the European Cup – Tevez spent long periods isolated as Manchester City's lone striker, and constantly dropped deep into midfield roles and linked play. Of course, Tevez was fundamentally comparable to Messi, and there were many debates in Argentina about whether they could co-exist for the national side. While not quite in Messi's class, Tevez largely replicated his compatriot's role for Manchester City that season, linking play smartly while also finishing as the Premier League's joint-top goalscorer alongside his ex-teammate, Manchester United's Dimitar Berbatov.

Berbatov's experience was also significant. After Ronaldo and Tevez had departed in 2009, Berbatov was generally deployed as

United's main striker, just ahead of Rooney – but later occasionally played more of a withdrawn role, with Rooney higher up against the opposition defence. Both were comfortable in either role, underlining how top-class centre-forwards were now somewhere between a number 9 and a number 10. The most fascinating aspect of Berbatov's 2010/11 campaign wasn't him finishing as joint-top Premier League scorer, however, but the fact that this status didn't even earn him a place in Sir Alex Ferguson's 18-man Champions League Final squad, with Rooney starting behind Javier Hernández and Michael Owen preferred on the bench. This came as a stark reminder that scoring goals wasn't enough.

After Tevez and Berbatov shared the honour in 2010/11, the Premier League's Golden Boot winner for the next two campaigns was Dutchman Robin van Persie, who produced a magnificent individual campaign in 2011/12 to drag a struggling Arsenal side into the top four, before he moved to Manchester United and fired them to the title. Van Persie was, like Tevez, considered a number 10 upon his arrival in English football in 2004 and coincidentally also played just behind Adebayor. The Togo striker's transfer to Manchester City in 2009 meant Arsène Wenger, typically, adjusted the role of an existing player rather than recruiting a direct replacement, with Van Persie now leading the line. He was sensational at the start of 2009/10, offering a perfect balance of creativity and finishing – seven assists and seven goals in 12 matches. But a serious ankle ligament injury ruled him out for five months.

During Van Persie's absence Wenger generally fielded Russian Andrey Arshavin as his most advanced forward. Arshavin was a confusing player; naturally a talented playmaker, he was deployed on the left of Arsenal's attack and offered sporadic brilliance, before badly losing his way and suffering a significant loss of confidence. He was purely creative and technical, providing little in terms of work rate or physicality, and was never a prolific goalscorer. He was the falsest of false nines during this period, but his poor performances rarely promoted the role. Arsenal desperately missed Van Persie.

After his long injury lay-off, the Dutchman was transformed from a talented but injury-prone second striker who scored great goals into a ruthless centre-forward who was a great goalscorer. Generally fielded upfront alone in a 4–3–3, he was an intelligent, eloquent footballer who appreciated how his role had changed. 'I don't really see it as a main striker position,' he explained. 'In Holland we call positions by their numbers – number 9 is the main striker and number 10 is the one just behind. I prefer to call myself "9 and a half" – I like to drop off sometimes and be part of the game. I'm still a bit of a behind-the-striker player when possible … The boss told me, "'Don't focus on scoring goals, because they will come, and play your game as you always used to play. Don't try to change your game and think of yourself as a striker only. You are more than that.'" That summarised it neatly; just because Van Persie was playing upfront, he wasn't supposed to lose his creative edge, and he provided plenty of goals for Theo Walcott, who balanced Van Persie's movement towards the ball with sprints in behind.

At Manchester United Van Persie formed a prolific strike partnership with Rooney, who played the withdrawn role in a 4–4–1–1, and the Dutchman increasingly became a pure number 9, although he returned to a familiar theme when describing Rooney and him as 'both 9 and a halves'. They boasted a fine relationship, and Ferguson's final title was sealed after a 3–0 victory over Aston Villa, with Van Persie scoring a hat-trick including a trademark volley from Rooney's floated ball over the top. That United team were somewhat shambolic at times, particularly in midfield, but both Rooney and Van Persie were outstanding.

After Van Persie had won two Golden Boots – presumably both left boots – the winner in 2013/14 was Liverpool's Luis Suárez. This campaign will be analysed in greater depth later, but the Uruguayan's level of performance was truly outstanding, with 31 goals in 33 matches at a rate of 0.94 goals per game, the best in Premier League history. Again, there's a familiar pattern here; Suárez wasn't considered a pure striker upon his arrival in English football in January 2011, having starred for Ajax on the right. This was underlined by the fact that when Liverpool did brilliantly to get £50m from Chelsea for the misfiring Fernando Torres the same day, they insisted upon immediately spending 70 per cent of the fee on Newcastle's unproven target man Andy Carroll, such was their desperation for a proper number 9. The fact they'd already signed the perfect Torres replacement two hours earlier went unnoticed.

Indeed, a major feature of Suárez's early Liverpool days was his relative lack of goals, despite his ability to dominate games and wreak havoc with his speed, movement and bustling past defenders. He managed just nine goals in his first year, partly because his position was frequently changed and he was often forced to flit around behind Carroll. But when fielded regularly in a proper centre-forward role he developed into the Premier League's most prolific striker, and continued to assist too.

The next two Golden Boot winners, Sergio Agüero and Harry Kane, are both generally considered pure strikers. Once again, this wasn't entirely the case from the outset. Agüero spent the majority of his first three campaigns in English football in his favoured position alongside a more traditional centre-forward. 'For most of my career I've played behind a striker, but close enough to form a partnership with them,' he outlined. 'That's where I think I play best.' But Agüero was eventually pushed forward to lead the line, and registered the two best goalscoring campaigns of his career.

Kane, meanwhile, took a while to convince observers of his true quality. He was a slightly awkward, clumsy player who boasted that old-school knack of being in the right place at the right time. But there was more to Kane's game than goalscoring, and when he suffered a goal drought the value of his link play became more obvious. Notably, like Agüero, he took the number 10 shirt rather than the number 9, and it was peculiar that Kane was compared to two former England strikers, Alan Shearer and Teddy Sheringham, who were entirely opposite in nature – which is precisely why they formed such a fine striking partnership. Kane had the goalscoring ability of Shearer and the link play of Sheringham. He was, as Van Persie would say, the classic 9.5. 'I played in different positions as a kid and it helped me learn different parts of the game,' Kane explained. 'Playing alone up front means you have to be good at so much more than taking chances. I know, in a game, I am going to receive the ball with my back to goal, and that the team will need me to link up and bring others into play.'

The ultimate example of the acceptance of this unorthodox forward came later, when Jürgen Klopp took charge of Liverpool. The major part of Klopp's game plan was his high-tempo counter-pressing, which demanded energy and dynamism from his centre-forward, as well as the ability to play quick, neat interchanges with onrushing midfielders. Klopp discarded Christian Benteke, who won aerial duels and scored goals but did little else, and also frequently left out traditional strikers Daniel Sturridge and Divock Origi in order to field Roberto Firmino – yet another converted number 10 – as his most advanced foward. Playing without a striker would have been considered lunacy a few years earlier, yet there was minimal dissent following Klopp's decision. In fact it was widely agreed that Firmino suited the system much better.

'There is a wide spectrum of types of strikers,' Klopp explained. 'Roberto is a very offensive player, so he is a striker. Everyone asked me, "What about Firmino, we need a real target striker!" Roberto is a striker. A lot of strikers are 1.6 metres; Lionel Messi, what is he? Firmino can play and score goals and he is flexible and at the moment in brilliant shape. He gets in the box and then something happens.' That was a relatively rare nod to the direct influence of Messi – few managers wanted to invite that comparison.

Why, then, did all these players take time to become proper strikers? The usual comment, in various forms from the players themselves, is that they believe there's 'more to their game' than simply scoring goals – Van Persie and Kane, in particular, are keen to mention their link play. But, of course, football had become universal – every player has more to their game than their basic job description, and in the possession era, it was about linking moves as much as finishing them.

Part Eight

Post-
possession

22

Rodgers' Reversal

*'When you look at the stats of the modern game, I'm
big on controlling domination of the ball. But against
Everton we were able to dominate without the ball.'*

Brendan Rodgers

Twice during the Premier League era the runners-up have proved
considerably more fascinating than the champions.

The first instance was Newcastle's inability to win the title in
1995/96, largely because of their tactical naivety – and there were
many similarities with Liverpool's dramatic failure in 2013/14. These
were two massive clubs from major footballing cities in the north,
both desperate for their first top-flight league championship in
decades. Both were relentlessly attacking, individualistic sides who
often overlooked the importance of defending. Add a young manager,
a volatile South American striker and a legendary late-season Anfield
thriller, and it's clear that Liverpool were the new 'Entertainers'.

After first Roy Hodgson and then Kenny Dalglish had been
dismissed, Liverpool were now managed by Brendan Rodgers. The
unusual sight of his Swansea side being applauded off the Anfield

pitch stuck in the minds of Liverpool's relatively new owners, Fenway Sports Group, who had transformed the Boston Red Sox with a progressive statistical approach frequently referred to as 'moneyball'.

FSG were fresh, ambitious owners who wanted a progressive manager, and Rodgers, with his love of possession figures, seemed a natural fit for both FSG's number-based approach and Liverpool's historic emphasis upon attractive football. Rodgers proudly spoke of his belief in passing the ball, and wanted to replicate the possession statistics he'd achieved at Swansea. 'When you've got the ball, 65 to 70 per cent of the time it's a football death for the other team,' he explained after a few weeks. 'We're not at that stage yet, but that's what we will get to. It's death by football.' This was the unashamed target: complete possession dominance.

His first transfer window lacked transformative arrivals, but his intentions were obvious; out went Andy Carroll, the classic target man who required regular crosses, and Charlie Adam, the midfielder who thumped ambitious balls downfield. In came Joe Allen, one of Rodgers' dependable Swansea midfielders whom he optimistically referred to as 'the Welsh Xavi', and Fabio Borini, whom he'd coached for Chelsea's youth side and who had played under Pep Guardiola's long-term successor Luis Enrique at Roma. Both already understood Rodgers' possession-based approach.

Rodgers also started his Liverpool tenure starring in a six-part fly-on-the-wall TV series entitled *Being: Liverpool* – if the curious punctuation implied other clubs would agree to similar treatment, the content did little to persuade them. Filmed throughout Rodgers' first pre-season, with no competitive matches and few meaningful storylines, it relied upon Rodgers' monologues for content. It was all slightly too *The Office* for comfort, thanks to a combination of unremarkable behind-the-scenes shots, 'Brendan' being disturbingly close to 'Brent', and his tendency to say things like 'I've always said that you can live without water for many days, but you can't live for a second without hope.' He became a figure of fun, mocked for his buzzwords and, unfairly, for a stunt where he held up three sealed envelopes to his squad, supposedly containing the names of the three players he believed wouldn't push themselves throughout the season. This was considered lunacy – but it was a move borrowed directly from Sir Alex Ferguson ahead of his 1993/94 title-winning season with Manchester United.

Rodgers' subsequent debut season was underwhelming. Liverpool failed to win in their first five games, then improved steadily and were boosted by the arrival of Daniel Sturridge and Philippe Coutinho in January. However, they finished seventh, just a one-place improvement from the previous campaign, and without a cup run to compensate – Dalglish had won the League Cup and reached the FA Cup Final in his only full season during his second spell as manager. The end of Rodgers' first campaign was dominated, meanwhile, by Luis Suárez.

While the Uruguayan forward – whom Rodgers had once greeted with 'You're a fantastic player, congratulations' in Spanish during his Swansea days – proved highly popular at Liverpool, he had an unfortunate tendency to get himself into trouble. Most notoriously, there was an incident between him and Manchester United left-back Patrice Evra, which resulted in the FA finding Suárez guilty of using 'insulting words including a reference to Evra's colour' and handing him an eight-match ban. Dalglish backed Suárez to the hilt, which involved Liverpool's players warming up for a subsequent game in T-shirts showing support for Suárez, an ill-judged campaign that was widely ridiculed and which, some suggested, might have contributed to Dalglish's dismissal. Suárez's first game back following the ban was inevitably at Old Trafford, where he started by refusing to shake Evra's hand and ended by scoring. That was Suárez: shameless and superb within the same match.

Towards the end of Rodgers' first campaign, meanwhile, Suárez earned an even longer ban – this time ten matches – when he reacted to a routine chase for the ball with Chelsea's Branislav Ivanović by biting the Serbian defender on the arm. The Premier League was accustomed to foreign attackers introducing new practices into English football, but this was something entirely unexpected, an innovative take on violent conduct. Most bizarrely, it was neither the first nor the last time Suárez was banned for biting, also sinking his teeth into opponents with Ajax and Uruguay. Even Prime Minister David Cameron got involved, saying Suárez was 'setting the most appalling example'.

In the summer of 2013, and midway through his suspension, Suárez decided he was sick of English football. He'd been interested in a move to Juventus the previous summer, and came to a gentleman's agreement with Liverpool that if they didn't achieve Champions League qualification he could leave. There were two problems, however: the club went back on their agreement and few foreign clubs showed serious interest. Arsenal, however, were extremely keen, and after discovering that Suárez's contract contained a release clause for offers in advance of £40m, took this literally by cheekily offering £40,000,001.

What followed was curious; Liverpool seemingly fibbed about the nature of the release clause, claiming that the only thing Arsenal's bid activated was an obligation for them to inform Suárez of the London club's interest. That would have been a largely pointless clause, and as Liverpool owner Henry later admitted, was a complete fabrication. 'What we've found is that contracts don't seem to mean a lot in England, actually, in world football,' Henry proudly told the MIT Sloan Sports Analytics Conference. 'It doesn't matter how long a player's contract is, he can decide he's leaving – we sold a player, Fernando Torres, for £50m, that we didn't want to sell. We were forced to. Since apparently these contracts don't seem to hold, we took the position that we're just not selling.'

Suárez now held two completely different grudges against Liverpool, as he outlined in an explosive *Guardian* interview. First, the gentleman's agreement: 'Last year I had the opportunity to move to a big European club and I stayed on the understanding that if we failed to qualify for the Champions League the following season I'd be allowed to go,' he said. 'I gave absolutely everything last season but it was not enough to give us a top-four finish – now all I want is for Liverpool to honour our agreement.' Second, the Arsenal bid: 'I have the club's word and we have the written contract, and we are happy to take this to the Premier League for them to decide but I do not want it to come to that.' Suárez was essentially banned from first-team training and told he wouldn't be reintegrated until he apologised.

It's remarkable that Suárez remained at Liverpool at all, let alone produced among the most impressive individual campaigns of the Premier League era. A major factor in his continued presence in 2013/14 was the intervention of Steven Gerrard, who had long been club captain but who was more important than ever following the retirement of Jamie Carragher, a more natural leader. Gerrard was surprisingly crucial in Liverpool's transfer activities that summer. In between sending texts to Shakhtar Donetsk's Willian, attempting to convince him of a move to Anfield – the Brazilian eventually turned down Liverpool and Tottenham and joined Chelsea for Champions League football – Gerrard persuaded Suárez that fighting Liverpool over a 'sideways' switch to Arsenal wasn't worthwhile, and he should focus on playing another great campaign with the club to secure a move to Real Madrid or Barcelona.

This convinced Suárez – who, after all, had been primarily determined to leave the Premier League entirely, rather than commit to a long-term contract elsewhere in England. Gerrard met Suárez for a morning chat at Melwood, Liverpool's training ground, essentially disobeying orders because the Uruguayan was banned until the first team had gone home at lunchtime, and then arranged a meeting between Suárez and Rodgers. Suárez wouldn't attend unless Gerrard joined him. Everything was smoothed over; Suárez didn't want to go to Arsenal, and he stayed at Liverpool. There was, of course, simply the small matter of him being banned for the first five games of the season. But this was nevertheless a huge victory for Liverpool, who had managed to retain their star player against all odds. Gerrard, in particular, deserved great credit for the fact that Liverpool mounted a Suárez-led title challenge in 2013/14, a campaign that was largely about the contributions of these two players.

In addition to acting as Liverpool's unofficial transfer negotiator, Gerrard also had his testimonial that August. He'd long since passed the ten-year mark that entitles a player to the honour, and the decision to hold it in 2013 felt like recognition that Gerrard was nearing the end. Notably, he still hadn't won a league title, and had seemingly abandoned all hope (clearly not having listened to Rodgers' aforementioned proverb). 'It will be a miracle if I now realise my dream of winning the title with Liverpool,' Gerrard wrote in his autobiography, published the previous year. 'I say that because of my age and where we finished in the league the past couple of years, and also the situation we're in with our rivals.' Liverpool started 2013/14 at 33/1 for the title – fifth-favourites – and therefore outsiders for a Champions League place. But Manchester United, Manchester City and Chelsea had all been destabilised by managerial changes. The appointment of David Moyes and Manuel Pellegrini – and the second coming of José Mourinho – meant that all three teams were unpredictable going into the new season. Arsenal, meanwhile, completed no major signing until the arrival of Mesut Özil with the season already under way. There was a chance for Liverpool to take the league by storm.

They started in impressive fashion. In Suárez's absence, Daniel Sturridge played alone up front in a 4–2–3–1 and scored the winner in Liverpool's first three matches of the season against Stoke, Aston Villa and Manchester United: 1–0, 1–0, 1–0. This proved inappropriate preparation for Liverpool's eventual all-out-attack philosophy, however, and they didn't win 1–0 again all season.

They subsequently drew 2–2 at Swansea and lost 1–0 at Southampton, before a trip to Sunderland. This wouldn't normally have been a particularly significant game, but it marked the return of Suárez after his ten-match ban. Surprisingly, Rodgers completely abandoned his previous system, deploying a 3–4–1–2 simply to get Suárez and Sturridge in their favoured centre-forward roles, without resorting to a simple 4–4–2 that wouldn't offer a three-man central midfield. Other players were square pegs in round holes: Victor Moses wasn't a number 10, Jordan Henderson wasn't a right-wingback. But in Liverpool's next four matches they scored 12 goals, with only three scorers: Suárez with six, Sturridge with four (one in each match) and two penalties from Gerrard. Liverpool, much like the Manchester United side who triumphed the previous season, were all about their centre-forwards, who were nicknamed – with a nod to Blackburn's partnership of Alan Shearer and Chris Sutton in 1994/95 – the SAS.

Much like that SAS, however, Sturridge and Suárez weren't particularly close for a similar reason: both wanted to be the main man. The first time they spoke at Liverpool's training ground, Sturridge approached Suárez and immediately said: 'Together, you and I can do something big here.' Little sign of tension, you might think, but it's telling that Suárez's self-confessed reaction was, 'It's not normal for a new player to be as bold as Daniel was that day, and I did momentarily think, "What's that guy saying that to me for?"' Suárez insists, however, that they got along perfectly well.

Gerrard's interpretation is more enlightening. 'SAS was not a partnership in the mould of John Toshack and Kevin Keegan,' he said. 'Suárez and Sturridge instead worked as two gifted individuals. Brendan often spoke about the fact that they were like two soloists vying with each other rather than playing together as a harmonious duo. They never said much to each other in training … it never got nasty but there was an edge between them. There were probably some games when Luis was a bit heavy on Daniel.' This hardly affected their individual scoring rates; Suárez hit 31 goals, Sturridge 21, the first time one club had the Premier League's top two goalscorers. They weren't, however, a proper partnership.

Still, playing them up front meant Liverpool could attack two against two when they won possession, and in a 2–0 defeat to Arsenal in early November it was surprising how often Liverpool attempted long balls into the channels, trying to exploit the space vacated by the opposition's attacking full-backs. But Arsenal's Laurent Koscielny was outstanding, consistently dispossessing both. On a rare occasion when Suárez escaped the Frenchman's attention, he ambitiously shot at goal rather than passing to an unmarked Sturridge, who threw his arms into the air in disgust. At half-time Rodgers reverted to 4–2–3–1, permanently abandoning the back three.

Sturridge's absence through injury during December meant Suárez was unquestionably the main man, and he produced a scintillating succession of performances, including ten goals and three assists in a sensational four-game spell. He seemingly considered every player on the pitch to be merely apparatus for helping him to score, regularly bouncing the ball off opponents to continue his dribbles and depending upon one-twos more than a wedding DJ testing his microphone.

At times he was simply unstoppable, with his four-goal haul against Norwich made up entirely of absolutely brilliant strikes.

It became clear that Suárez was enjoying among the best-ever individual Premier League campaigns, up there with Dennis Bergkamp in 1997/98, Thierry Henry in 2003/04 and Cristiano Ronaldo in 2007/08. There were only two negatives: him missing the first five games of the season through suspension, when Liverpool dropped five points to average opposition, and the fact that he didn't score in six matches against other top four sides, matches that counted for four of Liverpool's five defeats. By definition it's harder to score against stronger sides, and it's worth remembering that Liverpool's title challenge of 2008/09 failed because they weren't swatting aside Premier League minnows regularly enough, which wasn't a problem when the ruthless Suárez was available. Nevertheless, 1.1 goals per game against the Premier League's 'other' 16 sides contrasts sharply with his 0.0 against the top four.

The most significant tactical development as winter approached, however, involved Gerrard, who had become desperately unhappy with his performances in an attack-minded midfield role. Unusually, he approached Rodgers and asked him to watch videos of his recent performances to assess his all-round game, and wanted Liverpool's analytics department to provide statistical analysis of his recent performances. This was a quite unprecedented step for such an established player, let alone someone who hadn't obviously been playing poorly. Rodgers stayed up late that evening watching the tapes, and they reconvened the following afternoon.

The statistics involving Gerrard's physical output were satisfactory, but Rodgers identified a problem with the way his captain was receiving possession. 'It was plain to see that my head movement wasn't there,' Gerrard remembered. 'That movement is so important because it feels as if you've got to have eyes in the back of your head to play as a midfielder in the Premier League. It's so much more significant now than when I started, because it's so congested in the midfield and you have so much less time on the ball.' They discussed Gerrard playing a considerably deeper midfield role where he'd find more space, taking inspiration from the wonderful Italian deep playmaker Andrea Pirlo, who had dominated proceedings against England at Euro 2012.

Then Gerrard collected a hamstring injury and was unavailable for a month anyway. His replacement as captain, surprisingly, was Suárez – just four months after he'd been banned from training with his teammates. Without Gerrard, Liverpool recorded a comprehensive 5–0 victory at Tottenham, which Rodgers described as 'a watershed moment' in his side's development, but also lost 2–1 at Chelsea and Manchester City between Christmas and New Year, with the club somewhat unfortunate that their two trickiest fixtures of the campaign, away at both of their eventual title rivals, came back to back in the middle of the busiest part of the season.

Liverpool's first match after the festive period was a trip to Stoke, and saw a significant tactical innovation – Gerrard deployed in the Pirlo role, a hugely surprising move. Gerrard's major weakness was his positional indiscipline, and he'd therefore never previously played that position as the sole holding midfielder for Liverpool. Lucas Leiva, accustomed to defensive midfield, now played a box-to-box role alongside Henderson, with their energy creating a pocket of space for Gerrard, who launched long diagonal passes downfield. The match finished 5–3 and would foreshadow the rest of their campaign; with Gerrard used in that deeper role, Liverpool were sensational going forward but their defensive structure was rather risky.

Liverpool's outstanding performance came in February, a sensational 5–1 home win over Arsenal – particularly remarkable considering the Gunners were top of the Premier League. Rodgers' side were absolutely rampant, with Martin Škrtel scoring the first two from set-pieces, then Liverpool producing a masterful counter-attacking performance against a side eternally vulnerable to that approach. Goals from first Raheem Sterling, a speedy young winger perfect for this approach, and then Sturridge put Liverpool 4–0 up after just 20 minutes, Sterling completed the scoring in the second half, while Suárez produced an astonishing all-round display and hit the woodwork from 35 yards, but somehow finished goalless. Arsenal pulled one back when Gerrard tripped Alex Oxlade-Chamberlain, Mikel Arteta converting the resulting penalty. That incident, with Gerrard's defensive skills found wanting, was the sole negative in an otherwise fantastic all-round display, which was consistent with Liverpool's previous home match, a similarly impressive 4–0 thrashing of Everton. Then, Gerrard was left isolated ahead of the defence and too easily attracted to Everton's wide players drifting inside, and Ross Barkley, Everton's number 10, found space. Nevertheless, Liverpool were scoring plenty of goals, with Gerrard starting the attacks from deep. Despite these two thumping wins, Liverpool were very much outsiders for the side – still in fourth place.

Crucially, Liverpool now played an entirely different brand of football from Rodgers' initial intentions. Those long spells of possession hadn't materialised, and now Liverpool were most impressive when playing extremely direct counter-attacking football, which depended upon the speed of Suárez, Sturridge and Sterling – the SASAS? – to break past the opposition quickly. That was most obvious against Arsenal, and was combined with an aggressive midfield press that twice caught out Mesut Özil, stunned by the speed of the midfield battle, directly leading to breakaway goals. This approach was perfect for box-to-box midfielder Henderson, who provided both energetic pressing and storming forward runs.

Liverpool's average possession share was the fifth-highest in the league, and they commanded matches against weak opposition. But in their eight matches against the other top five sides – Manchester City, Chelsea, Arsenal and Everton – they dominated possession only once. More crucially, Liverpool lost four of those eight games.

In the Arsenal match, and most others during this period, Rodgers played a 4–3–3 system – which meant either Sturridge or Suárez was fielded wide. This was a tricky balancing act for Rodgers. On one hand he determined the positioning of Suárez and Sturridge tactically, usually by deploying Sturridge's pace against the opposition's slowest defender. On the other hand, however, it was simply about managing Suárez and Sturridge's mood. 'I can play two or three games on the wing for you, but by the fourth game I'll be annoyed,' admitted Suárez. 'Brendan looked for a formula to play me and Daniel in a way that meant we were both comfortable – at times decisions are made to keep good players happy as much as they are to create a particular tactical structure.' In that sense, there was a similarity to Carlo Ancelotti's Chelsea, an emphasis upon placating senior players as much as building a cohesive starting XI. Neither Suárez nor Sturridge were expected to track the opposition full-back when used wide, and were instructed to remain in the channel and offer a direct passing option so Liverpool could pounce immediately at transitions.

Meanwhile, with Barcelona being toppled by a counter-attacking Atlético Madrid in both La Liga and the Champions League, and Pep Guardiola's possession-based Bayern Munich side being utterly destroyed 5–0 on aggregate by a highly direct Real Madrid, tiki-taka's popularity had waned. Nothing symbolised this sudden shift as much as Rodgers ditching possession football for this more straightforward style. Possession statistics were now considered less important, and in 2013/14 Liverpool led the way in two completely different areas: they made the most tackles and scored the most counter-attacking goals. It was the complete opposite of what Rodgers had intended to create. This was post-possession football.

Rodgers also became significantly more reactive – and astute – with his tactics. Liverpool had the significant advantage of no European football and just five cup matches that season, so Rodgers used this freedom to tailor training sessions throughout the week with Liverpool's upcoming opponents in mind. Players don't like thinking specifically about the opposition too early, but from the Tuesday Rodgers would devise drills that conditioned the players for their weekend task. He wouldn't immediately explain the precise reasons for the exercises, but would, for example, spend a couple of days working on through-balls and getting midfield runners beyond the forwards. Only on Thursday and Friday would he offer specific instructions – the opposition midfielders don't track runs properly and their defence plays too high up the pitch, so that's what Liverpool should exploit.

It was an intelligent approach and wouldn't have been possible had Liverpool been juggling regular midweek football. Liverpool also used their extra time on the training ground to work hard on set-pieces, and it's notable that they regularly opened the scoring through this route, which then forced the opposition to attack, leaving space into which Liverpool could counter-attack. Gerrard's fine deliveries helped Liverpool score a staggering 26 goals from dead-ball situations, the most in the league and more than double the average.

That landmark 5–1 thrashing of Arsenal was the start of an astonishing 11-game winning run that took Liverpool from fourth position into first. The combination of Rodgers' astute tactics, Gerrard creating from deep, an aggressive midfield press, attacking dynamism and the league's best two goalscorers created a seemingly unstoppable force. Liverpool were actually more Newcastle 1995/96 than Keegan's team were themselves – whereas Newcastle's goals-for and goals-against tallies were both surprisingly low, this 11-game Liverpool run included wins of 4–3, 6–3 and two 3–2s. In nine of those 11 games they scored three or more goals. They were absolutely battering opponents with relentless waves of attack.

The penultimate game of this sequence was a 3–2 victory over Manchester City in early April, seemingly a title decider. This is also arguably the greatest game in Premier League history, another honour they'd be wrestling away from Newcastle 1995/96, with their famous 4–3 defeat to Liverpool widely considered the Premier League's best. But this 3–2 was equally enthralling, was played at an incredible intensity and featured action from beginning to end. Crucially, it was bookended by tremendous drama too.

Beforehand, Anfield observed the anniversary of the Hillsborough disaster. This is always a solemn occasion, but 2014 proved particularly emotional. It was the 25th anniversary and came less than a fortnight after the start of an inquest into the disaster – after decades of campaigning by families of the victims – which eventually found that the 96 had been unlawfully killed. Matches that weekend started at 3:06 – the time the semi-final in 1989 had been stopped. And, while football itself inevitably takes a back seat in this context, it was impossible to ignore Liverpool's title charge. At the Hillsborough Memorial Service, Liverpool fans ended 'You'll Never Walk Alone' and were soon singing their primary chant for that season: 'And now you're gonna believe us / We're gonna win the league!' Liverpool supporters clearly believed, regularly turning the arrival of the team bus at Anfield into a colourful, raucous parade.

The game itself was extraordinary, with Rodgers deploying a diamond midfield with Sterling at its tip. He'd been told to exploit the space by Suárez and Sturridge's runs into the channels, and it worked perfectly as he raced through for the opener within six minutes. Škrtel scored another header from a set-piece to make it 2–0, while City's Yaya Touré went off injured. The SAS were surprisingly quiet, however, with City's full-backs refusing to push forward for fear of leaving space in the channels. Both Liverpool strikers played to the right, attempting to exploit left-sided centre-back Martin Demichelis's lack of speed, largely without success. In fact, right-sided Kompany, well short of match fitness, was the weak link, finding himself unable to track Sterling's run for the first goal and losing Škrtel for the second.

At half-time, however, Manuel Pellegrini introduced James Milner, who offered thrust down the right, while David Silva provided a sensational spell of dominance, running the game single-handedly. He was up against Gerrard, who simply couldn't get close to him and received little assistance from his midfield colleagues. This was not entirely surprising – Gerrard was unfamiliar with the deep role, Henderson was a box-to-box player, Coutinho a number 10 and Sterling a natural winger. It was hardly unexpected that such an attack-minded midfield quartet failed to cope with the magical Silva's drifts, bursts and clever passes between the lines. Gerrard's defensive shortcomings had been a nagging concern for weeks – now they were a major issue.

Having put City in charge, Silva was responsible for both their goals, poking home from Milner's cut-back, before playing a cut-back himself that deflected off Glen Johnson and bounced into the net. 2–2, and City were looking for another. Silva nearly snatched the winner, but his five-foot-seven frame wasn't enough to properly connect with Sergio Agüero's low cross. Then, entirely against the run of play, City captain Kompany completed a miserable afternoon by slicing a simple clearance straight to Coutinho, who curled home gloriously. 3–2. It was a sensational game, a sensational victory, and Liverpool were on course for the title.

At full-time, Gerrard immediately broke down in tears, before being surrounded by Liverpool teammates in an impromptu huddle. Gerrard then, overcome by emotion, found the composure to deliver a rallying cry: 'Hey! This does not fucking slip now! Listen! This does not fucking slip. Listen, listen, this is gone, we go at Norwich exactly the same!' he roared, hammering his fist into his other hand. 'We go again!'

The trip to Norwich wasn't dissimilar, with Liverpool racing out of the traps and leading 2–0 within ten minutes through Sterling and Suárez, before being pegged back to 3–2 and enduring a nervy last 15 minutes. With Sturridge injured and Henderson suspended following a late dismissal in the victory over City, Rodgers used an unusual formation. He wanted to stick with his diamond, but was aware Norwich coach Neil Adams planned to play the same system. Recalling a strategy a South American coach had used against his Chelsea youth team nearly a decade earlier, Rodgers therefore placed Coutinho in between the diamond of Gerrard, Lucas, Allen and Sterling, creating a five-against-four situation and dominating midfield with this highly unusual 4–1–3–1–1 shape.

Then, however, came Liverpool's fateful home match against Chelsea. With three games remaining, Liverpool were five points clear of Mourinho's Chelsea, who had effectively abandoned their title charge and were concentrating upon their Champions League semi-final against Atlético Madrid three days later. Liverpool were also six points clear of Manchester City, who had a game in hand, and, crucially, a superior goal difference. A draw would have suited Liverpool as it would keep Chelsea five points behind and ensure the title remained in their own hands, with just two wins against Crystal Palace and Newcastle required to win their first Premier League crown.

Mourinho rested most of his first-choice XI: John Terry, Gary Cahill, David Luiz, Ramires, Willian, Eden Hazard and Fernando Torres were all omitted because they were starting against Atlético in midweek. Only Mark Schwarzer, César Azpilicueta, Branislav Ivanović and Ashley Cole started both games. It was effectively a second-string XI sent to spoil Liverpool's party, including Czech centre-back Tomáš Kalas, who hadn't played a single minute in the league all season. 'I am a player for training sessions,' he'd joked to Czech TV a fortnight beforehand. 'If they need a cone, they put me there instead.' Suddenly, he was thrust into one of the Premier League's most decisive matches.

Chelsea's performance was unashamedly negative. Rodgers later complained they'd 'parked two buses' in front of the goal – Mourinho yet again being the victim of the phrase he'd introduced to English football – which made it impossible for Liverpool to find their attackers running in behind. But again, this shouldn't have been problematic. A draw would have suited Liverpool, but they simply weren't a side who could play for a point – they were always gung-ho, all guns blazing, starting matches at 100mph. This concerned Gerrard. 'I was worried about how we were planning to play against Chelsea,' he admitted in his autobiography. 'I've never been able to say this in public before, but I was seriously concerned that we thought we could blow Chelsea away. I sensed an overconfidence in Brendan's team talk. He thought we could go out and attack Chelsea, just as we had done against Manchester City and Norwich. We played into Mourinho's hands. I feared it then, and I know it now.'

Henderson was still suspended and Sturridge only fit enough for the bench, so Rodgers used a 4–3–3/4–3–2–1, with Sterling and Coutinho drifting inside from the flanks into the crowded centre. Liverpool offered little width, because full-backs Johnson and young-ster Jon Flanagan played considerably more conservatively than usual, perhaps a sign that Rodgers knew Liverpool should play more defensively. As a result they never stretched Chelsea.

At the end of an entirely uneventful first half, the key moment took place on the stroke of half-time, involving Gerrard – who came close to missing this game, sidelined throughout the week with agonising back pain and only playing following a series of painkilling tablets and injections, the strongest permissible. Liverpool's centre-backs had spread wide, so Gerrard dropped deep to temporarily become the main defender. As he received a simple sideways pass from left-sided centre-back Mamadou Sakho, he slipped.

That's not the full story, however. What actually happened was more complex – Gerrard's slip was the second error. The first came a split-second earlier, when he momentarily took his eye off the ball and let it run beneath his foot. Before the ball arrived, Gerrard had already glanced up twice, checking his passing options and the positioning of Chelsea striker Demba Ba. The liberty of taking a third look, however, killed him. 'My concentration was more on Ba than the ball,' he admitted. This caused the miscontrol, and in Gerrard's desperation to recover the situation, he panicked, lost his footing, and Ba dribbled forward to score.

It's become an iconic moment laced with cruel irony for two reasons. First, there's the prosaic: Gerrard had ended the apparent title decider against City roaring 'This does not slip!,' then his slip proved disastrous. It would feel ludicrously contrived in a film script, but it proved one of the Premier League's most significant moments. The second irony was more significant – Gerrard was only playing this deeper role because he'd discovered his head movement hadn't been good enough further forward. Now, his head movement resulted in the Premier League's costliest miscontrol.

Rodgers mentioned the mistake in his half-time team-talk, reminding his players that Gerrard had rescued Liverpool countless times before and now they needed to repay him. But Liverpool had grown accustomed to breaking into space and looked perplexed about how to penetrate a deep defence. Their second-half performance is primarily remembered for Gerrard's desperate attempts to atone for his own mistake, about which he was typically self-critical – 'I was running forward too much, trying shots from impossible angles.' Indeed, he attempted eight shots after the break, generally from long range. But Liverpool had few other promising routes of attack. Sturridge and Suárez couldn't receive possession in dangerous positions, with the latter underlining Liverpool's tactical naivety by asking a Chelsea defender why they were playing so defensively. Sterling had no room to dribble, Liverpool's passing combinations simply weren't working, and crosses played into Chelsea's hands. Against a team playing so extraordinarily deep, shooting from range was a perfectly legitimate tactic, although Gerrard's attempts gradually changed from 'leading by example' to personifying that old criticism – 'trying to do everything himself'.

In stoppage time Chelsea doubled their lead, when an awful corner from Liverpool substitute Iago Aspas created a counter-attacking chance. Former Liverpool hero Torres broke forward, then laid the ball sideways, assisting Willian for an open goal. Willian, the man Gerrard had been imploring to join Liverpool the previous summer, had confirmed Liverpool's most crushing defeat. 'Congratulations to Chelsea for the win,' Rodgers said afterwards. 'They probably came for a draw; we were the side trying to win.' But that desperately missed the point, of course – if Chelsea had come for the draw, Liverpool should have taken the draw.

Manchester City won later that day, 2–0 at Crystal Palace, and also the following weekend against Everton, 3–2. It meant, with two games remaining apiece, Manchester City and Liverpool both had 80 points. City, however, had a goal difference advantage of nine.

On the final Monday night of the campaign Liverpool travelled to Crystal Palace. Gerrard admits feeling depressed in the wake of his Chelsea mistake, and had flown to Monaco for a couple of days – a destination he chose, tellingly, because he'd visited once before and remembered it being completely empty. But his performance against Palace showed little sign of his sorrow. He assisted the opener from a corner, Allen nodding in, then created the second for Sturridge with a typical long diagonal pass from his new deep role. After 55 minutes, Suárez played a classic one-two with Sterling and poked home. 3–0. 'We were murdering them – I honestly thought we were going to win 6–0,' Gerrard said afterwards. Suárez, tellingly, raced to collect the ball from the net, taking it quickly back to the halfway line. Liverpool believed they could make up that nine-goal deficit to Manchester City in just two games,. 'Somehow, that idea of chasing down Manchester City's superior goal difference seemed possible,' Suárez later recalled. 'That was the only thing in our heads: goals, goals, goals … we thought we could actually do it.'

This isn't as ludicrous as it seems. Liverpool had won 11 of their previous 12 games, putting six goals past Cardiff, five past Arsenal, and four against both Tottenham and Swansea. Their final-day fixture was at Anfield against Alan Pardew's Newcastle, who had completely collapsed in the second half of the campaign, losing 11 of their 14 previous matches, 10 of them without scoring. During that sequence they'd been thrashed 4–0 by Tottenham, Southampton and Manchester United, and 3–0 by Sunderland, Chelsea, Everton and Arsenal. They were utterly hopeless. A victory of the margin Liverpool would require – quite possibly double figures – had never occurred before in the Premier League. But then, no side had ever been incentivised to score ten goals. Usually, at 4–0 or 5–0 up, a team switches off and conserves energy, but this would have been the perfect recipe for the biggest-ever Premier League victory: a rampant attacking force, boasting the division's top two goalscorers, requiring as many as humanly possible in 90 minutes against a team who had completely downed tools. If Liverpool could score four in 20 minutes against league leaders Arsenal, how many could they manage in 90 minutes against a truly shambolic Newcastle side? Liverpool evidently believed they could win big, and it would have made for fascinating viewing.

We never found out. In Suárez and Liverpool's desperation to hammer more goals past Palace they left the back door open, conceding three times in the final ten minutes and falling to a disastrous 3–3 draw. Suárez was inconsolable at full-time, despite Gerrard's best efforts, sobbing with his shirt over his head, making the exceedingly long walk to Selhurst Park's inconveniently placed corner tunnel with his face hidden from cameras. Liverpool's chance had gone, and City won their remaining two matches to lift the Premier League title for the second time.

While a final-day shootout would have been brilliant, Liverpool should have realised that simply ensuring a victory against Crystal Palace was their primary task. This would have put Manchester City under significant pressure, and while City's remaining fixtures were hardly tricky, at home to Aston Villa and West Ham – the David Cameron double-header – they'd earned a reputation as bottlers. They'd nearly blown their simple final-day match against QPR two years earlier, and had lost the previous year's FA Cup Final to a relegated Wigan side. Liverpool had let them off the hook.

Liverpool's naivety wasn't about specific tactics but about their wider objectives. They didn't need to defeat Chelsea, but desperately attempted to. They didn't need to hammer more goals past Palace, but desperately attempted to. Liverpool had become such a relentless, all-out-attacking side that they couldn't revert to the style Rodgers initially wanted – the possession football that offered control rather than goals. Ultimately, that cost them the title.

23

Pressing Issues

'Our style is to win back the ball as soon as possible –
we move our lines forward and play upfield. It may
seem like we are running more, but really we are just
running in a more organised way.'

Mauricio Pochettino

For a couple of years possession football reigned supreme – almost everyone attempted to retain the ball for long periods, and the opposition sat back and waited for their opportunity to play in the same manner. Eventually, however, there was a significant response: the rise of pressing. Rather than sitting back and admiring the opposition's pretty passing, teams increasingly pushed up and attempted to disrupt it.

Pressing wasn't a new tactic. It had been a major feature of Ajax and the Netherlands' Total Football in the 1970s, and was particularly popularised by Arrigo Sacchi's brilliant AC Milan side of the late 1980s. There was a significant history of pressing in England, too. While former England manager Graham Taylor was closely associated with long-ball football, his successful Watford side also pressed extremely effectively. 'Our style was based on pressing the ball wherever it was,' Taylor said. 'So even if the opposition right-back had the ball deep in his own half, we still pressed him. We played extremely high-tempo football, which meant we had to be extremely fit.'

Taylor's methods were unfairly mocked, but at the time of his death in January 2017 Premier League football was focused upon pressing like never before, albeit in a more intense and collective manner – as outlined by former Arsenal manager George Graham, famous for his insistence on a high defensive line in the late 1980s and early 1990s. 'A lot of teams are buying into a pressing game as the modern way to play,' he said. 'We used to press years ago, believe me, but not collectively to the extent they do it now.'

Indeed, pressing lent itself naturally to the Premier League. In a footballing culture fixated on hard work, energy and tackling, getting tight to opponents was a dominant feature of Sunday League football, never mind Premier League football, while the cooler temperature made it easier to run constantly in England than in countries with a Mediterranean climate.

Yet pressing was rarely discussed in the first two decades of the Premier League era. Teams were often praised for their work rate, and energetic forwards were credited for shutting down defenders, but it's difficult to remember many teams between 1992 and 2012 being genuinely celebrated for their collective pressure upon opponents. In the subsequent five years, however, the tactic became football's most discussed concept.

Pressing was another quality repopularised by Pep Guardiola's Barcelona, particularly during their 2010/11 Champions League-winning campaign. The difference between their performances in the two final victories over Manchester United is extraordinary; in 2009 Barça's forwards retreated to the halfway line, in 2011 they sprinted forward to press relentlessly, preventing United from developing any passing moves. 'We play in the other team's half as much as possible,' explained Guardiola. 'We're a horrible team without the ball, so I want us to get it back as soon as possible.'

English football's sudden embrace of pressing can be traced back to one specific half of football in April 2010, when Guardiola's Barcelona travelled to the Emirates for a Champions League quarter-final first leg against Arsène Wenger's Arsenal. Pre-match discussion concentrated on the meeting of two possession-based sides; but whereas Arsenal were simply about retaining possession, Barcelona were equally concerned with disrupting the opposition's possession, and their first-half performance was a sensational, terrifying example of pressing. Arsenal were absolutely stunned by the ferocity and intensity of Barcelona's performance, with right-back Daniel Alves pushing up so high that, at one stage, he was shutting down Arsenal left-back Gaël Clichy next to the corner flag. Arsenal had no obvious solution; they were uncomfortable passing through the press, and were unaccustomed to bypassing it by playing long. They continually played into trouble, while Barcelona regained the ball close to the Arsenal goal and could have been 5–0 up by half-time. Only a rare goalkeeping masterclass from Manuel Almunia kept the game goalless at the break.

Wenger evidently spent his half-time team talk encouraging Arsenal to replicate Barcelona's press, but this proved unsuccessful. Pressing is about organisation rather than merely energy, and Arsenal attempted to close down Barcelona's defence in ones and twos rather than as a collective unit. Barcelona played through this half-hearted press easily, and with Arsenal's defence now playing higher, they knocked two long balls in behind for Zlatan Ibrahimović to score two almost identical goals.

Arsenal recovered, however. Barcelona were exhausted from their early exertions, and the introduction of the speedy Theo Walcott allowed Wenger's side to exploit space behind the defence. Walcott got a goal back, before Arsenal captain Cesc Fàbregas won and then scored a penalty against his boyhood club five minutes from time. Incidentally, Fàbregas cracked his right fibula when being fouled by Carles Puyol for the penalty and consequently missed the rest of Arsenal's campaign – but adrenaline got him through the next minute, and he smashed home the spot-kick with, effectively, a fractured leg. It finished 2–2, but a better summary of Barcelona's dominance is the amazing 14–2 'shots on target' figure. 'Last season we won many trophies, but never played away in the Champions League like we did here,' Guardiola marvelled afterwards. 'We took the ball and never allowed them to play. It was the best 45 minutes since I became a coach … we've given a good image of how football should be played.' It was telling that Guardiola focused on 'never allowing Arsenal to play'.

One coach particularly inspired by Guardiola's pressing was André Villas-Boas. The Portuguese coach became involved in football in brilliantly poetic fashion – as a 16-year-old Porto fan he was frustrated that his favourite player, Domingos Paciência, had been dropped by manager Bobby Robson. Villas-Boas happened to live in the same apartment block as Robson, so put a letter in his mailbox outlining his objections to Porto's tactics. Robson, in typically welcoming fashion, invited Villas-Boas around for a cup of tea, and then challenged him to provide analysis of Porto's next game to illustrate his point. Robson was so impressed by Villas-Boas's football brain, as he had been by José Mourinho's, that he appointed him as a trainee coach. Villas-Boas was still at Porto when Mourinho became manager in 2002, becoming his opposition analyst and following him to Chelsea, where he became renowned for the dossiers that defined Mourinho's first Premier League stint. By 2009 Villas-Boas was a manager in his own right, at Portuguese side Académica, then he became Porto manager in 2010. In his first season he guided them to an unbeaten league campaign, and he went on to win the Europa League with a 1–0 victory over Braga, who were, fatefully, managed by Domingos Paciência, the man who had unwittingly launched Villas-Boas's coaching career.

Immediately after that Europa League victory Villas-Boas paid tribute to both Robson and Mourinho, but surprisingly also to Guardiola, whom he'd never met. 'He is always an inspiration for me because his methodology gets his team playing fantastic football,' Villas-Boas explained. 'His quality and philosophy are a template for me every day.' Perhaps this alerted Roman Abramovich, who had recently sacked Carlo Ancelotti and still yearned for a Chelsea side with a positive identity. Villas-Boas became Chelsea manager at the age of just 34. This was a bold choice, and Villas-Boas didn't prove particularly popular in English football, often referred to as a 'laptop manager' more interested in statistics than man-management.

Villas-Boas immediately attempted to transfer his Porto template onto Chelsea, with disappointing results. The key ingredients were a 4–3–3 system and an aggressive defensive line, and while Chelsea were accustomed to the former, they struggled significantly with the latter. The team's defensive line became the major talking point when analysing Villas-Boas's system, because it was so radically different from the way they had played since Mourinho's appointment in 2004. Indeed, while Villas-Boas was inevitably referred to as 'the new Mourinho', no other Chelsea manager had introduced such a radically different approach from the Mourinho era.

This aggressive defensive line formed part of Villas-Boas's 'high block', a term previously rarely used in English football, which referred to the outfielders all pushing up and pressuring the opponents in advanced positions. This was a significant development; Villas-Boas was the first Premier League manager since George

Graham whose tactics were defined by what the players did without possession rather than with it. Even though Mourinho's approach was considerably more defensive, his approach was referred to as counter-attacking football, which implicitly acknowledges periods spent without the ball but literally refers to his side's attacking approach. Now, pundits focused on Chelsea's approach when the opposition had the ball, although Villas-Boas often emphasised that his team played 'vertical' passes – getting the ball forward quickly.

Although Chelsea compressed the opposition for long periods, their high line was often breached. While this was forgivable against quick players, it was notable that they also struggled against Norwich striker Grant Holt, a rather rotund, old-fashioned centre-forward who was experiencing his first Premier League season having spent his career in the lower leagues. In some matches Chelsea's approach lacked cohesion; in a 3–1 defeat at Old Trafford, for example, the defence played high up the pitch but the midfield didn't press properly, which invited through-balls and runners in behind. The most blatant example of the problem was a 5–3 home defeat to Arsenal. Robin van Persie was the hero, grabbing a hat-trick, while the speed of wide forwards Theo Walcott and Gervinho repeatedly exploited the space behind Chelsea's defence. For Van Persie's second goal, a slightly wayward Jon Obi Mikel pass towards John Terry forced Chelsea's captain to turn and sprint back. The Dutchman easily outpaced him, and Terry stumbled helplessly to the floor as Van Persie rounded Petr Čech. That became the defining image of Villas-Boas's high block.

Villas-Boas gradually realised that this approach wasn't suited to Chelsea, and in December used an extremely low block for a pivotal final Champions League group match against Valencia, when he feared a defeat would cost him his job. Chelsea allowed Valencia complete dominance of midfield, enjoying just 31 per cent of possession, but ran out 3–0 winners. It was old-school Chelsea. From that point there were inevitably major questions about the validity of Villas-Boas's high block, and after a narrow 2–1 victory over Manchester City Villas-Boas was asked what position his defence were supposed to be taking. 'In the beginning of the game we were trying to find the best position for the block,' he explained. 'We set out today in a medium block. They were feeling too much attraction to press their short build-up, and in the first ten minutes we suffered a lot. I think we adjusted that, I think the players felt they had to adjust, so they lowered the lines a little bit, felt comfortable with it, and then they gained the confidence.'

This sounded suspiciously like the players overruling his tactics and playing deeper than he intended. But Villas-Boas generally returned to the high block, probably with Abramovich's demands for a positive identity on his mind, and sometimes the consequences were extraordinary. In a 3–1 defeat to Napoli in the Champions League second round, for example, the Neapolitans repeatedly created clear chances when hitting direct passes for speedy left-winger Ezequiel Lavezzi, who exploited the huge space behind Chelsea right-back Branislav Ivanović.

Ultimately, Villas-Boas lasted only eight months at Chelsea. Roberto Di Matteo, his former assistant, took Chelsea to the Champions League title that season – with a Mourinho-esque deep block.

Less than five months after his dismissal, Villas-Boas was back in the Premier League with Tottenham Hotspur, as a replacement for Harry Redknapp – who, coincidentally, had taken Spurs to fourth position, which would have been enough for a Champions League place were it not for Di Matteo's improbable triumph. Again, Villas-Boas's emphasis upon pressing was immediately obvious. In Tottenham's opening match of 2012/13, a 2–1 defeat at Newcastle,

Villas-Boas wanted Spurs to press every opponent except the centre-backs, so the Magpies' defensive duo of Steven Taylor and James Perch finished with pass completion rates of 100 per cent and 98 per cent respectively, while the rest of Newcastle's side averaged just 77 per cent. This suggested Villas-Boas had adjusted rather than abandoned his high block.

Generally, though, Spurs pushed up very aggressively. A crucial feature was the extraordinarily high starting position of goalkeeper Hugo Lloris, who took the sweeper-keeper role very literally and regularly raced outside his box to produce spectacular headed clearances. Occasionally Spurs were tremendous under Villas-Boas, fired by the sensational Gareth Bale. They recorded their first-ever Premier League victory at Old Trafford in September 2012, winning 3–2, having started by aggressively pressing Paul Scholes and Michael Carrick with the more mobile duo of Moussa Dembélé and Clint Dempsey – although they eventually retreated into an extremely deep defensive block and enjoyed just 26 per cent of possession.

Too often, however, Spurs pressed too intensely and offered little control. After a 4–2 defeat by Villas-Boas's former club Chelsea, now with Mourinho back in charge, Villas-Boas admitted 'the characteristic of the game was the pace of the game. It was frenetic, many balls were lost by both teams … the intensity was a problem, we wanted to calm the game down.' But in a 2–1 victory over Arsenal, a peculiar game completely defined by both sides pressing aggressively, using high defensive lines and compressing the game into a very small strip 20 yards either side of the halfway line, Spurs were more cohesive and superior at playing through-balls – goals from Bale and Aaron Lennon, darting in behind from wide, sealed the victory.

Bale's departure was the major cause of Spurs' sudden decline the following season – but the secondary problem was their high defensive line. In a 1–0 defeat to Arsenal their back line was repeatedly penetrated by the runs of Theo Walcott, but also the considerably slower Olivier Giroud, while in a 1–1 draw with Chelsea the badly out-of-form Fernando Torres produced his first decent performance for months because he was given so much space to sprint into, although he was dismissed late on for a tangle with Jan Vertonghen.

But when Villas-Boas's system failed, it failed spectacularly. There was an absolutely shambolic defeat at Manchester City, when Jesús Navas exploited Spurs' high line and opened the scoring within 15 seconds. The immobile centre-back partnership of Michael Dawson and Younès Kaboul were absolutely torn apart by the speed of Sergio Agüero, and with Spurs 3–0 down at half-time Villas-Boas exacerbated the problem by chasing a lost cause, switching from 4–2–3–1 to 4–4–2 and allowing City the run of midfield. It finished 6–0.

Less than a month later Tottenham were thrashed in a similar manner, this time at home by Liverpool. With midfielder Étienne Capoue deployed as a makeshift centre-back alongside Dawson, Spurs again defended extremely high up the pitch but put very little pressure on the opponent in possession. Sure enough, Luis Suárez repeatedly raced in behind and Liverpool won 5–0. This was madness from Villas-Boas: doing the same thing again and again, and expecting different results. He was sacked the next day. Both of his dismissals, from Chelsea and Tottenham, owed much to his obsession with a high defensive line as part of a pressing strategy.

By this stage, however, Villas-Boas was no longer the posterboy for Premier League pressing. The baton had been passed to Mauricio Pochettino, who became Southampton manager in January 2013. This was a somewhat controversial appointment. After a difficult start to Southampton's first season back in the Premier League for eight years Nigel Adkins had achieved some impressive results, and it seemed strange to disturb Southampton's rhythm midway through the campaign. Pochettino's only previous coaching job with Espanyol had produced some exciting matches, particularly when they went toe-to-toe with city rivals Barcelona by pressing them intensely, but ultimately he'd been dismissed with Espanyol bottom of the league.

Nevertheless, Pochettino was a highly promising young manager who placed pressing at the forefront of his coaching philosophy. His primary inspiration was one of Guardiola's idols, Marcelo Bielsa, although Pochettino had a stronger link to his compatriot. Bielsa had been Pochettino's youth coach during the late 1980s at Argentine side Newell's Old Boys, and when promoted to become the club's manager he immediately handed first-team opportunities to Pochettino, who won the Argentine league title at just 19. Bielsa's sides were renowned for their high-tempo, energetic pressing style, which rubbed off on Pochettino, and they crossed paths again with the Argentine national side, and briefly at Espanyol.

By the time of Pochettino's arrival in England, incidentally, Bielsa was coaching Athletic Bilbao, taking them to a hugely impressive 5–3 aggregate Europa League victory over Manchester United, when their intense pressing and rapid one-twos completely overwhelmed Sir Alex Ferguson's side. Before that game Bielsa outlined his philosophy. 'Our simple ethos is to win the ball back as quickly as possible, as far up the field as we can – and by that I mean everyone is involved in winning the ball, back from the forwards,' he explained. 'Once we have got it, we try to find a way of getting forward as quickly as possible, in a kind of vertical direction.' When it worked, Bielsa's side were thrilling, and Pochettino tried to replicate that style at Southampton – who, coincidentally, had provided Athletic Bilbao with their famous red-and-white-striped shirts in the 19th century, thanks to shipworkers travelling between the two ports.

Pochettino's vision was obvious from the outset. In his opening game against Everton his attackers started the pressure, the midfielders pushed forward onto their opposite numbers and the defence held a high line. In the first half Southampton won possession quickly and created clear chances, but they couldn't quite translate their dominance into goals. The pressing meant they tired in the second half and the game finished goalless, but overall Pochettino was delighted. 'It was a very good example because we put in a very good effort,' he said. 'We were focusing on the high pressure, which is one of our main goals, so we've established the basic foundations of how we want to carry on.'

Pochettino's approach proved particularly effective against strong opposition, when Southampton could disrupt teams who wanted to play out from the back. His first three Premier League victories, significantly, were against Manchester City, Liverpool and Chelsea, but during this period Southampton failed to beat Wigan, Norwich and Queens Park Rangers.

In Pochettino's only full campaign at St Mary's, 2013/14, Southampton's style was best summed up by the contrast in two statistics. First, they achieved the highest average possession share in the Premier League. Second, they achieved just the ninth-highest pass-completion rate in the Premier League. That's a remarkable imbalance, considering a side's level of possession is generally considered to be about how effectively they retain the ball. How did Southampton manage to dominate possession so regularly when their ball retention was so average? Simple – because possession share is also determined by how quickly the ball is regained. Southampton pressed relentlessly from the front, backed up by the powerful duo of Morgan Schneiderlin and Victor Wanyama patrolling midfield. At turnovers they attempted ambitious, vertical passes that often went awry. But if possession was conceded, Southampton would simply press again and restart the process. They were the purest pressing side the Premier League has witnessed.

Schneiderlin offered an excellent summary of Pochettino's style: 'When I press, I always concentrate on leaving the opponents with the worst possible pass, and Pochettino asks us not to leave the opponent with several options. This means an enormous collective effort, but after six or seven months working according to his ideas, it's possible to harass and completely destabilise teams. We couldn't do this immediately, because it's a huge job in training. He wants to get the ball back as high as possible, so it's normally an attacker who triggers the pressing and we must all follow.'

Pochettino's approach worked well at Southampton, whose tremendous success with bringing intelligent footballers through their academy meant he could call upon a young, energetic squad willing to learn new methods. It proved useful for the national team, too; Adam Lallana, Rickie Lambert, Jay Rodriguez, Nathaniel Clyne and Luke Shaw all received England call-ups. Shortly after one squad announcement Southampton fans spent the first half of the 4–1 victory over Hull in November 2013 singing, 'Come on England!' and 'It's just like watching England!' in celebration of their contribution to Roy Hodgson's squad.

Pochettino transformed his team into a genuine top-half side with occasionally enthralling football, but he never denied his ambition, considering the Saints a springboard to bigger clubs. This potentially explains why his pressing style was so extreme with Southampton – it was, from his perspective, about attracting the attention of other clubs. They finished eighth in 2013/14, a respectable finish, but it was Southampton's style rather than their results that encouraged Tottenham to appoint Pochettino that summer.

This was essentially an attempt to continue Villas-Boas's philosophy; here were two managers fixated on pressing and a high defensive line. Between these two spells, Spurs were managed by Tim Sherwood, Blackburn Rovers' title-winning captain from 1994/95.

He was a back-to-basics throwback of a manager who seemingly overlooked every tactical development that had been made during the Premier League era. Sherwood played 4–4–2, said that 'players only call themselves number 10s because they can't score goals' and claimed that he didn't understand the point of defensive midfielders. Bafflingly, he achieved the highest win percentage of any Tottenham manager in the Premier League era, as he constantly reminded the media. But while Sherwood proved a useful short-term manager, he lacked the vision to oversee a new era.

Pochettino's Tottenham didn't press as aggressively as his Southampton side, but they still focused on pushing forward and shutting down opponents quickly. They were also more intelligent in the manner they pressed laterally, with the wide midfielders moving into central positions when opponents had the ball on the opposite flank, boxing in opponents towards the touchlines. The Argentine's first campaign with Tottenham, 2014/15, produced mixed results; sometimes Tottenham pressed excellently to force turnovers and launched quick attacks, exemplified by their opener in September's north London derby. Mathieu Flamini was tentative in possession deep inside his own half, Christian Eriksen charged towards him, stole the ball and slipped it to Erik Lamela, who played in Nacer Chadli to finish smartly. That was precisely what Pochettino wanted – an aggressive press in an advanced position, and a quick, direct attack. But on other occasions Spurs' pressing left their defence exposed, the youthful midfield combination of Ryan Mason and Nabil Bentaleb lacking the requisite positional discipline.

Things improved significantly during 2015/16, when Spurs briefly launched a serious title charge. As Schneiderlin had outlined at Southampton, it takes time on the training ground to perfect a pressing approach, and Tottenham were more fluent in Pochettino's philosophy. An improvement in the calibre of individuals also proved significant; the athletic and skilful central midfielder Dembélé regained his place as a regular, the physical defender Eric Dier was redeployed as a central midfielder with great success, the boundless energy of new signing Dele Alli proved crucial, while the outstanding centre-back Toby Alderweireld arrived following a successful season at Pochettino's former club Southampton, who were also pressing effectively under his successor Ronald Koeman. Alderweireld formed a formidable centre-back partnership with fellow Belgian Jan Vertonghen, both having been raised in the Ajax youth academy, which puts great emphasis upon pressing. 'We train pretty tactically,' said Alderweireld. 'We play pressing football, where everyone works for each other, from the striker to the goalkeeper. We are a hungry team, without real superstars; I have never worked so hard in my life as under Pochettino.'

Fitness levels, too, were clearly superior in the second season, partly thanks to Pochettino's extremely intense training sessions. 'There's not been a good moment in pre-season, if I'm honest,' sighed striker Harry Kane, the major beneficiary of Pochettino's regime. 'There were double sessions, times when you were pushing yourself to the limit.' The improvement of Spurs' two attacking full-backs, Danny Rose and Kyle Walker, was remarkable, and their continual running defined Spurs' shape. Tottenham regularly covered greater distances than any other side in the Premier League, and were sometimes amazingly dominant, recording a 4–1 victory over Manchester City and a 3–0 win against Manchester United. Some suggested Tottenham depended too much upon pressing, but the approach proved effective in both an attacking and a defensive sense. In Pochettino's second campaign Spurs recorded the most shots on target (6.6 per game, some way clear of the next-best-placed side, Arsenal, who managed 5.6) and also conceded the fewest goals.

In terms of pressing, Tottenham's most notable match in 2015/16 was their goalless draw at home to Liverpool in mid-October. The match itself was uneventful, but the occasion was significant, because it was Liverpool's first game under the regime of Jürgen Klopp.

Klopp had established himself as a top-class manager at Borussia Dortmund, where he won consecutive Bundesliga titles in 2011 and 2012, and reached the Champions League Final the following season, being defeated by Bayern Munich at Wembley – a complete German takeover of England's national stadium. Dortmund, meanwhile, had become extremely popular in England, at one point attracting over 1,000 English fans per match. The Westfalenstadion offered a raucous atmosphere, cheap tickets, plus standing and drinking on the terraces – everything the Premier League had seemingly lost. There was also Dortmund's exhilarating, high-tempo football featuring speedy transitions and direct running. More than anything, however, Klopp's game was based around pressing.

To be more specific, Klopp's system was based around *gegenpressing*, a German word that effectively translates as 'counter-pressing'. This was different from the pressing favoured by Villas-Boas and Pochettino, which was about constantly harassing the opponents in advanced zones. Klopp's Dortmund sometimes played in that manner, but their press was largely about the timing rather than the positioning; counter-pressing involves pressuring immediately after possession was lost.

Counter-pressing attempted to redefine the accepted nature of the simple, cyclical four-part flow chart used in coaching manuals to explain 'phases of play'. Traditionally, a team is either in possession or out of possession. To move between these two phases there's the transition – the concept Mourinho popularised during his first stint at Chelsea. So the flow is simple: in possession, defensive transition, out of possession, attacking transition. And repeat. You're always in one of these four stages. But Klopp's counter-pressing changed that – a successful counter-press replaced the 'defensive transition' and allowed the side to immediately return to 'in possession'.

This proved extremely effective in the Bundesliga, a division based heavily around transitions. Klopp's Dortmund side would often counter-press and regain possession when the opposition were launching their attacking transition and pushing their full-backs forward, making it easy to penetrate the defence and create goalscoring chances. 'Think about the passes you have to make to get a number 10 in a position where he can play the genius pass,' Klopp explained. 'Counter-pressing lets you win back the ball nearer to the goal, and it's only one pass away from a really good opportunity. No playmaker in the world can be as good as a good counter-pressing situation.'

Much like Guardiola at Barcelona, Klopp's Dortmund methods proved so effective that his philosophy was partly popularised in the Premier League before he'd arrived himself. But Klopp's appointment, as Brendan Rodgers' replacement, nevertheless sparked Liverpool into life after a disappointing 18 months following their narrow title failure in 2013/14. 'I believe in a playing philosophy that is very emotional, very fast and very strong,' Klopp outlined at his first press conference. 'My teams must play at full throttle and take it to the limit every single game – tactical, of course, but tactical with a big heart.'

From that first match at Tottenham, despite Klopp only having a couple of days on the training ground with Liverpool's full squad, the effects were clear. Liverpool played a 4–3–2–1 that dominated the centre, and they counter-pressed immediately when possession was lost – which was often, considering Tottenham's own aggressive press. This created an extremely fast-paced, scrappy match all about disrupting the opposition and shutting down passing options quickly, and the goalless draw wasn't surprising, as both sides were spoiling the other's approach play. Klopp was pleased with Liverpool's work rate – and they became the first team to outrun Pochettino's Tottenham – but the German explained that 'the problem was when we had the ball – we weren't good enough, we didn't use our skills, we were too hectic, we didn't see the right option.' This was reminiscent of Villas-Boas's complaints. While Liverpool's possession play would improve considerably, matches between two pressing sides often became disjointed. Later, Klopp frequently praised his side when they were frantic without possession, but calm in possession.

That was also very much the case with Manchester United at this point, under the reign of Louis van Gaal. They didn't press as intensely as Liverpool or Tottenham, and initially used a surprisingly simple press that involved midfielders man-marking their opposite numbers and inevitably being dragged out of shape. But their medium block was eventually compact and cohesive, and Van Gaal didn't receive enough credit for United's organisation during this period – no Premier League side conceded fewer goals during his two-year Premier League spell. United were rather *too* calm in possession, however, which didn't please a fanbase accustomed to more purposeful football.

It was Pochettino and Klopp, though, who were effectively leading the pressing revolution in English football, with the former keen to point out the differences in their approaches. 'I think it's a different pressing,' Pochettino explained. 'If you analyse Dortmund, it's not similar to how we played at Southampton because our pressing was high up to the opponent's goalkeeper, but Dortmund played a medium block. It's very strange to compare those two styles, Klopp's style to mine.' Klopp's Liverpool, however, increasingly combined counter-pressing with standard pressing in advanced positions. A 4–1 thrashing of Manchester City at the Etihad, after Klopp had been in charge for just a month, showed the possibilities of his high-energy system, with the counter-pressing and pressing combined with slick interplay from Roberto Firmino, Coutinho and Adam Lallana producing a truly dominant victory. Liverpool reached the League Cup and Europa League finals in his first season, although they were beaten on both occasions.

Klopp generally overlooked traditional strikers and deployed Firmino, an attacking midfielder, as his most advanced attacker. While this was in keeping with the increased emphasis on forwards linking play, it was primarily because the energetic Brazilian was excellent at starting Liverpool's press. In Klopp's system, Firmino's job was to 'split' the pitch in half, forcing the opposition to play the ball towards either full-back, then to pressure the passing lane between that full-back and the nearest centre-back, while his team-mates would push up and get tight to other nearby passing options. Much like Pochettino's Southampton, Liverpool performed better against big sides because they depended upon teams passing out from the back for their press to be activated and their game plan to work. In that sense Liverpool returned to their problems of the Rafael Benítez years, when they consistently won big games but struggled against smaller teams.

The impact of these pressing-focused managers was significant – after a few years of calm, thoughtful matches in the possession era, now teams were fierce, frantic units obsessed with breaking up play and covering plenty of ground. No Premier League team combined top-class possession play with top-class pressing, and therefore none came close to the level of Guardiola's Barcelona. Much of the pressing was taken for granted, but the tendency for teams to push up and prevent the opposition taking goal-kicks short, for example, is a relatively new development. Of course, a decade beforehand goalkeepers simply thumped the ball downfield, meaning any pressing would have been pointless – so this is a neat microcosm of how pressing arose as a direct response to possession.

'There's a lot of high-intensity, really quick pressing,' said Swansea's Leon Britton, who had epitomised the possession era but found himself less valued in the pressing era. 'The new generation of manager is producing training sessions to reflect that game; they are pressing quicker, getting players to recover quicker. It's an 11-man game now.'

That summarises the expansion of the Premier League's defensive units. Most of the Premier League's greatest attacking talents, from Eric Cantona to Cristiano Ronaldo, had thrived when freed from defensive responsibilities. With the rise of pressing, however, the free role was a thing of the past.

24

Leicester

'In an era when money counts for everything,
I think we give hope to everybody.'

Claudio Ranieri

There is simply no precedent for Leicester City's astonishing title triumph in 2015/16. No achievement in sporting history has ever been so improbable; nothing comes close to matching the pre-season odds of 5000/1, which became a major discussion point as Claudio Ranieri's side edged closer to the title. Previously, all 23 Premier League title-winning sides had one of the five highest wage bills in the division. Leicester's, however, was among the bottom five.

Despite being widely considered a relegation candidate, Leicester started encouragingly, stayed within touching distance of the leaders for longer than anyone expected – and then, with the usual suspects enduring awful campaigns and other challengers gradually dropping away, simply kept on going. Theirs was a truly wonderful underdog victory, the type that simply didn't appear possible considering the huge financial inequalities in the Premier League – Leicester's wage bill was around one-quarter of Chelsea's. Opposition players, rival managers and fans across the country united in support of Ranieri's side, willing them over the finishing line. In Premier League terms it was a unique event unlikely to be repeated.

There was, however, a template for Ranieri and Leicester City. English football had increasingly been influenced by successful European sides, as the sudden obsessions with Pep Guardiola's Barcelona and Jürgen Klopp's Dortmund demonstrated. For a true underdog victory, meanwhile, there was the tale of Atlético Madrid's improbable 2013/14 La Liga success. This was previously considered the biggest upset of modern football times, as Diego Simeone's team ended Barcelona and Real Madrid's decade-long duopoly by clinching the title at Camp Nou – serenaded by Barça supporters who couldn't help but admire them. This wasn't quite a Leicester tale – Atlético were 100/1 rather than 5000/1 – but like the Premier League, La Liga had previously been dominated by an even more untouchable, even more exclusive elite. Atlético smashed that ceiling, and pointed the way for others to upset the traditional big boys.

Simeone's Atlético overachieved through a combination of superb organisation, terrifying intensity and lightning-quick transitions. Pre-match teamsheets depicted Atlético in a simple, old-school 4–4–2 system, although the reality was more sophisticated; the two forwards, Diego Costa and David Villa, played extraordinarily deep when Atlético didn't have possession, almost as supplementary midfielders. This allowed the midfield quartet to sit back and protect the defence keenly, keeping Atlético incredibly compact and difficult to play through. They shepherded the opposition into wide areas, then pressed intensely, forcing turnovers and countering ruthlessly. More than anything, Atlético were defined by their lack of interest in possession, averaging less than 50 per cent throughout their title campaign, which came as a serious shock in Spain, a nation that had dominated world football with tiki-taka. Statistically, Atlético led the way in terms of tackling, an attribute Spain midfielder Xabi Alonso had rubbished as 'a last resort … it isn't a quality to aspire to.' La Liga's widespread emphasis upon possession played into the hands of the alternative: counter-attacking Atlético.

By the time Leicester became title favourites in the spring of 2016, the similarity with Atlético was obvious: a compact 4–4–2, deep defending, feisty tacklers in central midfield, brilliant counter-attacking and the maximising of set-piece opportunities. Their share of possession was the third-lowest in the division with only West Brom and Sunderland – managed by Tony Pulis and Sam Allardyce respectively, the Premier League's most notorious route one merchants – seeing less of the ball. However, like Atlético in 2013/14, Leicester recorded the highest number of tackles in the division and the highest number of interceptions. The fascinating story behind Leicester's fairy-tale season is their gradual evolution into that type of side.

In the previous season, 2014/15, Leicester were playing in the Premier League for the first time in over a decade. It initially appeared a fleeting return, as the Foxes were in the relegation zone for over half the campaign and bottom for 17 consecutive matches. But a late-season surge, in part because manager Nigel Pearson switched to a three-man defence, proved crucial. Having won just four of their first 29 matches, Leicester won seven of their last nine, with that winning streak only broken by a defeat to eventual champions Chelsea, and a goalless draw at Sunderland when Leicester knew a point would seal survival.

Pearson, having achieved this hugely improbable great escape, was surprisingly sacked in the summer. A local newspaper poll found that 70 per cent of supporters disagreed with the decision. Pearson's conduct in press conferences and in interactions with supporters had occasionally been entirely unprofessional, while his son, a reserve team player, was sacked having been filmed using racist language while on a post-season trip to Thailand – particularly embarrassing given that Leicester were owned by Thai billionaire Vichai Srivaddhanaprabha. Leicester then stunned the footballing world by appointing Ranieri. He'd most recently been seen spectacularly failing with the Greek national side, who suffered an embarrassing defeat to the Faroe Islands. At Leicester he lasted only 20 months, and was dismissed with the club hovering just above the relegation zone. In that period, though, he recorded the most sensational title victory in English football history.

'They were strong, very fighting,' Ranieri said of Leicester's 2014/15 campaign, at his first Leicester press conference, 'but I think they need a little more tactics.' Throughout his stint at Chelsea Ranieri was nicknamed 'the Tinkerman' for his tendency to rotate, change formation and make surprise substitutions. But upon arrival at Leicester he was noticeably keen not to reinvent the wheel. At Chelsea Ranieri discovered that there were members of his own backroom staff who were extremely unpopular with the players, so with Leicester he retained the services of Pearson's highly rated and popular assistants Steve Walsh and Craig Shakespeare.

Ranieri spent the pre-season trip to Austria observing training sessions rather than interfering. 'I'm sure I don't want to change too many things – I'm going to change very slowly, so that everyone understands me,' he announced. Therefore, throughout Leicester's pre-season friendlies he always started with Pearson's formation, although he routinely switched to a four-man defence. 'I'd start with a back three and switch to a back four at half-time,' he explained. 'And it was really simple – we just played better with a four.' For Leicester's first league game – against Sunderland – he therefore settled on a four-man defence but named only one new signing, energetic Japanese striker Shinji Okazaki, in his starting XI. Other recruits, such as midfield destroyer N'Golo Kanté and left-back Christian Fuchs, needed to be patient. While Ranieri would eventually name the same starting XI almost every week, at the start of the campaign only seven of those players were in his side.

Initially, Leicester were nothing like the solid, defensive-minded outfit that would later grind out narrow victories during the run-in. In fact, their journey was the opposite of Liverpool's in 2013/14, who started off winning matches 1–0, then became involved in countless goalfests – Leicester started the season with end-to-end thrillers, then learned how to win in a controlled manner, eventually becoming renowned as a superb counter-attacking outfit. This approach was impossible in the opening weeks, because it depends upon the opposition coming onto you. Leicester, however, frequently conceded the first goal and were therefore forced to dominate matches in search of a comeback. In four of their opening six matches the Foxes went 1–0 behind, meaning the opposition sat deeper and denied Ranieri's side space to break into. They proved excellent at clawing themselves back into games, and somewhat surprisingly maintained the league's longest unbeaten run. After five matches they were in second place.

But Ranieri wasn't happy, and he realised that a significant defensive improvement was required simply to keep Leicester in the Premier League. Ahead of the sixth game of the season, away at Stoke, Ranieri announced he'd bribed his players to underline the importance of shutting out the opposition. 'When we make a clean sheet, I will buy everybody a pizza!' he declared. 'I want to buy pizza, but my players don't want pizza – maybe they don't love pizza?' The problem, however, was more about Leicester's tactical approach than the players' culinary preferences; they were extremely open, and their defence was constantly penetrated by through-balls between centre-back and full-back. They didn't keep a clean sheet at Stoke – indeed, captain Wes Morgan's wayward back-pass for Jon Walters' goal was the worst defensive mistake of Leicester's campaign – and the Potters were 2–0 up at the break. But when Ranieri reshaped at half-time, he stumbled upon the midfield quartet that would take Leicester to the title. Crucially, this featured Kanté deployed as a central midfielder for the first time, the combative Frenchman being one of three key players who would define Leicester's campaign.

Kanté, signed from Caen that summer, wasn't actually the main target identified by Leicester's recruitment department. Their first-choice was Jordan Veretout, and they were disappointed when the playmaker chose to join Aston Villa – which, considering Villa finished bottom, proved an unimaginably awful decision. Kanté was a different type of player, who had impressed Leicester's analytics team with his ball-recovery statistics, winning more tackles than any other Ligue 1 player. Initially, he and fellow newcomer Gökhan İnler, a more exciting purchase because he boasted Champions League experience and captained Switzerland, were omitted, with the previous season's combination of Danny Drinkwater and Andy King preferred. When handed opportunities İnler was hugely disappointing and struggled with the pace of the Premier League, but Kanté played at a higher tempo than anyone, buzzing around the pitch and constantly dispossessing opponents. Indeed, he was so energetic that Ranieri was initially reluctant to deploy him as a defensive midfielder, feeling he required players who offered more positional discipline. As a result Kanté's initial opportunities came either on the left, or in Okazaki's position between midfield and Vardy – the Frenchman was the only player who could match Okazaki's incredible work rate.

Despite being fielded in relatively attacking roles, Kanté's ball-winning statistics proved impossible to ignore. From his advanced midfield position he won ten tackles against Bournemouth, six more than anyone else on the pitch, and from the left against Stoke he made the most ball recoveries. He was evidently an outstanding ball-winner, and Ranieri gradually realised that he should be anchoring Leicester's midfield. At half-time against Stoke he removed the cumbersome İnler and introduced Marc Albrighton, who had been harshly dropped, having recorded three assists in five games. Kanté shifted inside into his preferred central role, and Leicester improved dramatically – more ball-winning potential in the middle, more crossing threat from Albrighton. They produced yet another second-half comeback, drawing 2–2, and Kanté would never be moved from that central role. He evoked memories of former Chelsea defensive midfielder Claude Makélélé, making both the most tackles and the most interceptions of any player in the Premier League that season.

'We play three in midfield,' joked assistant Steve Walsh. 'We play Danny Drinkwater in the middle and Kanté either side.' It was a pertinent joke, although it's worth considering that Leicester's true third central midfielder was actually Okazaki, who dropped into extremely deep positions and shut down the opposition's holding midfielder quickly. He was a striker by nature – but five goals and no assists underlines the fact he offered little threat in the penalty box. Instead, he was more useful for starting the defensive pressure.

Kanté's central positioning was only the first step in Leicester's evolution, and it didn't reap instant rewards. The title-winning midfield quartet of Mahrez, Drinkwater, Kanté and Albrighton started together for the first time the following weekend, but Leicester's unbeaten record was ended with a 5–2 thrashing at the hands of Arsenal, whose quick attackers Alexis Sánchez and Theo Walcott found plenty of space in the channels, the Chilean grabbing a hat-trick. At this point Leicester were a thrilling all-out-attack side; they'd jointly scored the most goals in the Premier League alongside

West Ham, but only Sunderland had conceded more. They dropped to eighth position, surely regressing towards their rightful place, and Ranieri still hadn't bought pizza. His centre-backs, Morgan and Robert Huth, lacked mobility and were forced to cover a huge amount of space with their teammates bombing forward regularly. Reverting to the previous season's three-man defence seemed an obvious tactical switch, but Ranieri persisted with the back four and concentrated upon minimising space in the channels. Ahead of the next game, against Norwich, he made a significant decision.

In the opening weeks Ranieri's left-back was Jeffrey Schlupp, a flying wing-back in Pearson's system, whose frequent powerful runs had earned him Leicester's Players' Player of the Year award. But his attack-minded mentality didn't work at left-back, and Ranieri knew his forward running was exposing the centre-backs. Instead, he fielded Fuchs, who lacked Schlupp's attacking dynamism but was six foot one, solid, and could tuck inside to protect Morgan and Huth. On the opposite flank, Ritchie De Laet had made too many defensive mistakes, so Danny Simpson replaced him and played more conservatively. They were given specific instructions: you can only overlap when Leicester are losing.

The change was dramatic. Leicester dropped deeper, played narrower and conceded space on the outside of, rather than between, the four defenders. The strong duo of Morgan and Huth were happier remaining on the edge of their own box and heading away crosses rather than playing higher up and chasing quicker opponents into the channels. 'Jeff and Ritchie going forward are lightning,' explained goalkeeper Kasper Schmeichel. 'But it left huge, huge spaces to be exposed in behind ... we needed to change something. Now we have four *defenders* in there.'

It's a cliché to insist Italian managers love defensive football, but Ranieri continually emphasised his 'Italian tactics', and he deliberately took a further step backwards to concentrate on keeping a clean sheet. Astonishingly, he dropped Mahrez, the right-winger who had recorded five goals and three assists in his first seven games, and would eventually be voted PFA Player of the Year. For two games, with Ranieri so determined to improve Leicester's defensive structure, Mahrez was omitted. Not injured, not rested, not rotated, simply excluded from the starting XI for tactical reasons. Schlupp played on the left of midfield, Albrighton started on the right. The clean sheet still didn't come, but Leicester looked better defensively against Norwich and Southampton.

Then, ten matches into the campaign, they bagged their first clean sheet, against Crystal Palace. Ranieri recalled Mahrez, but not in a position where he had defensive responsibility, instead using the Algerian behind Vardy – the two combined for the only goal of the game. 'It was more of an Italian match than an English one,' grinned Ranieri. That Italian match was celebrated, of course, with pizza, although Ranieri didn't simply buy dinner. He took the entire squad to Peter Pizzeria in the centre of Leicester, where the players had to make their own pizzas. This served as a great team-bonding exercise and a tremendous PR stunt, a new spin on Premier League footballers with loads of dough.

Behind the fun and games, however, this was a genuinely significant moment. From this point on, Leicester kept clean sheets in exactly half of their remaining matches, including an incredible spell of 12 in 17 games as they evolved from surprise contenders to title favourites in the new year. Defensively, Leicester were well organised in open play and somewhat physical at set-pieces, with Huth admitting he often strayed beyond what is considered legal. The following season, when referees were instructed to punish shirt-pulling at corner kicks more keenly, Leicester struggled and right-back Simpson claimed this refereeing change affected them badly.

The shift to a deeper, more compact defensive block also suited Vardy, Leicester's second key player, who became the first footballer to score in 11 consecutive Premier League matches, an unthinkable achievement considering he'd managed just five goals in the whole of the previous season. He dominated headlines when Leicester's form seemed a novelty rather than making them serious title challengers; while everyone was focusing upon his unprecedented scoring streak, Leicester went top with a 3–0 win at Newcastle in November, and would hold that position for 20 of the next 23 matchdays.

Vardy's rise was truly remarkable. He'd been released by Sheffield Wednesday as a teenager and completely quit football for seven months, before storming up the footballing pyramid in a manner rarely witnessed, starting at eighth-tier Stocksbridge Park Steels, where his wage was £30 a week. Following a conviction for assault, he played for six months with an electronic tag around his ankle and was forced to observe a home curfew from 6 pm every evening, which meant being substituted midway through the second half at away matches and driving home quickly. Then came a move to seventh-tier Halifax Town for £15,000, while he worked full-time at a factory making carbon-fibre splints. Twenty-nine goals in 41 games earned him a transfer to Fleetwood Town, in the fifth tier of English football. He spent just a season there, because 34 goals in 42 matches meant Leicester were prepared to spend £1m to secure his services – a record for a non-league player.

Initially Vardy seemed too raw for the Premier League, but a significant improvement to his first touch and finishing ability turned him from an energetic workhorse into the league's deadliest striker. Having spent much of his career out wide, Vardy's game was all about exploiting space on the outside of centre-backs, receiving the ball on the run and finishing smartly. There was also a significant shift in his duties once his goalscoring form became apparent; at the start of the season

Vardy retreated alongside Okazaki to ensure Leicester remained compact and difficult to play through. Although Ranieri persisted with roughly the same system, Vardy was afforded licence to stay higher, on the shoulder of the last defender and considerably in advance of Okazaki, enabling Leicester to find him running through on goal immediately after possession was won. It was 4–4–1–1 rather than 4–4–2. Vardy's memorable dipping strike against Liverpool in a 2–0 home victory was a perfect example of how Leicester provided him with service – Mahrez collected a loose ball deep inside his own half, brought it under control and then immediately fired the ball into the channel for Vardy, who thumped it home first-time. You couldn't find a more direct attack; this was a one-pass move. 'Jamie Vardy's having a party' became Leicester fans' main chant.

Vardy developed a particularly good relationship with Drinkwater, whose searching diagonal balls worked perfectly with the striker's acceleration. 'You can hit a 50–50 ball and he changes the odds with his pace and hunger,' raved Drinkwater. 'He makes bad passes look brilliant.' Goalkeeper Schmeichel said something similar. 'When you have a player like that, he's a dream to play with. You hit balls and clearances and he makes something of them, he turns them into good balls because he chases everything down and never gives up.' Schmeichel's long-range throws were crucial to Leicester's counter-attacking, reminiscent of the way his father had revolutionised goalkeeper distribution in the Premier League's formative years. As if to underline Leicester's lack of interest in possession figures, Schmeichel recorded the lowest pass completion rate of any Premier League player – but his distribution skills were vital, as he created more chances than any other goalkeeper.

Leicester's underdog status was also crucial to their footballing style. Traditionally big clubs can't solely depend upon counter-attacking, especially at home, because opponents tend to defend deep. But Leicester were allowed to play that way because opponents always underestimated them, playing in their default style rather than adjusting their approach to deny Leicester space. A classic example was Leicester's 3–0 victory over Swansea, who continually pushed their full-backs forward, which created space for Vardy and Mahrez, who hit a perfect hat-trick (right foot, left foot, header).

Mahrez, Leicester's third key player, proved extremely important during this stage of the season. Although he was a brilliant counter-attacker, he wasn't simply a space invader like Vardy, and he could dribble past opponents with trickery, which was essential now that opponents were parking men behind the ball. A dribbler, an assister and a goalscorer in one, Mahrez was Leicester's best all-round footballer, and his sensational contributions justified the fact that he played a considerably more advanced role than Albrighton on the opposite flank. Like Cristiano Ronaldo and Luis Suárez, the contribution from his counter-attacks excused his not tracking the opposition full-back. He was deservedly voted Player of the Year by his fellow professionals.

Even when opponents started to guard against Leicester's counter-attacks, however, the Foxes still found a way through. Shortly before Christmas, Vardy and Mahrez were the two goalscorers in Leicester's famous 2–1 win over reigning champions Chelsea, who were badly struggling in the bottom half of the table. José Mourinho was furious; he complained that his 'work was betrayed', having highlighted that duo's threat beforehand. But neither goal was scored on the break. The first came from Mahrez crossing to Vardy, the second was all about Mahrez's trickery outfoxing César Azpilicueta, arguably the Premier League's best full-back.

That game, incidentally, finished off Mourinho's second spell at Chelsea, a poetic moment considering the Portuguese coach had replaced Ranieri at Chelsea in 2004 and frequently attacked him in subsequent years. At one point, he said Ranieri 'had the mentality of someone who doesn't need to win … he is almost 70 years of age, he has won a Supercup and another small trophy, and he is too old to change his mentality.' But that mentality proved perfect for playing down expectations and coping with pressure. Ranieri continually insisted Leicester's target was to avoid relegation, then to qualify for Europe, then to qualify for the Champions League. Gradually, though, it became clear Leicester were genuine title challengers.

Leicester, like Liverpool two years earlier, also had the advantage of no European football and therefore much better preparation for weekend matches compared with their title rivals. This not only had tactical benefits; it also gave the team physical advantages, as Ranieri explained. 'In England the football is always of a high intensity and wipes people out. They have more need to recover. We play Saturday, then Sunday is a day off for everyone. On Monday we resume with light training, the way they do in Italy. Tuesday is hard training, Wednesday absolute rest. On Thursday another hard session, Friday preparation for the match, Saturday another game.' A team playing on a Wednesday wouldn't have those two hard training sessions. Leicester were running harder, better and faster than any other side in the Premier League.

Over Christmas Leicester failed to find the net in three consecutive games, suggesting their bubble had burst, although this would be their only three blanks all season. Opponents started adjusting to their threat, and while Vardy scored excellent counter-attacking goals against Liverpool, Sunderland and West Ham in the second half of the campaign, there were fewer opportunities for Leicester to get him running in behind. At one point he managed just four goals in 16 games, one of them a penalty, a drought that forced Leicester to diversify and find goals from elsewhere. Penalties, incidentally, proved a very useful source of goals for the club – they were awarded 13, the most of any Premier League team since 2001/02. Defenders were frequently isolated against the speed of Vardy or Mahrez, and ended up bringing them down.

Vardy's dry spell meant clean sheets became more important, as Leicester needed to ensure that scoring one goal, rather than two or three, would be enough. They recorded six 1–0 wins during the title run-in, including a spell of five in six games. 'Those 1–0s are really important because it points out that they are a unit, they're not going to lose,' said an impressed Sir Alex Ferguson, giving a rare post-retirement interview. Significantly, none of these winners were scored by Vardy, or from counter-attacks. Tactically, this was the most impressive part of Leicester's incredible title triumph; although they had perfected counter-attacking football, they realised the dangers of relying on that approach and became a considerably more complete side. They achieved this in three crucial ways.

First, Leicester's evolution into a complete attacking force involved their potency from set-pieces. As Liverpool had demonstrated when almost winning the title two years beforehand, striking early from dead-ball situations is extremely useful for counter-attacking sides who struggle to penetrate deep defences – because it forces defensive-minded opponents to come out and chase the game, leaving space to break into. Centre-back duo Huth and Morgan, who hadn't registered in the first half of the campaign, contributed five important goals after Christmas; Huth nodded in the winner in the crucial January victory over Tottenham, who emerged as Leicester's main title rivals, then scored two more, including the early opener, at Manchester City in February. Morgan, meanwhile, scored a winner against Southampton and the equaliser in a 1–1 draw at Old Trafford in April – when, for the first time all season, Leicester looked extremely nervous.

Second, Ranieri's tinkerman tactics proved invaluable. Although he retained a settled starting XI after Christmas, he used his bench extremely effectively. Against deeper defences, back-up striker Leonardo Ulloa became the perfect plan B, as he offered considerably more height than Vardy and Okazaki, and thrived on crosses. In February, with ten minutes remaining in a home match against Norwich, Ranieri realised the match was set for a goalless draw. He made a courageous decision, introducing bonus centre-forward Ulloa in place of right-back Daniel Amartey, who had started in place of the suspended Simpson. Sure enough, Ulloa popped up in the 89th minute with a crucial winner. Later, when Vardy served a two-game suspension, Ulloa kept his composure to net a stoppage-time penalty in a 2–2 draw with West Ham, then hit two more goals against Swansea. His contribution was minimal in terms of playing time but highly significant in terms of points. The fourth goal in that crushing 4–0 victory over Swansea was telling, featuring a combination between three substitutes – King, Albrighton and January arrival Demarai Gray. The match was already won, but it underlined how Ranieri kept the entire squad involved, despite rarely making changes to his first XI.

The third element in Leicester's evolution was the most crucial, and received surprisingly little attention; far from relying on counter-attacking, the team now played more proactively, particularly in the opening stages of matches. It wasn't about possession play but instead about regaining the ball in advanced positions by pressing aggressively. This was particularly notable in the 3–0 victory versus Stoke in January, and absolutely crucial in the season-defining 3–1 victory against Manchester City at the Etihad the following month.

From kick-off at the Etihad, Drinkwater thumped a long diagonal ball into City's right-back zone, sending the ball straight out of play for a City throw – and Leicester pushed forward to box their opponents in. Perhaps Drinkwater simply overhit his pass, but Leicester seemed to be deliberately giving away the ball, underlining their lack of interest in possession. It meant, however, that they could quickly press high, and Kanté immediately won a 50–50 tackle with Yaya Touré. The game wasn't a minute old, and Leicester were already demonstrating their ball-winning qualities.

Upon regaining possession Leicester immediately switched play to Mahrez on the right. By this stage of the season the Algerian's determination to cut inside onto his left foot was well-established, so City boss Manuel Pellegrini fielded Fabian Delph as a narrow left-sided midfielder, specifically to prevent Mahrez moving inside. He and left-back Aleksandar Kolarov were clearly supposed to show Mahrez down the line. But to their surprise Mahrez was entirely happy to go there – he darted towards the byline, catching out Kolarov, who clumsily fouled him. From the ensuing free-kick Mahrez crossed for Huth to score.

The nature of these opening two minutes demonstrated Leicester's evolution. They realised City would attempt to prevent them counter-attacking, so they changed their game plan and pressed high. Mahrez realised he would struggle to find space when he drifted inside, so he went outside. This is what great champions do; when their opponents can proactively nullify their strengths they diversify, not simply excelling at their favoured moves but also at the alternatives. Of course, the beauty of going 1–0 ahead was that Leicester could play on the break after all, with Mahrez's outstanding second goal a perfect example. Once again he surprised an opposition defender, this time Martin Demichelis, by checking to his right, and then smashed the ball past Joe Hart with his weaker foot.

Huth scored another goal to make it 3–0, and while Sergio Agüero pulled one back as Manchester City rallied, Leicester won 3–1 and were generously applauded off the pitch by the opposition supporters. This was a momentous day – Leicester went five points clear at the top, became the bookmakers' favourites, and as Ranieri later admitted, this was the first time he truly believed his team could win the title. Even City goalkeeper Hart seemed to realise what was happening, telling his ex-teammate Schmeichel on the pitch afterwards: 'All right, come on, if you're ever going to win it, it's now. Get it done.' A late 2–1 defeat to Arsenal followed – with various Leicester players saying Arsenal's post-match celebratory dressing-room photos proved an unlikely source of motivation. From that point forwards, Leicester were unstoppable.

Their succession of late-season 1–0 victories was highly impressive, but there were inevitably times when they were slightly fortunate. They retreated extraordinarily deep at Crystal Palace in March, and after Mahrez gave them the lead, they played terribly and invited too much pressure, with Palace centre-back Damien Delaney hitting the bar in stoppage time. But it was moments like this that convinced Leicester fans that the unthinkable was going to happen. Twenty minutes after full-time at Selhurst Park, the away section remained packed, as Leicester supporters stayed behind to chant, 'Now you're gonna believe us – we're gonna win the league.' It was quite a sight. Some Palace fans applauded them as they shuffled towards the exits, others stopped and simply watched them belting out the same song again and again and again with a look of bemusement as if to say: this is happening. Leicester *were* actually going to win the league.

There have been 'neutrals' favourites' in the Premier League before, but nothing like Leicester. Gary Lineker, Leicester's most famous ex-player and now their most famous supporter, was unashamedly cheering them on while presenting *Match of the Day* every weekend – and no one complained. Opposition managers were falling over themselves to support them. 'It would be absolutely fantastic for everyone in football if Leicester could do it,' said West

Brom manager Tony Pulis. 'I am supporting Leicester City between now and the end of the season.' Southampton's Ronald Koeman joined in – 'They deserve to win the title, I hope they do win it' – and Swansea boss Francesco Guidolin repeated the message. Peculiarly, Leicester weren't even battling the pre-season Premier League favourites. Champions Chelsea spent most of the season in the bottom half, Manchester City collapsed after Pellegrini announced he was leaving in February, while Manchester United were so mediocre that even lifting the FA Cup couldn't save Louis van Gaal's job. Leicester ended up competing against Arsenal, who hadn't won the league in 12 seasons, and Tottenham, who hadn't triumphed for over half a century. Yet Leicester were still overwhelmingly the neutrals' favourites.

This extended to opposition players, too. Going into the final fortnight of the campaign, Leicester were on the brink of securing the title. The Foxes needed one more victory against Everton or Chelsea – but if Tottenham slipped up away at Stamford Bridge, Leicester's title would be confirmed early. Spurs raced to a 2–0 lead at Stamford Bridge, but then something clicked for the home side. Beforehand, Chelsea's players had been unanimous in their support for Leicester. 'I don't want Spurs to win it, to be honest,' admitted midfielder Cesc Fàbregas. 'For what they've done through the season I'd love Leicester to win the Premier League.' Winger Eden Hazard, who had won the 2014/15 PFA Player of the Year award when Chelsea triumphed, but spent much of 2015/16 off-form and completely disinterested, echoed the sentiment. 'We – the fans, the club, the players – don't want Tottenham to win the Premier League,' he admitted. 'We hope for Leicester because they deserve to be champions.'

After half-time Chelsea rallied, got a goal back, and then Hazard drove through the Spurs defence, played a one-two, and then bent the ball majestically into the top corner. 2–2. Leicester were champions. Chelsea's players celebrated, Leicester's players did too – Jamie Vardy was literally having a party – and so did most of Britain. Leicester, astonishingly, had clinched the Premier League with two games to spare, and would eventually triumph by ten clear points.

The celebrations were memorable. Leicester collected the trophy after a 3–1 victory over Everton – a game where many charitable Everton fans gave up their tickets to desperate Leicester fans, while over a thousand Italians made the pilgrimage to Leicester simply to be in the city and observe the celebrations for Ranieri, with no hope of getting a ticket. Inside the King Power before the trophy presentation, Andrea Bocelli took the stage in a Leicester shirt, stood alongside Ranieri and belted out 'Nessun dorma'.

This moment, while utterly surreal, somehow felt fitting. Football's hugely increased popularity in England had started before the formation of the Premier League, with England's run to the 1990 World Cup semi-final in Italy. 'It was a seminal moment in terms of football in this country,' recalled Lineker, England's star striker at the tournament. 'Lots of different kinds of people got interested in football, all different classes of people, and I think it had a significant effect on the growth of football.' The BBC famously soundtracked the tournament with Luciano Pavarotti's version of 'Nessun dorma'; this piece of music subsequently held a special place in the hearts of English football fans, immediately conjuring up that tournament – and that tournament alone.

Using 'Nessun dorma' in another footballing context was unthinkable. But then again, so was Leicester City winning the Premier League.

25

Three at the Back

'This league is the most difficult in the world –
six or seven teams can win the title.'

Antonio Conte

By the time the Premier League celebrated its 25th season it was unquestionably home to European football's greatest talents.

Not, however, in terms of footballers. Only two Premier League players finished in the top ten of the 2016 Ballon d'Or voting – and they were Leicester duo Jamie Vardy and Riyad Mahrez, who were both enduring hugely disappointing post-title seasons as the Foxes found themselves battling against relegation. Three other Premier League players received a handful of votes: Manchester United's new duo of Zlatan Ibrahimović and Paul Pogba, both being recognised for performances for other sides, while West Ham's Dimitri Payet managed a single vote but was on the verge of returning to France. The top six players in the world, according to this vote, were all based in Spain, and three of them – Cristiano Ronaldo, Luis Suárez and Gareth Bale – had moved there because they'd outgrown the Premier League.

In managerial terms, however, the Premier League offered Europe's finest. Arsène Wenger and Mauricio Pochettino were still in place at Arsenal and Tottenham respectively, Jürgen Klopp was starting his first full season as Liverpool manager, while José Mourinho had recovered from his Chelsea setback to be appointed at Manchester United and Ronald Koeman jumped ship from Southampton to Everton. Most excitingly, Manchester City had appointed Pep Guardiola, the coach who had done so much to influence Premier League tactics before he'd even arrived on these shores, while Chelsea appointed Antonio Conte, who had transformed Juventus before impressing as manager of the Italian national side.

The seven favourites for the Premier League, therefore, were led by managers from seven different countries: France, Spain, Portugal, Holland, Germany, Italy and Argentina. Between them they'd lifted no fewer than 26 major European league titles, with only the up-and-coming Pochettino not contributing to this figure. Of course, this stellar group didn't even include the Premier League's reigning champion, Claudio Ranieri.

The Premier League's managerial line-up therefore boasted its most exciting combination ever, a level of talent and diversity never previously witnessed. Following a period when Premier League sides struggled with their organisation, strategy and tactics – reflected in their mediocre Champions League performances – suddenly England was the ultimate destination for top-class coaching. Even the second tier was home to two European Cup-winning managers: Newcastle's Rafael Benítez and Aston Villa's Roberto Di Matteo. Winning club football's greatest prize was no guarantee of a top job.

The media's initial focus was on the revolutionary Guardiola – who ditched England number 1 Joe Hart and instead played sweeper-keeper Claudio Bravo, deployed attack-minded left-back

Aleksandar Kolarov as a centre-back and asked his full-backs to drift inside to become central midfielders. After a promising start, City fell away badly and Guardiola admitted he struggled to adapt to English football. 'Here the football is more unpredictable because the ball is in the air more than on the floor,' he complained. 'I only needed to see one game to understand English football: Swansea 5–4 against Crystal Palace. Nine goals, eight from set pieces. That is English football and I have to adapt.' City had been pre-season title favourites, but finished 15 points behind eventual champions Chelsea.

With Guardiola enduring a difficult first campaign, Conte proved the Premier League's most inspirational coach in 2016/17. Although the Italian had won three straight Scudettos with Juventus and his Italy side were hugely impressive at Euro 2016, particularly with their dominant 2–0 win over Spain in the second round, his appointment at Chelsea felt like a background development amid the obsession about Guardiola and Mourinho rekindling their *El Clásico* rivalry in Manchester. But he avoided petty squabbles, got on with business and took Chelsea to their fifth Premier League title.

While Conte's imperious first campaign owed much to a decisive tactical switch in autumn, his regime was initially dominated by fitness work. He surprised Chelsea's players with his emphasis on long, hard running sessions during pre-season – a practice that in recent years had largely been ditched in favour of more technical sessions. Football's post-possession shift towards pressing, however, meant supreme physical fitness was more important than ever. 'In all my years playing – I've had José Mourinho, Carlo Ancelotti, Roberto Di Matteo – I've never done this kind of running, you know, proper running,' said captain John Terry, then in his last season with Chelsea. 'In the past, under Mourinho, from day one in pre-season you get the balls out. But Conte has come in and from the start of pre-season we have done running. This is a group that hasn't done that for seven, eight, nine years. It was a bit of a shock, but after two or three weeks of doing it the lads were going, "Physically, we feel much better."' Conte also became significantly stricter with the diet of Chelsea's players, which had become surprisingly lax during Mourinho's second spell.

Conte started playing a 4–3–3/4–1–4–1 system that recalled Mourinho's first spell at the club, complete with N'Golo Kanté, signed from champions Leicester, effectively deployed in the Makélélé role in front of the defence. Conte had explicitly outlined his midfield intentions in pre-season, explaining that his system had no place for Cesc Fàbregas, who was among the most prolific assisters in the Premier League but lacked tactical intelligence and physical qualities, the two aspects Conte concentrated upon. He was omitted, with Kanté deep, the sturdy Nemanja Matić to the left and the creative but disciplined Oscar to the right. 'Oscar can do both facets: both offensive and defensive,' explained Conte in a nod to Fàbregas's shortcomings. The Spaniard's omission represented the shift away from possession football towards a more intense, pressing-based approach. 'Today, it's more difficult for the talented players to succeed,' Fàbregas complained. 'I don't think my physical abilities are the best – I'm not the quickest, I'm not the strongest, I'm not the sharpest ... to be a footballer today, if you're very strong or you run a lot, or stuff like that, it's easier. That's why I try to get even better, because football is growing in a way that before I don't think it was. Every day, you see less talent, and more power and players running around.' This was just half a decade after Barcelona's possession play had inspired the rest of Europe to concentrate on technical, creative midfielders.

In Chelsea's victory over West Ham on the opening weekend, it was notable that the full-backs, Branislav Ivanović and César

Azpilicueta, were encouraged to push forward extremely aggressively when their team had possession. This was an unusual tactic for Chelsea, who had largely been resistant to the shift towards attacking full-backs over the past 15 years. Indeed, the fact both players were regulars in those positions was largely for defensive reasons: right-sided Ivanović was a converted centre-back who naturally tucked inside and minimised space in the channel, while left-sided Azpilicueta was a converted right-back, which meant he protected space on the inside and rarely overlapped. The first time they'd been instructed to attack simultaneously only came during Conte's reign. In midfield, Matić and Oscar rarely advanced and instead moved to slightly wider positions, protecting the space the full-backs would generally defend, while Kanté sometimes dropped deep between the two centre-backs. Chelsea's system effectively featured a front five, with the full-backs on either side of the three forwards, and five players remaining in solid central-defensive positions.

But Chelsea started 2016/17 slowly, with unconvincing victories over West Ham and Watford, a more impressive win over a poor Burnley side, a draw at Swansea and then defeats in their first major tests against Liverpool and Arsenal, when they were completely outplayed. Against Liverpool they sat extraordinarily deep without possession, another classic Chelsea tactic, and the following weekend at the Emirates, Conte attempted to use a more advanced defensive line, but his centre-backs and Kanté were destroyed by the counter-attacking speed of Alexis Sánchez and Mesut Özil, with Chelsea 3–0 down by half-time.

Ten minutes into the second half, with the game already lost, Conte decided to experiment. He substituted Fàbregas, who was making his first league start of the campaign after a fine midweek performance in the League Cup, and introduced debutant Marcos Alonso, a surprising addition considering he'd previously performed at left-back in the Premier League with little distinction for Bolton and Sunderland. But Conte had witnessed him excel as a wing-back for Fiorentina, and his ability in that role allowed Chelsea to switch from 4–3–3 to 3–4–3. Although the scoreline remained 3–0 until full-time, this was among the most crucial tactical switches in Premier League history. 'That decision changed our season,' Conte later recalled.

From then on, Chelsea resolutely played 3–4–3, with the most consistent starting XI in the Premier League, and embarked on a truly extraordinary run of results. It seemed the best recipe for a title challenge was an early-season three-goal defeat to Arsenal: a 5–2 loss for Leicester on 26 September 2015 had encouraged Claudio Ranieri to change system, and now Chelsea's 3–0 defeat at Arsenal on 24 September 2016 forced Conte to follow suit.

It wasn't entirely surprising that Conte turned to a three-man defence, as he'd previously been associated with that system at Juventus and with the Italian national team. Although he started his spell at Juve playing a 4–4–2 – with such attack-minded wingers that Italians considered it a 4–2–4 – the fact he could depend upon three top-class centre-backs in Giorgio Chiellini, Leonardo Bonucci and Andrea Barzagli meant he switched to 3–5–2. When he took the Italy job after three years in Turin he was counting upon the same defensive trio, and so used the same system.

It's also worth considering, meanwhile, that Conte adopted his three-man defence in Serie A having witnessed outsiders Udinese and Napoli break into the Champions League places with extremely impressive three-man defences. Those clubs' managers during that period – Francesco Guidolin and Walter Mazzarri – also took charge of Premier League clubs in 2016, Guidolin at Swansea and Mazzarri at Watford. Guidolin seldom played a three-man defence, but Mazzarri usually did.

'We started the season with another system, but I noticed in some circumstances we didn't have the right balance,' Conte said. 'For this reason we switched to the new system of 3–4–3, and I think this is a good fit for our squad because we have the forwards adapted for this system. I thought it would improve us offensively as well as defensively … I always knew the squad could play with this 3–4–3 system. In my mind there was always this possibility; I knew the characteristic of the players and for this reason when I spoke to the club and we planned the season, this system was an alternative.' Chelsea won their next 13 games using the 3–4–3 system – the first six without conceding – narrowly failing to break Arsenal's 2002 record of 14 consecutive Premier League wins.

Chelsea were excellently drilled in their new system thanks to unusually long periods in training working on team shape. Conte's favourite training exercise was simply lining up his starting XI on the training ground, with no opposition, and working through passing combinations repeatedly to get one of his forwards, or either of the wing-backs, in a dangerous attacking position. Hazard, the most free-spirited and creative player in Chelsea's starting XI, described Chelsea's movement and passing combinations as 'automatisms', thanks to such repetition in training. Conte had the advantage, like Brendan Rodgers' Liverpool in 2013/14 and Claudio Ranieri's Leicester in 2015/16 (and Conte himself in his debut season at Juventus in 2011/12), of having no European football to contend with, which meant more coaching time on the training ground. 'Defensively we all work as a unit in training,' said right-wing-back Victor Moses. 'Every day in training, the manager is on top of us to make sure we are solid at the back.' Conte also placed huge emphasis on video analysis of his team's shape, channelling Mourinho by opening up these sessions and turning them into a group activity. Conte had written his dissertation at

Italy's national training centre, Coverciano, on the evolution of video analysis.

The new system suited Conte's players much better. There were crucial changes in personnel: David Luiz, surprisingly re-signed from Paris Saint-Germain, played the free role at the heart of the defence impeccably, transforming from laughing stock to among the division's most impressive centre-backs and Chelsea's defensive leader. 'The central defender must be more tactical, reflect more, find the right position and call the defensive line up and down,' explained Conte. The Brazilian did that excellently, and was perfectly suited to the three-man defence.

On the right, Moses finally became a Chelsea regular, having spent the previous three seasons out on loan. He adapted impressively to the wing-back role, which meant Azpilicueta dropped deeper to become a wide centre-back, a role that necessitated considerable mobility, as acknowledged by Cahill, who played to the left. 'I feel like I do more running,' Cahill explained. 'I have to come inside as well as go outside when we go out wide, so I'm covering more ground.' It was significant that the two major victims of the new system were Chelsea's two most immobile defenders, Branislav Ivanović and John Terry. Both were long-serving players and pillars of Chelsea's previous title triumphs, but neither of them started another game in Chelsea's title bid. Ivanović departed in January, while Terry stuck around but didn't start again until Chelsea had already clinched the title. His most notable contribution was starting the final game of the campaign, his last in a Chelsea shirt, but being substituted in the 26th minute – which he'd specifically suggested to match his shirt number. Alas, his departure from the pitch took so long that the records show he was actually substituted in the 28th minute. Conte, incidentally, was keen to play most of the match without Terry – his side's cohesion owed much to the familiarity of the starting XI, and he wanted to use his first-choice side as preparation for the following week's FA Cup Final.

The peculiar thing about the dramatic change in system, however, was that in possession it wasn't entirely different to Conte's initial 4–3–3/4–1–4–1 shape. There was still the front five, with Alonso and Moses pushing forward either side of Eden Hazard, Diego Costa and Pedro Rodríguez, with two solid midfielders, two centre-backs and another player, David Luiz, playing between defence and midfield. But Chelsea achieved that shape more naturally, were less vulnerable to counter-attacks and had players with much greater mobility in defensive positions. Hazard, Chelsea's key attacker, was allowed almost complete freedom from defensive responsibilities, and an overlapping player in Alonso granted him licence to drift inside into his favoured central positions. After a dreadful 2015/16, the Belgian returned to his 2014/15 form and was the Premier League's most consistently dangerous attacker, scoring outstanding solo goals in big matches against Liverpool and Arsenal, and brilliant counter-attacking strikes against Bournemouth and West Ham. Pedro, meanwhile, played higher up the pitch and ran in behind the opposition more frequently, as he did so menacingly in his Barcelona days.

Costa was the only player who found his role unchanged, and after a period when managers were increasingly encouraging their striker to take up deeper positions, Conte encouraged Costa to remain solidly in centre-forward zones. 'Diego knows that in my idea of football, the forward must always be a point of reference for the team,' Conte explained. 'I don't like them to move around the pitch, I like them to stay there because you are a forward, you are committed to score the goals, stay in the right position. You are a forward, not a midfielder or a defender.' Costa had a typically controversial campaign, with frequent bouts of indiscipline in the opening weeks, before flirting with a move to China in the January transfer window, and finally receiving a post-season text from Conte telling him he wasn't in his plans for the next campaign. Nevertheless, he hit 20 league goals.

In deeper positions, it was notable that Conte found the right balance in the 'in-between' roles that English teams struggled with when switching from a four-man to a three-man defence. Should the wing-backs be natural full-backs or natural wingers? In Alonso and Moses, he had one of each. Should the wide defenders be natural centre-backs or natural full-backs? Again, in Cahill and Azpilicueta, Conte had one of each. Azpilicueta, the only Chelsea player to complete all 3,420 Premier League minutes in 2016/17, was the best personification of Conte's beliefs. Having previously played as a left-back despite being a right-back, under Conte the Spaniard switched to right-sided centre-back, then deputised as left-sided centre-back and right-wing-back, showing incredible consistency in each position. That type of versatility harks back to the type of player Sir Alex Ferguson depended upon when launching Manchester United's title bids, and it's significant that Ferguson had been so inspired by the tactical awareness and versatility of various utility men in Marcello Lippi's Juventus side. One of those players, of course, was Conte.

To guard against their back four becoming overloaded by Chelsea's attacking five, many managers started matching Chelsea's system. In early November Everton manager Ronald Koeman was the first to attempt it, although it backfired dramatically as Chelsea's wide forwards counter-attacked in behind Everton's wing-backs. Koeman was forced to revert to a back four before half-time, and Chelsea eventually ran out 5–0 winners.

Chelsea's most memorable victory of the season was the crucial 3–1 victory at Manchester City in early December. Beforehand Guardiola had described Conte as 'maybe the best coach in the world right now', while Conte had returned the compliment by pointing out that Guardiola had won far more than him. The game proved to be arguably the most complex tactical battle the Premier League has ever witnessed, with Guardiola deploying a bizarre 3–2–4–1 system to dominate midfield and press Chelsea's wing-backs, but leaving his three defenders exposed to Chelsea's front three.

In truth, Chelsea could have easily lost this game. Gary Cahill clumsily diverted Jesús Navas's right-wing cross into his own net, and the outstanding Kevin De Bruyne should have doubled City's lead against his former club, somehow hitting the bar when presented with an open goal. But Chelsea stormed back and scored three goals that took advantage of City's lack of defensive numbers. Costa brought down a long ball, outmuscled Nicolas Otamendi and smashed home, and shortly afterwards turned Otamendi and played in the onrushing Willian for goal number two. In stoppage time Hazard streaked away from Aleksandar Kolarov and finished coolly. On each occasion Chelsea needed only one attacker to beat his direct opponent to get in on goal, which was why matching Chelsea's back three was such a gamble. But because opponents found themselves struggling to cope with Hazard and Pedro drifting inside, and couldn't decide whether Chelsea's wing-backs should be tracked by full-backs or wide midfielders, more managers started using a 3–4–3 themselves, playing wing-backs against wing-backs.

By the end of 2016, Conte had won 13 consecutive matches, one short of the record, while Conte became the first to be crowned Manager of the Month in three consecutive months. But Chelsea suffered defeat in their opening match of 2017. Mauricio Pochettino's Tottenham played 3–4–3 and pressed Chelsea aggressively, while exploiting a weakness in Chelsea's three-man defence with two identical strikes. Christian Eriksen twice crossed to the far post where Dele Alli took advantage of his height advantage over Azpilicueta to head home both goals. This underlined the fact that Chelsea's greatest challenge for the title was to come from Tottenham, but ultimately Conte's side were relatively untroubled and their system continued to overwhelm opponents – particularly those still using a four-man defence.

The best example was Marcos Alonso's opener in a 3–1 victory over Arsenal in February, a goal that prompted plenty of discussion because of Alonso's robust aerial challenge on compatriot Héctor Bellerín, which forced the Arsenal right-back to depart with concussion. But behind the controversy, this was a perfect example of how 3–4–3 caused a four-man defence problems. Arsenal's defence was in a perfectly good shape in the build-up, but then their left-back Nacho Monreal was dragged towards Chelsea's right-wing-back Moses, while centre-backs Laurent Koscielny and Shkodran Mustafi dutifully tracked the runs of Pedro and Hazard. This left Bellerín isolated at the far post, against both Costa and the lurking Alonso. Ultimately, Bellerín stood little chance: Chelsea had worked a five-against-four situation and he was overloaded. That goal showed the value of the 3–4–3 in the attacking phase, and it was notable how frequently one of Chelsea's wing-backs would find themselves unmarked to score at the far post, when the opposition's defence had been dragged across to the other side. Moses' winner against Tottenham in November was a classic example, while Alonso netted in similar circumstances in 3–0 wins over both Leicester and Middlesbrough.

These matches were also notable for the flexibility of Chelsea's three-man defence in possession. In the victory at Leicester, David Luiz was the game's outstanding performer because he constantly stepped forward from defence to become a deep-lying midfield playmaker, while in the win over already-relegated Middlesbrough, right-sided Azpilicueta shuttled forward to turn the 3–2–5 in possession into a 2–3–5. He was Chelsea's most dangerous attacking weapon, and the 'average position' diagram at full-time showed the Spaniard in advance of Chelsea's two central midfielders, Matić and Fàbregas (who enjoyed a late-season revival as Conte was gradually seduced by his incredible knack for assists). These shifts usually occurred when Chelsea's three-man defence faced a lone striker; Conte avoided a surplus at the back.

Chelsea surged to the title – after that setback at White Hart Lane in their opening game of 2017, Conte's side only dropped ten more points. They became the first side to win 30 Premier League games in a season and ended on 93 points – the second-best Premier League tally after their own effort in 2004/05, when they recorded 95. There was an obvious tactical similarity between the campaigns – just as José Mourinho had dominated the league after an autumn switch to 4–3–3, Conte had stormed to the title with an autumn switch to 3–4–3. On both occasions, Chelsea's extraordinary success inspired others to replicate their system.

A 3–4–3 appeared the best way to contain Chelsea's 3–4–3, especially if attempting to press in advanced positions, so the more teams switched to that system, the more opponents felt compelled to respond. On one hand it illustrated that the division was become more varied tactically, on the other it prompted questions about why coaches in England depended so much on arrivals from abroad to introduce innovative tactics. It was a remarkable turnaround – in 2015/16, there were just 31 examples of a Premier League side starting with a three-man defence – in 2016/17, that figure rose to 130. By the end of the campaign, no fewer than 17 of the 20 Premier League sides had started at least one match with a three-man defence.

The most surprising of these 17 sides was Arsenal. After two decades and over 1,000 matches where Arsene Wenger had used a four-man defence, he appeared so impressed by the performances of Chelsea and Tottenham in their 3–4–3 systems that he elected to follow suit in spring, following a disastrous spell during which the Gunners gained just seven points from eight league matches. While there were initial teething problems in an unconvincing 2–1 victory at Middlesbrough, the overall impact was excellent – Arsenal won nine of their final ten matches of 2016/17 when playing 3–4–3. The only failure came in a 2–0 defeat to Tottenham Hotspur, the result that confirmed Wenger would finish behind Spurs for the first time in his Arsenal career.

This formation-inspired run wasn't enough to haul Arsenal into the top four – again, a first-time failure in the Wenger era – but it took them to the FA Cup, with 2–1 victories in the semi-final against Manchester City and then, significantly, against Conte's Chelsea in the final at Wembley. The scoreline didn't do justice to Arsenal's over-all dominance, and their performance was particularly impressive considering Arsenal defeated the title winners without centre-backs Koscielny, Mustafi and Gabriel. Wenger fielded left-back Monreal and youngster Rob Holding in the wide centre-back positions, and, incredibly, used Per Mertesacker in the central role despite Arsenal's club captain having played just 37 minutes all season. But Mertesacker was magnificent throughout, and goals from Alexis Sánchez and Aaron Ramsey meant Wenger became the most successful manager in FA Cup history, lifting the trophy for the seventh time.

It was a cruel way for Conte to end such a dominant debut campaign – and also somewhat ironic that after Chelsea's defeat to Arsenal in autumn prompted Conte to switch to 3–4–3, Chelsea's subsequent brilliance inspired Wenger to replicate that system, with the Frenchman then using the 3–4–3 to deny Conte the double. As the story of Premier League tactics shows, Conte was hardly the first manager to be a victim of his own success – but whereas previously this would have taken place over the course of several years, it could now occur during a single campaign.

Nevertheless, Conte's Chelsea became the first side since Harry Catterick's Everton in 1962/63 to win the English top-flight with a three-man defence, the Italian thereby ending over fifty years of flat-back-four dominance. 'I think in England something is changing because there are different coaches from different countries and they are bringing new, different ideas, and new methods and new philosophies of football,' he said. But this had now been the case for a quarter of a century. From Cantona to Conte, the Premier League's evolution has depended almost entirely upon foreign influence.

Postscript

The Premier League's 25th season took place alongside the most significant political event in Britain for decades.

In June 2016 the British electorate surprisingly voted to leave the European Union. This was more than simply a background development, and it threatened serious ramifications for English football. The explosion in the number of foreign players in the late 1990s was prompted by the Bosman case, which ruled that football's restrictions were in breach of EU laws and forced immediate and significant change. Once Britain was outside the EU, however, English football could reintroduce quotas.

It took only three months for Labour MP Andy Burnham to raise the issue. 'Could Brexit mean that English football takes a step away from the European directives with relation to free movement in sport?' he asked. 'Could we look at introducing a quota for our homegrown players, so that the Premier League doesn't become a playground for the world's best talent but, actually, we make sure that we bring through more English and homegrown players in our domestic league? I think that's a debate that is worth having ... the question is: can you have both, can you have the best league in the world and the most successful international team?'

Implicit in Burnham's question was the acknowledgement that the presence of so many foreign imports had improved the Premier League. 'A playground for the world's best talent' was used in a negative sense, but is exactly the type of phrase that could feature in a pre-season Sky advertisement, complete with a 'back to school' theme.

Of the various figures charted throughout this story of the Premier League's tactical evolution, perhaps there are only two genuine British revolutionaries: Rio Ferdinand and Brendan Rodgers. Ferdinand changed centre-back play and Rodgers championed possession football at Swansea. Yet Ferdinand was told by Kevin Keegan he'd have a better chance of international caps 'if he was French, Brazilian or Dutch', and Rodgers consistently underlined his love for Spanish and Dutch football. The Premier League's evolution has almost solely been about foreign influence.

The other significant event of summer 2016 was purely footballing: the European Championships. This tournament, held in France, was widely considered underwhelming, with few intriguing matches and barely any memorable moments. The lack of tactical variety was particularly problematic, and it's significant that the tournament's two overachievers were arguably the only sides who played unusual systems – winners Portugal deployed a midfield diamond and no true centre-forward, while semi-finalists Wales used a 3–4–2–1. Otherwise it was disappointingly homogeneous. In a post-tournament survey of its readers by *When Saturday Comes* magazine, two-thirds of respondents agreed that 'many games were samey.' This is a damning indictment of an international tournament intended to be a multicultural jamboree of contrasting football styles. It's supposed to be about the technique of Spain, the discipline of Italy, the efficiency of Germany, the tactical inadequacy of England. Instead, everyone played in roughly the same way.

But the 2016/17 edition of the Premier League was its most stylistically diverse campaign ever. At one stage, in early February, the top nine in the Premier League were, incredibly, led by managers from nine different nations: Italy, Argentina, Spain, France, Germany, Portugal, Holland, Wales and Croatia. To varying extents, these managers represented their country's traditional playing styles. The Premier League was as stylistically diverse as, or perhaps even more than, the European Championships. The obvious absence from that list, of course, was England.

But the Premier League retains a distinct English identity. Pep Guardiola was shocked by the emphasis upon 'second balls' in the Premier League. This is a distinctly English phenomenon, but with so few English players and managers, why has it remained? The players don't naturally play in that style, the managers don't encourage it.

It's about the environment, rather than the footballing personnel. We're approaching 10,000 Premier League matches, and all have been played in England or Wales. This is significant, because Britain provides certain crucial characteristics that influence football. Most obviously, there's the climate – this is decidedly colder than in the majority of other top-class European countries, which allows for a faster style of play. And although there's been a great improvement over the last couple of decades, England and Wales's wetter weather also means pitches are boggier, which encourages more balls to be played in the air.

English officials are more lenient than any in Europe – to the extent that, in Italy, a referee who allows strong tackles without punishment is literally referred to as a 'very English' referee. This, of course, means that flair players find it more difficult to work their magic in England, and rudimentary defenders can intimidate through physicality.

Most importantly there are the supporters, who continue to represent English football identity by celebrating things their European counterparts don't. No one else cheers the winning of a corner like English fans, because it's an opportunity to launch the ball into the penalty box. There's a load roar for a thundering tackle and an enthusiastic round of applause whenever a team switches play from one flank to the other. You never hear that for a straight, penetrative pass – despite the fact they are, in the modern age, much more valuable. There's still a good helping of 'traditional' English grounds, which foreign imports often remark upon as being intimidating and creating a particularly fiery atmosphere.

But many of these factors may become less relevant, because at some point in its second 25 years, the Premier League will surely play matches abroad. Since 1992 the division has evolved from battling against other sports for a British sporting audience, to battling other football leagues for a global football audience, to battling against other sports for a global sporting audience. The world's two major sports leagues are now the Premier League and the NFL, with both experiencing a recent surge of popularity from the 'wrong' side of the Atlantic.

While the NFL has played a succession of matches in London, mainly at Wembley, the Premier League hasn't yet ventured abroad, but sports bars in New York and other major cities are packed with fans watching 'EPL' action. There's a huge market in the US – and across the world – for the Premier League to take advantage of. The idea for a 'game 39' – an extra Premier League fixture for every side, played abroad – entirely undermines the simple structure of playing each league opponent twice. Every club playing one 'home' game abroad, however, seems inevitable, and could increase dramatically over time. Playing matches abroad would compromise many of the Premier League's 'English' ingredients. The climate would inevitably be variable. The stadiums would be different, probably with fans further from the pitch. The level of support would be hugely impressive in numbers, but almost certainly not as cohesive and vocal as traditional home matches.

But this would simply be the next step in a process that has been the Premier League's defining feature – its internationalism – and the Premier League's role in promoting Britain itself should not be underestimated. A 2015 Populus poll of citizens from seven countries and one territory across the world – Nigeria, Qatar, India, China, Thailand, Indonesia, the USA and Hong Kong – revealed that the Premier League was Britain's most popular 'brand', ahead of such things as the BBC, British universities, the monarchy and British music. 'Eighty-four per cent of those polled across all the markets say that the Premier League makes them feel more positive towards the UK,' it read. 'Furthermore, you don't have to like the UK to like the Premier League: the Premier League's high Index score is not dependent on people's general views about the UK as a country … our research shows that of the many effective advertisements the UK has for what it wants to say about itself – modern, successful, exciting, open, inclusive – the Premier League is the strongest.'

That's significant in light of the proposal from Burnham – who campaigned for Britain to remain in the EU – that English football should consider reintroducing foreign quotas. Consider the fact that Britain is set to become more isolated and that the Premier League is effectively Britain's best advertisement for itself. The reintroduction of foreign quotas would be an extremely significant decision that would have ramifications far beyond football.

The English product of the Premier League is barely English at all – it simply takes place in England. In much the same way English high streets feature restaurants serving food from various world cuisines – meaning bland English fare is now largely the preserve of the traditional pub – old-school English football has been relegated to the lower leagues.

The English top flight takes exotic ingredients from various foreign countries, and serves the most diverse, exciting and unpredictable footballing feast in the world. The Premier League is, of course, the mixer.

Bibliography

Adams, Tony. *Addicted*, London, CollinsWillow, 1998

Alciato, Alessandro. *Carlo Ancelotti*, New York, Rizzoli, 2010

Alexander, Duncan. *OptaJoe's Football Yearbook*, London, Century, 2016

Allardyce, Sam. *Big Sam*, London, Headline, 2015

Allen, Richard. *Roy Hodgson*, Farnham, Richard Allen, 2014

Ancelotti, Carlo. *Quiet Leadership*, London, Portfolio Penguin, 2016

Anderson, Chris and Sally, David. *The Numbers Game*, London, Penguin, 2014

Astaire, Simon. *Sol Campbell*, London, SpellBinding Media, 2015

Atkinson, Ron. *Big Ron*, London, André Deutsch, 1998

Auclair, Philippe. *Cantona*, London, Macmillan, 2009

Auclair, Philippe. *Thierry Henry*, London, Macmillan, 2012

Balague, Guillem. *A Season on the Brink*, London, Orion, 2005

Balague, Guillem. *Cristiano Ronaldo*, London, Orion, 2015

Ball, Alan. *Playing Extra Time*, London, Sidgwick & Jackson, 2004

Barclay, Patrick. *Mourinho*, London, Orion, 2005

Batty, David. *The Autobiography*, London, Headline, 2001

Beasley, Rob. *José Mourinho*, London, Michael O'Mara Books, 2016

Beckham, David. *My Side*, London, CollinsWillow, 2003

Bellamy, Craig. *GoodFella*, London, Trinity Mirror Sport Media, 2014

Benítez, Rafael. *Champions League Dreams*, London, Headline, 2012

Bergkamp, David. *Stillness and Speed*, London, Simon & Schuster, 2013

Bevan, David. *The Unbelievables*, Liverpool, deCoubertin, 2016

Bose, Mihir. *Game Changer*, Singapore, Marshall Cavendish, 2012

Brassell, Andy. *All or Nothing*, Oxford, Trafford Publishing, 2006

Brennan, Stuart. *Roberto Mancini*, London, Carlton, 2012

Caioli, Luca. *Roberto Mancini*, London, Corinthian, 2012

Caioli, Luca. *Ronaldo*, London, Corinthian, 2012

Calvin, Mike. *Living on the Volcano*, London, Century, 2015

Cantona, Eric. *My Story*, London, Headline, 1994

Carragher, Jamie. *Carra*, London, Transworld, 2008

Carson, Mike. *The Manager*, London, Bloomsbury, 2013

Clark, Frank. *Kicking with Both Feet*, London, Headline, 1999

Cole, Andy. *The Autobiography*, London, André Deutsch, 1999

Cole, Ashley. *My Defence*, London, Headline, 2006

Coomber, Richard. *Lucas*, Ilkley, Great Northern Books, 2010

Curbishley, Alan. *Game Changers*, London, HarperSport, 2016

Dalglish, Kenny. *My Autobiography*, London, Hodder & Stoughton, 1996

Derbyshire, Oliver. *John Terry*, London, John Blake, 2016

Drogba, Didier. *Commitment*, London, Hachette, 2015

Dudek, Jerzy. *A Big Pole in Your Goal*, London, Trinity Mirror Sport Media, 2016

Eriksson, Sven-Göran. *Sven*, London, Headline, 2013

Evans, Tony. *I Don't Know What It Is But I Love It*, London, Penguin, 2014

Ferdinand, Les. *Sir Les*, London, Headline, 1997

Ferdinand, Rio. *Rio*, London, Headline, 2007

Bibliography

Ferdinand, Rio. *#2Sides*, Dorking, Blink, 2014

Ferguson, Alex. *6 Years at United*, Edinburgh, Mainstream, 1992

Ferguson, Alex. *A Year in the Life*, London, Virgin Publishing, 1995

Ferguson, Alex. *A Will to Win*, London, André Deutsch Ltd, 1997

Ferguson, Alex. *My Autobiography*, London, Hodder & Stoughton, 1999

Ferguson, Alex. *The Unique Treble*, London, Hodder & Stoughton, 2000

Ferguson, Alex. *My Autobiography*, London, Hodder & Stoughton, 2013

Ferguson, Alex. *Leading*, London, Hodder & Stoughton, 2015

Flanagan, Chris. *Who Put the Ball in the Munich Net?*, Skipton, Vertical Editions, 2014

Flynn, Alex. *Arsenal*, Kingston upon Thames, Vision, 2008

Foster, Stephen. *And She Laughed No More*, London, Short Books, 2009

Fowler, Robbie. *Fowler*, London, Macmillan, 2005

Gerrard, Steven. *My Autobiography*, London, Bantam Press, 2006

Gerrard, Steven. *My Liverpool Story*, London, Headline, 2012

Gerrard, Steven. *My Story*, London, Penguin Random House, 2015

Giggs, Ryan. *My Life, My Story*, London, Headline, 2010

Giggs, Ryan. *Giggs*, London, Penguin, 2011

Ginola, David. *Le Magnifique*, London, CollinsWillow, 2000

Glanville, Brian. *England Managers*, London, Headline, 2008

Goldblatt, David. *The Game of Our Lives*, London, Penguin, 2014

Gray, Eddie. *Marching on Together*, London, Hodder & Stoughton, 2001

Gullit, Ruud. *How to Watch Football*, London, Viking, 2016

Haas, Robert. *Eat to Win*, London, Penguin, 1991

Hamann, Dietmar. *Didi Man*, London, Headline, 2012

Hardy, Martin. *Touching Distance*, London, deCoubertin, 2015

Harris, Harry. *Ruud Gullit*, London, Orion, 1997

Harris, Harry. *The Immortals*, London, G2, 2016

Harris, Harry. *King Conte*, London, G2, 2017

Harris, Nick. *The Foreign Revolution*, London, Aurum, 2006

Harrison, Eric. *The View from the Dugout*, Manchester, Parrs Wood Press, 2001

Hasselbaink, Jimmy Floyd. *Jimmy*, London, HarperSport, 2005

Higginbotham, Danny. *Rise of the Underdog*, Croydon, Sport Media, 2015

Hoddle, Glenn. *My 1998 World Cup Story*, London, André Deutsch, 1998

Hodges, Michael. *Kevin Keegan*, London, Boxtree, 1997

Honigstein, Raphael. *Englischer Fussball*, London, Yellow Jersey, 2008

Hornby, Nick. *Fever Pitch*, London, Orion, 1996

Hughes, Simon. *Men in White Suits*, London, Transworld, 2015

Hughes, Simon. *Ring of Fire*, London, Transworld, 2016

Hyypiä, Sami. *From Voikkaa to the Premiership*, London, Mainstream, 2003

Joannou, Paul. *Shirt of Legends*, Edinburgh, Mainstream, 2004

Keane, Roy. *The Autobiography*, London, Penguin, 2002

Keane, Roy. *The Second Half*, London, Orion, 2014

Keegan, Kevin. *My Autobiography*, London, Little, Brown, 1998

King, Ledley. *King*, London, Quercus, 2013

Kuper, Simon. *Football Against the Enemy*, London, Orion, 1994

Kuper, Simon. *The Football Men*, London, Simon & Schuster, 2012

Lampard, Frank. *Totally Frank*, London, HarperSport, 2006

Lawrence, Amy. *Invincible*, London, Viking, 2014

Le Saux, Graeme. *Left Field*, London, HarperSport, 2007

Lee, David. *Triffic*, Stoke-on-Trent, Proverbial, 2014

Lloret, Paco. *Rafa Benítez*, Valencia, Engloba Edición, 2004

Lourenço, Luís. *José Mourinho*, Stockport, Dewi Lewis Media, 2004

Lovejoy, Tim. *Goals, Glory and Greed*, Edinburgh, Mainstream, 2011

Lyttleton, Ben. *Twelve Yards*, London, Bantam Press, 2014

McClair, Brian. *Odd Man Out*, London, Manchester United Books, 1998

MacLeay, Ian. *Cole Play*, London, John Blake, 2006

MacLeay, Ian. *Carlos Tevez*, London, John Blake, 2010

Makélélé, Claude. *Tout Simplement*, Paris, Editions Prolongations, 2009

Marcotti, Gabriele. *Capello*, London, Bantam, 2010

Marcotti, Gabriele. *Hail, Claudio!*, London, Yellow Jersey Press, 2016

Marshall, Ian. *Class of 92*, London, Simon & Schuster, 2012

Matteo, Dominic. *In My Defence*, Ilkley, Great Northern Books, 2011

Merson, Paul. *How Not to Be a Professional Footballer*, London, HarperSport, 2012

Michels, Rinus. *Teambuilding*, Leeuwarden, Uitgeverij Eisma, 2001

Miller, Joel. *Damien Duff*, London, John Blake, 2008

Mitten, Andy. *Glory Glory!*, Kingston upon Thames, Vision, 2009

Muffling, Steve. *Exile in the Promised Land*, Milton Keynes, AuthorHouse, 2009

Neveling, Elmar. *Jurgen Klopp*, London, Ebury, 2016

Neville, Gary. *Red*, London, Corgi, 2012

Northcroft, Jonathan. *Fearless*, London, Headline, 2016

O'Leary, David. *Leeds United on Trial*, London, Time Warner, 2002

Owen, Michael. *Off the Record*, London, CollinsWillow, 2004

Pallister, Gary. *Pally*, Studley, Know the Score, 2008

Parlour, Ray. *The Romford Pelé*, London, Century, 2016

Pearce, Stuart. *Psycho*, London, Headline, 2000

Perarnau, Martí. *Pep Guardiola*, London, Arena Sport, 2016

Pirès, Robert. *Footballeur*, London, Yellow Jersey Press, 2004

Platt, David. *Achieving the Goal*, London, Richard Cohen, 1995

Ranieri, Claudio. *Proud Man Walking*, London, CollinsWillow, 2004

Redknapp, Harry. *Always Managing*, London, Ebury, 2013

Redknapp, Harry. *A Man Walks on to a Pitch*, London, Ebury, 2015

Reedie, Euan. *Alan Shearer*, London, John Blake, 2007

Reina, Pepe. *Pepe*, Liverpool, Trinity Mirror Sport Media, 2011

Ridley, Ian. *Kevin Keegan*, London, Simon & Schuster, 2008

Ridley, Ian. *There's a Golden Sky*, London, Bloomsbury, 2011

Ridsdale, Peter. *United We Fall*, London, Macmillan, 2007

Rivoire, Xavier. *Arsène Wenger*, London, Aurum, 2007

Robson, Bryan. *Robbo*, London, Hodder & Stoughton, 2006

Ronay, Barney. *The Manager*, London, Sphere, 2009

Rooney, Wayne. *My Decade in the Premier League*, London, HarperSport, 2012

Saha, Louis. *Thinking Inside the Box*, Kingston upon Thames, Vision, 2012

Schmeichel, Peter. *Schmeichel*, London, Virgin Books, 1999

Scholes, Paul. *My Story*, London, Simon & Schuster, 2012

Seaman, David. *Safe Hands*, London, Orion, 2000

Sharpe, Lee. *My Idea of Fun*, London, Orion, 2005

Shearer, Alan. *My Story So Far*, London, Hodder & Stoughton, 1998

Shindler, Colin. *Fathers, Sons and Football*, London, Headline, 2002

Sleight, Andrew. *Robbie Keane*, London, John Blake, 2008

Southall, Neville. *Everton Blues*, Edinburgh, B&W Publishing, 1997

Spurling, Jon. *Top Guns*, Cardiff, Aureus, 2001

Spurling, Jon. *Rebels for the Cause*, Edinburgh, Mainstream, 2003

Stam, Jaap. *Head to Head*, London, CollinsWillow, 2002

Stubbs, David. *1996 & The End of History*, London, Repeater, 2016

Suárez, Luis. *Crossing the Line*, London, Headline, 2014

Sumpter, David. *Soccermatics*, London, Bloomsbury, 2016

Sutton, Chris. *Paradise and Beyond*, Edinburgh, Black & White, 2012

Tanner, Rob. *5000–1*, London, Icon, 2016

Taylor, Daniel. *This Is the One*, London, Aurum, 2008

Terry, John. *My Winning Season*, London, HarperSport, 2005

Tidey, Will. *Life with Sir Alex*, London, Bloomsbury, 2011

Torres, Diego. *The Special One*, London, HarperSport, 2014

Vardy, Jamie. *From Nowhere*, London, Ebury, 2016

Venables, Terry. *Born to Manage*, London, Simon & Schuster, 2014

Vialli, Gianluca. *The Italian Job*, London, Transworld, 2006

Vieira, Patrick. *Vieira*, London, Orion, 2005

Walcott, Theo. *Growing Up Fast*, London, Transworld, 2011

White, Jim. *Premier League*, London, Head of Zeus, 2013

Wilkinson, Howard. *Managing to Succeed*, Edinburgh, Mainstream, 1992

Wilson, Jonathan. *Inverting the Pyramid*, London, Orion, 2008

Wilson, Jonathan. *The Anatomy of England*, London, Orion, 2010

Wilson, Jonathan. *Nobody Ever Says Thank You*, London, Orion, 2012

Wilson, Jonathan. *The Anatomy of Liverpool*, London, Orion, 2013

Wilson, Jonathan. *The Outsider*, London, Orion, 2013

Winter, Henry. *Fifty Years of Hurt*, London, Transworld, 2016

Worrall, Frank. *Bale*, London, John Blake, 2016

Yorke, Dwight. *Born to Score*, London, Macmillan, 2010

Newspapers & magazines
Daily Mail
Daily Mirror
Evening Chronicle
Evening Gazette
Evening Standard

Bibliography

FourFourTwo
Guardian
Independent
Liverpool Echo
Observer
Telegraph
The Times
When Saturday Comes

TV
Premier League 100 Club
Premier League Legends
Premier League Years
Time of Our Lives

Websites
arseweb.com
bbc.co.uk
chelseafc.com
englandfootballonline.com
espn.co.uk
football-lineups.com
fourfourtwo.com
premierleague.com
skysports.com
statto.com
thesetpieces.com
toffeeweb.com
whoscored.com
youtube.com
zonalmarking.net

Acknowledgements

Huge thanks to my agent Chris Wellbelove, who approached me about writing a book in 2012. Four years later I decided it was time to get started. His patience is much appreciated, and his input throughout has been invaluable. I am grateful to my editor Jack Fogg for his initial interest, for extremely helpful pointers throughout the process and for indulging me by publishing a book 50 per cent longer than planned. Our most important meeting took place in a pub on a Friday night, which sums up how pleasant the process has been.

Thanks also to Orlando Mowbray for his enthusiasm from an early stage and to Isabel Prodger for her tireless work on the publicity campaign. Mark Bolland made crucial revisions at the copyediting stage, and Simeon Greenaway designed a fantastic cover. Thanks to everyone else at HarperCollins for vital behind-the-scenes work.

Thanks to Carlo Ancelotti for taking time to explain his Chelsea system to me. I am indebted to Duncan Alexander for regularly digging into Opta's archive to help with statistical requests. *Merci* to Jack Lang for translation assistance. Thanks to Nick Ames, Neil Baker, Rupert Cane, Jamie Cutteridge, Andy Exley, Duncan Hamilton, Mark Holmes, Taimour Lay, Ben Lyttleton, James Maw, Alex Mocchi, Matt Phillips and Owen Whoever for help in some form. Inspiration for the structure came from the BBC's *Seven Ages of Rock* series; inspiration for everything else came from Claire Boucher.

Cheers to Amy Rose-McMullen for Bosman-related research and advice, which finally justified her decade of legal study and immediately disproved her promise that she wasn't going to read any of this book. Thanks to Tom Ross for feedback, especially as we were midway through a three-week trip around Colombia and therefore he was presumably already sick of my views on football. Thanks to the hundreds of people whose writing I have borrowed from, and those who recorded 1990s football footage on VHS and later uploaded the videos onto the internet. Hello to friends who wanted a mention in this acknowledgment section; I won't embarrass you by mentioning your names.

Cheers to Philippe Auclair and Jonathan Wilson for inviting me out for a drink back in 2010, and thanks to Sean Ingle, James Martin, Gary Parkinson and Oli Przybylski for employing me despite my complete lack of journalism experience or qualifications. I'm still working for the *Guardian*, ESPN, *FourFourTwo* and Betfair seven years on, so thanks to their colleagues and successors too.

This all stemmed from people visiting my website, Zonal Marking, so enormous thanks to everyone who has visited ZM over the past seven years, particularly during its formative period. I hugely appreciate the support and am still pleasantly surprised so many people are interested in this kind of football coverage. Massive thanks from the bottom of my heart, the relegation zone, to Stephanie, who watched football matches on the prescient condition that I wrote down the starting XIs in correct formation order and explained what was going on, then was the only person to believe that starting ZM was a good idea. I haven't forgotten you being employed to sit in a bookshop window and read a book; can you do the same for this one?

Acknowledgements

Most importantly, eternal thanks to my mum and dad, who initially had absolutely no interest in football whatsoever, yet spent countless cold weekend mornings on the touchline of playing fields across south-west London, put up with me transforming the garden into a muddy goalmouth and arranged holidays to coincide with Serie A games. The fact Mum recently referred to my old bedroom as 'Dad's football-watching room' suggests my mission is complete.

And finally, if you enjoyed reading this book, you might enjoy the accompanying eight-part *The Mixer* podcast series. It's available through iTunes, SoundCloud and the other usual channels.

Index

Index

Index

Index

Index

Index

Index

Index

Index

Index

Index

Index

Index